# NEEDS, VALUES, TRUTH

# Needs, Values, Truth

*Essays in the Philosophy of Value*

## DAVID WIGGINS

### Third edition

CLARENDON PRESS · OXFORD

Oxford University Press, Great Clarendon Street, Oxford OX2 6DP

Oxford University Press is a department of the University of Oxford.
It furthers the University's objective of excellence in research, scholarship,
and education by publishing worldwide in

Oxford New York

Auckland Cape Town Dar es Salaam Hong Kong Karachi Kuala Lumpur
Madrid Melbourne Mexico City Nairobi New Delhi Shanghai Taipei Toronto

With offices in

Argentina Austria Brazil Chile Czech Republic France Greece
Guatemala Hungary Italy Japan Poland Portugal Singapore
South Korea Switzerland Thailand Turkey Ukraine Vietnam

Oxford is a registered trade mark of Oxford University Press
in the UK and in certain other countries

Published in the United States
by Oxford University Press Inc., New York

First published 1987
by Basil Blackwell Ltd.
in cooperation with the Aristotelian Society
Second edition (paperback only 1991)
Third edition 1998 Oxford University Press

British Library Cataloguing in Publication Data
Data available

Library of Congress Cataloging in Publication Data
Data available

ISBN 978-0-19-823719-8

Printed in Great Britain on acid-free paper by
Biddles Ltd., King's Lynn, Norfolk

# Contents

# Preface (1987)

In this collection, essays that are not new have all been revised, either by the correction of selected sentences or paragraphs (as in the case of I, VI, VII, IX) or (at the other extreme, represented by VIII) by abridgement and editing of what was there before and the addition of new sections or notes or longer notes. In every case, the aim was to do the least that was necessary, or slightly less than that.

In one or two special cases, an opinion I no longer hold has been allowed to stand because there seemed to be a point in registering the option to entertain that opinion and entering the appropriate reservation in a subsequent essay (with a cross reference at each place).

Where I found that the same point was made in more or less the same words in different essays, I have usually let the repetition stand. Those whom such repeated passages do not even convince may see it as an aggravation of the offence if I quote William James' preface to the *Will to Believe*: 'Apology is also needed for the repetition of the same passage in different essays. My excuse is that one cannot always express the same thought in two ways that seem equally forcible'. But I calculate that the self-containment that this preserves for each essay will be a more durable service to the reader than any mitigation of the annoyance of repetition might have been.

Taken together, the essays printed in this book steer me, and the reader perhaps, towards certain sorts of conclusions. But these conclusions do not enjoy the status of 'results'. Especially in the case of the group comprising Essays II, III, IV, and V, I should attach more importance to the (as unstipulative as I could make it) basis on which I have tried to ground my answers to questions than to any inventory of my conclusions. When these seem strange, or too strong or too weak, it is my hope that the reader will ask himself how he thinks I could have done better, or what conclusion I ought to have come to, given the dialectical position that obtained at that point. There is nothing here—as perhaps there is sometimes in Essays I, VIII and IX—that I have decided on other grounds, lying off the page, that I must somehow find an argument for.

Somewhat similarly, much more importance attaches to whatever I may have achieved in making a certain theoretical option visible in the philosophy of morals or politics than to demonstrating that option's total adequacy (of which I am sceptical), or to attacking the familiar approaches for which I see it as an alternative. I do not seek to disprove the theories of Stevenson, Hare, or Mackie—still less that of Hume, from whom I have taken so much. The excellences and difficulties of these familar approaches are reasonably well known, even if not everyone arrives at the same estimate of their seriousness or arrives at the same theoretical preference. What we most badly need now in this field is *more options*—more approaches, not necessarily more 'theories' or '—isms'. And, among these further approaches, some or several must surely come to terms with a point that one associates with Bernard Williams' writings in this field, his theory and his practice: that in the philosophy of value our practical and our theoretical difficulties are not distinct, and they flow largely from our having not too many but too few moral/political/critical ideas—and too little interest, I would add, in making the most of those we have got and in understanding the mutual irreducibility and mutual relations of these.

Perhaps there are several approaches that will lay claim to a full understanding of Williams' observation. My own commitment is to the approach that perseveres with his point even to the length of taking fully seriously many or most of the *convictions* that come with the ideas that he would advise us to hold on to. The rationale for this approach is bound up with two complementary (if not strictly consequential) theses: (i) that as agents we feel and know more than we can say about moral questions, and we can say more than can be systematized; (ii) more controversially, that, among the various convictions that come with the various ideas we must make the most of, an equal respect deserves to be accorded to our confidence, *such as it is* (i.e. in so far as we have it), that we share a capacity to apply very much the same sort of standard of correctness within the area of value as we apply in many other areas, the name of the relevant dimension of assessment being 'truth'. We must make neither too much of the contestability of the findings in which we are able to concur there, nor yet too little.

The acknowledgements I owe the many scholars and friends to whose work or advice or suggestions I am indebted—and in some cases very heavily indebted—are made so far as possible point by point, or (at worst) essay by essay. The same applies to acknowledgements to publishers who have given permission to reprint or to make quotations. Further substantial debts that I cannot completely discharge in this way are to Anthony Price and Jennifer Hornsby, who read the whole book through for the Aristotelian Society and made many helpful corrections and comments. I shall be lucky if the reader takes my side in even a handful of the cases where I did not try to accommodate everything that they said.

After many delays, some of them resulting from the deteriorating conditions in British universities for intellectual labour of all sorts, even for those who do not have to live hand to mouth and are lucky enough to enjoy the relative peace of mind that comes from having an established teaching post, what made it possible for me to complete this book was leave of absence, for which I thank University College, Oxford, and Oxford University. During this period it has been my good fortune to experience the unique conditions for thinking, reading, and writing that are provided by the Center for Advanced Study in the Behavioral Sciences at Stanford, California and the good humoured and dedicated staff of the Center. I am grateful also for the financial support of my Fellowship there in 1985/6 provided by the Andrew W. Mellon Foundation.

Like other contributors to this Series, I have greatly benefited from the signal patience, forbearance, skill and good sense of the Monographs Editor, Martin Davies.

# Preface to the Second (1991) and Third (1998) Editions

The new printing has created the opportunity to make minor corrections and to identify substantial errors, both failures to follow through connectedly or fully upon the positions actually reached in 1987 and failures to complete particular revisions I was trying to make to two or three of the older papers that were being reprinted in the first edition. Among the pages more seriously affected in such (or other) ways are pp. 52, 96, 123, 124, 286, 328, 336–7.

From among those kind enough to draw attention to *corrigenda* of every sort, far more than could ever be attended to, I owe a special debt of gratitude to Dr Bella Wheater. I hope that her own writing on cognate subjects will soon be given to the worlds of letters and philosophy.

Rereading the book, I saw how many passages there were where the word *man* signified, in a fashion once commonplace in the writings of philosophers of both sexes, what *Mensch*, *homo* or *anthropos* signify. Lest I ruin the publisher, I could not undertake to obliterate every trace of this obsolescent usage or to expel any other archaisms that date these essays to the various times when they were written.

Further to the Postscript and the partial synopsis there offered, I have attempted in an article called 'Moral Cognitivism, Moral Relativism and Motivating Moral Beliefs', forthcoming in *Proceedings of the Aristotelian Society* vol. LXXXXI (1990–1), to gather certain of the threads, especially those relating to the idea of truth, that connect Essays II, III, IV, V, VII.

The demand for a second edition of a book given to the public under a title whose first word is *need*, and in which Essay I concerns claims of need, might encourage the hope that there is now a new interest in this idea, even an interest that is theoretically sober and innocent equally of conservative rage, liberal irritability and socialist rancour.

If there is such an interest, I hope it will not continue to be shackled to the obsession with economic equality as such. Is it not the silliest of euphemisms to insist on subsuming under the badness of economic inequality as such the badness of every act of injustice, callousness, or mindless indifference to the vital interests of other classes than one's own? (Consider whatever private or public acts or abstentions they are that result in the state of affairs where some have no alternative but to sleep winter nights out of doors in a cardboard box. Why prefer, even in such a case, the contentious over the uncontentious, unignorable and obvious criticism?) Another hope one might harbour is that any new interest in the theory of needs will be dissociated from the unbelievable thesis that the problem of goods—concrete or abstract goods, the problem of bringing them into being or of preserving them in being—may be solved independently of the problem of property rights and of 'counter-claims' (the intuitive idea explained at pages 39–40). Unless anything can be turned into anything—and why should the licence to practise the crafts of statesmanship or political science require the profession of belief in a something as incredible as transubstantiation?—how can 'redistributive' taxation ever turn entitlement relations that are defective into entitlement relations that are sound, or make them remotely fit for a kingdom of ends?

One might then think that it would be better for any new concern with needs to be linked to two new aims: (i) the creation of conditions in which it will be possible, even at some cost to larger enterprises and those who live by them, for the wealth on which vital needs depend to be produced closer to the point where it is to confer its benefit; (ii) the equal protection (from predations of all kinds) of the vital needs, as such, of anyone and everyone, not excluding future generations. (A limited form of equality, but hard to find anywhere on the face of the earth—and an eminently proper aim on which, if necessary, to spend money raised by taxation.) I like to think that any such interest or concern will be sensitive to what is bad, injurious or unjust in bad, injurious or unjust existing states of affairs and *equally* sensitive to what is good, felicific or just and all too easily thrown away in good, felicific or just existing states of affairs. In the first instance, what matters the most is not that such an interest make people better, but that it should prompt them to conduct political argument on a wider basis of ideas and considerations than will find a hearing under the simple despotism, however democratic, of desires. Let me repeat, however, that in its serious form such an interest will require, *inter alia*, a serious interest in *what it turns on* whether a need does or does not count as vital. I try to offer an account of this matter on pages 17, 22–3, 39–40. (Vital and basic are not the same.) The unkind accusations that such efforts have so often provoked and do still provoke are answered on page 320 following.

For the third edition, undertaken by the Oxford University Press and through the good offices of Mr Peter Momtchiloff, I have added a tenth essay which makes explicit something that always lurked in the earlier pieces. The postscript to Essay X further consolidates the doctrines I defend concerning freedom, autonomy, deliberation, and the limitations of utility theory. There is one important correction to Essay IV (I was made to see the necessity for it by Wilfrid Hodges); and there are a number of other corrections of some philosophical moment in other essays.

# I

# Claims of Need*

The art of our necessities is strange.
SHAKESPEARE (*King Lear* III:3:70)

O, I have ta'en
Too little care of this! Take physic, pomp;
Expose thyself to feel what wretches feel,
That thou mayst shake the superflux to them
And show the heavens more just
(*Ibidem*, III:4:32)

1. It has been felt for a long time that there must be some intimate connection between the needs of human beings and their abstract rights. H.L.A. Hart was giving voice to a strong and widespread intuition when he wrote:

> A concept of legal rights limited to those cases where the law . . . respects the choice of individuals would be too narrow. For there is a form of the moral criticism of law which . . . is inspired by regard for the needs of individuals for certain fundamental freedoms and protections or benefits. Criticism of the law for its failure to provide for such individual needs is distinct from, and sometimes at war with, the criticism with which Bentham was perhaps too exclusively concerned, that the law often fails to maximize aggregate utility.[1]

In practice, however, the connection between needs and rights

* In a slightly different form, this essay originally appeared in a tribute to John Mackie, *Morality and Objectivity*, ed. Honderich (London: Routledge & Kegan Paul, 1985). Sections 4, 5, 6, 7, 8, and 14 are adapted from work on needs which will appear elsewhere and in another form in the *Journal of Medical Ethics*, under joint authorship with Sira Dermen, to whom I am greatly indebted. I benefited greatly from letters that Bernard Williams and Ronald Dworkin kindly sent to me about the penultimate draft. I am grateful too for advice and suggestions given by Jennifer Hornsby, Susan Hurley, Robert Gay, Michael Smith, Margery Eagle, and Roger Scruton and Anthony Price (who both made many more suggestions than I was able to do justice to).

[1] 'Bentham on Legal Rights' in *Oxford Essays in Jurisprudence* II ed. Simpson, 1973, p. 200.

has proved elusive. Of course it ought not to have been expected that a linkage of this kind would be simple or hard and fast, or provide the one missing clue to everything that still puzzles us in the idea of justice. But if the connection is not only complicated but important too, and what validates it is there to be discovered among the sentiments that actually sustain our various ideas about justice, it will be a great shame if the failure to be simple or hard and fast continues to stand in the way of our trying to understand the special force and political impact of a claim of serious need. To postpone the problem is to postpone the day when we attempt to get ourselves an account of justice that is based on as many distinct ideas as justice itself may prove to contain within itself.

In advance, however, of all questions of justice and entitlement, where I have been happy to work within a framework rather similar to J.L. Mackie's, not presupposing the welfare state but reasoning positively and point by point about the kind of entitlement that needing creates,[2] it will be necessary to attend for its own sake and at some length to the question what needing is—a precaution disregarded almost equally by champions and by critics of the idea that there is something serious to be made of this notion in political philosophy. One can hardly explain the special force of a claim when one will not first determine what exactly one who makes it says, or in what contexts it seems particularly natural to make it, or what conceptions and misconceptions these contexts especially lend themselves to.

2.   Those who complain that the question of what it is to need something is relatively neglected in our tradition are sometimes directed to the writings of Hegel and Marx. But there one is likely to be disappointed. It is true that each of these writers makes heartening acknowledgement of the familiarity and importance of the concept of need, and true again that in Marx one will encounter the famous or infamous formula 'From

---

[2] 'Can there be a rights-based moral theory?' in *Midwest Studies in Philosophy* Volume 3, 1978, pp. 350-9; 'Rights, Utility, and Universalization' in Frey ed. *Utility and Rights* (Oxford: Blackwell, 1984). See also his 'Rights, Utility, and External Costs' and other papers in his *Collected Papers* II, Oxford 1985, Essays XII-XVI.

each according to his ability; to each according to his need'[3] (though Marx did not in fact invent this principle).[4] But neither Marx nor Hegel says what a need is, or indicates what it really turns on in a given case whether this or that is needed by someone. In Hegel, there is a strong tendency for needs to be simply run together with desires: needs are first placed with desires on the side of subjectivity, in opposition to the objects of needing and desiring and the reality that resists them (as in the description of the evolution of self-consciousness in the *Phenomenology of Spirit*); and then they are put with desires again, on the social level, in the totality comprehending *all* interests and motivations that constitutes civil society as a 'system of needs' (as in the *Philosophy of Right*). Marx can be read as innocent of this conflation: but what we encounter in his case is the philosophically debilitating refusal to say anything that will forejudge any part of the substance of the public criterion of need that it is supposed history will supply or to anticipate in any other way the needs that some future 'consciousness exceeding its bounds' will acknowledge as properly expressive of 'human essence'.

Analytical philosophers are not as constrained here as it seems Marx was. But in our kind of philosophy, sensitive though it always is to questions of the form *what is it to* φ?, the idea of needing something suffers from guilt by association. Either the idea smells of *dirigisme*, state interference in the processes of production, and distaste for 'consumer preference',[5]

[3] *Critique of Gotha Programme* (towards the end of Marx's third comment on the document). For further references to Marx and Hegel, see Patricia Springborg, *The Problem of Human Needs and the Critique of Civilization* (London: George Allen and Unwin, 1981). See also Agnes Heller's important study, *The Theory of Need in Marx* (London: Allison and Busby, 1976).

[4] Cp. Shakespeare *Lear* 'So distribution should undo excess/And each man have enough', 4.1.66. And for nineteenth century pre-Marxian formulations of the abilities/needs principle, L. Blanc's and others', see pp. 147-8, note 3, of Del Vecchio *Justice: an Historical and Philosophical Essay*, ed. A.H. Campbell, (Edinburgh, 1952).

[5] Cp. Anthony Flew, *The Politics of Procrustes* (London: Temple Smith, 1981), p. 117:

> An emphasis upon needs as opposed to wants . . . cannot but appeal to those who would like to see themselves as experts qualified both to determine what the needs of others are, and to prescribe and enforce the means appropriate to the satisfaction of those needs.

Or compare Jeremy Bray, *Decision in Government* (London: Gollancz, 1970), p. 72, quoted in note 5 of essay VI. For criticisms of a very different tone and tenor, see James Griffin 'Modern Utilitarianism', *Revue Internationale de Philosophie*, no. 141, 1982, pp. 340-343.

or it revives bad memories of the 'means test' and numerous earlier attempts to restrict the number of indigent persons entitled to the outdoor relief provided by the Poor Law of 1601 and its more recent counterparts (social security, etc.). Or else it somehow contrives to arouse both sorts of association. And, in case that is not a sufficient disadvantage for the idea to labour under, those who have been willing to experiment with it have been dismayed to find, seeing the problem of justice in the way they were apt to see it, that, instead of simplifying things, the separate consideration of need only complicated them. It also infected certain questions with an indefiniteness that these philosophers were reluctant to accept as inherent in this subject matter.

3.   However inhibiting these doubts and suspicions and difficulties have been within philosophy itself, it is a surprising and most important fact that they operate only at the level of theory. In practice—and to an extent that could not be predicted or even suspected on the basis of an examination of present day political theory—the political-cum-administrative process as we know it in Europe and North America could scarcely continue (could scarcely even conclude an argument) without constant recourse to the idea of need:[6]

> 'The outstanding object of the Beveridge Plan is to provide as far as possible a unified system of income maintenance to cover needs arising from a variety of causes.' (G.D.H. Cole, pamphlet explaining the Beveridge Plan.)

> 'Scientists are almost unanimous that in spite of the development of *in vitro* methods of testing and experiment, and in spite of

---

[6] Although it is official ratiocination and argument rather than legislative enactment that displays the most frequent employment of the word 'need', it is by no means unknown even in Acts of Parliament. For instance, Clause 2 of the 1978 Transport Act requires County Councils in England and Wales to prepare and publish annually a five year public transport plan reviewing existing services 'in relation to need'. (For the source of this use, compare the White Paper *Transport Policy* 1977 *Cmnd.* 6836, which lays it down as one objective of official policy to 'meet social needs by securing a reasonable level of mobility'.)

Note that in the third example given in the sequel below we find as often, the form '*x* needs to be V-ed', which may be presumed to be a transformation from 'it needs to be that *x* is V-ed', which presumably comes from '[we] need to V *x*' or '[we] need *x* to be V-ed'.

advances in tissue culture techniques, we still need to perform experiments on live animals.'

'The United Kingdom Atomic Energy Authority . . . has told the Government that it thinks that a fast reactor needs to be built and it is naturally keen to move on from the experience gained on the two small-scale plants it has operated at Dounreay in Scotland and to the logical next stage of development.' (*The Times*, March 18, 1981.)

'The minister decided not to reopen the inquiry, and in his decision he said that he had taken into account the general changes relating to design flow standards and traffic forecasts since the inquiry, and he was satisfied that they did not affect the evidence on which the inspector made his recommendation. He was convinced the schemes were needed and the road should be constructed.' (*The Times*, Law Report, December 10, 1977.)

An economist once said to me—and since that time I have gathered that this is a standardized professional reaction—'What do you mean by a need? Is a need just something you want, but aren't prepared to pay for?' This is witty, as well as perceptive of something (cp. §§26–7). But the literal inaccuracy of the suggestion will appear plainly to anyone who makes the experiment of reformulating 'needs' claims like those cited above and replacing 'need' by 'want', 'desire', 'prefer' or their nominal derivatives. No matter how one does this, the result lacks not simply the rhetorical force of the original, but even its particular meaning, coherence and argumentative point. And this is something that we have to explain, rather than rail against the idea of need and accuse it of trying to force our hand or of aiding and abetting some illicit transition from a statement of what is to a statement of what must be.[7] Indeed, I should say that, given the special force

---

[7] Cp. Springborg *op. cit.* Appendix. All else apart, the accusation conceded much too much to the word. There is no real contradiction at all in saying: 'This patient needs a blood transfusion. But she can't have one. The only suitable blood has been allocated to someone else'. (E.D. Watt in 'Human Needs, Human Wants, and Political Consequences', *Political Studies*, vol. 30, 1982, p. 541, imputes the same error to K.R. Minogue, who wrongly characterizes a need as something that has by definition 'a right to satisfaction'. See *The Liberal Mind* (London: Methuen, 1963), pp. 46, 103.)

carried by 'need', we ought to try to grasp some special content that the word possesses in virtue of which that force accrues to it. It would be a sort of word-magic if so striking a difference as that between 'want' and 'need' could arise except from a difference of substance.

4.  The last contention might be defended on general grounds relating to meaning and force. But, where someone is seriously tempted by the idea that needs are a certain class of strong desires or preferences or strong unconscious desires or preferences,[8] more particular considerations can be adduced. If I want to have $x$ and $x = y$, then I do not necessarily want to have $y$. If I want to eat that oyster, and that oyster is the oyster that will consign me to oblivion, it doesn't follow that I want to eat the oyster that will consign me to oblivion. But with needs it is different. I can only need to have $x$ if anything identical with $x$ is something that I need. Unlike 'desire' or 'want' then, 'need' is not evidently an intentional verb. What I need depends not on thought or the workings of my mind (or not only on these) but on the way the world is. Again, if one wants something because it is F, one believes or suspects that it is F. But if one needs something because it is F, it must really be F, whether or not one believes that it is.[9]

5.  The apparent distinctiveness of needing being registered in this way, we may now move one step closer to a positive

---

[8] Or desires or preferences that I should have if I were rational? But who can say what it is rational for someone to want in advance of knowing what he needs? There must of course be many other ways of arriving at rational wants otherwise than via needs; but insofar as rationality comes into the matter at all—i.e. rationality as conceived independently of given actual motivations—the idea of need surely has to be at least *coeval* with the idea of want, and should be accorded its own semantic identity.

[9] See A.R. White's telling criticisms of the assimilation of needs and desires in *Modal Thinking* (Oxford: Blackwell, 1971), p. 114. There are numerous other ways of bringing out this sort of difference. But one way of making the distinction can and must be firmly dispensed with, and is certainly superfluous. This is the claim that a man who needs $x$ *eo ipso* lacks $x$ and ails without $x$, whereas a man who wants $x$ may not lack $x$. The trouble with this is that it isn't true that I lack whatever I need: all sorts of things that I already have are things that I need. See again here White, p. 107. For the other view, see *e.g.* Benn and Peters, *Social Principles and the Democratic State* (London: Allen & Unwin, 1959), p. 143.

elucidation. Something that has been insisted upon in most analytical accounts of needing[10] is that needing is by its nature needing for a purpose, and that statements of need which do not mention relevant purposes (or 'end-states' as White calls them) are elliptical—some will say dishonestly elliptical—for sentences that do mention them.[11]

One thing seems right with this claim, and another seems wrong.

The thing that seems right concerns what may be called purely instrumental needing. Someone may say 'I now need to have £200 to buy a suit', or, speaking elliptically, 'I need £200'. If he can't get the suit he has in mind for less than £200, then it is true, on an instrumental reading of his claim, that he needs £200. All that has to hold for this to be the case is something of the form:

It is necessary (relative to time $t$ and relative to the $t$ circumstances $c$) that if (. . . . at t″) then (__ at t′).[12]

---

[10] The exceptions are (1) G.E.M. Anscombe 'Modern Moral Philosophy', *Philosophy*, 1958, p. 7: 'To say that [an organism] needs that environment is not to say, e.g. that you want it to have that environment, but that it won't flourish unless it has it. Certainly, it all depends whether you *want* it to flourish! as Hume would say. But what "all depends" on whether you want it to flourish is whether the fact that it needs that environment, or won't flourish without it, has the slightest influence on your actions'; (2) Joel Feinberg in *Social Philosophy* (Prentice Hall, 1973), p. 111: 'In a general sense to say that S needs X is to say simply that if he doesn't have X he will be harmed'. (Cp. David Miller, *Social Justice* (Oxford University Press, 1976), p. 130; David Richards, *A Theory of Reasons for Action* (Oxford University Press, 1970), pp. 37-8; Honoré, *op. cit.*, at note 29 below, his p. 78.)

The main difference between these analyses or elucidations and the one we shall propose consists in the fact that we propose to see *need* as an explicitly modal notion, which leads us to insist that Anscombe's conditional be governed by 'necessarily'. For other works which appear to be under the direct or indirect influence of Anscombe's formulation see D. Wiggins, *Sameness & Substance* (Oxford: Blackwell, 1980), p. 183, and J. Finnis, *Natural Law and Natural Rights* (Oxford, 1980), *passim*.

[11] This is the common point in the otherwise very different (and differently modulated) accounts of Flew and White and Barry. See Flew, *Politics of Procrustes*, p. 120: ('If I say that I need something, it is never inept to ask what for. . . . There is always something hypothetically imperative about my need'); White, *op. cit.*, ('To say that A needs to V is elliptical for saying that A needs to V in order to F [where to F is the end state] (p. 105), . . . a failure to notice the elliptical nature of statements about what A needs leads to arguments at cross purposes (p. 106) . . . "Does A need X?" is an elliptical not a normative question' (p. 106)); Brian Barry, *Political Argument* (London: Routledge & Kegan Paul, 1965), Ch. III, §5a.

[12] Strictly speaking, we have to add something here entailing that whatever '. . . .' holds a place for is a *matter of concern*. But very shortly, when we come to the non-

In the present case, the antecedent of the conditional relates to the man's having the suit and the consequent to his having £200.

So far so good. If something like this is right, then it makes excellent sense of the claim that certain uses of 'I need to have $x$' are elliptical (*e.g.* the claim 'I need £200' as made by this man); and one whole class of non-elliptical *need* sentences receives a plausible treatment. But there is something else the elucidation fails to make sense of. This is the fact that, if we have already been through everything this man can say about his need, then we can properly and pointedly respond to his claim with: 'You need £200 to buy that suit, but you don't need £200—because you don't need to buy that suit'. The ellipse theory suggests that he ought then to insist that there is an end of his for which the suit is necessary. But it is plain that without deliberate misunderstanding of what we are now saying, he cannot make this retort. If he did respond in this way, then it would be open to us, meaning our remark to him in the only way we could mean it, to say that he was simply missing the point. What he has to show, if he wants to make more than the instrumental

---

instrumental needs, which are our real interest, the addition will be superfluous, because we shall supplant the '. . . .' in the antecedent by a sentence representing something the person cannot help being concerned with. I draw attention to this, nevertheless, because, even if there is a usage according to which the antecedent need not endorse some end as a matter of concern ('to do something totally pointless knowing that it is totally pointless you need a lot of patience'—can one truly say that?), the common elliptical usage discussed in the next paragraph is only available when the suppressed antecedent *does* relate to something that is a matter of concern.

For more on the necessity invoked in the formula, see below §8. The three time variables $t$, $t'$, $t''$, are all needed in the full form of the 'need' sentence as given without any ellipse or abbreviation (even though, evidently, they do not vary entirely independently). $t''$ need not be $t'$, because the goal mentioned in the antecendent may be achieved later than the prerequisite mentioned in the consequent. $t$ need not be $t''$, because the end-state, a child's having good second teeth for instance, may create an earlier necessity that certain measures be taken. And $t$ need not be $t'$ either, because it may be necessary *now* ($t$) that certain measures be taken next year ($t'$) for the subsequent ($t''$) good of the second teeth—even though it was not necessary last year (before $t$) that these measures be taken at $t'$. Before $t$ there was a chance of dispensing with these $t'$ measures, e.g. by taking proper or better care of the first teeth.

It is well beyond my present scope to trace the relationship of the time indicators in this sort of elucidation to the tenses that appear in the various natural language forms that it seeks to elucidate.

claim, is that he *cannot get on without that suit*, that *his life will be blighted without it*, or some such thing.

What is suggested by the existence of this extra, more problematical requirement? It suggests that, although there is an instrumental sense of 'need' where we can ask for some purpose to be specified in a non-elliptical version of the 'needs' claim and there are no limits on what purpose this is (except the limits of what can be of any conceivable concern to anyone), there is another sense of 'need' by which the purpose is already fixed, and fixed in virtue of the meaning of the word. What is more, this must be the sense of the word employed by the majority of scientists, the UKAEA, the Minister, and the other makers of needs claims quoted in §3.[13] These people are representing, and the meanings of their words commit them to representing, that we simply can't get on without more roads, more reactors, or more animal experiments or whatever. ('We have no alternative.') They might be wrong. There might be minor obscurity in what exactly is intended by this. But the thing that is controversial in what is said is not the necessity for the avoidance of harm to human beings—it is precisely the fact that such avoidance is not a controversial purpose that lends needs claims their *prima facie* special practical and argumentative force—, but the claim that our prior adherence to this end *commits us* to have more roads, more fast reactors, more animal experiments or whatever. What is controversial is the claim that there is no alternative.

6.   We have then to assign at least two senses to 'need' if we are to assign the right significance to the sorts of thing people use the word to say and to understand the special argumentative force of needs claims. But of course there is a connection between the purely instrumental and the not purely instrumental sense, or what we may call (simply for the sake of a name, not

---

[13] The hazards of claiming the strict lexical distinctness of senses are now familiar. We are claiming that the considerations in the text will suffice for a proof of distinctness of sense of 'need' that comes up to the standard proposed in David Wiggins 'Sentence Sense, Word Sense and Difference of Word Sense' in *Semantics: an Interdisciplinary Reader*, ed. Steinberg and Jacobovits (Cambridge University Press, 1971) or Bede Rundle, *Grammar in Philosophy* (Oxford University Press, 1981), pp. 14–5.

to exclude the relativities to be set out in §7) the absolute or categorical sense of the word. Thus:

> I need [absolutely] to have $x$
> if and only if
> I need [instrumentally] to have $x$ if I am to avoid being harmed
> if and only if
> It is necessary, things being what they actually are, that if I avoid being harmed then I have $x$.

What distinguishes the second sense of 'need', so defined by reference to the first, is that it is in virtue of what is carried along by this sense itself of the word 'need', not in virtue of context (whatever part context plays in determining that this is the sense intended), that appeal is made to the necessary conditions of harm's being avoided. If so, the identity of the antecedent '. . . .' of the conditional 'Necessarily, since circumstances are what they are, if . . . ., then ___' is fixed by the presence of the word 'need' taken in this absolute sense.[14] It must follow that there is then no question of ellipse in this case. (One does not have to supply again what is already there.)[15]

Given this account of the word's content, it becomes unsurprising that 'need' taken in the absolute sense should have the special point and force it appears to have both in the individual case and in the case of the community's needing something. (I postpone *sine die* the neither easy nor impossible

---

[14] What might possibly confuse one is that if someone says that he needs something [absolutely] then he may perfectly well explain himself (as our equivalences indeed suggest) by reference to what he needs [instrumentally] to stay alive or avoid harm.

[15] The feeling that this proposal imports a semantical singularity of some sort may be substantially reduced by reference to a certain more familiar and uncontroversial example of ambiguity, where there is a similar nesting of one sense of a word in the account of another sense of the same word: where 'V' holds a place for a verb or verb-phrase, and 'iff' abbreviates 'if and only if',

> $z$ has a [liberty] right to $V$ iff $z$ has no duty not to $V$; $z$ has a [claim] right to $V$ iff $z$ has a [liberty] right to $V$ and some person or agency has no [liberty] right not to secure to $z$ the opportunity and ability to exercise his [liberty] right to $V$.

Cp. Joel Feinberg, *Social Philosophy*, p. 58: 'One can have a liberty which is not also a [claim] right but one cannot have a [claim] right which is not also a liberty'.

task of explicating the relation of these two cases of needing.) It is also to be expected that, so understood, 'need' should be normative or evaluative, and normative or evaluative *in virtue of its content*.

7. Normativeness apart, there are at least three distinct ways in which needs-statements of the simple singular variety we have elucidated must appear to be *relative* (notwithstanding the other respect, see §5, in which they are absolute).

First, the suggested elucidation in terms of harm exposes a certain parameter that is always there to be discovered within claims of absolute needing. This is the idea, not innocent of the metaphysics of personhood, of well-being or flourishing, by reference to which we make judgments of harm.

What follows from this relativeness? Relativeness to something else is no obstacle in itself to the most extreme or perfect kind of objectivity. Indeed making such relativeness fully explicit sometimes has the effect of revealing the subject matter in question as a candidate for unqualified or absolute truth.[16]

The first relativeness was only a matter of *need*'s involving a parameter. The second and different way in which need-sentences may appear to be relative qualifies any hopes that might be inspired by this account of the first.—What constitutes suffering or wretchedness or harm is an essentially contestable matter, and is to some extent relative to a culture, even to some extent relative to people's conceptions of suffering, wretchedness and harm. Obviously there is much more to be said about that (even if it is doubtful how much of it involves the idea of 'relative deprivation'—a relativity we have ventured to omit altogether from the argument); but instead let us hurry on, simply insisting that, even when the instability is conceded of some of the opinions that have been reached within our culture about absolute needs, some needs claims are so far from being indeterminate or seriously

[16] For instance, relativizing length, duration and motion and reformulating Newton's laws to render them relative to the reference frame of the observer and all reference frames in uniform motion with respect to him, and then qualifying the laws in certain ways suggested by the Special Theory of Relativity, made of a theory that was not previously unqualifiedly true a theory that may yet prove to be absolutely true.

contestable that they are more or less decidable. We shall return briefly to this point after making mention of a third relativity.

The third relativity is relativity to the particular circumstances of the time or times (see note 12, paragraph 2) associated with the need and the background of (no doubt normative) assumptions associated with those circumstances. When we make a claim of the form *Necessarily at t if such and such then so and so*, where *t* is a moment for which this *necessarily* is temporally indexed, we thereby confine our consideration to all alternative futures from *t* onwards, and what we are saying is equivalent to the claim that every alternative in which such and such holds is one in which so and so holds. If pure historical necessity at *t*, $\Box_t$, were our concern, then a future would count as an alternative for times $\geq t$ just if it could coherently be described, and every correct description of it was compatible with the conjunction of (i) the state of the world that actually obtained at *t* and (ii) all true laws of nature. Thus $\Box_t(p)$ is true if and only if *p* is true in every alternative world whose history is indistinguishable from the history of the actual world up to the moment *t*, natural laws being counted as part of the history of the world and fixed as of *t*.[17] But where needing is concerned, it seems that the definition of alternativeness must be modified to restrict the class of alternative futures to futures $\geq t$ that (i) are economically or technologically realistically conceivable, given the actual state of things at *t*, and (ii) do not involve us in morally (or otherwise) unacceptable acts[18] or interventions in the arrangements of particular human lives or society or whatever, and (iii) can be envisaged without our envisaging ourselves tolerating what we do not have to tolerate.

This relativity to circumstance imports one more feature that deserves special comment. The fixed antecedent of the whole conditional that is governed by the modal operator

---

[17] Cp. David Wiggins, 'Towards a Reasonable Libertarianism', Essay VIII in this volume, §4.

[18] Note that we have already had implicit recourse to this thought in the discussion of the instrumental sense in so far as we allowed that *N* needed £200 to buy a suit. The fact that there is a future in which he has a suit without paying £200, because he steals one, was not allowed to count against this claim.

'necessarily relative to the circumstances $c$ obtaining at $t$' speaks of avoidance of harm. This is not in itself obscure, but it will not give quite the sense we require to cover all the kinds of absolute (more than merely instrumental) needing that usage allows, unless some associated standard is thought of as supplied for harm to be judged according to the context, the standard creating the presumption that it is itself suggested by *some however minimal level of flourishing that is actually attainable here*. Avoidance of harm can then be understood always by reference to a norm of flourishing that is relative to $c$, and this in its turn can import the entailment or implicature that, if $y$ non-instrumentally needs $x$ at $t$ under circumstances $c$, then there *exists* some alternative future in which $y$ does flourish to some however minimal extent.[19] (When I am utterly doomed however the future is realistically envisaged, then I can begin to lose some of my ordinary needs, even as I acquire very special short term needs.)

For non-instrumental or categorical needing, this third species of relativity furnishes more of what was already furnished by the second. It is not just that the idea of harm, or the norm of flourishing by reference to which harm is judged, is historically conditioned and essentially contestable. It is also circumstantially conditioned *as of some time t* what futures are to count as realistic, morally acceptable alternatives, how long a forward view we have to take of flourishing in considering what counts as harm, and what the relevant standard of harm ought to be with respect to the time-span that is agreed to be the right one to apply in the given case. It may even be contestable—before we consider how much the present constrains the future—what exactly the circumstances are that prevail at $t$. The second and third sorts of relativity interact.

There is plenty here for an objectivist to face up to. And yet, in spite of the real and manifold contestability of most of these things, some may be tempted to conclude (as I do) that the

---

[19] Thus for our conditional in §6 governed by the specially indexed modality the problem simply does not arise that the impossibility of the antecedent will make the conditional true vacuously.

For the reasons for preferring the 'harm'-formulation to a direct formulation in terms of 'flourishing' ('Necessarily (if $z$ flourishes then. . . .)'), see below §14, on Aristotle.

agreement that can be reached about the truth or falsity of a wide variety of needs claims (when they are seriously and correctly construed as making the contextually much constrained but very strong claims they do make) is far more striking than the disagreement some others will arouse. The temptation exists, though I shall not try to evaluate it here, to claim that objectivity is a matter of degree and that some significant degree of it can coexist even with the second of the three kinds of relativity we have distinguished.

8.   The thought we have now arrived at is that a person needs $x$ [absolutely] if and only if, whatever morally and socially acceptable variation it is (economically, technologically, politically, historically . . . *etc*.) possible to envisage occurring within the relevant time-span, he will be harmed if he goes without $x$. A proper development of this that enabled us to try to measure the relative public weights of various claims of need would have to make room for certain obvious and essential refinements. And it would have to prepare the ground for these by distinguishing certain distinct questions.

There is the question of the *badness* or *gravity* of needs. How much harm or suffering would be occasioned by going without the thing in question? And there is a consequential question of *urgency*: given that some not inconsiderable harm or suffering would be occasioned by going without the thing in question, how soon must this thing be supplied? And then there is the question of the *basicness*, the *entrenchment*, and the *substitutability* of needs. Being technical terms, however, these categorizations all require more elaborate introduction.

When we attempt to survey the class of alternative possible futures and then, restricting this to envisageable acceptable futures, we ask whether every future in which person $y$ is not harmed is one in which he has $x$, we shall often discover that it is a matter of degree how difficult it is to envisage realistically some alternative in which $y$ will escape harm without having $x$, or how morally acceptable it would be to propose—or to acquiesce in—that alternative's being deliberately brought about. Often we shall then have to resolve such difficulties by imposing a threshold on what departures from the familiar we are to regard as realistically envisageable, as morally acceptable or as practical politics. The lower such thresholds are set, the more futures then count as real alternatives, and the harder it will then become for a need statement to count as true. Seeing the effects of lower settings of the thresholds but being reluctant to deny that $y$ really needs $x$ at all, we shall often have to choose between (i) raising the threshold of moral and social possibility again; (ii) quite differently, lowering (relaxing) the standard by which the harm to $y$ is judged, allowing more things to count as harm; and (iii) keeping the lower threshold of moral and political possibility, together with the more exigent truth-condition it imports, but disjoining having $x$ with having some slightly inferior potential substitute for $x$.

In the light of all this, it will be a useful stipulation to say that $y$'s need for $x$ is *entrenched* if the question of whether $y$ can remain unharmed without having $x$ is rather insensitive to the placing of the aforementioned threshold of realistic envisageability-cum-political and moral acceptability of alternative futures. When we are concerned with the problem of arbitration between general needs claims or arbitration between general needs claims and other claims, it will then be important to distinguish between entrenchment with respect to the shorter term (where extant arrangements create definite requirements that cannot be escaped immediately but may be in due course escaped) and entrenchment with respect to the longer term. Some desirable disruptions of the established order that would enable people to escape harm without having $x$ cannot be envisaged happening as it were overnight; but in many cases the change can be coherently and easily described and can be quite realistically envisaged taking place gradually and by stages.

Developing a special case of entrenchment, one might then stipulate that $y$'s need for $x$ is *basic* just if what excludes futures in which $y$ remains unharmed despite his not having $x$ are laws of nature, unalterable and invariable environmental facts, or facts about human constitution.[20] And within the basic, one might try to discriminate between (1) that which is owed to unchangeable tendencies of things to turn out in one rather

---

[20] 'Basic' will be here, as in all the schemes we have encountered in other writers, a technical term to be grasped in the first instance by the definition of the category, and in the second instance by reference to the *point* of setting up such a category. (To forget

than another specifiable kind of way (either in general or given the particular place, time or culture) and (2) that which is owed to something non-negotiable in the various ideas about human harm and flourishing that condition our sense of the socially possible (as well as our sense of what $y$ must have).

Finally, we may find it useful to be able to say that $y$'s need for $x$ is *substitutable with respect to $x$* if some slight lowering of the standard by which $y$'s harm is judged permits us to weaken claims of need by disjoining $y$'s having $x$ with his having $u$ or $v$ or $w$ or whatever.

It should be obvious that these labels correspond to overlapping but independent categorizations. A need for $x$ can be not very bad but basic, for instance; or bad and also urgent yet substitutable with respect to $x$; or bad in the extreme and highly entrenched insofar as it is urgent, but, insofar as it is not urgent, relatively superficially entrenched in the mid term and not entrenched at all in the long term. It should be equally obvious how important it is to be clear whether the need we are talking about stems from a judgment about a particular human being, or about all human beings in specified kinds of circumstances, or (making the truth-condition most exigent of all) all human beings under all actual variations of circumstance.

9.   How then are needs and desires and needs and interests related? Perhaps we had better see needs themselves (contrast things needed) as *states of dependency (in respect of not being harmed)*, which have as their proper objects things needed (or, more strictly, *having* or *using* things). In that case our categorization in §8 is a categorization of states of dependency. Such states often find expression in desire or striving (or avoidance or whatever): and often the propositional object of

---

this, and to dispute as if the categories were antecedently given, is to engage in the sort of logomachy that gives philosophy a bad name.) In particular, we would remark that our basic category is not the same in definition or point as the category of *survival needs*, or biological needs as Benn and Peters call them (*op. cit.* pp. 144–146, see also Stanley Rosen's criticisms in *Mind*, vol. 86, 1977, p. 88). Nor is it the same in definition or point as Benn and Peter's own category of *basic needs*, which simply concerns a decent standard of living; or the same as the modern Marxist category of *really human needs*, or *one's needs as a human being*, which are usually introduced to make a contrast with *false needs*. (A contrast we have partially but only partially absorbed by bringing out the full exigency of the truth-conditions of statements of need.)

the desire or striving will be the same as that which we find in some correct statement of the need. But even in this special case it is not perfectly obvious that the desire ought to be simply identified with the need. A more plausible identification is between someone's having a certain need and his having a certain interest. If a person needs $x$, then he has an interest in $x$'s being or becoming available to him. And if he very badly needs at $t$ to have $x$ at $t$, and the need is also significantly entrenched as of $t$ and scarcely substitutable at all, then his having $x$ may be said to represent a *vital interest* of his. His having the need for $x$ is then the same as his having a vital interest in having $x$. This is a good ruling, I believe, but only if we use the word 'interest' to mean what it means in English, where its connection with 'want' or 'desire' is complicated and indirect (cp. White, *op. cit.*, p. 120.), and if the proposed equivalence is without prejudice in favour of any general alignment between needs and interests.

10.  So far so good. Inasmuch as the idea of need has begun to appear at least clarifiable and intelligibly related to familiar notions, its champions will now hasten to point out what an important part it played in the motivation of the later 19th and 20th-century humanitarian efforts that have transformed the living conditions of so many 20th-century city-dwellers.

Yet it is important that there is another side to this picture. Detractors of the *need* concept will point out that, among those who know the failures as well as the successes of modern planning, the regulations and minimum standards which ideas about what people need have inspired national and municipal governments to lay down and impose with the effect of law are now widely blamed for urban blight, the bleak monotonous environment, the graceless stereotyped architecture, and even the economic inertia of that which has come to replace the city of slums and smoking factories. Over and over again, these critics will say, rigid housing standards, building regulations, public health regulations and zoning restrictions, all founded in the idea of human need and many of them supposed to afford particular protection to the poorest and wretchedest members of society, have combined in a singular and unforeseen way to their conspicuous disadvantage. In operation, these standards and restrictions have first reduced the housing stock actually available at any time for human habitation, thus raising rents and house-prices against those least able to afford them; then conspired to inhibit all individual efforts at piecemeal improvement in neighbourhoods that will probably be condemned in their entirety; and then narrowed the choice, where new building is concerned, to the meanest and least flexible of conceptions (excluding from consideration almost all that we are wont to admire when we encounter them in the architecture and town-planning of the past). Thus a quarter of alleys, tenements and terraces that long ago replaced a semi-rural slum of huts and hovels built on small plots is not itself replaced gradually, or at a pace that corresponds to what can be practically envisaged or anticipated by anyone with a direct interest there, but—such is the power of an idea like *need*—is demolished and swept away in its entirety. Inhabitants and local industries are dispersed. And then, to a lengthening list of statutory specifications and on a shrinking budget (itself ill-defended from corruption), the towers or blocks we now see in the East End of London (or Liverpool, or Glasgow or, more benignly, Sheffield) are built upon the vast space that has been swept clear, connected only by windswept walkways or (where new, higher capacity roads dictate this) pedestrian underpasses, in an environment that repels all human attempts to come to terms with it and almost paralyses practical initiative. It can still be hoped that trees or grass will catch root somewhere and grow where they can. But otherwise, and surely at least in part as a result of an official determination of need, a whole quarter is sterilized against all beneficial adaptation, initiative or change. And, except in the rare cases where industry and business reestablish themselves there in strength, it will be beyond the powers of most of the tenants of the place to escape from the client condition to which they have been reduced.

11.    Anyone who wants to take needs seriously would not be well advised to deny that such occurrences are familiar in practice, or simply to counter by pointing to outrageous schemes that governments of different complexion now instigate *in defiance* of local need. For where need really was the dominant motivation, the indictment he faces must be a serious

one, and attributions of need are deeply implicated in the charge. He may of course declare that so many different misapprehensions and oversights lie buried in the dense history of shortage, emergency and unreasoning optimism that makes up the record of the early post Second World War reconstruction— while the later history of the idea of need is overlaid by so much unconscious corruption,[21] dogmatism and megalomania (all sustained by the in practice nearly limitless ambiguity of the expression 'the public interest')—that his opponent can not really claim to have laid bare the one mistake that explains everything that he deplores and laments here. There is some justice in that. But, given the original motivation and the need-oriented thoughts that were expressed in good faith by statesmen, public officials and the experts they relied upon, a more substantial defence is required. Unless we can find some serious misconception of need among the ideas that motivated these people, or can, as I suspect, identify some definite coarseness in their appreciation of it, the case for superseding the idea of need altogether in political philosophy will be extremely hard to rebut.

The first thing I should say myself in defence of the idea of need is that, as we have elucidated statements about what is needed by a given person or set of persons, they commit us, not only to answers for certain general questions about harm, about what can be tolerated or not, and about what sort of thing can and cannot be realistically envisaged, but also to something highly particular and special to the given circumstances of the people, whoever they are, who will not, it is said,

---

[21] Corruption flourishes in a special way when nobody quite knows what *counts* as corruption, and even honest men do not know what distance to keep from certain other men of entrepreneurial energy and flair. For one part of the reason for this state of doubt and confusion see §24 following below. This is a state of doubt and confusion that makes room for methods of persuasion and promotion that represent corruption in a further moral/ intellectual (not legal) sense. Cp. Francis Gladstone, *The Politics of Planning* (London: Temple Smith, 1976), p. 105 on rhetorical use of the 'have-nots' as a means of dressing up the dedesiderata of those who 'have'.)

Postscript (1997). Some of the emphases and formulations of pp. 17–19 date these pages to the 1980s. But the events and situations to which they react are still important, however overlain by our new circumstances. They need to be understood.

being placed just as they are placed, escape harm without the thing stated to be needed. This combination of particular and general is one of the most important and intriguing features of particular non-instrumental needs. And it is open to question whether it has been properly grasped by those who have been happy to think in terms of codes of minimum standards. Certainly, the rigid standard is in constant danger of institutionalizing the neglect of such differences. It threatens the distinction between particular needs that are *bad* (even amount to the vital interest of certain particular people at a particular time) and something yet harder to identify and formulate, *viz.* needs that are *basic* or *deeply entrenched* and susceptible of being *generalized* to arrive at practical precepts that it is safe and sensible to have enforced by public officials over indefinitely many cases in indefinitely many kinds of circumstances.[22]

---

[22] For the inherent indefiniteness of the subject matter of practice, cp. Aristotle *Nicomachean Ethics* V.x. 4–5.

Somewhat similar remarks to those in the text ought probably to be directed at the Marxists' conception of 'truly human needs', needs that are 'expressive of human essence' etc. Countless needs, under any conceivable state of affairs, will always be both urgent and non-basic—i.e. put there by particular circumstances. And there will always be particular circumstances, however admirable the new condition of man. To the extent then that we cannot confront the problem that 'Under private property . . . every person speculates on creating a new need in another' (Marx *1844 MSS.*, London: Lawrence and Wishart, 1970, p. 147) by insisting on the proper interpretation of claims of need, the problem of false needs is much too hard to be simply solved by identifying the class of basic or essentially human needs.

The poignancy of the contrast between the thin set of universal needs that *nature* will underwrite and the set of things that may be needed by someone placed in a particular situation is brought out, however obliquely to Shakespeare's intention, most vividly in *Lear* (2.4.262):

> Allow not nature more than nature needs,
> Man's life is cheap as beast's.

Plainly, there is no 'human need' to have a retinue of a hundred knights. But an abdicated king in Lear's position needed such a retinue—and, to judge by what happened to him, much else besides.

There is a closely related difficulty in bringing Rawls' theory of primary goods to bear upon the problem of needs, as I conceive this. For one of the things we have to be prepared to attempt here is to look behind social arrangements defined in terms of primary goods, and behind representative positions of representative kinds of person, to the actual circumstances of particular persons—all in a manner apparently forbidden by Rawls in *A Theory of Justice*. On this point, see Brian Barry *The Liberal Theory of Justice* (Oxford University Press, 1975), especially pp. 54–5, 114–15.

In the second place, I should say that, if the relativities set out in §7 were imperfectly understood by those charged with post war reconstruction, it was not likely that there would be much understanding of the interaction of the second and third species of relativity. Many claims of needing depend crucially for their acceptance or rejection on our being ready to try to find the practically envisageable standard of flourishing or well-being by reference to which questions of harm (or lesser or greater harm) can be judged and questions of substitutability can be resolved in a way that respects real political possibility. Of course every necessary condition of a possible state of affairs of not being harmed is consistent with every other necessary condition whenever harm is not inevitable. But if, in pride or a spirit of would-be revolution that will in fact come to nothing, or for whatever other reason, statesmen or managers pitch the standard too high (and this has already happened in effect wherever the replacement of what is condemned will *in fact* represent no real improvement), or if they fail to be realistic about what futures are practically envisageable, then, in the limited space which is all there really is here, one condition of harm's being avoided will be met at the expense of another condition. (Even at the expense of a condition that is more important and nothing less than a prerequisite for an even more minimal state of not being harmed.) If the standard is set impossibly high in one sphere of concern,[23] and we fail at the same time to heed or respect (if only by *not* doing things) the totality of other needs (and if we do not recognize that we don't know too much about many of these things), then something like this is pretty well bound to happen. The more resources that are then diverted to the task of meeting the standard of need that has been set in one sphere, the worse this tendency is likely to become, and the greater the danger that one specific

---

[23] For some connected observations, based on the experience of developing countries, see Paul Streeten, *First Things First* (Oxford: OUP for World Bank, 1981), pp. 190–91. I must however qualify the claims I make in the text. Under special conditions—and when the *immediate* result is not in itself very costly—it may be heuristically indispensable to set the standard too high (even shameful not to). When anaesthetics did not exist, certain sorts of suffering and harm were inevitable. Yet there was a point in saying anaesthetics were needed; and, had our ancestors not felt some such thing, they would not have striven as hard as they did to make such things realistically envisageable or to discover them.

requirement will eventually crowd out other less specific, less behaviourally transparent, but perhaps equally or even more important requirements (especially requirements such as choice and independence); or the greater the danger that what is provided may suit some people and not suit others—an outcome that is not inconsistent with the objectivity of value, but reflects the tendency for values to compete with one another and for the lives of different people to represent widely different responses to irreducibly distinct value claims. (A different emphasis or value focus.)

12.   If we have enough faith in this defence to persist in the wish to take needs with a seriousness at all proportionate to the frequency with which they are actually invoked in political and administrative argument (cp. §3), then it seems that, having grasped the complexity and stringency of the truth-condition, we must start to see any statement of the form '$y$ needs $x$ [absolutely]' as tantamount to a challenge to imagine an alternative future in which $y$ escapes harm or damage without having $x$, or an alternative where $y$'s vital interests are better adjusted to others' vital interests than they would be if $x$ were what he had. We must proceed like this not because to be concerned with needs is to take up an attitude of stinginess or meanness (if it connotes any particular attitude, the attitude is much closer to the concern for *all* rights, 'counter-rights', cp. §20 below, and right-like claims), but because, if we do not, some vital needs and interests may not be properly determined, or may go unheeded. It is without prejudice one way or the other to the satisfaction of desires for things that are not needed.

Sometimes (as we have noticed) this sort of challenge to the imagination will not lead to outright rejection of a statement, but to a weakening of the specification of the thing said to be needed: 'He will get by if he has $x$ or $w$ or $v$'. This is a very familiar move, and the elucidation of needing given here explains why that is. Overspecificity in a 'needs' sentence makes it false.[24] But what our elucidation equally predicts is

---

[24] A good example of this is provided by modern transport planners' ingrained habit of speaking of 'mobility' (by car) as a standing need of western civilization. There is no doubt that, with present tendencies towards concentration of facilities, closure of

that often the thing that survives the weakening (the introduction of disjunctions *etc*.) will still be a very strong statement—most especially where the particular judgement of *y*'s non-instrumental need results from a process in which the actuality of *y*'s concrete situation and the constraints that this puts upon the future are fully apprehended (taking into account the real, however hypothetical, intentions of all relevant other persons or groups of persons), and where the process clarifies both the worst and the best that can befall *y* and *y*'s vital interests. (Perhaps prompting us to climb down from '*y* needs *x*', where *x* is the best but most expensive remedy, well out of *y*'s reach unless he forgoes everything else, to 'what *y* really needs [given the circumstances] is *w*', where absence of *w* will blight even that minimal level of well-being that is the best real possibility for *y*.) It seems certain that, even when claims of need are scrutinized in this way, we shall be left with much more than a tiny handful of needs statements. If so, there need be no further postponement of the question whether vital needs are better or worse satisfied now than they once were, why they are worse satisfied (wherever they are), and whether they can be better satisfied.

13. It is sometimes held that it is the role of government to make itself as responsive as possible in as many ways as possible to as many of its subjects' desires as possible. But obviously the more strongly someone inclines to the opposing view that what prudence and justice demand is that public policy be selective in what it attempts positively and be primarily based upon needs, the more important he must think it is for governments, insofar as they are directly or indirectly involved in some matter, not to specify needs incorrectly, and to be careful to take the greatest advantage of all alternative ways of satisfying them (and/or letting them go on being

---

smaller shops and offices and more dispersed patterns of development, such mobility approximates to a short or medium term need with a considerable and rising degree of entrenchment. But, if alternative tendencies can be envisaged, we shall get a fairer view of all the available options if we realize that the right name for the standing, invariable need (the need that underlies the shorter term need) is not 'mobility' but, more plastically and indefinitely, 'access [to facilities that are frequently needed]'.

satisfied, however they already were satisfied). Among needs that such a policy concerns itself with, the more plastic must make accommodation for the less plastic, and (what is different) the less bad must give way to the worse. A proper balance must be found between present needs and future needs. And *ceteris paribus* desires as such must cede rank to what emerge from careful scrutiny as grave, entrenched, non-substitutable needs. Nobody's grave, entrenched, non-substitutable need, or as one might say (exploiting the ambiguity in the adjective that was surely made for just this purpose) nobody's *vital interest*, must be sacrificed by society to the mere desire of anybody else, or of any however large group of other people.—Or as we have this contention stated in Del Vecchio's formulation of what is called, in his classic study of the history of the idea of justice, *providential, assisting* or *social* justice:

> It is a requirement of justice, that, before being assigned to any other purpose whatever, all the means which the state has legally at its disposal should be assigned by it to the protection of the life and physical and moral integrity of its members, especially of those who are not in a position to provide for this by their own means or by means of persons particularly obliged thereto.[25]

Del Vecchio is no friend of *need*. I have singled him out here as one who is explicitly hostile in principle to that way of making claims upon society.[26] But what we may now suspect is that the indispensable role of the concept of need is precisely to assist us in singling or marking out those very interests that have to be the *special* concern of social justice, both where the State has to intervene on their behalf and also in the cases where it is the business of the State to insist on some pause or hesitation, e.g. in connection with grand projects (private or public) that will serve the actual or hypothetical desires of millions but sacrifice to them the present or future vital interests of other identifiable or unidentifiable people.[27]

[25] Del Vecchio, *Justice, op. cit.* p. 148.
[26] See his criticisms at p. 148 (note), somewhat mitigated at p. 143.
[27] Cp. §23 below and cp. Mackie 'Can There be a Rights-based Moral Theory?', *op. cit.* Note also the discrepancy with Mackie, who uses the notion of a right for what we use *right, counterclaim* and *vital need* together to accomplish.

If this suspicion can be shown to be well-founded, it will certainly put in a new light the ineliminable vagueness, contestability, or non-effectiveness for which the idea of need is so often criticized. The true situation may really be that these charges against it are an indirect tribute to the idea's actual importance and indispensability to us. It may be that, *pace* some liberal and conservative critics, one aspect of its indispensability concerns the defence it can afford to the individual, in a community that has found a way of adjusting its institutions to its sentiments, against the arbitrary use of State power. (Cp. §23 below.)

14.   Having thus arrived at the frontier of political philosophy and canvassed—so far without much attempt at precision or argument—a priority principle about true needs that is either an inchoate political principle (a principle of social justice) or nothing, not a principle of individual morality as such, I want to pause for the space of one section and try to see more clearly where we have come from, before moving further forward.

We have taken Anscombe's and Feinberg's part against White, Barry and Flew (see notes 9, 10, 11) in seeking to identify an absolute sense of 'need'. We have been with White, however, in insisting that *need* is a modal notion. And here again we are not the first to take up such a position.

Aristotle is not usually credited with having any view of what a need is; but in his philosophical lexicon at *Metaphysics V* he has the following entry for 'necessary':

> 1015a20: We call NECESSARY (a) that without which, as a joint cause, it is not possible to live, as for instance breathing and nourishment are necessary for an animal, because it is incapable of existing without them: and (b) anything without which it is not possible for good to exist or come to be, or for bad to be discarded or got rid of, as for instance drinking medicine is necessary so as not to be ill, and sailing to Aegina so as to get money (trans. Kirwan).

For good reasons (especially the importance of the chapter's being seen as Aristotle's single entry for several senses of the Greek word for 'necessary'), the word ἀναγκαῖον has never been translated here as 'needed'. But, in another way, it is a shame that it was not. In the presence of an Aristotelian elucidation, the reductive, rationalized strong desires conception of need might not have passed so long without serious challenge.

Aristotle's (a)-paraphrase appears too restrictive to exhaust what we have called the absolute sense. (The case for some relaxation of the condition is, of course, of long standing. Cp. Adam Smith, *Wealth of Nations* [V.2.2], 'By necessities I understand not only the commodities which are indispensably necessary for the support of life, but whatever the custom of the country renders it indecent for creditable people even of the lowest rank to be without'.) And Aristotle's (b)-paraphrase is in danger of causing us to classify certain absolute occurrences of 'need' (needing to drink medicine for instance) with other occurrences of the word that it may be better to treat as elliptical and purely instrumental (*e.g.* needing to sail to Aegina). These two faults, if they are faults, are better corrected in the 'harm' formulation of Feinberg, I suggest, than by substituting 'flourishing' for 'living' in Aristotle's (a)-paraphrase. (One is bound to think that they are better corrected by the 'harm' formula if one is reluctant to be led by the tautology that flourishing is a necessary condition of flourishing to say that human beings *need to flourish*, but one does not mind being led by the same form of argument to the conclusion that human beings need to avoid harm.) But the value of Aristotle's contribution to this subject is not obscured by the necessity to make the case for these amendments. It resides in his having signalled (even if only to those already open to the thought) that *need* is a modal concept of a special kind[28] and imports the linked ideas of a situation and a non-negotiable (or in-the-circumstances-non-negotiable) good, which *together* leave no real alternative but to . . . . .

15.   Even those who urge us to dispense with the idea of need concede the *prima facie* compelling character of a true unexaggerated statement of need. Hence, I suppose, their

---

[28] The point is of course unaffected even if one supposes that the natural conditional is *already* secretly modal. This would hardly make the modality indexed for time and circumstance, as in §7, redundant.

animus against it. But what sort of claim is made upon society by such a statement? And is this really a claim of justice, or sometimes a claim of justice and sometimes an appeal to something beyond or beside justice? Or what is it? The rest of the paper will be devoted to these questions.

It is a marked tendency in most of the writers in whom one can discover an interest in the force of claims of need to subsume them for all purposes of justice under the general category of equality-claims (claims of equality of treatment, or claims about the intolerability of certain *in*equalities).[29] Many liberal conservatives, as well as seeing the concern with needs as such as symptomatic of an ill-conceived, busy-body or interventionist attitude to public policy or of a simple-minded idea of justice, distrust the idea of a need because they view it as indissolubly linked with conceptions of equality that they find deeply suspect. And the same linkage between needs and equality claims would appear to be assumed by radical or anti-conservative writers. Indeed, in so far as there are differences of opinion between radicals in the matter of needing, the significant divergence seems to turn on the question whether they see the idea of need as a positive help[30] or as a hindrance in

---

[29] Cp. V. Pareto *Les Systèmes Socialistes* (Paris 1901-2) vol. ii, pp. 167-8: 'La formule: *à chacun selon ses besoins*, devient . . . un travestissement métaphysique de la formule: *à chacun part égale, avec certaines corrections*'; Gregory Vlastos 'Justice and Equality' in Brandt, ed. *Social Justice* (Prentice Hall, 1962): ' "To each according to his need" . . . is in fact the most perfect form of equal distribution' (p. 40); A.M. Honoré, 'Social Justice' in *Essays in Legal Philosophy*, ed. R.S. Summers (Blackwell, 1970) p. 78: 'The principle of social justice . . . lays down that men have a claim to advantages and an equal share in advantages. Therefore the principle of justice according to need may be regarded as one aspect, or one corollary, of the principle of social justice. From the point of view of this principle, those who are in need are entitled to point to the fact that they lack advantages to which the principle of social justice entitles them'; Honoré quotes here D.D. Raphael 'Justice and Liberty' in *Proceedings of the Aristotelian Society*, 1951: 'Thus the basis of the claim of social need is really a recognition of the claim to equality'; Feinberg, *op. cit.* at note 10 above, p. 111; A. Sen 'Equality of What?' in *Tanner Lectures on Human Values* (Utah/Cambridge, 1980), ed. McMurrin, especially pp. 217-19; David Miller, *Social Justice* (Oxford University Press, 1976), 'One could say that the principle of need represents the most urgent part of the principle of equality' (p. 149). See also Peter Singer in *Reading Nozick*, J. Paul ed., (Oxford: Blackwell, 1981), p. 49; Flew, *op. cit.* at note 4 above; R.H. Tawney *Equality* (London: Allen and Unwin, 1952), p. 42.

[30] Cp. Williams, *Problems of the Self* (Cambridge University Press, 1973), p. 240 following, and *e.g.* Vlastos, Honoré, Miller, cited at note 29.

the justification and further elucidation of the idea of equality.[31]

There is nothing to be gained by denying how natural and appropriate it is, where a writer already has a strong, positive argument in support of the idea of men's having a title and an equal title to all advantages that are generally desired and are in fact conducive to well-being (*a fortiori* where he has an argument in support of the idea of men's having a title to an equal share in such advantages),[32] for him to call on the concept of need to help him articulate his proposal. (A redistribution of everything—if that were thinkable—in accordance with need would no doubt be a more efficient approach to equality of welfare than, say, assigning everyone an equal share of goods.) The thing that does deserve to be denied is that need claims are essentially, or by their nature, claims to be treated in accordance with the precepts of the distinctive sorts of social justice that are advocated by egalitarians. There are several ways of seeing that, as such, they are not. I shall offer two considerations. Neither is a proof. Each points I hope at something the reader is already able to see.

The first consideration I advance is this: claims of vital need can be satisfied (or satisfied to a great extent at least) in a society where there is considerable inequality of wealth and even some appreciable inequality of economic opportunity[33] (especially—however big an *if* this may be—if economic inequalities are prevented from undermining legal rights and effective equality before the law). When one looks at how matters stand within such a society, and what it will involve on the levels of thought and action and refraining from action (cp. §§7–13) to maintain this happy state of affairs, nothing appears

---

[31] It may be surmised that Ronald Dworkin would regard it as a hindrance, at least so far as elucidation goes. See 'What is Equality? (Part One)', *Philosophy and Public Affairs*, vol. 10, no. 3, 1981. (Marx, having no patience with the idea of equality as such, is of course an exception to the general claim in the text.)

[32] I lean heavily here, and below, on the useful formulations of Honoré, *op. cit.* at note 29 above.

[33] And even perhaps inequality of respect? (Cp. H.L.A. Hart, *The Concept of Law*, Oxford University Press, 1961, p. 158.) Some may be tempted to say that equality of respect is a need. This is not something I shall deny. But note that if *this* is wherein the urgency of equal respect resides, then there is a danger, not that equality considerations will swallow considerations of need, but that the latter will swallow the former.

rationally inevitable in the progression from taking claims of need as deeply seriously as this society does to taking similarly seriously everyone's claim to a level of well-being effectively equal to that of anyone else.[34]

In the second place, needs claims and claims to equal treatment are sustained by and appeal to interestingly different sentiments. The matter is clearest perhaps where disappointment is in question. Under such conditions, claims to equal treatment typically proceed out of feelings of being affronted, insulted, belittled or (more generally) left out, or slightingly used; and, in their debased or pathological form, they may lapse into simple envy. What these claims demand is for those who advance them to be treated with the respect due to a human being who is accepted, simply *qua* human being, as an equal participant with an equal stake in what is seen under the aspect of a common venture.[35] Claims of need on the other hand, even when tinged with moral indignation, may be pressed from a simple passion to subsist (or for one's dependents to subsist) under tolerable conditions—a passion that lapses in its extreme or pathological form not into envy necessarily, but into self-pity or helplessness or self-absorption. When claims of need go unheeded, that which is disappointed is the expectation that it would be taken into account that the claimant's actual survival or most minimal well-being was at issue. The appeal of need depends of course on recognition of the claimant as equally a participant in society; but what sustains the appeal of the claimant and lends it strength may

[34] And if so, then here at least even some conservatives could afford to relax their guarded attitude towards needing. If the attitude towards need that I shall propose is taken just as it stands, and no more is then read into it by the force of habitual political association, then it is left open whether the proper province of state action or interference is wide or narrow, except insofar as there is strong pressure for such intervention from the quarter of otherwise unsatisfiable vital human need. But the final import of such claims of need will then depend on the totality of justice claims that are invoked. What is more, considerations of need will themselves suggest principles of limitation of the scope of action by the state. (See §23 below.)

[35] This is not to say that, by simply knowing that the relevant feelings and sentiments were drawn from this store, one could determine the content or character of the claim for equal treatment. What matters for the argument is only that there should be some distinctive difference or other in the feelings characteristically involved in the making or the recognition of the two kinds of claim.

have to comprise simple compassion or sympathy (on the part of the recognizer of the claim, and the expectation of this on the part of the claimant), or a particularized form of what Hume called the 'resentment of the misery of mankind'—a much more powerful sentiment, as Schopenhauer and others have truly observed, than even-handed benevolence or humanity. It is true of course that, insofar as claims of equality and claims of need are accepted as claims of justice, the acceptance must involve the recognition of the claimant as party to a whole network of intersubjectively established interrelations between selves which create actual duties and entitlements.[36] But for purposes of any special entitlement or expectation that is conferred by need, this network or system does not have to legitimize the expectation of substantive equality of title to all advantages. The most that it validates is the expectation that wherever rights are themselves formulated in terms of needing as such equal *needs* for $\varphi$ will import equal titles to $\varphi$-derived benefit: but that is not the title to economic equality *per se*, or in general. We do not have to speak here of the claimant's equal stake in anything, for instance.

16.     What then, if it is *sui generis*, and not to be reduced to the claim that inequality as such ought to be removed, is the distinctive political force of a statement of a serious need? The positive answer to be offered to that question will depend on dividing it in a way corresponding to three phases or levels. Phase one justice will be justice as the guardian of rights as narrowly and strictly construed; phase two justice will be justice as the definer of the limits of aggregative reasoning and vigilant arbitrator between rights and other claims (to be called counter-rights) which are not themselves rights; phase three justice will be justice as the custodian and distributor of public goods. Phase three justice will operate only within the area allowed to it by a certain principle of phase two justice, limiting the operation of aggregative reasoning.

This is to anticipate, however; and we must begin by excogitating the prerequisites of something's counting as a

---

[36] Cp. Del Vecchio's treatment of *alteritas*, in *Justice* Ch. VII. And compare H.L.A. Hart, *Concept of Law*, p. 155.

possible social morality and try to identify the role that such a thing must give (at phase or level one) to the idea of a right. Some needs will then appear as special candidates to make abstract claim-rights (claim-rights that ought to be recognized and realized concretely); and some others that do not attain to this status will appear at the second phase or level as candidates to represent abstract *counter-claims*. But these counter-claims will lie well within the province of justice, however strictly it is conceived, and will rest upon the same sort of foundation as abstract rights rest upon.

There are two necessary preliminaries to this approach. First, although need statements, when they weigh with us at all, do always weigh at least in part *as* statements of need, yet we must note that their public force is highly variable, even when their truth is not being questioned. Certainly this force is not always proportional to the need's admitted seriousness. Any account of these matters must explain or allow for this variability, and leave room for the influence or countervailing influence of factors other than need itself. Secondly, it is still worth insisting, against one kind of positivist, that the moral force of a claim of need cannot be identified with its being acknowledged to have this force, or with society's acting upon it or having regard to it—just as the social morality that a claim of need depends on for its force ought to be clearly distinguished both from the actual norms of reciprocity and cooperation that the morality makes possible and from the extant laws and social institutions that regulate these norms. (I take it that such a morality cannot properly coincide with any of these things if it will sometimes muster criticisms of existing social arrangements, and will also serve to *sustain* mores, institutions and laws, weakly or strongly, even as it subjects them to scrutiny.)

17. These preliminaries being completed, the first part of my answer to our question is this: that, in the case of some needs-statements, they report a need for something whose being needed is one part of what precisely creates the abstract right or entitlement to it. I suggest that, for purposes of a social morality $S$ that is actually lived and succeeds in proposing to agents shared concerns that they can make their own, there is

an *abstract claim-right or entitlement to x under conditions* C just where *x is something the denial or removal of which under conditions* C *gives (and can be seen as giving)*[37] *the person denied or deprived part or all of a reason, and a reason that is avowable and publicly sustainable within S, to reconsider his adherence to the norms of reciprocity and cooperation sustained by S.* This is to say that, if in such a case the victim who is deprived of *x* disappoints us in some spoken or previously unspoken expectation of co-operation, then that counts as something morally intelligible within the shared sensibility that depends on this expectation.[38]

To grasp the full import of this very exigent condition for the existence of a right it will assist to state the assumption it rests upon. This is the assumption that unless there existed *some* condition under which withdrawal of consensus was found intelligible and natural *even within S—i.e.* some condition under which *S* at least allowed someone party to *S* to think of himself as having been unjustly (even unjustifiably) sacrificed—, then *S* could scarcely count as a social morality at all. For a

---

[37] Note that the *non-availability of x* is not sufficient. The condition is limited to the denial or deprivation or removal of *x*.

Strictly we need to add after 'seen' some such words as these: both within S and within any recognizable transformation of S that continues to define a point of view can be 'common to each man with others' as he departs from his 'private and particular situation'. (Cp. Hume, *Inquiry Concerning the Principles of Morals*, IX part 1, 222.)

It suffices for this construction if, where there are interestingly different moral sensibilities to be discovered within a historically given culture, there is some minimal shared components or nucleus of differing sensibilities.

For the claim (neither required by nor inconsistent with anything that is urged here) that what is timelessly essential to the core of morality as such can be reached by factoring *ethos* out from morality itself, within what he sees as only superficially different moralities, see Aurel Kolnai 'Moral Consensus', *Proceedings of the Aristotelian Society*, 1969/70.

For another account of rights that is complementary and would deliver substantially the same account as this of the connection between needs and rights, see note 45.

[38] In connexion with this whole approach, compare *e.g.* J.L. Mackie, 'Rights, Utility and Universalization', *op. cit.*, J.L. Mackie, *Ethics* (Harmondsworth: Penguin, 1977), Bernard Williams, *Moral Luck*, p. x and *passim e.g.* 'Internal and External Reasons' pp. 101–113. In so far as my treatment differs from Mackie's and Williams', it is mainly in respect of the crucial importance I should attach in these matters of motivation to judgments of value being what they seem to be, viz. statements about features of reality, albeit essentially anthropocentrically categorized, that are discovered to us by our interest in them. Cp. Essays III and V, below.

For certain aspects of social morality equally neglected by Williams, Mackie and myself, see A.M. Honoré, 'Groups, Law and Obedience' in *Oxford Essays in Jurisprudence* II, 1973.

social morality, as conceived for these purposes, is not just any old set of abstract principles. It is something that exists only as realized or embodied (or as capable of being realized or embodied) in a shared sensibility, and in the historically given *mores* and institutions that are themselves perpetuated by it. It is only by virtue of participating in this sort of thing, and seeing one another as participating in it, that ordinary human beings as actually constituted are able to embrace common concerns and common goals that will take on a life of their own or be perceived as enshrining values that possess what Hume sometimes called 'moral beauty'. A social morality cannot of course give any particular person a guaranteed title to wealth, health, happiness, or security from ordinary misfortune. But equally it must not be such as to threaten anyone who is to be bound by it that it will bring upon him or any other individual participant, as if gratuitously, the misfortune of having his vital interests simply sacrificed for the sake of some larger public good.[39] What sustains and regulates or adjusts a social morality and what rebuts objections to it, must be something intelligible to all its individual participants, in human (never mind archangelic or ideal observer) terms.[40] It must engage with the passions of those who are to live by it—or at least not *dis*engage with those passions.

[39] Cp. J.L. Mackie, 'Can there be a rights-based moral theory?', *op. cit.*

'A central embarrassment for the best known goal-based theories, the various forms of utilitarianism, is that the well being of one individual should be sacrificed without limits, for the well being of others (p. 352) . . . Why should it not be a *fundamental* moral principle that the well being of one person cannot be simply replaced by that of another? There is no proof of purely aggregative consequentialism at any level (p. 354)'.

For a lawyer's formulation of what is almost the same point see Arnold Goodman, *Not for the Record* (London: Deutsch, 1972), pp. 18–19:

'The popular proposition that we must sink our selfish self-interest in the public good . . . requires the closest scrutiny and the strongest scepticism. For it is the proposition which can justify any hardship or injustice to a private person, and the one most prone to ignore the arithmetical truism that the community is the sum of its individuals. That injury to an individual—inequitable or unrequited—is, in the absence of strong contrary proof, an injustice to the community in whose name it is so lightly committed. But [this proposition] is invoked with monotonous ruthlessness by governmental systems.'

[40] States go to war, and in fighting them they have exacted the sacrifice of millions of lives. But states that deserve the loyalty of their subjects do not go to war 'to maximize the public good'—rather to avoid invasion or national humiliation or subjugation or to defend vital interests that subjects can identify with.

18.   It is only a small step from requiring that a social morality lack this licence to requiring, more positively and definitely: (i) that it should place explicit limitations on the social goals it promotes or tolerates, on the burdens individuals can normally be asked to endure in the common pursuit of this or that kind of public goal, and on the scope and ambit of any modes of aggregative reasoning it countenances: (ii) that it should sustain rights under a rule of law, securing individuals from arbitrary arrest, imprisonment or punishment, and assuring them of other civic and legal protections; and (iii) that it should uphold the right to make certain sorts of agreement with other individuals, to buy the necessities of life, sell the product of one's labour, and be not dispossessed of that which one has appropriated or mixed one's labour with in ways seen as worthy of being accorded legal recognition.

Items that find a place in this enumeration do not find it *simply* because they are needed. But as Hart anticipated (§ 1), the idea of need plays its own distinctive and recognizable role in helping to generate and constrain the enumeration. What is more, its presence helps to render the idea of an abstract claim-right unmysterious. Certainly the derivation is not obliged to represent itself as *a priori* or *pre-moral* or as resting upon natural law (a concept it needs neither to invoke nor to denounce). In a very general way it is *a posteriori*. No doubt the *a posteriority* of the question what social moralities have to be like in order to be possible will appear to many philosophers of some temperaments to disqualify the entire approach. But surely *a posteriority* is what we ought to have predicted if we expect morality to have the hold upon motive and action that Hume argued that it must. Morality must have this hold intelligibly, by virtue of the content of the judgements it delivers, and by virtue of the possibility of the values and concerns that it proposes to agents becoming for them nothing less than ends in themselves, furnishing them with what they can see as reasons for being concerned or affected in certain particular ways.[41]

---

[41] *A posteriority* is again what we ought to predict if we will allow that the relation between social morality and its embodying social institutions needs to be a reciprocal one. It needs to be reciprocal if the morality is to take up from *mores* and institutions the distinctive colouration and distinctive emphases that will characterize the

This whole view of rights may provoke the accusation that I say there is a right wherever there is an opportunity for blackmail, or that I submit morality itself to what Nietzsche called 'the trading mentality', and might equally well, with almost equal moral ugliness, have called 'the contracting mentality'. But wherever else this accusation may be appropriate, it does not belong here. The view of rights that I am defending is consistent with a morality's *not* being something whose force, nature or content is supplied from any kind of prudence. Not only does the view respect the fact that we do not opt or contract into a social morality. No weight at all has had to attach to the possibility (which I wholly discount) of reconstructing the reasons we would or might, as pre-socially conceived, have had for so opting or contracting. A social morality, as conceived here, is not even something which *it is as if* we have opted or contracted into.[42] It is simply the sort of thing that we find ourselves in the midst of. By virtue of being what it is and having the content it does have and deserving to command the consensus of those who live within it, it is something that does *not* furnish its adherents with what they would have to regard as decently avowable reasons to *opt out of it*. It is neither here nor there if there are all sorts of other

---

communal ends and socially conditioned individual ends that the morality recognizes as intelligible ends of human endeavour and concern. (In fact both logically and historically speaking, social morality and social institutions must come into being simultaneously.) To reject *a posteriori* here is to reject the idea that values and shared concerns need to have a historical aspect. But without a historical aspect most values and concerns that go beyond simple human survival are simply arbitrary and, in every relevant sense of the phrase, rationally unintelligible.

[42] If we suppose that it is even a bit like something to opt into, then we immediately find ourselves forced to think that it ought to be possible to reconstruct the reasons (it is now as if) we once had for the choice that (it is now as if) we once made when we opted into it. But surely, if such reasons had to be found, none could possibly be provided. How could any candidate to be such a reason both show, as it would need to show, that this was the morality we would have been most *prudent* or *rational* to adhere to, and also respect the status as a morality of what it is as if we should have chosen? Any consideration at all that promised to be suitable to count as a reason of the required sort would *either* employ a notion of rationality and prudence that begged the question (this I insist is the innocent, fruitful way with the matter in all other connexions) *or* depend on a conception of rationality that would have us choosing virtue or justice not for what it is in itself but in the expectation of a return of another sort.

moralities that pass this test and that we might have found ourselves in the midst of. Our attachment does not depend on that's not being so, or on our satisfying ourselves that there is no other social morality that might have offered someone in our position a better package of rights.

19.    Principles (i), (ii) and (iii) are concerned with great goods, and what they presuppose is already an enormous charge on the State. But consideration of what it takes to ensure their persistence in the real world is certain to lend colour to an independent demand for certain much more specifically political rights, as well as for publicly provided systems of education, legal aid and basic health care. These things are intelligible extensions, of which I shall say more later, in what it is still just possible to recognize as the same spirit. I should say that these things were at most one step beyond the rights whose non-realization gives men good reason for disaffection from society, because (i) (ii) (iii) and their proper extensions are simply the preconditions of someone's securing his own material survival in his own way, or in the best way relative to his circumstances, by his own efforts. Someone who demands such rights as these asks for scarcely any strictly first order goods—only for that with which to get his own, within a community that recognizes him as a participant with this right and that he in his turn recognizes as conferring, guaranteeing and limiting that right, and as presupposed, in some condition or other, to any life that he can fully value. Still less does he ask for an equal title to an equal share of first order goods.

However familiar or unfamiliar our general method of justification may have appeared, the embryo rights that it generates are familiar enough. What will be noted, however, is that, although some needs have now turned up as generating rights and/or liberties with a protective fence of claim-rights, we still have no *general* vindication of the force of serious needs claims as such. It is true of course that some who set store by rights are apt to insist on more numerous and stronger rights than any afforded under (i), (ii) and (iii), and it is also true and important that, in practice, many extant social moralities will recognize, and impress upon the institutions and laws that they sustain, more rights than the abstract things one can demonstrate by the general method we have sketched.[43] (In their special circumstances, they may have to. See below §21 foll.) But that is not enough for our purposes. For, having rejected the idea of a social contract, and what one is *owed* for one's accord in the same, because we rejected the idea of a reconstruction of any however hypothetical, prudence-based reasons for opting into morality, we dare not see first order benefits that go too far beyond (i) (ii) (iii), or all needs simply as such, under the aspect of moral rights or abstract entitlements—lest they appear under the guise of a sort of *quid pro quo* for the retention of participative adherence or consensus. No idea could more quickly subvert a social morality, or more effectively despoil the achievement that it represents. (Cp. Schopenhauer, *On the Basis of Morality*, §7.)

There is a second reason not to find rights, or what have sometimes been called 'claim-rights in the making' or 'manifesto rights', wherever there happen to be some serious needs, and this reason will hold good even for cases where certain needs are far harder to ignore than some unproblematical, acknowledged rights are. If we hold onto the conception of rights introduced in §17, then it will be natural to suppose that a categorical abstract claim-right only exists where there could in principle be some institutional obligation upon someone or something to arrange for people to have the chance to take official or legal action against some specific defendant or legal entity in order to require some specific performance of him or it.[44] But however we rearrange society and its processes, there will always be claims of dire need that fail this test. If we use the idea

---

[43] Historically some have recognized rather fewer. But the reader will have guessed that I shall claim this does not matter. What people will put up with is an *a posteriori* question, one dependent on factors of human psychology and awareness that change gradually but constantly through time. These changes are for the most part irreversible. As in all matters of awareness, a kind of ratchet mechanism operates.

What people will acquiesce in is to some degree a moral question. For what people can acquiesce in depends on what they think is fair to them. And what they think fair must depend however indirectly or minimally on what *is* fair. If our explanations in these sections were intended as reductive or eliminative, this would be fatal to them. But our aim here is only to exhibit the *inter-connections* of the concepts *claim-right, need, participants' consensus, social justice* . . . .

[44] On claim rights, cp. note 15 above; and see also Alan Ryan 'Overriding Interests', *Times Literary Supplement*, 22 April 1983, p. 411.

of right to prevent these from falling into oblivion, then we risk
having to do without any criterion at all for right-hood and
losing all sharpness in the idea of a right.[45] Given the nature of
the opposition, that is not a risk that it is wise to take.

There will be a temptation at this point to try to find room
for needs in our picture by seeing needs that are not good
candidates to be simple rights as having a force somehow
comparable to a claim-right, and as requiring that whoever has
this or that serious need should be recognized as owed *special
consideration* when the mass of claims that bear upon any
particular matter is reviewed. But, although this is correct
enough for certain kinds of claims of needing, it is too vague.
What is far worse, it still leaves everything unexplained. Why
*should* these kinds of needing deserve special public consideration?

The general form of the answer that I shall offer to this
question, in what I shall number the second phase of the
explanation promised in §16, is that serious non-instrumental

---

[45] Cp. also the question put by Charles Fried, *Right and Wrong* (Cambridge Mass:
Harvard, 1978), p. 122:

> The major objection to a theory of rights based on needs [is that] though needs and their
> satisfaction have an objective quality, the fact is that any commitment, via the recognition
> of positive rights, to meet need also makes us hostages to vastly varied and voracious
> needs. . . . How to contain this voraciousness? If needs create rights to their satisfaction,
> how are we to prevent them from claiming so much that there is no energy left to pursue
> other goals?

Having given an account of rights that answers Fried's question—see §17 above—, let
me refer to a complementary and no doubt better account of rights, which I did not
know when I formulated mine, namely Joseph Raz's version of the so-called
beneficiary theory of rights as given in his 'On the Nature of Rights', *Mind* vol. 93, 1984,
pp. 192–214. The careful adherent of a position like Raz's may certainly hold that to
say a person has a right is to say that some interest of that person's is a sufficient reason
for holding another person or body to be subject to some duty that serves the interest.
But not just any old interest will count, or just any old ground. Everything depends on
what kind of interest, with what provenance, and (if the interest passes that test) what
protection, if any, is not only stably and foreseeably beneficial to the right-holder in
society, but also nearly invariably indispensable to the protection and enjoyment of
that interest. What the Aristotelian account explains is how needs can be important
enough *in certain classes of case* to be indispensable to the justification for imposing
such duties, not how needs automatically generate rights *wherever* needs ought to
impinge as needs on the determination of public policy. Compare also E.D. Watt, *op.
cit.* (note 7 above): 'What it is important to insist . . . is that it can make good sense to
speak of needs without implying an active obligation on the part of any person to meet
these needs'.

needs that do not constitute rights or entitlements can sometimes stand in a certain counterpoise relation, first with straightforward rights actually recognized, and then (in a potentially contrasting way) with the ends of concerted public action. Especially, vital needs (as defined p. 17) can do so.

20.   Principles (i), (ii) and (iii) of §18 start life as scarcely more than the preconditions of men's securing their own survival in their own way, or in the best way relative to their circumstances. But they have a tendency to outgrow their beginnings. And on our *a posteriori* consensual approach, the strength and status of class (iii) rights and entitlements to property, inheritance etc. is not fixed exactly or for all places and times. What *is* determined about them—given the finitude of the world's natural resources, the long term impossibility of each man's appropriation from natural resources leaving behind as much and as good for the next, and the accumulation of power that has inevitably accrued in a finite social space to those who stand at the end of long chains of inheritance of property and influence—is only that the stronger the support and confirmation that a given social morality provides for entrenched entitlements, and the greater the legal and political protection accordingly extended to those exercising a large number of class (iii) rights, the greater will be the State's and its servants' moral duty to respect in all legal and political deliberation the needs and vital interests of the people there will always be who have not got themselves into a position to acquire or exercise very many such rights and entitlements. And the readier the State must then be, having marked out property and other entitlements, to diminish the extent to which such entrenched rights can countervail against true claims of vital need that must otherwise go unsatisfied. Surely needs must offset property rights *at least* to the extent that the appropriations and transfers of the centuries render ineffective all present efforts to command the resources that one requires to live by one's own efforts.[46] But one ought to go

---

[46] Cp. J.L. Mackie *Ethics, op. cit.* pp. 175–6: and 'Rights, Utility and Universalization', *op. cit.* And for a relatively ancient statement of the relevant (still neglected) platitude, see J. von Neumann, *Collected Works VI*, p. 505: 'Literally and figuratively we are running out of room. At long last, we begin to feel the effects of the finite actual size of the earth in a critical way.'

further. The stronger the property rights that are politically recognized and legally enforced, and the greater the efficacity of the social morality in sustaining the institutions that protect these rights, the more self-conscious society must become (at least under the conditions we are now used to in all the more populated, civilized and economically exploited parts of the earth) about the *inflexibility* and *possible failure* of the systems of entitlement relations that govern possession and use,[47] and the readier it must be to give practical expression to this self-consciousness, by the regulation of commerce, by ministering directly to unsatisfied vital needs, or (better) by ensuring that wealth should be created closer to the point where there are vital interests that will otherwise go unsatisfied. Society must cultivate this self-consciousness on pain of being seen as precisely worsening the plight of those who have least and who might otherwise have combined to take by force what they needed for self-sufficiency.[48]—Or on pain of the State's finding itself forced to subdue these people by methods that will in the end subvert morality itself.

21.   It would be a great mistake to suppose that the public perception of the failure of entitlement relations is wedded even historically (let alone philosophically, see §15) to the ideal of equality (in the sense of everyone's having an equal title to all advantages), or that this failure is a new thing, and somehow the problem child of the welfare state as such. Classical and medieval anticipations aside, even nineteenth century capitalism hard-headedly recognized what was nothing other than a failure of entitlement relations when it saw a problem in the housing of the poor (the employed and industrious poor

[47] I am indebted in this formulation to important general ideas expounded by Amartya Sen in his *Poverty and Famines* (Oxford University Press, 1983) and, later, to his contention that what famine dramatizes is not so much the power of natural disaster as the failure or weakness of systems of entitlement relations.

[48] I say 'otherwise'. But of course they may do this anyway. And they may do it in a way that goes well beyond taking by force what they need. What is being urged here without prejudice to any of those questions is simply the weakest claim: that, if under these circumstances men combine to take what they need by force, then moral justification may be available for that, whatever condemnation may also be possible for whatever else they do.

For the way in which phase two justice (I now see) makes ineliminable use of one distinctively egalitarian (but restricted) idea, see now *Postscript*, note 13.

especially).[49] It is true that *de facto*, and perhaps inevitably, philanthropy entered in here. But even if it takes emergency to make us attend to what is intolerable in certain failures of entitlement, *e.g.* in famine as Amartya Sen has anatomized that, we must still distinguish that mixed sort of disaster from natural disasters like flooding, earthquake or hurricane. Society intervenes there as well, but in the cause of philanthropy. Whereas in the case of simple starvation or lack of shelter, the duty to ask whether these are failures of entitlement, and to be prepared, if necessary, to abridge or modify various type (iii) rights is a requirement of justice, and will remain so even where we cannot characterize the situation either correctly or illuminatingly in terms of specific rights. (Of course, in the context of a given system of law and administration that has grown sensitive to counterclaims, it may come about that citizens acquire certain legal rights to certain sorts of benefits, in money or in kind, *e.g.* health-care, or subsidized housing or even subsidized transport. And, as we have seen, there can be backing in justice for these rights, as conditionally considered, at least in the presence of certain now familiar social conditions arising from distortions of various heterogeneous kinds. But this backing can scarcely comprise any categorical abstract rights to such goods or services, however badly they are needed.)

22. With counterclaims and everything they involve, one enters immediately into an area of conflict, of revolution even. So it is not surprising how hard it is to say anything, however theoretical, to satisfy all parties to the conflict. One half of the difficulty is that rights like those of class (iii) give rise to entirely legitimate expectations about the character and extent of the interventions against historical contingency and luck that society will undertake in the name of justice. Not only are rights like those falling in class (iii) founded in a special way in a human need. It is also a deep human need to be *able* to frame such long term expectations of tenure and security. (To remove the possibility of these is to abandon one of the most distinctive advantages of the very civilization that almost everyone aspires

---

[49] For an illuminating account, see for instance J.N. Tarn *Five per cent Philanthropy* (Cambridge University Press, 1973).

to enjoy who looks to ordinary politics for the redress of injustice.) The other half of the difficulty is of course that in certain cases the situation of those whom a certain system of rights impedes from living by their own efforts may be nothing short of desperate.

Sticking to what our approach suggests ought to be least controversial, I would urge (1) that the clearest case, both for rights falling within the kinds (i), (ii), (iii) and for counterclaims, reposes upon vital needs that men will not otherwise be able to satisfy by their own efforts; (2) that, however strong the case in need for however stringent an abridgement of rights of acquisition or tenure, the correction or redistribution ought to be gradual and non-retrospective lest considerations of social justice invade and annihilate the very idea of a right. Again (3), when the satisfaction of counter-claims makes it necessary to abridge rights or raise taxes above levels that were justified by the expense of providing and protecting rights and benefits falling within categories (i), (ii), (iii), this should be done in a manner that is (a) perspicuous in intention; (b) generally consistent with a man's original title to what he earns;[50] (c) such as to force upon us the question whether enough (or too much) is being attempted, and whether in the right way.[51] Otherwise we lose sight of the terms of the original conflict, and blur the distinction between that issue and other issues that arise at a later phase of the evolution of social justice (namely, phase three, see below, §26). Finally (4) I note that the more complicated and diverse the admissible counter-claims that can appear under the aspect of claims in justice, and the more complicated and diverse the response to them that is attempted in society's name, the more likely this public response is to get

[50] A citizen is taxed, surely, on what he has earned and made his own. He ought not to be deemed not even to have earned the portion he gives up. He cannot give *back* to society what is never his.

[51] Consider for instance subsidized, publicly owned housing. Is this a better solution to the problem than subsidizing rents of those of low income in a flourishing, properly regulated private sector? For a powerful but wholly neglected argument that public or special housing was not the best or the only solution to the problem, see Jane Jacobs *Death and Life of the Great American City* (London: Jonathan Cape, 1962), pp. 323–7. And *why* in any case (we must always ask) are the incomes of some hard-working industrious persons doing essential work too low for them to be able to afford adequate housing?

muddled up with different kinds of public projects whose rationale is not vital need based at all.

Justice mediates between rights and counter-rights on the principle that, when the rights system leaves insufficient room for everyone to satisfy vital needs, rights may have to be abridged on a principle of equal concern for anyone's and everyone's vital need. But this concern will often itself lead to collective reasoning designed to increase the overall sum of opportunities —which may in its turn threaten vital needs of some individuals.

23. Perhaps the limitative principle that must regulate both rights/counter-rights arbitration *and* collective reasoning conducted in pursuit of public goods is this. Even if there is nothing unjust in actions of the State or its agencies making one man poorer in a way that makes another man less poor than he was (in kind or money)—and even if there need be no injustice as such (whatever pause it suggests for thought) if among those who suffer thereby one will find some who are already the least fortunate among all the parties involved—, *it is pro tanto unjust* if the State or an agency of the State intervenes against contingency, or changes its policy, or confounds citizens' sensible expectations, in a way that sacrifices anyone's strictly vital interests to the mere desires of however many others; and (more speculatively) *it is pro tanto unjust* if, among vital interests actually affected by such interventions, the greater strictly vital need of anyone is sacrificed in the name of the lesser needs of however many others.

Such a principle—which must be based, as always, in the connexion between justice, consensus and citizens' sense of the legitimacy of government (and should be adjusted or corrected and weakened or strengthened in the light of that connexion)— is still in the spirit of the arguments of §§20–21. A society that allows type (iii) rights to outgrow their proper rationale does precisely threaten vital interests. And the same applies to a society that is uncritical of the counter-claims it finds valid. But let it be clear that not only the fortunate need to be protected by the operation of a limitative principle, and it is not only the question of counter-claims that gives rise to the need for it. Almost invariably, actual societies' perception of the duty of governments to intervene in the name of counter-

claims has coincided with (or even been preceded by) a
perception of quite different reasons for public intervention,
*e.g.*, the necessity to solve coordination problems or provide
benefits that coordination problems prevent the market from
providing. It is hard to show any objection in principle to this,
even where the resulting projects are not vital needs-based. But
all experience suggests that, as society's public actions become
more heterogeneous, as lower incomes begin to be heavily
taxed, and as public projects impinge more and more severely
upon the environment, displacing citizens for public works
such as schools, hospitals, parks and public road building (the
last having an understandable tendency always to seek out the
areas of lowest rateable value), those who stand in the direst
need of the Principle of Limitation are almost never the rich or
the fortunate. And the more it then begins to seem proper for
the State to undertake, the smaller the probability that all
consensually requisite protection of every individual's vital
interests will be available already, in the shape of effective,
recognized legal and/or constitutional rights and remedies,
like those falling in our classes (i), (ii), (iii), that can be opposed
to the actual or prospective, direct or indirect effects of public
action.

24.   In the face of this sort of problem, some have suggested
that accepted methods such as cost-benefit analysis be more
widely used and simultaneously strengthened to reflect the
observed fact that the most a person is willing to pay for a
benefit he has not got, or to avert an evil he does not
suffer, is less than the smallest amount he would accept to be
deprived of the benefit or be forced to put up with the evil; or
that such methods ought to give a special weighting to burdens
and benefits that will accrue from a scheme to the poorer
sections of the community. But this palliative[52] scarcely goes to
the middle of the difficulty, which is that a sufficient number of
mere desires can always swamp any however heavily weighted
need; and that a sufficient number of needs of the non-vital

---

[52] Cp. *mutatis mutandis* Sen's remark at *op. cit.* pp. 156–7 ('As a category for causal
analysis *the poor* isn't a very helpful one').

variety can always outweigh any however heavily weighted vital need.[53]

Others have considered that what was required was a new sensitivity to the common law rights of individuals and some legislative strengthening of individual rights. But in practice this would almost certainly have been ineffective in some cases and too effective in others—if it means that certain sorts of public project, even projects justified by the direst need, could always be obstructed (*e.g.* by the refusal or threatened refusal by the victims of a public project to accept proffered compensation as adequate).[54] I do not of course deny that there may be a case for some strengthening in individual rights. But as a general response, this sort of approach does not address

---

[53] Sober theorists like E.J. Mishan have always been unequivocally clear that projects admitted on cost-benefit analysis are 'consistent with transparent inequity', and that 'for a project to be socially acceptable it is not enough to show that the outcome of a cost-benefit analysis is acceptable . . . it must also be shown that no gross inequities are committed'.

Mackie had an idea which might seem to help here, in 'Can there be a rights-based Moral Theory' *op. cit.*

> [We shall] not allow the vital interests of anyone to be sacrificed for the advantage of others, to be outweighted by an aggregate of less vital interests. Rather we might think in terms of a model in which each person is represented by a point-centre of force, and the forces (representing *prima facie* rights) obey an inverse square law, so that a right decreases in weight with the remoteness of the matter on which it bears from the person whose right it is. There will be some matters so close to each person that with respect to them his rights will nearly always outweight any aggregate of other rights.

The mathematical model is suggestive, and it will be plain that I am indebted to it (however doubtful I am that it will quite work). But I fear it will provoke ingenious, disobliging persons to miss the whole point of holding some position such as Mackie's; and, if the model were applied to the exposition of the present proposal (which complicates the picture by bringing in needs-based counter-claims as vital interests that do not necessarily correspond to rights), it would no doubt provoke the same persons to misunderstand the basis and intention of the Principle of Limitation. In my treatment, that Principle is not, of course, part of an outline decision procedure but one of the several principles comprised in justice, with the special property of essentially contestably demarcating the area in which certain others can operate.

[54] Yet nothing less than the possibility of refusing what was offered would have been sufficient in the case of many of the injustices that have actually been committed in this area.

It is instructive in this connexion and in all sorts of connected ways to read command paper Cmnd. 5124 (October 1972) *Development and Compensation*—especially if one is moved beyond anything that is actively encouraged by the cool correct language of the document itself to try to remember or imagine the countless actions that eventually gave rise to the need for this, by the going standards, extraordinarily frank official confession of past injustice.

the real problem. *What* new rights are to be found or created, and on what principle? And how can these ever be arranged to anticipate the *indefinite* number of possible future injustices that will be committed against identifiable and non-identifiable people in the name of the public interest?[55]

Another slightly different approach has proposed the institution of a procedural-cum-constitutional right to have one's vital needs or interests taken as vital interests when public schemes are mooted, this right being backed by the legal power to force relevant officials either to prove at a hearing that these interests have been taken into account and treated in accordance with some relevant principle or to abandon their project. But, however impressive this may sound, it would be curiously ineffective in the absence of any agreed principles about how vital interests that are not legal rights are to be treated, as well as suffering from the same difficulties with unidentified or unidentifiable victims as beset the common law and new statute law approach.

So the direction in which one is finally inclined is along the path that leads not through rights as such but directly back to what starts to appear as nothing less than a necessity of political culture, namely the explicit acknowledgement as a constituent principle of justice (along with whatever other principles we can muster) of some principle like the ones I

---

[55] It may be well to give an example where common law rights give out before the concerns of justice can. When public works lay a whole neighbourhood waste and some or all of its inhabitants are to be resettled, the only legal claim-right anyone has normally had to compensation has derived from the legal ownership of land or a house. But there are always many who own neither. It is true that in more recent times those who actually live there at a specified date have been given some legal right to be resettled by the local authority, and may even qualify under recent provisions for some grant for 'disturbance' (a sum that it was proposed in 1972, on the basis of some vague sense of its inadequacy, simply to double). These are improvements in justice, even though the local authority is not necessarily the landlord of their choice, nor will they necessarily be rehoused at the rent they paid previously. It is possible to imagine these and other deficiencies being remedied. It is even possible, I suppose, to imagine a code of compensation that made good in real terms what a scheme actually took away from owners and non-owners who could be *identified*. Note however that even this would by no means exhaust those whose vital interests were actually affected, *e.g.*, by the contribution that such public projects may make to shortage (pushing up rents and house-prices), to blight, and to the dereliction of local employment. Any approach that will stress the openness of the class of persons to be affected in these ways must go well beyond the concern with common law rights and codes of compensation.

stated in §§22-3. (Cp. also §13.) Administrative and legal details are important but secondary. What matters first is that something like what I shall call the Principle of Limitation should be confirmed in the status of a principle of fairness, and should come to be taken so much for granted as a principle of fairness that it be normally impossible for administrative practice and political decision-making to proceed in apparent defiance of the Principle. (By 'normally' I mean 'under conditions where there is no strong case for overriding considerations of justice'.) In the presence of the expectation of this, it will be largely a matter of legal tradition whether or not citizens have the envisaged procedural-constitutional rights or how else the operation of the principle is guaranteed.[56] In the absence of the expectation that vital needs will rank in this way, the long term prospects are not very good, in the world as it is now, for government with the full consent of the governed. There will be things that stick in the throat when we seek to justify what government is forced to say and do to those who take exception to its encroachments.

25.    If the Limitation Principle is an attempt to spell out, in terms of a vagueness suited to the subject matter, one of the prerequisites for the adherents of a workable social morality to lack avowable reasons to abdicate from it, then in all modern societies that are governed by consent, men's moral consciousness ought to concur in the Limitation Principle. But perhaps one should not expect to find any very direct practical or phenomenological test for the Principle or the correctness of the argument that I have offered for it. For we must be prepared to accept that different societies may differ considerably in the interpretation they put on 'vital' as it figures in 'vital interest or need'. (Cp. §9.) One would predict that these and other differences in interpretation or emphasis will combine

---

[56] A compromise might make provision for appeal against such procedures as Compulsory Purchase Order or Power of Eminent Domain, and might permit those directly affected to secure a formal hearing for themselves at which it was relevant and appropriate to refer to the Limitation Principle. Indeed I believe that the strong official predisposition in favour of the language of need, pointed out in §3, precisely rests on some inchoate, partial understanding of this appropriateness.

with divergent conceptions of the interventive role of government to issue in many important variations in the practice and
sentiments of justice. The existence of these variations is
perfectly consistent with the correctness of the Limitation
Principle, whose operation is in any case highly sensitive, even
at a particular time in a particular context, to where exactly the
frontier of vital interests is seen as lying. Where a need is (as
correctly formulated) vital and is specially protected as such by
the principle, then it limits the space within which it is just for
society to seek to maximize aggregated social advantage. If on
the other hand the need falls short of that threshold, then it takes
its chance with other needs, and there are conditions under
which it may be sacrificed, and sacrificed without injustice, to
the aggregated weight of other interests.

This discontinuity may seem strange. But reflection suggests
that things have to be like this. There are some things we
cannot justly do to a man, however much in aggregate other
men may benefit.[57] (Almost nobody thinks that it can be just to
kill one innocent man simply in order that millions should
each receive some less than vital benefit.) The only question is
how far this special protection extends beyond life itself. And
of course there must be *some* cut-off. Otherwise we could
scarcely ever reason aggregatively without incurring the charge
of being to some extent unjust to someone.

What one ought to hope then is not that we can dispense with
the threshold just mentioned, but that, given a place, a time, a
climate of opinion and a set of expectations, the placing of the
threshold will not be arbitrary but at worst essentially
contestable. One might also expect that, as a society grows
richer—and as it enlarges its sympathies to treat as if they were
counter-claims in justice the claims of those who are prevented
by natural handicap rather than by the power or prior
appropriations of others from living through their own
efforts—, the members of that society will construe 'vital
interests' more generously. Perhaps in feeling they do. In

---

[57] It is worth remembering here that if we allow ourselves to be forced by some
imaginable but appalling circumstance to override the claim of justice, it will be better
to say 'We had to be unjust' than to say 'What we did was, in the circumstances, just'
(or 'just in the circumstances'). (For a good statement of the impact of emergency upon
criteria of vital need, see Finnis, *Natural Law and Natural Rights, op. cit.*, p. 174.)

practice, however—even if the human sentiments are prepared in principle for this, and are also prepared to understand the Limitation Principle more generously than I did in assigning it the excluding role I proposed for it—, the bureaucratic consciousness construes 'vital interests' extremely narrowly, so narrowly sometimes as to include little more than the bare prerequisites of life.[58]

The long term dangers of this narrow construal are the same, I believe, as the dangers of an outright rejection of the Principle of Limitation. But the chief reason for the narrow interpretation is not, I think, any particular wickedness of bureaucrats, but the intense competition that they are apt to find themselves witnessing at close quarters (or involved in as the recipients of lobbying, special pleading, pressure from newspapers about particular cases *etc.*) between considerations like the Limitation Principle (understood as a principle of justice, but not properly understood as a principle of limitation, and almost always *under-represented* because very few projects clearly endanger the vital interests of a larger number of people than the number they benefit) and very different kinds of need-based claims. The rationale of these other claims (which should not be lightly assumed to be a rationale in justice) arises at what is logically (if not historically) a third phase, after the two phases I have described in the preceding sections.

26. A society reaches the third phase, by my count, when government not only sees itself as the guardian of rights (the first phase) and counter-claims (the second phase), but also confirms itself in its role as the agent of coordination and the

---

[58] Nobody who does not already have some knowledge of the desolate scenes touched upon in *Cmnd* 5124 (*op. cit.* note 54 above) will want to take this on my say so. But to those who do I will remark how rare it is for a public agency bent on a large project with many direct and indirect consequences to pause to consider all the legal and moral obstacles that a private promoter would have had to face if he had tried to realize the same project as a commercial venture.

Postscript (1990) The decade just concluded, dense as it has been with socially and aesthetically destructive schemes promoted by private Act of Parliament or by other special procedures, has not been kind to the assumption that is made in the last sentence, namely that private or mixed private and public schemes will be scrutinized with greater care or with greater thought for legitimate expectations of the kind expressed by the Principle of Limitation than public schemes were. What the decade has reinforced is the case for recognizing such a principle as the Limitation Principle.

indispensable minister (at least in certain particular spheres) to human needs that will otherwise go unsatisfied. (And desires too, no doubt, though, as we noticed at the beginning, once taken on board, desires are usually accorded the official title of needs.) Here the numbers who benefit from any project and the quantity of need that can be satisfied by a given resource are felt to be a strong consideration—and, given the shortage of resources, rightly so. For what the administrator is now involved with is aggregative or agglomerative reasoning—i.e. subject to some constraint, he is maximizing something—, and what presumably matters most *within the proper sphere of such reasoning* is accurate measurement and prediction of consequences, and the will to jump off the treadmill whenever necessary for the imaginative exploration of alternatives that will bring greater total satisfaction and avoid the projection into the future of situations already giving rise to dissatisfaction and the mounting consumption of resources.[59]

Once a society is launched into phase three (and launched there for reasons having nothing specially to do with justice) and has instituted corresponding rules and practices, it moves into a whole new range of possible unfairness. And protestation at unfairness is sure to become unprecedentedly shrill and rancorous, giving even an obsession with the older and more important part of justice the unjustified reputation of enviousness and stridency. 'If $z$ with need $x$ had such and such done for him, why is nothing done for me with my need $w$?' What every administration that has entered the third phase requires is a range of defensible answers to such questions. It seems it must always be able to reply either 'Yes, we will!' or '$z$'s need is greater', or 'Your need is more expensive to satisfy'. Whatever

---

[59] It is not very useful to predict how people would behave, and what preferences they would thereby reveal, in a future state of affairs that inherits most of the unsatisfactory features they seek to escape from in the present. ('We always plan too much and think too little', as Schumpeter says in another connection.) But of course to escape from that dead end, we must understand better on the levels of reason and constituent beliefs, desires, needs, vital interests . . . what people avoid or seek in the present, and what alterable features of the present condition these beliefs, desires, needs, vital interests . . . (and how they condition them). (See my *Sameness and Substance*, pp. 180ff.; also 'Deliberation and Practical Reason' in J. Raz, *Practical Reasoning* (Oxford University Press 1981), which is an extract from Essay VI below.) And this may interest us afresh in considerations of justice that antedate phase three.

it gives to anyone placed in such and such a way, it must also give to anyone else so placed; and then (for given only finite resources, this must result from the same policy) it must be careful never to give anyone anything before it has looked to the ends of the earth to ensure that there are not too many others who will be able to represent that they have the very same entitlement.

27. There is no going back from phase three. We are too used to the benefits we attribute to it. And our feelings are commendably (however confusedly) fixed upon at least one small but conspicuous concomitant of it, namely our new willingness to intervene against contingency to help remedy certain entitlement failures that are in no way society's fault or strict responsibility. We did not have to feel this, but we do in fact. What was claimed about the distinction between claims of need and claims of the intolerability of inequality still holds good; but that distinction leaves room for an idea (not itself lacking some link with consensus but without any *special* tie to need) that there can be such a thing as too great a gap between people's life-chances.[60] It does not enforce or entail this idea, but it allows it.

But if there is no going back, and phase three is where we resolve to take our stand, then the time has arrived to try to understand much better the essential instability of the conception of social justice that we have got ourselves. And this we can scarcely do if we will never try to decipher the palimpsest of divergent ideas that it comprises.

In the first place, *need* itself now figures not only on the side of *justice as limitative, protective, and remedial*, (phases one and two), but also on the frequently conflicting side of *justice as the keeper and distributor of public goods*. In the conversation with the economist that I reported at §3, we could barely understand

---

[60] It may be worth contrasting this relatively weak principle with stronger formulations such as Richard Norman's 'Comprehensive Egalitarian Principle' in *Contemporary Political Philosophy: Radical Studies* (Cambridge, 1982), ed. K. Graham, p. 102: 'satisfaction of the basic needs of all, plus equality of monetary incomes over and above that (though this might need further qualifying if it were desired to increase some incomes to compensate for particularly dangerous or unpleasant work)'.

one another because he was preoccupied with the second of these roles and I was so preoccupied with the first. Had we realized this, and had I then expressed my concurrence in his belief that claims of need are often found in the company of abuse and special pleading, we could have got a little further and might even have found ourselves discussing vital interests, the limits of compensation and the problem of bequeathing to our descendants a world with at least as many tolerable niches for individual human existence as the one we inherited. Few questions are more urgent. But no progress at all can be made on them without some public understanding of the distinctness of these ways in which need claims impinge on us, and some sense of the putative priority in justice itself of phase one and phase two considerations over phase three considerations.

In the second place, we must learn to acquiesce in a tension there will always be *within* our way of thinking of phase three justice as keeper and distributor of whatever wealth is deemed public.

Consider the two following principles of justice:

(U)  *Ceteris paribus* it is unjust not to have equal regard to equal needs, and subject to possibility and cost, it is just to accord equal weight to equal needs.

(E)  *Ceteris paribus* it is unjust to accord different weight to people in respect of their needs; and, subject to possibility and cost, it is just to satisfy people equally in respect of their needs.

Each will seem compelling, especially in the absence of the suggestion that the other is compelling.

(U) looks like just the kind of principle the hard pressed bureaucrat or manager requires. What he is there for is to rid the world from all the various kinds of unsatisfied need, starting presumably with the worst among those unsatisfied. At any stage he reaches in the process[61] he must identify all outstanding needs that are as bad as or worse than (equal to or greater than) those so far attended to, and attend to them—*subject* of course *to cost*. But what effectively can that mean? The

---

[61] Recall here Beveridge's 'five giants' on the road of reconstruction: 'Want, Ignorance, Squalor, Idleness and Disease'.

answer that suggests itself is: Consider the resources available, and do the most you can with them by way of need satisfaction. And of course the next thought is: Needs do after all shade off into desires, so it would be less arbitrary to do the best one can with the resources available to satisfy all unsatisfied needs *and* desires. And then having reached that point—that is, act utilitarianism with respect to public policy—even the Limitation Principle must begin to seem anomalous, or ripe to be swallowed by the new doctrine. Indeed, the Limitation Principle, in so far as it suggests any policy at variance with what is suggested by the diminishing marginal usefulness to individuals of public largesse, will now seem simply irrational. It can only appear to stand in the way of the war against unsatisfied needs and desires.

But the principle (E) can initiate its own progression. Surely when we treat people differently, there must be a reason to treat them differently. And what better reason to treat them differently than that one of them has more unsatisfied needs? So we must proportion the largesse people receive to how much they stand in want of. Or rather we must do this subject to the cost. We cannot spend a million pounds on making one paraplegic's life just appreciably less bad simply because his suffering is greater than that of others who also have serious needs, or in spite of the fact that the same money would have given these others a very great deal of what they need. So, as we said, it is all subject to cost. But what effectively can that mean? The manager will want a rule. And if he must have a rule, then perhaps the only possible rule is to allocate the same to each person for his needs (or, since they shade off into desires, for his needs and desires) for him to do the best he can with.—Or rather, remembering the starting point and the anxiety that some had more unsatisfied need and others less, the rule must be to allocate public resources in such a way that the total that each person eventually enjoys (of public and private resources taken together) is equal to that which anyone else eventually enjoys. And having got to that point, or to some further sophistication of it—that is to a public philosophy of pure equality—it must seem anomalous and absurd to recognize a separate Limitation Principle. Since we are doing the best we can for each, everybody's vital interests will be intact if anyone's are. The distributive principle (E) simply swallows the limitative protective principle.

28.   (U) and (E) so developed stand in stark opposition to one another. Each initiates a progression or simplification that seems within its own terms of reference irresistible. But each then loses touch with the original impulse that placed it there. (U) prepares us in principle to sacrifice individuals without limit, as Mackie would put it. (E) serves up a notion of equality of resources that is so abstract that it can scarcely impinge at all upon the sentiments that made needs seem important in the first place.

If the prospect seems unbearable of living with this conflict or tolerating the essential contestability of the frontier that contains it and is intended to prevent (U) and (E) from overrunning phase one and phase two reasoning about justice, then, having deciphered the palimpsest I spoke of, we could, I suppose try to retrace the marks we have made and contemplate the restoration (by deletion of the most recent) of the simpler moral universe in which the State undertakes the minimum and in which rights and counter-claims make up the whole of justice. It seems certain that it could induce a sense of proportion to think through the moral advantages of this. But this is not to say that it is really possible to get back to that point.

A much more characteristic response on the part of philosophers and political scientists is to tinker and try to find a principle that mediates or compromises somehow between (U) and (E), and then to make the new principle absorb everything that we have subsumed under phases one and two. And there is no end I am sure to the ingenuity that can be brought to bear upon the task of qualifying and adjusting the arguments that lead (U) and (E) from the state of tension into the state of outright practical incompossibility. But perhaps it would be better to learn to live with (U), (E) and the Limitation Principle as making out three separate, mutually irreducible sorts of claim upon us, and to prevent the deafening noise of the conflict between (U) and (E) from drowning the pleas of other more important and prior demands of justice. It would be better to refrain from assimilating limitative protective justice (phase one and two) to distributive justice (phase three), not taking protective justice (properly understood as protective and limitative and not as presupposing phase three) to be in any conflict at all with aggregative public rationality. Surely they cannot be in conflict. One simply defines the other's proper theatre of operation, essentially contestably.

Why then might the prospect of living with these irreducibilities seem unbearable—or any more unnerving than the prospect of riding a bicycle? I suspect that it will seem unbearable only if we see it as the task of a theory of justice to hit on suitable principles or axioms that generate a description or blueprint for a just state or society, *e.g.* in the manner Plato adopts in the *Republic*, relying upon the non-self-sufficiency of men and the supposed truism that each kind of man should do what he does best, or in the manner of John Rawls, who arrives at a just order of things by working out what departures from strict equality would have been written into a social contract drawn up under ideal conditions, in ignorance of social reality as we have it and of the positions of particular people therein. In the thought-experimentation that is characteristic of these approaches, nothing is left to chance, and nothing is *prima facie* anybody's (even if the thing in question would never have existed at all but for him) until it is *assigned* to him as his share.—Though of course the exactitude of the theoretical calculations that the procedure purports in some variants to make possible is diminished out of all recognition when we reach the problem of social criticism and we attempt concrete comparison of actual holdings with hypothetically just holdings, a baffling and multiply counterfactual problem.

So long as one is committed to this approach, one will think one has to try to construct a sort of *model* of justice. Our own attempt has been quite different—indeed almost opposite in intention. We have started out with the historical contingency that men live in societies, societies being things that we discover in existence possessing whatever nature they do possess, completing and conditioning the lives of men in all sorts of different ways and manifesting different degrees of cohesion and consensus. And we have then speculated on what it now takes for societies that exist by consensus to perpetuate themselves on terms and by means that their participants can avow to themselves without having to unlearn their instinctive capacity to recognize other men as conscious subjects and objects of reciprocity and interpretation[62]—and what it takes for them to continue to do so even as the awareness grows among these societies' members of their own power. In this consensual, evolutionary approach, the philosophy of justice does not have to invent and hold up for comparison some contractualist (or whatever) *ideal polity* with which reality can be confronted for purposes of adjustment and criticism. It has to try to draw upon the various potentially divergent and discrepant ideas and feelings we already have, in order to describe how and to what extent historical contingency, and whatever other goals besides justice we may pursue, will have to be offset by deliberate regulation and intervention, sometimes despite men's legitimate expectation, to secure some accord with our evolving sense of what it is fair for people to be asked to do and endure, with our sense of the entitlement that must normally accrue to effort or achievement or inheritance or settled expectation or whatever, and with our untheoretical sense of the relative strengths of the various classes of need claims. Justice here is only the lack of a certain sort of evil. (A theory of it does not need to furnish a determinate paradigm for the legal and constitutional arrangements of a country.) And not only are there many other matters a society must concern itself with besides justice (the security of the state, economic survival, *etc.*) Not only must these other considerations limit how just it is possible to be. But also justice is *itself* a complex and many rooted idea; and it can even conflict with itself—or so our approach prepares us to expect—in ways for which there may be no predetermined mode of resolution.

When it comes to applying such a conception of justice as this to social reality, whether in policy-making or in criticism, its practical application is at once direct, underdetermined and contextually constrained (leaving much to be decided by something like Aristotelian *aisthesis*).[63] There is no difficulty in

[62] Cp. *Sameness and Substance, op. cit.* Chapter Six, with addenda for pp. 174–184, *Longer Note* 6.36 §3; Peter Winch, Presidential Address, *Proceedings of the Aristotelian Society*, 1980–81, stressing correctly the pre-rational character of this recognition.

[63] Cp. J.R. Lucas 'The Lesbian Rule' *Philosophy* 1954, Essay VI below, §4–5. In correction and amplification of what is said here, the issue of underdetermination is treated further at pp. 318 and 348.

seeing that certain things are clearly just and that certain others are clearly unjust. But room is left even for one and the same society at a given time to choose between several different ways of answering certain sorts of question.

Nor is it a positive point in favour of accepting some other picture that it eliminates this under-determination, either within justice itself or in the competition between justice and other values. Given a social morality as determinate as you like (as determinate even as such a thing can be), it is not demonstrably rational to look confidently for the elimination of essential contestability. But then, if we pause a little longer on the point, maybe we shall find not hopelessness but comfort—even some obscure hope for politics itself (does one *have* to think of one's political opponents as wicked or morally deranged?)—in the thought that I shall end by quoting from another colleague to whom, as to Mackie, this essay owes much:

> The basic moral intuitions of mankind—which Right and Left alike cannot but take for granted as a premise for their moral appeal—provide no solution except in a prohibitive and limiting sense, for the permanent and topical problems of political organization and choice.[64]

[Postscript. These questions are resumed and certain related themes pursued at pp. 314–28 below.]

---

[64] Aurel Kolnai, 'The Moral Theme in Political Division', *Philosophy*, 1960. For other references to Kolnai's thinking on this and related matters, see Bernard Williams' and David Wiggins' Introduction to his *Ethics, Value and Reality* (London: Athlone, 1973).

# II

# Universalizability, Impartiality, Truth*

> Tzu-kung asked, Is there any single saying
> that one can act upon all day and every day?
> The Master said, Perhaps the saying about
> consideration: 'Never do to others what you
> would not like them to do to you'.
>
> CONFUCIUS

> As regards the rule to the effect that we should
> do to others only what we are willing that they
> do to us, it requires not only proof but also
> elucidation.
>
> LEIBNIZ

1.   What is the relation of the demand that agents act upon judgments that are universalizable to the demand that agents adopt the moral point of view? 'Universalizable' being a term of art, let us begin with 'moral point of view'. I cannot define this, but that need not prevent me from enlarging upon what one might ordinarily mean by the phrase. Borrowing from Hume and from other writers, perhaps we may say that, in so far as someone adopts the moral point of view, he will have to refer his actions, feelings, evaluations, complaints and exhortations to the point of view that is 'common to him with others'. Departing from 'his private and particular situation', he must try to speak and think not only on behalf of himself but as if on behalf of others too.[1] If, in spite of his intention to try to

---

*Not previously published. I gratefully acknowledge the part played in the production of this paper by the members of a 1983 revision class at University College, Oxford at whose request I produced a written conspectus of some of the main contentions (some of which are excessively familiar) advanced here.
[1] Cp. *Inquiry concerning the Principles of Morals* IX, §1. Hume says more in this chapter than I try to use either here or later. I am treating the insights that the passage offers as having the direct and immediate appeal of a fresh and telling perception of a natural phenomenon. On the interpretation of Hume, see further below, especially note 5.

speak for everyone in a certain sort of matter, it seems that he has failed in this, or others will not endorse what he says, then either he must withdraw what he has said or else he must see whether he can convince others, or others can convince him. Epistemologically, consensus is not so much a primary source of moral information as a check upon the correctness of beliefs arrived at without consultation of the opinions of others. But, on the level of content, consensus appears somehow intrinsic to what judgments of value, moral obligation and moral necessity actually say.[2] Any judgment of these kinds appeals by virtue of its content to a point of view that is not only subjective but also inter-subjective, not only mine (it is at least mine) but also common to me with others, and to this extent impersonal. It is to be expected, for instance, that, if I say that someone is not only my enemy or antagonist but *also* (I continue) *vicious* or *odious* or *depraved*, then, after the shift from the personal to the public, the implied reference to how he strikes me or impinges upon me will become a reference to how he strikes *us*, or how he ought to strike us. Or, as Hume puts the point in section IX of the *Inquiry into the Principles of Morals*,

> when [a man] bestows on any [other] man the epithets of *vicious* or *odious* or *depraved* . . . he expresses sentiments in which he expects all his audience are to concur with him. He must here, therefore, depart from his private and particular situation and must choose a point of view common to him with others; he must move some universal principle of the human frame and touch a string to which all mankind have an accord and symphony.

2.  This moral perspective upon things (on whose content more will be said in §4 below), being no particular person's, is public and, in one good sense, impersonal. But this is an impersonality that it seems we must be ready to distinguish in principle from the substantive *impartiality* that some philosophers have seen as expressed by a so-called golden rule 'Do

----

[2] Cp. Aurel Kolnai 'Moral Consensus', *Proceedings of the Aristotelian Society* 1969–70. For the explanations I should myself offer of how this involvement of content and consensus is possible, see Essay V and the account given there of the intersubjective properties of the objects of evaluative assessment.

unto others as you would have them do unto you' and tried to catch with the idea of universalizability. (Since universalizability has been redefined countless times in moral philosophy, and we shall need in due course to review some of these possibilities, let 'judgment conformable with the general requirement of impartiality' determine for the moment the general sense of 'universalizable judgment.') For the public standard determined by the common point of view might be one that stressed not utility (in the sense of the greatest public happiness or whatever, thus requiring that the identities of putative recipients of it be treated as irrelevant)[3] but, say, reciprocity; and, apart from reciprocity, it might uphold a moral outlook like that which Aristotle conveys by the saying 'The knee is closer than the shin'. (Or as Mackie might have put the point, the public standard may enjoin not impartiality but a policy of 'self-referential altruism')[4] So, for all that can be gathered from the argument of this section of the *Inquiry* taken on its own (or from the bare supposition that this shared perspective or common point of view is there to be adopted), it may be that the common standard of conduct will insist[5] that one should always put one's own family, friends, or compatriots first. It may be suggested that this insistence should be seen in impartialist fashion as resulting from the solution to a problem of coordination. But to that I should reply that the public standard need not require these kinds of conduct because each one's looking after his own is taken to be the most efficient way

---

[3] Hume himself stressed utility, of course, and there has been a tendency for him to be read (*e.g.*, by Bentham and those whom Bentham has influenced) as offering the germ of some explanation that traces the nature and content of morality back to something or other about the greatest happiness of the greatest number, or the greatest happiness. It is not at all clear, however, that this does Hume a service, since he then has to be read as offering a most improbable and would-be precise explanation of morality (an explanation as specific as 'the greatest happiness' etc. can be interpreted to be), instead of a hazy and inchoate explanation that is really too hazy and inchoate even to be wrong. Usefully and clearly, John Mackie has stressed the superiority of reciprocity explanations of the origin and nature of morality over general utility explanations. Except when reinterpreted by utilitarians anxious to claim him as their own, Hume is better placed than they are to say that he never meant to exclude the reciprocity type of explanation that Mackie commends.

[4] See *Ethics: Inventing Right and Wrong* (Harmondsworth: Penguin Books, 1977).

[5] Except, no doubt, for the special but delimited (however frequent) sort of circumstance that makes impartiality apposite and compulsory.

of maximizing 'general happiness' (whatever that means—after all, the standard itself need never rise to the level of abstraction required to make sense of the phrase), but because of some relatively unsystematic connexion linking them with a historically conditioned, agent-centred shared ideal of human personhood and human excellence.[6]

3. That is the conclusion we are led to; yet it is often said that, once we understand properly the exact character and force of the requirement that we should 'universalize' our moral judgments (in the sense so far suggested and in a sense to be further explained), we shall see that such universalizability is (a) constitutive of the moral point of view itself; (b) founded in the logic or meaning of moral language; and (c) such as to render substantive impartiality a *logical* requirement—even (as in R.M. Hare's more recent work) committing us to adhere to the strong principle (explained below §14) that equal consideration is always to be given to equal interests, whosoever these interests are and whatever our relation with or nearness/distance from the person who has these interests.[7] And never mind how little of this we realized we were letting ourselves in for when we first warmed to the attractive but *prima facie* different idea we found in Hume's *Inquiry* (Section IX). I mean the idea that the content of morality may be given in propositions that are both well-grounded in consensus and fitted in respect of their content and would-be universal application to make their appeal to consensus. The consensus in question there is one which it is natural for human beings living together in society to arrive at. Consensus of this sort is something someone uncommitted to claims (a) (b) (c) may be inspired to try to see

---

[6] This is to say that, if we take over only as much as I have from Hume, then, if we wish, we can still lay the whole emphasis upon agent-centred ideals—in the way in which Hume himself did, or even in the extreme way that Nietzsche does:

> It is plain that moral designations were everywhere first applied to *human beings* and only later, derivatively to actions. (*Beyond Good and Evil* §260).

But note that I am not here declaring my own allegiance with agent-centred 'theories' against the other sort. On any sober view of the subject, every workable morality has comprised *both* agent-centred and non-agent-centred norms and ideals.

[7] See R.M. Hare *Moral Thinking: its Levels, Method and Point* (Oxford University Press, 1982).

as derived from the shared propensity to feel the various feelings that are presupposed to the fixing of the sense of the predicates that occur essentially in judgements expressive of morality. The adherent of (a) (b) (c) will not be so inspired, however, having a different theoretical expectation of the moral point of view, and a different philosophical interest in it.

4.   To arbitrate this disagreement or difference of emphasis, it seems we need another fix on the moral point of view. It seems unlikely that we shall be able to unpack this notion from out of the resources furnished to us by any single idea. (Unless, of course, it is the idea of universalizability itself, but this is the idea whose claims to recapitulate the whole of morality we are to investigate.) But if the problem is to find a way to accept or reject claims (a), (b) and (c) of §3 otherwise than on the basis of a stipulation, then perhaps such an unpacking or derivation of essence is not as necessary as it might at first seem. Never mind whether I am *illogical* or *irrational* to refuse to conform my conduct to judgments that are universalizable. Perhaps we can take as our first question: do universalizable judgments reconstruct what we recognize as moral requirements? Is it *morally reprehensible*, in the pretheoretically available sense of 'morally reprehensible', for me to refuse to conform my conduct to judgments that are universalizable? If the answer to this turns out to be other than positive, or if it can only be positive if we reinterpret the idea of universalizability in such a way that the combined self-sufficiency and moral and conceptual primacy so often claimed for principles like 'Do as you would be done by' lapses, then, being as questionable as they are, perhaps all further claims about rational commitment will fall by the wayside.[8]

In the second place, we can make some ground by testing contention (a) against the rest of the rich and partially articulate conception of morality that we already have.

---

[8] Conversely if (a) can be sustained, then the gross implausibility of the claim that there is some *logical* incoherence in failing to subject one's moral judgments to the universalizability test (or in failing to make moral judgments where universalizability requires them) will scarcely detract at all from the interest of the connexion that is registered by (a). On (b) *vide* J.L. Mackie *op. cit.*, chapter four. On (c) *vide* Bernard Williams, *Ethics and the Limits of Philosophy* (London: Fontana, 1985), p. 89 foll.

Without attempting to find its philosophical essence, perhaps we can clarify this conception of morality and draw it out from ourselves in the very process of testing the affirmative answer to our question. Any strangeness we find in any consequence of the universalizability thesis may act as a powerful reminder to us of what we already know.

5. The negative outcome of the test may reveal more, however, if we set the scene for it by trying to muster some agreement about the background facts (moral, social, legal, etc.) that help to make the moral point of view what it is and give morality the content that it has.

To this end, and to provoke the production of better suggestions, I offer seven points or observations.

(i) In living together human beings need to be able to see conflicts of interest as calling for arbitration by agreed procedures and as demanding the kinds of outcome that would not strike the parties (at least in advance of being involved in a particular dispute) as unfair.

(ii) Human beings need norms of reciprocity and cooperation that can counteract the settled tendency of things to turn out badly rather than well.[9]

(iii) Human beings need such norms of reciprocity and cooperation not only to define canons of behaviour that can determine expectations, but also to embody principles of conduct that can take on a life of their own. Unlike secondary principles as these are derisively envisaged by act-utilitarians in their attack upon the rule-utilitarians' alleged 'rule worship', such principles must perpetuate themselves by being seen by those who try to live by them as enshrining values and virtuous concerns that have a 'moral beauty' (in Hume's phrase) all of their own. Agents for whom such values can furnish a reason for anything need to be able to embrace them as values that they can make their own, and to make them their own in response to something that they think they can *find* in them.

---

[9] Cp. G.J. Warnock *The Object of Morality* (London: Methuen, 1971.)

(iv) Whatever may be the origin of moral concerns and principles, unless it can become an end in itself to act in accordance with the claims of reciprocity, gratitude, loyalty, veracity or whatever, and unless this can help to fill out the picture of what it is constitutively for things to go well and happily—that is, unless things sometimes go happily and satisfyingly precisely in virtue of the fact that reciprocity, gratitude, loyalty or veracity *are* valued and valued in a way that can impinge upon practice—the prospects are not good for the standard that requires these things. This standard can easily survive the fact that all sorts of egoistic ends compete, and almost always compete successfully, with these values. What it cannot survive is the idea that such values are mere means to other ends, or that it is other ends that force them upon us.[10]

One may speculate further that, under conditions in which the moral point of view reflects a shared social morality and this morality both sustains and is sustained by practices and institutions under which its participants are governed to some significant degree by consent, the content of the principles, values and concerns that it comprises will be continuously regulated, shaped and reshaped by the force of two further considerations:

(v) The social morality must safeguard and uphold arrangements that specially protect whatever is vitally or centrally important to the happiness or welfare of individual agents; and (subject only to countervailing claims of merit, reward &c) it must carefully proportion the protection it provides for an individual's interests to how central those interests are for the individual.—Lest the participants of a morality who never opted into it[11] opt out of the norms that it sets of cooperation and reciprocity. And again, for the same sort of reason, it seems

(vi) that a social morality must require of its participants some however minimal and delimited respect towards other

---

[10] Cp. Schopenhauer *On the Foundation of Morality* especially §7.

[11] And are not even, I think, in the state of its being *as if* once upon a time they had each contracted into it. For (v), see above Essay I, §19, §23 *et passim*.

participants—at least an acceptance of them as *equally participants*. Such respect does not necessarily involve anyone in according everyone an equal title to an equal share in all advantages (or even an equal but defeasible title to an equal share). But it does appear to entail that a participant must recognize every other participant as equally a bearer of rights and duties who must himself or herself recognize any other participant as equally a bearer of rights and duties. . . .[12]

In short, (vii) we expect a point of view that can be shared between the members of an actual society to give expression to a potentially enduring and transmissible shared sensibility. To adopt the moral point of view is to see one's thoughts, feelings and actions as answerable to the findings of such a shared sensibility. Or that is what this adoption would be in the idealized situation by reference to which we have to try to understand the idea of the moral point of view as such. (Of course few, if any, extant social moralities are seen by those subject to them as susceptible of perfect rational consensus.)

6.   So far, so good. In so far as we depart from Hume in supplying this content, it is only in ways that flow from our seeking to lay smaller stress than he inclined to upon the role of utility within the origins and maintaining mechanisms of morality.[13] But before we return to our question, I must stress that in arriving at points (i)–(vii) we incur no commitment to a reductive or functional view of social morality or civil society and its institutions. These points are generated not by reference to the *purpose* or *aim* of morality, but by reference to what such a thing must be like if the morality and the institutions and mores that embody it concretely are to support one another. A social morality is not just any old set of principles that meet formal constraints upon being moral principles. It is something that can only exist as realized or embodied in historically given actual mores and institutions that embody, condition and

---

[12] How do participants recognize other participants as such? In the first instance as human beings. Humanity creates the presumption. The presumption can be destroyed, however, by the other person's proving to be simply out of moral reach. For more on some of this, see my *Sameness and Substance* (Oxford: Blackwell, 1980), longer note 6.36.

[13] See note 3 above.

perpetuate it, even as it in its turn sustains, scrutinizes, adjusts and perpetuates mores and institutions. (It is from this consideration, and not from any functional argument, that I have drawn the conclusion that the moral point of view must not disengage with the various individual needs and concerns that have figured in the requirements (i)–(vii).)

Secondly, I would stress that, although there seemed to be no alternative but to follow Warnock and allude to the way in which the content of morality is constrained by men's need to combat the tendency of human affairs to turn out badly rather than well, there was really no question of our being able to say in full what 'well' and 'badly' meant except in a way that already imports reference to morality and society themselves. If morality is not a tool or instrument of human welfare whose function might just as well have been served by other tools or instruments, there must be a strong presumption against all theories that seek reductively to make rightness out of goodness and goodness out of human well-being as specified independently of the content of the moral point of view. It is true that certain basic goods and evils can be specified in a way that presupposes almost nothing about society or its arrangements; and no doubt these goods and evils play an important role in the origin and maintaining mechanisms of all extant social moralities. But not all important goods or evils are basic in this fashion; and, as is really quite clear in Hume (so soon as we cease to construe him as a wayward proto-utilitarian writer, but as a genealogist of morals better placed by his position in the history of the subject to delineate the object to be explained than to move towards precise explanations of it), and as was subsequently emphasized by a markedly dissimilar genealogist of morals, Nietzsche:

'Only that which has no history can be defined.' (*Genealogy of Morals* II.xiii.)

'There is no set of maxims more important for an historian than this: that the actual causes of a thing and its eventual uses, the manner of its incorporation into a system of purposes, are worlds apart ... all processes in the organic world are processes of outstripping and overcoming: and, in turn, all outstripping and overcoming means reinterpretation, rearrange-

ment, in the course of which the earlier meaning and purpose
was necessarily either obscured or lost.' (*Ibidem* II.xii.)

7. So much for the setting of the scene. Now we may ask
again: What is the relation between adopting the moral point
of view, or seeing one's own and others' conduct as answerable
to such a point of view etc., and the requirement that one's
moral judgments be universalized?

If we put the question in what is tantamount to its oldest
form in technical philosophy, which goes with the insistence of
Kant on the intimate connexion between moral agency and
rational autonomy, then it is equivalent to the question
whether adopting the moral point of view involves acting (and
judging one's own and others' conduct) according to the
following injunction: not to act except on a moral judgment
one can endorse (if only a judgment of *permissibility*), and not
to endorse the moral judgment in favour of φ-ing unless one
could, simultaneously with intending to φ, will that anyone in
like circumstances should φ. ('Act only on the maxim through
which you can at the same time will that it should become a
universal law'. 'Act as though the maxim of your action were
by your will to become a universal law of nature'.)

8. Taken just as it stands, this test gives some impressive
results. But it also gives some strange ones. For instance, it
appears that when universalized in Kant's fashion, the maxim
'To release my debtor from his debt, as an act of simple
generosity' must stand convicted of what Kant calls a
'contradiction in conception'.[14] (Anyone who knows what debt
is must know that, if everyone acted on the maxim 'to release a
debtor as an act of generosity', then most of the expectations
presupposed to lending and borrowing would lapse, and then
the practices presupposed to the intention to release one's debtor
from his debt as an act of simple generosity would lapse too.)
Nobody is normally required to release his debtor, but it is
strange to be required not to.

---

[14] For the importance and nature of the distinction of two sorts of obstacles,
contradictions in conception and in willing, see *Foundations of the Metaphysics of
Morals* p. 424.

Where the contradiction in conception test seems problematic, we can still subject intentions and their maxims to the test of consistency of willing. But here the trouble is that, when Kant seeks to demonstrate 'contradictions in willing', his derivations seem to import a heteronomy that is in danger of subverting the whole foundation of the theory.[15] If rational agency presupposes that nothing empirical should fix the character of what is done, and if this means that what is done must flow from the agent's giving himself as a law (his pre-empirical self's giving him as a law) what empirically uncontaminated reason proposes, then Kant needs to be able to confirm the Kantian *purity* of the rationality of the agent's will to ensure (say) that he is helped when he needs help; and Kant needs to be able to confirm this on the basis of an account of rationality that is both non-empirical and desire-independent. Is there any account of practical rationality that can do this? Or rather: Is there any account that can do this without importing the metaphysical ideas occasionally drawn upon by Kant that commit one to a quite distinct conception of ethics, say a teleological—either Aristotelian or Thomistic—conception?

9.    Evidently the only real chance of effecting a meet between the moral point of view and universalizability is to follow Kant's heirs in shifting the emphasis from the contradiction in conception test, forswearing Kant's attachment to a conception of rationality that transcends the empirical, and making heteronomy welcome by recasting the universalizability test. Nothing could appear less Kantian; but, under the new dispensation, one not only consults one's empirically given desires in endorsing a maxim, one explores them actively. For me to endorse a maxim is for me to accept its suitability for being acted upon in any relevantly similar situation, including situations where my own position is quite different, and for me to accept this on a desiderative or modified desiderative basis. So, if I make the judgment that I ought to φ, or that it is

---

[15] Consider for instance the following: 'A will which resolved [against the maxim to give aid and assistance here, where they are needed] would conflict with itself, since instances can often arise in which he would need the love and sympathy of others, and in which he would have robbed himself, by such a law springing from his own will, of all hope of the aid he desires'. (p. 423)

permissible for me to φ, I must *will* among other things that I
suffer the corresponding maxim's being acted upon, even in the
cases where I am in the position of those who now suffer by
virtue of the maxim's being endorsed and acted upon. Once I
grasp this, if I find that my desires stand in the way of this
willing, the judgment is not one that it is open to me to make so
long as I hold to the moral point of view.

10.    Stating the universalizability requirement in this way,
forgetting about pure Kantian 'moral disinterest', and leaving
on one side the claim that universalization is a requirement of
logic or rationality as such, the possibility is restored of making
some linkage with the common point of view that Hume
conceived. But what exactly is meant here by a 'situation' or
'position' that one might be in? If the requirement is that, in
order to endorse a maxim and make the corresponding
judgment, I must simply will here and now that the maxim be
acted upon *whatever my own station and material circumstances
would be*, and if that is what acting only upon universalized
judgments comes down to, then this is notoriously insufficient
for having the moral point of view. (Indeed what is then
envisaged is so strange that it is scarcely worth asking whether
it is necessary either.) For what adopting the moral point of
view especially involves is the recognition of *alterity*, the
otherness of the subjectivity of others. One must pay heed to
the fact that different people may like different things or
dislike different things from those that one likes or dislikes
oneself.
    The universalizer's standard reply to this initial difficulty is
to say that what the theory has always envisaged always
involved the readiness to see the moral judgment acted upon
even in the cases *where my own desires are different from my
present desires*, and everything also is different too. Difference
of desires suffices for difference of situation or position.
    The reply meets one part of the doubt, even if it provokes the
second doubt whether the preparedness in question might be
much too easily secured—when I know full well that I shall
never *be* in those positions. But, waiving that difficulty, isn't
there a new trouble—the possibility that absolutely every
putative moral judgment may be ruled out by the hypothetical

imaginative-cum-volitional exploration of a position I imagine myself in? In that case no judgment will be possible at all. (This may happen if, when I explore several different particular hypothetical situations, each one influences me decisively and, taken together, they rule out the possibility of willing *any* maxim.) Alternatively, and equally damagingly to the larger claims made on behalf of the universalizability test, I may be so utterly dedicated to my present projects and concerns that I am indifferent to what *I* in some imaginable positions should want or feel, and perfectly prepared to persist in willing the universalization of what I am proposing to do now, despite all these objections. Such an attitude is intelligible, need not be evil, and is not even obviously irrational. It is hard to frame any general condemnation of it.[16] It is hard to see that such dedication to one's present projects is evil in the way in which certain ways of behaving to others that the friends of universalization are seeking to explain the badness of are evil.

11.  One can get muddled here in spite of the excellent landmarks placed in this bog by J.L. Mackie,[17] Don Locke[18] and other writers.[19] So let us rehearse this last difficulty once more. Consider a small extension of the regrettably short narrative given in Cyril Connolly's fantasy *Ackermann's England*,[20] in which a dictator instructs his commander Lord Cavalcade to level all buildings built after 1840 and to prepare to restore England to the appearance that it is represented as wearing in Ackermann's *Divers Views*. Warming to his task and falling deeply in love with these representations and the ravishing beauty of what they depict, Lord Cavalcade reaches a point where he is perfectly prepared to will that, if he were in the position of one living in a house built in the 1870s or 1920s

---

[16] For Hare's recent thoughts on this, see *Moral Thinking op. cit.* pp. 95–6: criticized now by Williams in op. cit. note 8 above. See also Don Locke 'The Principle of Equal Interests' *Philosophical Review* vol. 90, 1981, at pp. 541–45.

[17] See *op. cit.* at note 8 above; and also Mackie's index under 'universalizability' for further remarks.

[18] See *op. cit.* note 16.

[19] See again Williams *op. cit.* note 8: also Sabina Lovibond, *Realism and Imagination in Ethics* (Oxford: Blackwell, 1984), esp. §31.

[20] In *The Secret Playground and Other Essays* (London, 1943).

or whatever, then his habitation should be razed to the ground. There is nothing he is overlooking when he becomes prepared to will this—nothing moral and nothing non-moral. It is what one would expect given his personal enthusiasm for the aesthetic project in which he is engaged. What is more, I think I can prove to almost anyone's satisfaction that there is nothing at all to criticize in his frame of mind. Changing Connolly's story, let us now suppose that in the course of the operation, Cavalcade becomes prey to doubt—but not to doubt about his own hypothetical willingness to be dispossessed of his own habitation wherever it dates from after 1840. Finding how ruthless he has had to be, and being shocked by the physical presence of those whom he has exposed to the weather, he starts to question whether he *ought* to complete his assignment. The philosophically remarkable thing is that, under these conditions, he could still will that if *he* were the inhabitant of an 1870 house then, *whatever he then thought*, his house should be razed. He still satisfies the revised condition on willing. For he has lost none of his own passionate attachment to the aesthetic ideal of restoring the built environment of 18th century England. But, even though he wills this *for himself* in the position of an inhabitant of an 1870 house and wills it regardless of what he might then think or feel, it still doesn't seem *morally right* to him that others (*e.g.*, those without this attachment) should be treated as the dictator had dictated. What has happened is that, so far from the refurbished preparedness-to-will test restoring a fanatic to his senses, someone who is *still* in one good ordinary sense a fanatic is here restrained by recognizably moral considerations from acting out his fanaticism and doing to others what he is perfectly prepared for others to do to him in any situation he might be in. His moral hesitation springs from a source *quite other* than any that the philosophical universalizer has tapped.

12.   Perhaps the meet between the idea of the moral point of view and the requirement of acting upon judgments one is prepared to universalize could be improved and at least this last difficulty, which is the second of the two difficulties mentioned in §10, can be answered (the first difficulty will reappear), by redrafting the universalizing requirement in the

following way: not to act except on a moral judgment whose maxim we are sincerely ready to endorse *on the basis of* the consideration of all positions.

Let me say again how we reach this reformulation. The original suggestion was that we have arrived at the moral point of view just if we never act except on a moral judgment we can endorse, and we never endorse a moral judgment unless we will accept it for any relevantly similar situation in which our own position is as different as you please from the actual one. The tests of acceptance so far tried are willing it while envisaging all hypothetical circumstances in which one has one's present desires, and willing it while envisaging hypothetical circumstances in which one has the desires of the other persons affected. What the case of Lord Cavalcade has now confirmed is that the universalizer must at the very least move beyond the requirement that one act on maxims one is prepared to endorse *while* envisaging all positions. He must move forward to the stronger requirement that one act on maxims that one endorses *on the basis* of envisaging all positions.[21] Consideration of each position must somehow *impinge* on the decision.

Three further points are worth noting about the reformulation. First, 'Do unto others as you would have them do unto you' drops out, however it is reinterpreted—but only because the bilateral has been abandoned in favour of the general form of the problem of reconciling conflicting interests. Secondly, we are still apparently in the business of making morality and the common point of view from out of the idea of finding mutual accommodation for desires, interests or preferences as pre-morally conceived. (There is as yet no restriction on the relevance of position for instance, unless it is a restriction that is explained causally. Ideas about who 'owes' what sort of care to whom are among the things to be *discovered* by this approach. It cannot take them for granted.) And thirdly, since

---

[21] Even this amendment may seem quite insufficient in the absence of some more about what there is for 'on the basis of' to mean (and how much of this the universalizer has a right to). When the reader reaches nearer to the end, he will see what cuts me off from attempting to supply the further explanations that would be needed. Meanwhile we are supposing that, after Cavalcade had moral doubts, he no longer willed that he be dispossessed *on the basis* of the consideration of all positions, even though he willed it *while envisaging* all positions.

*ex hypothesi* these desires, interests or preferences frequently conflict with one another, we must now add *ad fin.* 'doing the best one can for all taken together'.

13.    Consolidating all revisions to date the suggestion we have to consider is this then: To take the moral point of view is to obey the following injunction: never act or judge except on the basis of a judgment you are ready to endorse, and never endorse a judgment unless you will the corresponding maxim on the basis of simultaneous hypothetical consideration of all positions, doing the best for all taken together.

But how are we to do this? And is there one best way of doing it? One way of addressing this question—not necessarily the only one—is to take a hint from Adam Smith, whom it is fair to see as having inherited from Hume the task of further elucidating what we are to mean by 'the point of view that is common to one man with another'. Smith writes:

> Before we can make any proper comparison of those opposite interests (his interests and my interests), we must change our positions. We must view them neither with our own eyes nor yet with his, but from the place and with the eyes of a third person who has no particular connexion with either, and who judges with impartiality between us. (*Theory of the Moral Sentiments* III.3.3.)

It is an initial difficulty with this thought, at least for our purposes, that the impartial spectator's eventual verdict is going to depend crucially on what moral ideas he has, what concerns he has besides benevolence, and what construal he puts on 'benevolence' itself. Perhaps Smith himself should be credited with some awareness of this, and was not single-mindedly engaged in the universalizers' project of generating the whole of morality out of the idea that its essence corresponds to its role of finding rational resolutions of conflicts of interests. But, having aired the doubt whether Smith really belongs in the company of 20th-century universalizers, we might still abstract his idea dnd redeploy it here as follows: what one who adopts the moral point of view has to do is to move in imagination back and forth as often as necessary from one person's position to another's, trying to find a maxim that each would come to endorse once he realized that the maxim it would have suited him best to have endorsed will not be endorsed from other positions. Thus a maxim is endorsed if we should be prepared to accept it no matter whose position we were in, provided that in that position we were looking for a judgment that we should be prepared to accept no matter whose position we were in, provided that in that position . . . . And one way of making *this* less indefinite or regressive (though not necessarily the only way of doing this) might be to say that, when we attempt the moral point of view, we take account of others' attitudes and preferences, but no more account than they would take of their own attitudes and preferences if they were taking account of those of others.[22] Then, following Smith, perhaps you can be a Stoic and a Christian at the same time.

> As to love our neighbour as we love ourselves is the great law of *Christianity*, so it is the great precept of *Nature* to love ourselves only as we love our neighbour, or, what comes to the same thing, as our neighbour is capable of loving us.

14.   There is something important here. But, for the moment at least, our question is the delimited and special question how well it can serve to complete the post-Kantian universalizer's project. This was the project, whose hopelessness or arbitrariness will shortly become more fully apparent, of making the whole of morality from universalizability, and trying to determine a recognizably moral content for morality by seeing it as the instrument for the harmonization of interests as pre-morally conceived. What if, instead of discovering one maxim that meets these requirements, we find several conflicting ones, or no maxim at all? Or what if the divergencies in maxims that different would-be universalizers will actually hit upon for any

[22] Cp. Don Locke, *op. cit.* pp. 554–5, with whom I shall venture to disagree at note 23 below, and to whom I am indebted. I do not think that the formulation in the text is as definite as Locke and others have supposed, or that this is the only interpretation that can be put on what is said by the preceding sentence: but what it says is already quite definite enough to be controversial. As Christopher Gray has reminded me (and cp. Lovibond *op. cit.*), if we are happy with it so far as it goes, then we must for instance be happy to give no more weight to the views of non-universalizers than we should give if they were universalizers. That is already a substantive moral position for which more argument might be demanded.

given practical problem—in so far as each can find a maxim to universalize at all—stem from their different conceptions of what is forbidden and what is not, from their different evaluations of the virtues, from the divergency of their ways of sorting attitudes, preferences, interests by their moral quality, or from the different emphases they put upon claims of need, claims of desert, claims of formal entitlement, claims based on prior undertakings . . . etc.? What if, in the absence of such prior notions on the part of the universalizer, there is a threat of total indeterminacy? Well, if that is how it is, then we have simply not been told enough by the friends of the universalization thesis about *how* to allow for the conflicting attitudes and preferences of others in order to do the best for them all.[23] (What is more, these friends will have to recognize all sorts of restrictions on the outcome if they are to cause the universalizing idea to generate anything that is recognizable as morality.)[24]

15. There are a number of ways of reducing the indeterminacy that seems to threaten the project. One is for its defenders to go outside their remit for a moment and come back with the direction that the universalizer should adopt the maxim whose adoption would make in practice for the greatest happiness, or for the greatest satisfaction of desires. In that case a familiar species of calculation suggests that maxims must be chosen in the way that best ensures that the benefits or resources allocated to each interest should be somehow proportional to the efficiency with which it can convert those resources into satisfaction. But this makes the moral judgments based on these maxims extremely strange candidates for the moral point of view. (Cp. §5.) And it is open to the objection that it presupposes the one thing that is never provided, and without

---

[23] See *Longer Note* 23.

[24] Such instructions about how to proceed might be dispensed with, of course, if the proposal were modified to embrace the possibility of simple bargaining between those with conflicting interests. But that is another proposal altogether, requiring the abandonment of the idea that a universalizer is to ask himself what maxims he is to endorse on the basis of consideration of all other positions—for now we let each position speak for itself—, and also requiring the institution of some sort of substantive equality between bargainers. The outcome of bargaining between those who are unequal in power can show little or nothing about the content of the moral point of view. Cp. Lovibond *op. cit.* §31.

which all further and better elaborations of utilitarianism are simply a distraction: one good argument (or one strong, unflawed intuition) in positive support of the greatest happiness principle.[25]

Another way to reduce indeterminacy is to recall the suggestion that, when we sympathetically envisage all the conflicting interests that bear on a practical problem and make each interest (as if) our own, then the rule we are bound to follow—not only in our initial assessment but also in our eventual verdict or award—is that equal consideration is to be given to equal interests. This is to say that we are to endorse the maxim whose adoption would result in the weight attached to an interest being proportional to the magnitude of the interest (proportional that is to the strength of the corresponding desires, when these are corrected for any factual misapprehensions and misconceptions).[26] But this too is an import from outside the original remit; and, again, it results in a position that is a curious candidate for the moral point of view. For one wants to protest that some interests are more inviolable or more legitimate than others, and that some desires are more laudable or important or deserving than others—a deficiency one can scarcely remedy completely by exploring variants that insist on the universalizer's maximizing the satisfaction of persons instead of the satisfaction of desires or interests. However such variants are interpreted within the terms of the given universalizing project, they will be consistent with the universalizer's endorsing maxims whose adoption has the effect of sacrificing some people (as Mackie puts it) without limit, even though the universalizer does the best for all persons taken together. (Cp. here §5 above, especially points (v) and (vi).)

16.   So far all the suggestions considered for the reduction of indeterminacy are variants on utilitarianism, or intended as such. In its own way, each is at once gratuitous theoretically

---

[25] Here, as before in this essay, I stress the need to consider whether the thing in question, here happiness, is taken as pre-morally conceived. On this point and on the weakness of the best argument that has ever been produced for the greatest happiness principle, see Philippa Foot 'Utilitarianism and the Virtues', *Mind* vol. 94, 1985.

[26] See *Longer Note* 26.

and unfaithful intuitively to the idea of the moral point of view. Is there then nothing at all in the idea of universalizability?

The answer I shall propose to this question is: No, not simply nothing; something can be salvaged; but to see what that is we must begin by forgetting the hope of reconstructing the moral point of view on the basis of one idea. With that hope forgotten, however, and within the new framework to be described, one could retain the injunction not to act except on a moral judgment one can endorse (if only a judgment of permissibility), and not to endorse the moral judgment in favour of φ-ing unless one is ready to accept the corresponding maxim on the basis of simultaneous consideration of all positions, doing the best for all taken together. But, in the new understanding, this injunction does not define the moral point of view, it presupposes it, and at best it makes what it presupposes more explicit. What is more, the phrase 'doing the best for all taken together' has to be reinterpreted entirely. What it requires is for the would-be universalizer to arbitrate between conflicting attitudes and preferences in accordance with a pre-existing understanding of the virtues, a pre-existing sense of the difference between vital interests and mere desires, and a pre-existing grasp of what distinguishes the more morally admirable from the less morally admirable concerns of those whose interests conflict and distinguishes legitimate from non-legitimate expectations. A universalizer also needs to have a sense supplied from elsewhere of what sort of thing an agent is answerable or not answerable for, of what he owes to whom, and of what is morally possible or impossible for him. Which is to say that, in the framework now being envisaged, the universalizer is required to arbitrate between different positions in accordance with an indefinite range of antecedently given moral notions and conceptions—or in accordance with any variation upon these notions and conceptions that he is moved to visit upon them, and any new moral insights he comes upon, in the actual course of the process of arbitration itself.

It would be hard to exaggerate the difference between this and what golden rule theorists have hoped for. Universalization is no longer a method or any part of a method for the initial generation of moral ideas and principles. It works on what is already fully moralized and in no way merely *prima facie*. At best, it is a method of reminder and adjustment *already implicit* in what it is deployed upon. And it comes without any stated guarantee of producing a full consilience of moral ideas or principles (either intrapersonally or interpersonally). What is more, this species of universalization does not even aim to transcend the character of its intuitive starting point.[27] At most it suggests corrections—corrections that would be intelligible to one simply reconsidering his starting point, and that might have been accepted by him there.

Given a certain ambition for moral philosophy, it can be hard to give up the idea of the theorist's trying to parachute himself into morality supported and sustained by just one idea, and even harder to give up the insistence on seeing morality as having a harmonizing role that we can recognize pre-morally with content determined by the golden rule. But once we have succeeded in ridding ourselves of this hope, we might make the following picture for ourselves. In his new role, the universalizer (the more reflective agent or the theorist) is bidden onto the scene not in the role of an explorer or first map-maker but in the role of a surveyor visiting a scene already discovered and directly known. His work is to straighten out, to correct and to extend an existing corpus of judgments about a subject-matter already anecdotally and experimentally known, using only an extension of the *same methods* by which the original judgments were arrived at.

17. The last claim may provoke the objection that the concession to universalizability is vacuous unless more can be said about how the universalizer is even to attempt to 'do the best for all positions taken together'. There is a temptation to agree and leave the matter there. But a partial answer can be given to this question, and provided that the inquirer agrees not to misunderstand what I provide as exceeding the limitations already stated, and not to take it as a description of

---

[27] I stress this in order to emphasize the difference between universalization as here conceived, which does not aspire to reach a different level of reflection from the level of the judgments it works upon and only regulates these in the manner that they already invite, and Richard Hare's level of 'critical thinking.' For some important comments on the attitude of this last to the level of intuitive thinking, see Bernard Williams *op. cit.*, especially pp. 107–8.

a sophisticated actual method of thinking but as a rational reconstruction of an ordinary way of thinking that almost any one who wants to pause or reflect can engage in, the following answer might be given. Think of the universalizer as a fair-minded negotiator who can get bids from anyone and everyone, and who can extrapolate from these bids to other bids that would be made. To act in this new capacity, the universalizer will begin by envisaging so far as possible the position of every person who is affected by some practical decision.[28] In seeking for the maxim whose adoption does the best for all positions taken together (in searching for the winning bid, that is), he will envisage himself visiting and revisiting all positions *seriatim*, over and over again, communicating to the occupant of each position the nature and degree of the unacceptability of his first or earlier bid (the maxim that it would have been best for anyone in that position to see adopted). He imagines himself on each visit inviting the occupant of each position to revise his bid for the maxim to be adopted in the direction of greater acceptability to others. The method he thinks of himself imposing on the process is that the search must eventually terminate in one agreed maxim (obstructionism cannot avail), but that, even though he, the universalizer, has to decide *for* each occupant, vicariously and on the basis of his own (the universalizer's) moral ideas, he always explores the position of each occupant afresh so soon as it is clear that the maxim the occupant would have favoured cannot be adopted. Not only that. When (as if) suggesting to the occupant his revised bid and formulating it on his behalf, he explores the occupant's own moral outlook—his ideas about desert, legitimate expectation, entitlement, and vital needs or interests . . .—, as well as the moral and material aspects of that occupant's particular position. This process of adjustment continues and continues until (it is as if) everyone enters the *same* bid, or bids that are co-satisfiable. [See also p. 318 below].

If this is the reconstruction then there is no reason to expect that there will be any 'decision procedure' for our universalizer

---

[28] Or, in the less purely causal terms to which he is now entitled (given the limits of what is being attempted), he begins by envisaging the position of everyone with any sort of claim to have *some standing* in the matter.

(impartial spectator, negotiator, honest broker) to follow in the process of *tâtonnement* that is intended to discover the maxim that all can be imagined as reconciling themselves to agree upon. Nothing even ensures that there exists a unique best maxim. But there is a set of thoughts that can *guide* the universalizer in his exploration. He can consult the moral ideas that he has already and that others have, holding tentatively fast to his own but also holding these ideas open to subversion by anything that might affect them when he contemplates other positions, especially positions that are strange to him, and the moral outlooks of those who occupy these other positions. He endorses a moral judgment as correct only if, even when in the ways described he imagines himself occupying different standpoints and is properly influenced by that, he still endorses the judgment as correct. And if any two universalizers endorse different judgments then they have to hunt down the source of the discrepancy.

As threatened, the rational reconstruction of what is involved in taking alterity seriously is highly artificial. But, as I remarked before, universalizers of the new sort do not *make* moral judgments out of desires, or out of the rational will (whether autonomous or heteronomous). Having the candidate judgments already, what they do is subject them to a publicity or objectivity test which the judgments *already* invite. But this is the test by which we should regulate *any* would-be objective judgment about anything at all, e.g. an object of perception. 'It seems to me thus and so. I think it is thus and so. But not everyone agrees: and how would it strike me if I looked at the scene from over there, or from underneath?'—Or as Leibniz says, at the end of his brief but insightful discussion of the golden rule in the *New Essays*

> [The rule], far from serving as a standard, will need a standard. The true meaning of the rule is that the right way to judge more fairly is to adopt the point of view of other people.[29]

18.    Let us contemplate once more the huge distance we have come with this reinterpretation. If we persevere at all with the

---

[29] Remnant and Bennett trans. *New Essays on Human Understanding* (Cambridge, 1981) pp. 91–2.

golden rule, then what Leibniz's remark encourages us to persist in emphasizing at the expense of the idea of the rational morality-determining will is nothing other than the connexion between *the moral* and *the intersubjective* and the connexion between *the intersubjective* and *the public perspective*. And once we abandon the expectation that the pure or impure rational will can do something it really cannot do unaided, we are ready to notice that some of the same connexions are marked not only in Hume, in whom we encounter a third and equally important connexion, between *the public perspective* and *convergence*,[30] but in all sorts of practical precepts of equal antiquity with the golden rule (if not of equal renown or authority), *e.g.*, the various precepts that Confucius puts along with it:

> Jan Jung asked about Goodness. The Master said, Behave when away from home as though you were in the presence of an important guest. Deal with the common people as though you were officiating at an important sacrifice. Do not do to others what you would not like yourself. Then there will be no feelings of opposition to you, whether it is the affairs of a State that you are handling or the affairs of a Family.[31]

What is envisaged here is a public scene—a centre of attention like the events comprising a public rite—in which moral agents are at once actors and spectators, and in which the way actors act informs the way they see things, and the way they see things regulates the way they act. Actors here are persons doing things and persons having things done to them. Spectators are not strangers to these roles. Nor are actors strangers to the role of spectator. For everyone plays each of these three roles at some point, and his direct and indirect knowledge of the other roles constantly informs his playing of each.

---

[30] Cp. *loc. cit.* 'The notion of morals implies some sentiment common to all mankind, which recommends the same object to general approbation, and makes every man or most men agree in the same opinion concerning it. It *also* implies some sentiment, so universal and comprehensive as to extend to all mankind, and render the actions and conduct even of the persons the most remote, an object of applause or censure, according as they agree or disagree with that rule of right which is established. These two requisite circumstances belong alone to the sentiment of humanity here insisted upon . . .'

[31] *Analects* II.2, trans. Waley. Contrast the quotation given at the head of this essay (*Analects* XV.23).

Once we become party to this image, we shall look with a new interest, innocent of any close association with the idea of the rational will, at such precepts as that attributed to Pittakos of Mytilene: 'Don't do yourself what you disapprove of in others'. Instead of comparing Pittakos' precept with the golden rule—somewhat ineptly, for Pittakos presupposes you can already tell what you disapprove of when you are properly confronted by it *in foro publico*, whereas the point of the golden rule is that it may be only in the real or imagined role of *victim* that you can see certain things—,[32] we may see each precept as a partial articulation of a certain sort of awareness or intersubjectivity that seeks constantly to attain equilibrium in judgments. Pittakos reminds us how the roles and corresponding judgments of spectator and agent can be mutually correcting. The golden rule reminds us how the roles and corresponding judgments of agent and patient can be mutually correcting. Together they suggest a picture of tripartite mutual adjustment between the judgments of agent *and* patient *and* spectator. But the process they ought to make us want to know about is really a historical one. It is the process that has already conditioned the senses of all the predicates we can recognize as moral predicates. All that philosophical universalizability does is to recapitulate in an artificial sounding way what was already there—this being something that one who went about things by the artificial instructions I have produced would have to take care not to denature.

19.    The idea of an equilibrium in judgments such as is looked for in our latest conception of universalizability, like the consensual aspiration that Leibniz' observation can encourage us to see precepts like Confucius' and Pittakos' as pointed toward, is not at all straightforward in its application to the subject matter of morals. The convergence that comes into question cannot be demonstrated by anything I have said yet to be a convergence in the direction of objective truth. But what

[32] Herbert Fingarette has kindly drawn my attention to his own reading of *shu*, or the golden rule, in Confucius, which stresses its dependence on other ideas such as chung-hsin (≃ the set of 'good faith commitments') and its complementarity with them. See his 'Following the "One Thread" of the *Analects*' in *Journal of the American Academy of Religion*, September 1980, Vol. 47, no. 3(s), pp. 373–405, especially p. 392.

these precepts point to as the *aspiration* of moral discourse is nothing less than the objectivity and publicity that are proprietary to truth. The aspiration to truth is problematic, and it will not cease to be so. It will appear as *worse* than problematic, however, just so long as we postpone the task of exploring the relation of the domain of *that which is objective*, in the sense of 'objective' that connects objectivity with truth, to the domain of *that which is subjective and inter-subjective*, in the sense of 'subjective' in which the moral properties of things, persons, events and actions present themselves to us as at once subjective and inter-subjective, as keyed, that is, to responses by conscious subjects.[33]

---

[33] See below Essays III, IV, V. It will be contended in Essay V that 'subjective' and 'objective' belong to two distinct contrasts.

# Longer Notes

## Longer Note 23

Not everyone would accept the contention that we are not told enough by the friends of universalization about *how* to allow for the conflicting attitudes and preferences of others. Mackie's transition (in *op. cit.* Ch. Four) from third level universalization to act-utilitarianism would appear to rest on its rejection. For R.M. Hare's position, see Longer Note 26 below. And Don Locke, more explicitly than Mackie, presents an argument to the effect that, if we are looking for a judgment that we should be prepared to accept no matter whose position we were in, provided that in every position we were looking for a judgment that we should be prepared to accept no matter whose position we were in . . ., then we must 'put ourselves in someone else's position', 'take account of his attitudes and preferences', but 'take no more account of his attitudes and preferences than he would take of someone else's preferences when he put himself in anyone else's position. In other words, we must take the same account of each other's attitudes and preferences including our own: [and must] give everyone's attitudes and preferences the same weight, relative to how strongly they are held by the person concerned, regardless of whose they are. *In short* we [must] adopt the [principle of giving equal weight to the equal interests of different people]' (p. 555 [with page 531]).

What all three authors have in mind (and Mackie merely envisages, with scarcely a trace of enthusiasm for 'stage three' universalization) is tantamount to a double transition: first a transition from something like the principle envisaged in the first paragraph of §13 to a special principle for the *evaluation* or *appreciation* of the weight of claims upon a given agent (roughly to 'love ourselves and our own only as we love our neighbours'): and then a second transition from the said principle of appreciation to a special principle of allocation, *e.g.*, to 'to each in proportion to the strength of his interest (as pre-morally measured)' (with or without supplementary directions about the treatment of indivisibilities).

Each transition seems questionable. Together, they create no conviction at all of our being forced to maxims of any particular kind.

As regards the first transition: we might yet make our principles be principles that would be endorsed on the basis of simultaneous consideration of all positions, doing the best for all etc., without ever abandoning agent-centred or self-referentially altruistic principles. No argument is yet supplied why not.

As regards the second transition, suppose one agreed, for argument's sake, waiving the first objection, that a concern, interest, need, desire, attitude, preference. . . of X's and a *similar* concern, interest, desire, attitude, preference . . . of Y's ought to count for exactly the same with each of us, whoever X and Y are (even if X is one's grandson and Y is, say, a person in India quite unknown to one). One might still (having waived the question *whose* they are) question whether concerns, interests, needs, desires, attitudes, preferences, are all on a par with one another, qualitatively, when it comes to *how much* they severally count in favour of this or that allocation. One might resist their assimilation under the blanket term 'interests'. (See in this connection Essay I.) And one might also complain that much more is required to effect a discrimination between interests themselves, before proceeding to formulate *any* practical principle of award. The truth is that the first transition effects *one possible* amplification of the aim mentioned at the beginning of §13; and the second transition effects a *further possible* amplification. Neither amplification is compulsory—and most especially not if one fails to share the universalizer's presumption in favour of a reductive account of morality.

**Longer Note 26**

Richard Hare would insist that we are logically obliged to use this rule of equal consideration for equal interests so soon as we add to the other requirements (of universalizability and prescriptivity) the requirement that we should bring individual rationality or prudence to bear in our arbitration between the conflicting interests that we treat as if they were our own. And he would claim that, contrary to the tenor of my exposition, the result of supplying this rule will coincide with classical utilitarianism. Each of these claims seems doubtful in its own right.

(1) I begin, let us suppose, by treating *each* interest as my own. I try to apply prudence. But then I note that each interest usually conflicts with many others. That may stumble me once and for all. If, however, I do not give up, then I have to advance from treating each relevant interest as my own, applying prudence, to treating all relevant interests as my own, again applying prudence. But there is more than one way to do that. If we leave on one side the fact that, if it were for me as if I had *all* these strongly conflicting desires within me, the prudent course would be for me to take leave from my practical commitments and enroll as a patient at the madhouse,—if we leave that on one side, I say, and if we think of me as trying to *mediate* between conflicting interests, while identifying with each—it still need not follow that the most prudent course for me is to apply everywhere the judgment of Solomon or the Principle of Equal Interests. For first, the most prudent course might be to find some way of *discriminating* between interests. For prudence as we know it and understand it from the simple normal case would surely do just that. (The prudent course where my wants conflict is for me to ask myself what I need, for instance.) In the second place, it is an important fact about prudence that it is not entirely hived off from moral deliberation. Indeed, prudence as we know it in its normal workings would typically *insist upon* a moral discrimination between the conflicting interests it was trying to arbitrate between. (The first of these suggestions is at variance with the Principle of Equal Interests. The second is not only at variance with that but also inconsistent with the self-sufficiency and primacy attributed to Golden Rule type argument.)

(2) It also seems doubtful that the Principle of Equal Interests is strictly a refinement of utilitarianism. To secure this association either one must treat 'give equal consideration to equal interest' as the formula for the special case where all marginal efficiencies in converting resources into satisfaction are equal; or one must let 'consideration' mean just that and no more, and amplify the Principle of Equal Interests so that it continues as follows: 'but *proportion* the resources allocated to each interest to the efficiency with which it can convert these resources into satisfaction'.

# III

# Truth, Invention, and the Meaning of Life*

Nul n'est besoin d'espérer pour entreprendre,
ni de réussir pour persévérer.

WILLIAM THE SILENT

Eternal survival after death completely fails to
accomplish the purpose for which it has
always been intended. Or is some riddle solved
by my surviving for ever? Is not this eternal life
as much of a riddle as our present life?

WITTGENSTEIN

1. Even now, in an age not much given to mysticism, there are
people who ask 'What is the meaning of life?' Not a few of them
make the simple 'unphilosophical' assumption that there is
something to be known here. (One might say that they are
'cognitivists' with regard to this sort of question.) And most of
these same people make the equally unguarded assumption that
the whole issue of life's meaning presupposes some positive
answer to the question whether it can be plainly and straightforwardly *true* that this or that thing or activity or pursuit
is good, has value, or is worth something. Finally, something
even harder, they suppose that questions like that of life's meaning must be among the central questions of moral philosophy.

The question of life's having a meaning and the question of
truth are not at the centre of moral philosophy as we now have
it. The second is normally settled by something bordering on
stipulation,[1] and the first is under suspicion of belonging in the

---

* A lecture delivered on November 24th, 1976. First published in *Proceedings of the British Academy* LXII (1976), and reprinted here, with some editorial changes, by permission of the British Academy. The quotations from Richard Taylor are made by kind permission of Macmillan.
[1] Cp. Essay IV. In 1976, at the time of speaking, the remark stood in less need of qualification than it does now.

same class as 'What is the greatest good of the greatest
number?' or 'What is the will?' or 'What holds the world up?'
This is the class of questions not in good order, or best not
answered just as they stand.

If there is a semantical crux about this sort of occurrence of
the word 'meaning', then all logical priority attaches to it; and
no reasonable person could pretend that a perfectly straightforward purport attaches to the idea of life's meaning
something. But logical priority is not everything; and, most
notably, the order of logical priority is not always or
necessarily the same as the order of discovery. Someone who
was very perplexed or very persistent would be well within his
rights to insist that, where a question has been asked as often as
this one has, a philosopher must make what he can of it: and
that, if the sense really is obscure, then he must find what
significance the effort to frame an answer is apt to *force* upon
the question.

In what follows, I try to explore the possibility that the
question of truth and the question of life's meaning are among
the most fundamental questions of moral philosophy. The
outcome of the attempt may perhaps indicate that, unless we
want to continue to think of moral philosophy as the casuistry
of emergencies, these questions and the other questions that
they bring to our attention are a better focus for ethics and
meta-ethics than the textbook problem 'What [under this or
that or the other circumstance] shall I do?' My finding will be
that the question of life's meaning does, as the untheoretical
suppose, lead into the question of truth—and conversely.
Towards the end I shall also claim to uncover the possibility
that philosophy has put happiness in the place that should have
been occupied in moral philosophy by meaning. This is a
purely theoretical claim, but if it is correct, it is not without
consequences; and if (as some say) weariness and dissatisfaction
have issued from the direct pursuit of happiness as such, then it
is not without all explanatory power.

2.   I have spoken in favour of the direct approach, but it is
impossible to reach out to the perplexity for which the question
of meaning is felt to stand without first recording the sense
that, during relatively recent times, there has been some shift in

the way the question of life's meaning is seen, and in the kind of answer it is felt to require. Here is an answer made almost exactly two hundred years ago, two years before the death of Voltaire:

> We live in this world to compel ourselves industriously to enlighten one another by means of reasoning and to apply ourselves always to carrying forward the sciences and the arts. (W.A. Mozart to Padre Martini: letter of 4 December 1776.)[2]

What we envy here is the specificity, and the certainty of purpose. But, even as we feel envy, it is likely that we want to rejoice in our freedom to disbelieve in that which provided the contingent foundation of the specificity and certainty. I make this remark, not because I think that we ought to believe in what Mozart and Padre Martini believed in, but in outright opposition to the hope that some relatively painless accommodation can be made between the freedom and the certainty. The foundation of what we envy was the now (I think) almost unattainable conviction that there exists a God whose purpose ordains certain specific duties for all men, and appoints particular men to particular roles or vocations.

That conviction was not only fallible: there are many who would say that it was positively dangerous, would say the risk it carried was that, if the conviction were false, then one might prove to have thrown one's life away. It is true that in the cases we are considering, 'throwing one's life away' seems utterly the wrong thing to say of the risk carried by the conviction. It seems wrong even for the aspects of these men's lives that were intimately conditioned by the belief in God. But if one doubts that God exists, then it is one form of the problem of meaning to justify not wanting to speak here of throwing a life away. It is a terrible thing to try to live a life without believing in *anything*. But surely that doesn't mean that just any old set of concerns and beliefs will do, provided one *could* live a life by them. Surely if any old set would do, that is the same as life's being meaningless.

---

[2] Compare the composer's choice of expression on the occasion of his father's birthday anniversary in 1777: 'I wish you as many years as are needed to have nothing left to do in music.'

If we envy the certainty of the 1776 answer, then most likely this is only one of several differences that we see between our own situation and the situation of those who lived before the point at which Darwin's theory of evolution so confined the scope of the religious imagination. History has not yet carried us to the point where it is impossible for a description of such differences to count as exaggerated. But they are formidable. And, for the sake of the clarity of what is to come, I must pause to express open dissent from two comments that might be made about them.

First, someone more interested in theory than in what it was like to be alive then and what it is like now may try to diminish the differences that we sense, by arguing from the accessibility to both eighteenth and twentieth centuries of a core notion of God, a notion that he may say persists in the concept of God championed by modern theologians. To this use of their ideas I object that, whatever gap it is which lies between 1776 and 1976, such notions as *God as the ground of our being* cannot bridge it. For recourse to these exemplifies a tendency towards an *a priori* conception of God which, even if the eighteenth century had had it, most of the men of that age would have hastened to amplify with a more hazardous or *a posteriori* conception. Faith in God conceived *a posteriori* was precisely the cost of the particularity and definiteness of the certainty that we envy.

The other thing someone might say is that, in one crucial respect, our situation is not different from a late Enlightenment situation, because there is a conceptually determined need in which the eighteenth century stood and in which we stand equally. This, it might be said, is the need for commitment. In the eighteenth-century case, this extra thing was commitment to submission to God's purpose. We shall come in §4 to what these theorists think it is in our case. Faced however with this second comment, one might wonder how someone could come to the point of recognizing or even suspecting that it was God's purpose that he should be a composer (say) and yet be indifferent to that. Surely no extra anything, over and above some suspicion that this or that is God's purpose, is required to create the concern we should expect to find that that suspicion would have implanted in him. On the other hand, if this extra thing were supplied, as an extra, then it would bring too much. For the commitment to submission seems to exclude rebellion; and rebellion against what is taken as God's purpose has never been excluded by the religious attitude as such.

What then are the similarities and the differences between the eighteenth-century orientation and our own orientation upon the meaning of life? It seems that the similarities that persist will hold between the conceptual scheme with which they in that century confronted the world of everyday experience and the scheme with which we, in spite of our thoroughgoing acceptance of natural science, confront it: and the dissimilarities will relate to the specificity and particularity of the focus of the various concerns in which their world-view involved them and our world-view involves us. For us there is less specificity and much less focus.

If this is still a dark statement, it is surely not so dark as to obscure the relationship between this difference between them and us and a cognate difference that will have signalled its presence and importance so soon as I prepared to approach the divide between the eighteenth and twentieth centuries by reference to the purposive or practical certainty of individual people. Unless we are Marxists, we are more resistant in the second half of the twentieth century than the eighteenth- or nineteenth-centuries knew how to be against attempts to locate the meaning of human life or human history in mystical or metaphysical conceptions—in the emancipation of mankind, or progress, or the onward advance of Absolute Spirit. It is not that we have lost interest in emancipation or progress themselves. But, whether temporarily or permanently, we have more or less abandoned the idea that the importance of emancipation or progress (or a correct conception of spiritual advance) is that these are marks by which our minute speck in the universe can distinguish itself as the spiritual focus of the cosmos. Perhaps that is what makes the question of the meaning we can find in life so difficult and so desolate for us.

With these bare and inadequate historical assertions, however, the time is come to go straight to a modern philosophical account of the matter. There are not very many to choose from.

3. The account I have taken is that given in Chapter 18 of Richard Taylor's book *Good and Evil*—an account rightly singled out for praise by the analytical philosopher who reviewed the book for the *Philosophical Review*.[3]

Taylor's approach to the question whether life has any meaning is first to 'bring to our minds a clear image of meaningless existence', and then determine what would need to be inserted into the meaningless existence so depicted in order to make it not meaningless. Taylor writes:

> A perfect image of meaninglessness of the kind we are seeking is found in the ancient myth of Sisyphus. Sisyphus, it will be remembered, betrayed divine secrets to mortals, and for this he was condemned by the gods to roll a stone to the top of the hill, the stone then immediately to roll back down, again to be pushed to the top by Sisyphus, to roll down once more, and so on again and again, *forever*.

Two ways are then mentioned in which this meaninglessness could be alleviated or removed. First:

> . . . if we supposed that these stones . . . were assembled [by Sisyphus] at the top of the hill . . . in a beautiful and enduring temple, then . . . his labours would have a point, something would come of them all . . .

That is one way. But Taylor is not in the end disposed to place much reliance in this species of meaning, being more impressed by a second mode of enrichment.

> Suppose that the gods, as an afterthought, waxed perversely merciful by implanting in [Sisyphus] a strange and irrational impulse . . . to roll stones . . . To make this more graphic, suppose they accomplish this by implanting in him some substance that has this effect on his character and drives . . . This little afterthought of the gods . . . was . . . merciful. For they have by this device managed to give Sisyphus precisely what he wants—by making him want precisely what they inflict on him. However it may appear to us, Sisyphus' . . . life is now filled with mission and meaning, and he seems to himself to have been given an entry to heaven . . . The *only* thing that has happened is this: Sisyphus has been reconciled to [his existence]

---

[3] See Richard Taylor, *Good and Evil* (New York: Macmillan, 1970). The review was by Judith Jarvis Thomson, *Philosophical Review* vol. 81, 1973, p. 113.

... He has been led to embrace it. Not, however, by reason or
persuasion, but by nothing more rational than the potency of a
new substance in his veins ...

So much for meaninglessness, and two ways of alleviating it.
Meaninglessness, Taylor says,

> is essentially endless pointlessness, and meaningfulness is
> therefore the opposite. Activity, and even long drawn out and
> repetitive activity, has a meaning if it has some significant
> culmination, some more or less lasting end that can be
> considered to have been the direction and purpose of the
> activity.

That is the temple-building option, of course.

> But the descriptions so far also provide something else; namely,
> the suggestion of how an existence that is objectively meaningless,
> in this sense, can nevertheless acquire a meaning for him whose
> existence it is.

This 'something else' is the option of implanting in Sisyphus
the *impulse* to push what he has to push. Here Taylor turns
aside to compare, in point of meaninglessness or meaningfulness,
the condition of Sisyphus and the lives of various animals,
working from the lower to the higher animals—cannibalistic
blindworms, the cicada, migratory birds, and so on up to
ourselves. His verdict is that the point of any living thing's life
is evidently nothing but life itself.

> This life of the world thus presents itself to our eyes as a vast
> machine, feeding on itself, running on and on forever to
> nothing. And we are part of that life. To be sure, we are not just
> the same, but the differences are not so great as we like to think;
> many are merely invented and none really cancels meaningless-
> ness ... We are conscious of our activity. Our goals, whether in
> any significant sense we choose them or not, are things of which
> we are at least partly aware and can ... appraise ... Men have
> a history, as other animals do not. [Still] ... if we think that,
> unlike Sisyphus', [our] labours do have a point, that they
> culminate in something lasting and, independently of our own
> deep interests in them, very worthwhile, then we simply have
> not considered the thing closely enough ... For [Sisyphus'
> temple] to make any difference it had to be a temple that would
> at least endure, adding beauty to the world for the remainder of
> time. Our achievements ..., those that do last, like the sand-

swept pyramids, soon become mere curiosities, while around
them the rest of mankind continues its perpetual toting of
rocks, only to see them roll down . . .

Here is a point that obsesses the author. Paragraph upon
paragraph is devoted to describing the lamentable but
undoubted impermanence (futility *sub specie aeternitatis*) of
the architectural or built monuments of human labour. It is not
entirely clear that the same effect could have been contrived if
the gradual accumulation of scientific understanding or the
multiplication of the sublime utterances of literature or music
had been brought into the argument. What is clear is that
Taylor is commmitted to a strong preference for the second
method of enriching Sisyphus' life—that is the compulsion
caused by the substance put into Sisyphus' veins. For, as for the
first method, and temple-building for the sake of the temple,

> Suppose . . . that after ages of dreadful toil, all directed at this
> final result [Sisyphus] did at last complete his temple, [so] that
> now he could say his work was done, and he could rest and
> forever enjoy the result. Now what? What picture now presents
> itself to our minds? It is precisely the picture of infinite
> boredom! Of Sisyphus doing nothing ever again, but contem-
> plating what he has already wrought and can no longer add
> anything to, and contemplating it for eternity! Now in this
> picture we have a meaning for Sisyphus' existence, a point for
> his prodigious labour, because we have put it there; yet, at the
> same time, that which is really worthwhile seems to have
> slipped away entirely.

The final reckoning would appear to be this: (a) a lasting end or
*telos* could constitute a purpose for the work; but (b) there is no
permanence; and (c), even if there were such permanence, its
point would be effectively negated by boredom with the
outcome of the work. And so we are thrown inexorably into the
arms of the other and second sort of meaning.

> We can reintroduce what has been resolutely pushed aside in an
> effort to view our lives and human existence with objectivity;
> namely, our own wills, our deep interest in what we find
> ourselves doing . . . Even the glow worms . . . whose cycles of
> existence over the millions of years seem so pointless when
> looked at by us, will seem utterly different to us if we can
> somehow try to view their existence from within. . . . If the

philosopher is apt to see in this a pattern similar to the unending cycles of the existence of Sisyphus, and to despair, then it is indeed because the meaning and point he is seeking is not there—but mercifully so. The meaning of life is from within us, it is not bestowed from without, and it far exceeds in its beauty and permanence any heaven of which men have ever dreamed or yearned for.

4. Connoisseurs of twentieth-century ethical theory in its Anglo-Saxon and Continental variants will not be slow to see the affinities of this account. Practitioners of the first of these kinds are sometimes singled out for their failure to say anything about such questions as the meaning of life. But, if the affinities are as strong as I think, then, notwithstanding Taylor's philosophical distance from his contemporaries, what we have just unearthed has a strong claim to be their secret doctrine of the meaning of life.

Consider first the sharp supposedly unproblematic distinction, reinforced by the myth as told and retold here, between what we discover already there in the world—the facts, including the gods' enforcement of their sentence—and what is invented or, by thinking or willing, somehow *put into* or *spread onto* the factual world—namely the values.[4] Nobody who knows the philosophical literature on value will be surprised by Taylor's variant on the myth. . . . Here, however, at the point where the magic stuff is to be injected into the veins of Sisyphus, I must digress for the sake of what is to come, in order to explain the deliberate way in which I shall use the word 'value'.

I propose that we distinguish between *evaluations* (typically recorded by such forms as '*x* is good', 'bad', 'beautiful', 'ugly', 'ignoble', 'brave', 'just', 'mischievous', 'malicious', 'worthy', 'honest', 'corrupt', 'disgusting', 'amusing', 'diverting', 'boring', etc.—no restrictions at all on the category of *x*) and *directive* or *deliberative* (or *practical*) *judgements* (e.g. 'I must ψ', 'I ought to ψ', 'it would be best, all things considered, for me to ψ', etc.).[5] It

[4] On the differences between discovery and invention, and on some abuses of the distinction, see William Kneale, 'The Idea of Invention', *Proceedings of the British Academy* vol. 39, 1955.

[5] Note that this is not a distinction whose rationale is originally *founded* in a difference in the motivating force of judgments of the two classes, even if such a difference may be forthcoming from the distinction. In both cases, the thinking that *p* is arguably derivative from the *finding* that *p*. (Cp. Essay V. §11.)

is true that between these there is an important no-man's-land (comprising, *e.g.*, general judgments of the strongly deprecatory or commendatory kind about vices and virtues, and general or particular statements about actions that it is ignoble or inhuman or unspeakably wicked to do or not to do).[6] But the fact that many other kinds of judgment lie between pure valuations and pure directives is no objection; and it does nothing to obstruct the discrimination I seek to effect between the fact-value distinction and the is-ought or is-must distinction. The unavailability of any well-grounded notion of the factual that will make the fact-value distinction an exclusive distinction can only promote our interest in the possibility of our finding an *ought* or *must* that will not count as some species of *is*. If we then conceive of a distinction between *is* and *must* as corresponding to the distinction between appreciation and decision and at the same time emancipate ourselves from a limited and absurd idea of what *is*, then there can be a new verisimilitude in our several accounts of all these things.[7]

This being proposed as the usage of the word 'value' to be adhered to in this paper, let us return now to Sisyphus and the body of doctrine that is illustrated by Taylor's version of his story. At one moment Sisyphus sees his task as utterly futile and degrading: a moment later, supposedly without any initiating change in his cognitive appreciation, we are told that he sees his whole life as infinitely rewarding. What I was about to say, before the digression, was that there is only one philosophy of value that can even attempt to accommodate this possibility.

Consider next Taylor's account of the escape from meaninglessness—or what he might equally well have followed the Existentialists in calling *absurdity*. Taylor's mode of escape is simply a variation on the habitual philosophical reaction to the

---

[6] For some purposes, judgments that philosophers describe as judgments of *prima facie* obligation (better *pro tanto* obligation) might almost, or without excessive distortion be assimilated to valuational judgments.

[7] See below, §§6 and 10. In the language of note 20, ad fin, my own view is that the fact-value distinction is not like a *bat/elephant* distinction, but like an *animal/elephant* distinction. On the other hand, if §11 is right, then the *is/must* distinction is more like a *mammal/carnivore* distinction. For this possibility, see the diagram (p. 108) illustrating overlap of concept extensions.

perception of the real or supposed meaninglessness of human existence. As a method for escape it is co-ordinate with every other proposal that is known, suicide (always one recognized way), scorn or defiance (Albert Camus), resignation or drift (certain orientally influenced positions), various kinds of commitment (R.M. Hare and J.-P. Sartre), and what may be the most recently enlisted member of this équipe, which is irony.[8]

Again, few readers of *Freedom and Reason* will fail to recognize in Sisyphus, after the injection of the gods' substance into his veins, a Mark I, stone-rolling model of R.M. Hare's further elaborated, rationally impregnable 'fanatic'.[9] As for the mysterious substance itself, surely this is some extra oomph, injected afterwards *ad libitum*, that will enable Sisyphus' factual judgments about stone-rolling to take on 'evaluative meaning'.

Finally, nor has nineteenth- or twentieth-century Utilitarianism much to fear from this manner of fable-telling. For the *locus* or origin of all value has been firmly confined within the familiar area of psychological states conceived in independence of what they are directed to.[10]

In order to have a name, I shall call Taylor's and all similar accounts non-cognitive accounts of the meaning of life. This choice of name is not inappropriate if it helps to signal the association of these accounts with a long-standing philosophical tendency to strive for descriptions of the human condition by which will and intellect-cum-perception are kept separate and innocent of all insider transactions. The intellect supplies uncontaminated factual perception, deduction, and means-end reasoning. Ends are supplied (in this picture) by feeling or will, which are not conceived either as percipient or as determinants in any interesting way of perception.

My first contention will be that, in spite of the well-tried familiarity of these ideas, the non-cognitive account depends for its whole plausibility upon abandoning at the level of

---

[8] See Thomas Nagel, 'The Absurd' in *Journal of Philosophy* vol. 68, 1971.

[9] R.M. Hare, *Freedom and Reason* (Oxford University Press, 1963). I mean that Sisyphus is the *stuff* of which the fanatic is made.

[10] For efforts in the direction of a better account of some of these states, see below §6 and Essay V, *passim*.

theory the inner perspective that it commends as the only possible perspective upon life's meaning. This is a kind of incoherence, and one that casts some doubt upon the distinction of the inside and the outside viewpoints. I also believe that, once we break down the supposed distinction between the inner or participative and the outer, supposedly objective, viewpoints, there will be a route by which we can advance—though not to anything like the particularity of the moral certainty that we began by envying.

5. Where the non-cognitive account essentially depends on the existence and availability of the inner view, it is a question of capital importance whether the non-cognitivist's account of the inner view makes such sense of our condition as it actually has for us from the inside.

The first ground for suspecting distortion is that, if the non-cognitive view is put in the way Taylor puts it, then it seems to make too little difference to the meaningfulness of life how well or badly our strivings are apt to turn out. Stone-rolling for its own sake, and stone-rolling for successful temple building, and stone-rolling for temple building that will be frustrated—all seem to come to much the same thing. I object that that is not how it feels to most people. No doubt there are 'committed' individuals like William the Silent or the doctor in Camus' *La Peste* who will constitute exceptions to my claim. But in general, the larger the obstacles nature or other people put in our way, and the more truly hopeless the prospect, the less point most of us will feel anything has. 'Where there is no hope, there is no endeavour' as Samuel Johnson observed. In the end point is partly dependent on expectation of outcome; and expectation is dependent on past outcomes. So point is not independent of outcome.

The non-cognitivist may make two replies here. The first is that, in so far as the outcome is conceived by the agent as crucial for the value of the activity, the activity is merely instrumental and must lead back to other activities that are their own outcome. And these he will say are what matter. But in opposition to this,

(a)   I shall show in due course how activities that can be

regarded as 'their own goals' typically depend on valuations that non-cognitivism makes bad sense of (§6 below);

(b)    I shall question whether all activities that have a goal
independent of the activity itself are perceived by their
agents as only derivatively meaningful (§13 below).

The non-cognitivists' second reply will be directed against the
objection that he makes it matter too little how well or badly
our strivings turn out. Is it not a point on *his* side that the
emptier and worse worlds where one imagines everything
having even less point than it has now are worlds where the will
itself will falter? To this I say Yes, I hear the reply. But if the
non-cognitive view was to make the sense of our condition that
we attribute to it, then something needed to be written into the
non-cognitive account about what kinds of object will engage
with the will as important. And it is still unclear at this stage
how much room can be found within non-cognitivism for the
will's own distinctions between good and bad reasons for
caring about anything as important. Objectively speaking
(once 'we disengage our wills'), any reason is as good or as bad
as any other reason, it seems to say. For on the non-cognitive
account, life is objectively meaningless. So, by the non-
cognitivist's lights, it must appear that *whatever* the will
chooses to treat as a good reason to engage itself is, for the will,
a good reason. But the will itself, taking the inner view, picks
and chooses, deliberates, weighs, and tests its own concerns. It
craves objective reasons; and often it could not go forward
unless it thought it had them. The extension of the concept
*objective* is quite different on the inner view from the extension
assigned to it by the outer view. And the rationale for
determining the extension is different also.

There is here an incoherence. To avoid it without flying in
the face of what we think we know already about the difference
between meaning and meaninglessness, the disagreement
between the inner and the outer views must be softened
somehow. The trouble is that, if we want to preserve any of the
distinctive emphases of Taylor's and similar accounts, then we
are bound to find that, for purposes of the validation of any
given concern, the non-cognitive view always readdresses the
problem to the inner perspective *without itself adopting that*

*perspective*. It cannot adopt the inner perspective because, according to the picture that the non-cognitivist paints of these things, the inner view has to be unaware of the outer one, and has to enjoy essentially illusory notions of objectivity, importance, and significance: whereas the outer view has to hold that life is objectively meaningless. The non-cognitivist mitigates the outrageousness of so categorical a denial of meaning as the outer view issues by pointing to the availability of the participant perspective. But the most that he can do is to point to it. Otherwise the theorist is himself engulfed in a view to which he must deny any truth or correctness.

So much for the first distortion I claim to find in non-cognitivism and certain inconclusive defences of that approach. There is also a second distortion.

To us there seems to be an important difference between the life of the cannibalistic blindworms that Taylor describes and the life of (say) a basking seal or a dolphin at play, creatures that are conscious, can rest without sleeping, can adjust the end to the means as well as the means to the end, and can take in far more about the world than they have the immediate or instrumental need to take in. There also seems to us to be a difference, a different difference, between the life of seals or dolphins and the life of human beings living in communities with a history. And there is even a third difference, which as participants we insist upon, between the life of a man who contributes something to a society with a continuing history and a life lived on the plan of a southern pig-breeder who (in the economics textbooks, if not in real life) buys more land to grow more corn to feed more hogs to buy more land, to grow more corn to feed more hogs . . . The practical concerns of this man are at once regressive and circular. And we are keenly interested, on the inner view, in the difference between these concerns and non-circular practical reasonings or life plans.

For the inner view, this difference undoubtedly exists. If the outside view is right to commend the inside view, then the outside view must pay some heed to the differences that the inner view perceives. But needing to depreciate them, it cannot accord them an importance that is commensurate with the weight that the non-cognitive theory of life's meaning thrusts upon the inner view. 'The differences are merely invented,'

Taylor has to say, 'and none really cancels the kind of meaninglessness we found in Sisyphus'.

To the participant it may seem that it is far harder to explain what is so good about buying more land to grow more corn to feed more hogs to buy more land, to grow more corn to feed more hogs . . . than it is to explain what is good about digging a ditch with a man whom one likes, or helping the same man to talk or drink the sun down the sky. It might seem to a participant that the explanation of the second sort of thing, so far from having nowhere to go but round and round in circles, fans out into a whole arborescence of concerns; that, unlike any known explanation of what is so good about breeding hogs to buy more land to breed more hogs . . ., it can be pursued backwards and outwards to take in all the concerns of a whole life. But on the non-cognitive view of the inner view there is no way to make these differences stick. They count for so little that it is a mystery why the non-cognitivist doesn't simply say: life is meaningless; and that's all there is to it. If only he would make that pronouncement, we should know where we were.

But why do the differences just mentioned count for so little for the non-cognitivist? Because they all arise from subjective or anthropocentric considerations, and what is subjective or anthropocentric is not by the standards of the outer view objective. (Taylor insists that to determine whether something matters, we have to view it 'independently of our own deep interest'.) I shall come back to this when I reconstruct the non-cognitive view; but let me point out immediately the *prima facie* implausibility of the idea that the distinction between objectivity and non-objectivity (which appears to have to do with the existence of publicly accepted and rationally criticizable standards of argument, or of ratiocination towards truth) should coincide with the distinction between the anthropocentric and the non-anthropocentric (which concerns orientation towards human interests or a human point of view). The distinctions are not without conceptual links, but the *prima facie* appearance is that a matter that is anthropocentric may be either more objective or less objective, or (at the limit) *merely* subjective.[11] This is how things will appear until we have

---

[11] For an independent account of the subjective, see Essay V.

an argument to prove rigorously the mutual coincidence of independently plausible accounts of the anthropocentric/non-anthropocentric distinction, the non-objective/objective distinction, and the subjective/non-subjective distinction.[12]

The third and last distortion of experience I find in Taylor's presentation of non-cognitivism I shall try to convey by an anecdote. Two or three years ago, when I went to see some film at the Academy Cinema, the second feature of the evening was a documentary film about creatures fathoms down on the ocean-bottom. When it was over, I turned to my companion and asked, 'What is it about these films that makes one feel so utterly desolate?' Her reply was: 'apart from the fact that so much of the film was about sea monsters eating one another, the unnerving thing was that nothing down there ever seemed to *rest*.' As for play, disinterested curiosity, or merely contemplating, she could have added, these seemed inconceivable.

At least about the film we had just seen, these were just the points that needed to be made—untrammelled by all pseudo-philosophical inhibitions, which are irrelevant in any case to the 'inner' or participant perspective. And the thought the film leads to is this. If we can project upon a form of life nothing but the pursuit of life itself, if we find there no non-instrumental concerns and no interest in the world considered as lasting longer than the animal in question will need the world to last in order to sustain the animal's own life; then the form of life must be to some considerable extent alien to us.[13] Any adequate

---

[12] A similar observation needs to be entered about all the other distinctions that are in the offing here—the distinctions between the neutral and the committed, the neutral and the biased, the descriptive and the prescriptive, the descriptive and the evaluative, the quantifiable and the unquantifiable, the absolute and the relative, the scientific and the unscientific, the not essentially contestable and the essentially contestable, the verifiable or falsifiable and the neither verifiable nor falsifiable, the factual and the normative. . . . In common parlance, and in sociology and economics—even in political science, which should know better—these distinctions are used almost interchangeably. But they are different. Each of these contrasts has its own rationale. An account of all of them would be a contribution not only to philosophy but to life.

[13] Here, I think, or in this neighbourhood, lies the explanation of the profound unease that some people feel at the systematic and unrelenting exploitation of nature and animals which is represented by factory farming, by intensive livestock rearing, or by the mindless spoliation of non-renewable resources. This condemnation of evil will never be understood till it is distinguished by its detractors from its frequent, natural, but only contingent concomitant—the absolute prohibition of all killing not done in self-defence.

description of the point we can attach to our form of life must do more than treat our appetitive states in would-be isolation from their relation to the things they are directed at.

For purposes of his eventual philosophical destination, Richard Taylor had to forge an intimate and direct link between contemplation, permanence, and boredom. But, at least on the inner view, the connection between these things is at once extremely complex and relatively indirect.[14] And, once one has seen the final destination towards which it is Taylor's design to move the whole discussion, then one sees in a new light his obsession with monuments. Surely these are his hostages for the objects of psychological states in general; and all such objects are due to be in some sense discredited. (Discredited on the outer view, or accorded a stultifyingly indiscriminate tolerance on the outer account of the inner view.) And one comprehends all too well Taylor's sour grapes insistence on the impermanence of monuments—as if by this he could reduce to nil the philosophical (as opposed, he might say, to subjective) importance of all the objects of psychological states, longings, lookings, reverings, contemplatings, or whatever.

6. Leaving many questions still dangling, I shall conclude discussion of the outer account of the inner perspective with a general difficulty, and a suggestion.

There is a tendency, in Utilitarian writings and in the writings of economists,[15] to locate all ultimate or intrinsic value

---

[14] On permanence, *cf.* Wittgenstein *Tractatus Logico-Philosophicus* 6.4312 quoted *ad init.*; F.P. Ramsey, 'Is there anything to discuss?', *Foundations of Mathematics and other Essays* (London, 1931):

> 'I apply my perspective not merely to space but also to time. In time the world will cool and everything will die; but that is a long time off still and its percent value at compound discount is almost nothing. Nor is the present less valuable because the future will be blank.'

[15] *Cf.* Wilfred Beckerman, *New Statesman*, 21 June 1974, p. 880.

> The second, and real question is: at what rate should we use up resources in order to maximise the welfare of human beings . . . Throughout existence man has made use of the environment, and the only valid question for those who attach—as I do (in accordance with God's first injunction to Adam)—*complete and absolute priority to human welfare* is what rate of use provides the maximum welfare for humans, including future generations.

I quote this relatively guarded specimen to illustrate the hazards of making too easy a

in human appetitive states.[16] They are contrasted (as we also see Taylor contrasting them for his purposes) with everything else in the world. According to this sort of view, the value of anything that is not a psychological state derives from the psychological state or states for which it is an actual or potential object. See here what Bentham says in *An Introduction to the Principles of Morals and Legislation*:

> Strictly speaking, nothing can be said to be good or bad, but either in itself; which is the case only with pain or pleasure; or on account of its effects; which is the case only with things that are the causes or preventives of pain and pleasure.

One has only to put the matter like this, however, to be troubled by a curious instability. Since nothing at all can count for the outer view as inherently or intrinsically good, the doctrine must belong to the inner or inside view. But, as experienced, the inner view too will reject this view of value. For, adopting that inner view,[17] and supposing with Bentham that certain conscious states are good in themselves, we must take these states as they appear to the inner view. But then one cannot say without radical misconception that these states are all that is intrinsically valuable. For (a) many of these conscious states have intentional objects; (b) many of the conscious states in which intrinsic value supposedly resides are strivings *after* objects that are not states, or are contemplations *of* objects that are not themselves states; and (c) it is of the essence of these conscious states, experienced as strivings or contemplations or whatever, to accord to their intentional

---

distinction between human welfare on the one side and the environment on the other. But it also illustrates the purely ornamental role which has devolved upon the Hebrew scriptures. They constitute matter for the literary decoration of sentiments formed and apprehended by quite different methods of divination. It is irrelevant for instance that the world-view given voice in the first chapters of *Genesis* is perceptibly more complicated than the one Beckerman expresses.

[16] Or in the case of vegetarian utilitarian writings, to locate all ultimate value in conscious animal appetitive states.

[17] Perhaps some one individual man's inner view. For here and only here could it be held to be perfectly or fully obvious that the special goodness in themselves of certain of his pleasurable states is something simply above or beyond argument for him. Beyond that point—notwithstanding utilitarian explanations of the superfluity of argument on something so allegedly evident—it is less obvious to him.

objects a non-instrumental value. For from the inside of lived experience, and by the scale of value that that imposes, the shape of an archway or the sound of the lapping of the sea against the shore at some place at some time may appear to be of an altogether different order of importance from the satisfaction that some human being once had from his breakfast.[18]

The participant, with the going concepts of the objective and the worth while, descries certain external properties in things and states of affairs. And the presence there of these properties is what invests them with importance in his eyes. The one thing that properties cannot be, at least for him, is mere projections resulting from a certain kind of efficacy in the causation of satisfaction. For no appetitive or aesthetic or contemplative state can see its own object as having a value that is derivative in the special way that is required by the thesis that all non-instrumental value resides in human states of satisfaction. But, if that is right, then the outer view cannot rely for its credibility upon the meaning that the inner view perceives in something. To see itself and its object in the alien manner of the outer view, the state as experienced would have to be prepared to suppose that it, the state, could just as well have lighted on any other object (even any other kind of object), provided only that the requisite attitudes could have been induced. But in this conception of such states we are entitled to complain that nothing remains that we can recognize, or that the inner perspective will not instantly disown.[19]

---

[18] This feature of experience is of course lamented by thinkers who seek to make moral philosophy out of (('formal value theory' + moral earnestness) + some values of the theorist's own, generalized and thereby tested) + applications. But the feature is part of what is given in the phenomenology of some of the very same 'satisfaction' experiences that are the starting-point of the utilitarians themselves. And there is nothing to take fright at in this feature of them, inconsistent though it is with absurd slogans of the literally absolute priority of human welfare.

[19] An example will make these claims clearer perhaps. A man comes at dead of night to a hotel in a place where he has never been before. In the morning he stumbles out from his darkened room and, following the scent of coffee out of doors, he finds a sunlit terrace looking out across a valley on to a range of blue mountains in the half-distance. The sight of them—a veritable vale of Tempe—entrances him. In marvelling at the valley and mountains he thinks only how overwhelmingly beautiful they are. The value of the state depends on the value attributed to the object. But the theory I oppose says all non-instrumental value resides here in the man's own state, and in the like states of others who are actually so affected by the mountains. The more numerous such states are, the greater, presumably, the theory holds, is the 'realized' value of the mountains.

I promised to conclude the critique of non-cognitivism with a suggestion about values. It is this: no attempt to make sense of the human condition can really succeed if it treats the objects of psychological states as unequal partners or derivative elements in the conceptual structure of values and states and their objects. This is far worse than Aristotle's opposite error:

> We desire the object because it seems good to us, rather than the object's seeming good to us because we desire it. *Metaphysics*, 1072a29

Spinoza appears to have taken this sentence as it stood and deliberately negated it (*Ethics*, part III, proposition 9, note). But maybe it is the beginning of real wisdom to see that we may have to side against both Aristotle and Spinoza here and ask: 'Why should the *because* not hold both ways round?' Surely an adequate account of these matters will have to treat psychological states and their objects as equal and reciprocal partners, and is likely to need to see the identifications of the states and of the properties under which the states subsume their objects as interdependent. (If these interdependencies are fatal to the distinction of inner and outer, we are already in a position to be grateful for that.)

Surely it can be true both that we desire $x$ because we think $x$ good, and that $x$ is good because $x$ is such that we desire $x$. It does not count against the point that the explanation of the 'because' is different in each direction. Nor does it count against the particular anti-non-cognitivist position that is now emerging in opposition to non-cognitivism that the second 'because' might have to be explained in some such way as this: such desiring by human beings directed in this way is one part of what is required for there to be such a thing as the perspective from which the non-instrumental goodness of $x$ is there to be perceived.

There is an analogy for this suggestion. We may see a pillar-

---

The theory says that the whole actual value of the beauty of the valley and mountains is dependent upon arranging for the full exploitation of the capacity of these things to produce such states in human beings. (Exploitation now begun and duly recorded in Paul Jennings's Wordsworthian emendation: 'I wandered lonely as a crowd.') What I am saying about the theory is simply that it is untrue to the actual experience of the object-directed states that are the starting-point of that theory.

box as red because it is red. But also pillar-boxes, painted as they are, *count* as red only because there actually exists a perceptual apparatus (*e.g.* our own) that discriminates, and learns on the direct basis of experience to group together, all and only the actually red things. Not every sentient animal that sees a red postbox sees it as red. But this in no way impugns the idea that redness is an external, monadic property of a postbox. 'Red postbox' is not short for 'red to human beings postbox'. Red is not a relational property. (It is certainly not relational in the way in which 'father of' is relational, or 'moves' is relational on a Leibniz-Mach view of space.) All the same, it is in one interesting sense a *relative* property. For the category of colour is an anthropocentric category. The category corresponds to an interest that can only take root in creatures with something approaching our own sensory apparatus.

Philosophy has dwelt nearly exclusively on differences between 'good' and 'red' or 'yellow'. I have long marvelled at this.[20] For there resides in the combined objectivity and anthropocentricity of colour a striking analogy to illuminate not only the externality that human beings attribute to the properties by whose ascription they evaluate things, people, and actions, but also the way in which the quality *by* which the thing qualifies as good and the desire *for* the thing are equals—are 'made for one another' so to speak. Compare the

[20] Without of course wishing to deny the difference that good is 'attributive' to a marked degree, whereas colour words are scarcely attributive at all. I think that, in these familiar discussions, philosophers have misdescribed the undoubted fact that, because there is no standing interest to which yellowness answers, 'yellow' is not such as to be *cut out* (by virtue of standing for what it stands for) to commend a thing or evaluate it favourably. But, surely, if there were such a standing interest, 'yellow' would be at least as well suited to commend as 'sharp' or 'beautiful' or even 'just' are.

Against the suggestion that axiological predicates are a species of predicate not clearly marked off from the factual, there is a trick the non-cognitivist always plays and he ought not to be allowed to play. He picks himself a 'central case' of a descriptive predicate, and a 'central case' of a valuational predicate. Then he remarks how very different the predicates he has picked are. But what on earth can that show? Nobody thinks you could prove a bat was not an animal by contrasting some bat (a paradigm case of a bat) with some elephant (a paradigm case of an animal). Nothing can come clear from such procedures in advance of explanation of the point of the contrast. In the present case the point of the factual/non-factual distinction has not been explained; and it has to be explained without begging the question in favour of the non-cognitivist, who picked the quarrel in the first place. What was the nature or rationale of the difference which was by these means to have been demonstrated? Till it is explained there must remain all the following possibilities:

way in which the quality by which a thing counts as funny and the mental set that is presupposed to being amused by it are made for one another.

7. The time has come to sort out the non-cognitive theory to accommodate these findings and expel contradiction. But it is possible that I have not convinced you that any sorting out is necessary, and that you have found more coherent than I have allowed it to be the non-cognitivist's use of the idea of perspective, and of different and incompatible perspectives.

Perspective is not a form of illusion, distortion, or delusion. All the different perspectives of a single array of objects are perfectly consistent with one another. Given a set of perspectives, we can recover, if only they be reliably collected, a unified true account of the shape, spatial relations, and relative dimensions of the objects in the array. If we forget these platitudes then we may think it is much more harmless than it really is that the so-called outer and inner perspectives should straightforwardly contradict one another. There is nothing whatever in the idea of a perspective to license this scandalous idea—no more than the truism that two perspectives may include or exclude different aspects will create the licence to think that the participant and external views, as the noncognitivist has described them, may unproblematically conflict over whether a certain activity or pursuit is really (or objectively) worth while or not.[21]

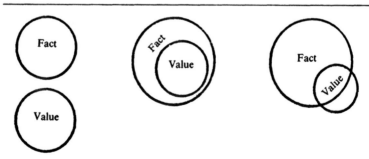

It would be unfair to say there have been no attempts at all to elucidate the point of the fact-value contrast as exclusive. Wittgenstein tried (unsuccessfully) to explain it so in his 'Lecture on Ethics', *Philosophical Review* vol. 74, 1965, p. 6. And prescriptivists explain it as exclusive by reference to the link they allege holds between evaluation and action. But, although there is some such link between deliberative judgment and action, the required link does not hold between evaluation and action. That was one part of the point of the contrast I proposed at the beginning of §4.

There are several different reasons then why the non-cognitivist theory must be redeployed, if it is to be taken seriously.

A traditional twentieth-century way of straightening out the theory to secure its self-consistency would have been *meta-ethics*, conceived as an axiologically neutral branch of 'logic'. Meta-ethics is not as neutral as was supposed. But it may be that it is still the best way for us to understand ourselves better.

Let us take the language of practice or morals as an object language. Call it L. The theorist's duty is then to discover, and to explain in the meta-language which is his own language, both a *formal theory* and a more discursive *informal theory* of L-utterances, not least L-utterances concerning what is worth while or a good thing to do with one's life. In place of philosophical analysis, let him concentrate on the informal elucidation of such judgements, then study the assertibility predicate in its application to various types of moral judgment and in each case determine its approximation there to genuine truth.

What does this involve? First, and this is the humble formal task that is presupposed to his more distinctively ethical aspirations, the theorist needs to be able to say, or assume that someone can say, what each of the sentences of the object language means. To achieve this, a procedure is needed for parsing L-sentences into their primitive semantic components, and an axiom is required for each primitive component accounting for its particular contribution to assertion conditions. Then, given any L-sentence s, the axioms can be deployed to derive a pairing of s with an assertion condition p, the pairing being stated in the metalanguage by a theorem in the form:

$s$ is assertible if and only if $p$.

Moral philosophy as we now know it makes many sophisticated claims about meaning and meanings, all hard to assess. Compared with everything that would be involved in making those assessments, what we are assuming here is minimal. What

---

[21] Still less does the language of perspective license the supposition that the philosopher who answers the question of the meaning of life could make a virtue out of committing himself to neither, or neither and both perspectives. Does he think of himself as one who somehow looks at everything from no perspective at all? For the closest approximation he could coherently conceive of attaining to this aspiration, see §10 below.

we are assuming is only that the informal remarks the moral theorist hopes to make about the status of this, that, or the other judgment in L will presuppose that such a biconditional can be constructed for each sentence of L. These assertion conditions give the meaning of the judgments he wants to comment upon. If no such principled understanding of what they mean may be thought of as obtainable, then (whatever other treasures he possesses) the moralist cannot even count on the first thing.

I speak of *assertion* conditions as that by which meaning is given, and not yet of *truth* conditions, but only because within this meta-ethical framework the non-cognitivist's most distinctive non-formal thesis is likely to be the denial that the assertibility of a value judgment or of a deliberative judgment can amount to anything as objective as we suppose truth to be. To do justice to this denial of his, we leave undecided—as Dummett in one way and Davidson and McDowell in another have shown to be possible—the relationship of truth and assertibility.[22] In this way we arrange matters so that it can turn out—as it does for empirical or scientific utterances—that truth is a special case of assertibility; but it is not theoretically excluded that, for certain classes of judgments, assertibility should fall short of truth. The matter is left open, and it is for meta-ethics and the informal theory that is built around the formal theory to close it. I come now to this informal theory.

Adapting Tarski's so-called 'Convention T' to the purposes of the formal theory, we may say now that the meta-language has a materially adequate definition of the predicate 'assertible' just in case it has as consequences all sentences obtained from the schema '*s* is assertible if and only if *p*' by substituting for '*s*' a name of any sentence of L and substituting for '*p*' the translation or interpretation of this sentence in the meta-

---

[22] See M.A.E. Dummett, *Frege: Philosophy of Language* (London: Duckworth, 1973) and John McDowell, 'Bivalence and Verificationism' in *Truth and Meaning: Essays in Semantics* (Oxford University Press, 1972), edited by Gareth Evans and John McDowell. McDowell shows how we can build up an independent account of what a semantical predicate F will have to be like if the sentences of an object language are to be interpreted by means of equivalences which will say what the object language sentences mean. His way of showing that it can be a *discovery*, so to speak, that it is the truth predicate which fulfils the requirements on F is prefigured at p. 210 of Donald Davidson, 'Truth and Meaning', *Synthèse* vol. 17, 1967.

language.[23] So if the ethical theorist is to erect a theory of objectivity, subjectivity, relativism, or whatever upon these foundations, then the next thing we need to say some more about is how a theory of L-assertibility is to be constrained in order to ensure that the sentence used on the right-hand side of any particular equivalence that is entailed by the theory of assertibility should indeed interpret or translate the sentence mentioned on the left. What is *interpretation* or *translation* in this context? If we can supply this constraint then, as a bonus, we shall understand far better the respective roles of participant and theorist and what assertibility would have to amount to.

It seems obvious that the only way to by-pass Tarski's explicit use of the word 'translation' is by reference to what Davidson has called radical interpretation.[24] A promising proposal is this. Rewrite convention T to state that the meta-language possesses an empirically correct definition of 'assertible' just in case the semantical axioms, in terms of which the definition of assertibility is given, all taken together, entail a set $\Sigma$ of equivalences '*s* is assertible just in case *p*', one equivalence for each sentence of L, with the following overall property: a theorist who employs the condition *p* with which each sentence *s* is mated in a $\Sigma$-equivalence, and who employs the equivalence to interpret utterances of *s*, is in the best position he can be to make the *best possible overall sense* there is to be made of L-speakers. This goal sets a real constraint—witness the fact that the theorist may test his theory, try it out as a way of making sense of his subjects, even as he constructs it. By 'making sense of them' would be meant ascribing to the speakers of L, on the strength of their linguistic and other actions, an intelligible collection of beliefs, needs, and concerns. That is a collection that diminishes to the bare minimum the need for the interpreter

[23] See p. 187 of A. Tarski, 'The Concept of Truth in Formalized languages', in *Logic, Semantics, and Metamathematics* (Oxford University Press, 1956). For my present doubts that there is anything to be gained, except an expository point, by the fabrication of a predicate of semantic assessment that is independent of 'true' in the fashion that 'assertible' might seem to promise to be, see Essay IV, §18 following.

[24] See D. Davidson, 'Radical Interpretation', *Dialectica* vol. 27, 1973. The original problem is of course Quine's. See W.V. Quine, *Word and Object* (Cambridge, Mass: MIT Press, 1960). Davidson's own conception has been progressively refined by many philosophers, notably by Richard Grandy, Donald Davidson, Christopher Peacocke, Gareth Evans, and John McDowell. See also pp. 141–7 below.

to ascribe inexplicable error or inexplicable irrationality to them.[25] By 'interpreting an utterance of *s*' is intended here: saying what it is that *s* is used to say.

This general description is intended to pass muster for the interpretation of a totally alien language. But now suppose that we envisage the object-language and meta-language both being English. Then we can turn radical interpretation to advantage in order to envisage ourselves as occupying simultaneously the roles of theorist or interpreter and subject or participant. That will be to envisage ourselves as engaged in an attempt to understand ourselves.

Whether we think of things in this way or not, it is very important to note how essentially similar are the positions of the linguistic theorist and his subjects. The role of the theorist is only to *supplement*, for theoretical purposes, the existing understanding of L-speakers. It is true that, subject to the constraint upon which the whole exercise of interpretation itself rests—namely sufficient agreement in beliefs, concerns, and conceptions of what is rational and what is not—the theorist need not have exactly the same beliefs as his subjects. But the descriptions of the world that are available to him are essentially the same sorts of description as those available to his subjects. He uses the very same sort of sentence to describe the conditions under which *s* is assertible as the sentence *s* itself:

---

[25] See Richard Grandy, 'Reference, Meaning, and Belief', *Journal of Philosophy* vol. 70, 1973: John McDowell, *op. cit.* The requirement that we diminish to the minimum the theoretical need to postulate inexplicable error or irrationality is a precondition of trying to project any interpretation at all upon alien speakers. It was phrased by Davidson in another way, and called by him the requirement of charity. The replacement given here is closer to what has been dubbed by Richard Grandy the requirement of *humanity*. The further alterations reflect the belief that philosophy must desist from the systematic destruction of the sense of the word 'want', and that what Davidson calls 'primary reasons' must be diversified to embrace a wider and more diverse class of affective states than *desire*. (For a little more on these points, see now my *Sameness and Substance* (Oxford: Blackwell, 1980), Longer Note 6.36.)

Note that, even though we must for purposes of radical interpretation project upon L-speakers our own notions of rationality (and there is no proof they are the sole possible), and even though we take all the advantage we can of the fact that the speakers of the object-language are like us in being men, there is no guarantee that there must be a unique best theory of the assertibility conditions of their utterances. It has not been excluded that there might be significant disagreement between interpreters who have made equally good overall sense of the shared life of speakers of L, but at some points rejected one another's interpretations of L.

and the meta-language is at no descriptive distance from the object-language. If the theorist believes his own semantic theory, then he is committed to be ready to put his mind where his mouth is at least once for each sentence *s* of the object-language, in a statement of assertion conditions for *s* in which he himself uses either *s* or a faithful translation of *s*. It follows that the possibility simply does not exist for the theorist to stand off entirely from the language of his subjects or from the viewpoint that gives this its sense. He has to begin at least by embracing—or by making as if to embrace—the very same commitments and world-view as the ordinary speakers of the object language. (This is not to say that having understood them, he cannot then back off from that world-view. What requires careful statement is how he is to do so.)

8. Even if this will be a disappointment to those who have supposed that, by means of meta-ethics, the theorist of value could move straight to a position of complete neutrality, it faces us in the right direction for the reconstitution of the non-cognitive theory. In fact the framework I have been proposing precisely enables him to register his own distinctive point. He can do so in at least two distinctive ways. The first accepts and the second actually requires that framework.

First, using the language of his subjects but thinking (as a moralist like a Swift or an Aristophanes should, or as any moral theorist may) a bit harder than the generality of his subjects, he may try to make them look at themselves; and he may prompt them to see their own pursuits and concerns in unaccustomed ways. There is an optical metaphor that is much more useful here than that of perspective. Staying within the participant perspective, what the theorist may do is *lower the level of optical resolution*. Suppressing irrelevancies and trivialities, he may perceive, and then persuade others to perceive, the capriciousness of some of the discriminations we unthinkingly engage in; or the obtuseness of some of the assimilations that we are content with. Again, rather differently but placing the non-cognitivist closer within reach of his own hobby-horse, he may direct the attention of his audience to what Aurel Kolnai called 'the incongruities of ordinary practice'.[26] Here Kolnai alluded to the irremovable disproportion between how heroic is the effort that it is biologically instinct in us to put into the pursuit of certain of our concerns; and how 'finite, limited, transient, perishable, tiny, tenuous' we ourselves and our goods and satisfactions all are. To lower the level of resolution, not down to the point where human concerns themselves are invisible—we shall come to that—but to the point where both the disproportion and its terms are manifest, is a precondition of human (as opposed to merely animal) resilience, of humour, of sense of proportion, of sanity even. It is the traditional function of the moralist who is a participant and of the satirist (who may want not to be). But this way of seeing is not the seeing of the total meaninglessness that Taylor spoke of. Nor, in the existentialist philosopher's highly technical sense, is it the perception of absurdity. For the participant perspective can contain together both the perception of incongruity and a nice appreciation of the limited but not necessarily infinitesimal importance of this or that particular object or concern. (It is not perfectly plain what Kolnai thought about the affinity of existentialist absurdity and incongruity—the manuscript is a fragment—but, if Kolnai had doubted the compatibility of the perceptions of incongruity and importance, I think I could have convinced him by a very Kolnaistic point. The disproportion between our effort and our transience is a fugitive quantity. It begins to disappear as soon as one is properly impressed by it. For it is only to us or our kind that our own past or future efforts can seem heroic.)

So much then for the non-cognitivist's first way of making his chief point. It will lead to nothing radical enough for him. The second way to make his point is to abstract it from the long sequence of preposterous attempts at traditional philosophical analysis of *good, ought, right, etc.* in terms of pleasure or feeling or approval . . ., and to transform it into an informal observation concerning the similarity or difference between the status of assertibility enjoyed by evaluative judgments and practical judgments, on the one hand, and the status of plain, paradigmatic, or canonical truth enjoyed by (for example) historical or geographical judgments on the other hand.[27]

---

[26] 'The Utopian Mind' (unpublished typescript), p. 77.
[27] See in this connexion Essay IV.

What then is plain truth? Well, for purposes of the comparison, perhaps it will be good enough to characterize it by what may be called the truisms of plain truth. These truisms I take to be (1) the primacy of truth as a dimension for the assessment of judgements: (2) the answerability of truth to evidenced argument that will under favourable conditions converge upon agreement whose proper explanation involves that very truth; and (3) the independence of truth both from our will and from our own limited means of recognizing the presence or absence of the property in a statement. (2) and (3) together suggest the truism (4) that every truth is true in virtue of something. We shall expect further (5) that every plain truth is compatible with every other plain truth. Finally, a putative further truism (6*) requires the complete determinacy of truth and of all questions whose answers can aspire to that status.[28]

Does the assertibility of evaluative judgments and/or deliberative judgments come up to this standard? If we press this question within the framework just proposed, the non-cognitivist's distinctive doctrine becomes the contention that the answer is *no*. The question can be pressed from a point that is well within reach. We do not need to pretend to be outside our own conceptual scheme, or at a point that ought to have been both inaccessible and unthinkable.[29] The question is one we can pursue by working with informal elucidations of truth and assertibility that can be fruitfully constrained by the project of radical interpretation.[30] And as regards the apparent incoherence of Taylor's non-cognitivism, we can supersede the separate outer and inner perspectives by a common perspective that is accessible to both theorist and participant. Suppose it is asserted that this, that, or the other thing is worth doing, and that the assertion is made on the best sort of grounds known to participant or theorist. Or suppose that a man dies declaring that his life has been marvellously worth while. The non-

---

[28] These formulations are superseded by the statement of the marks of truth given in §5 of Essay IV. (6*) does not survive there, for reasons that emerge in §10 below.

[29] Compare the manner in which we could ascertain from within the space that we occupy certain of the geometrical properties of that very space: e.g., discover whether all equilateral triangles we encounter, of whatever size, are in fact similar triangles. If not, then the space is non-Euclidean.

[30] Cp. Essay IV, §4.

cognitive theory is first and foremost a theory not about the meaning but about the *status* of those remarks: that their assertibility is not plain truth and reflects no fact of the matter. What is more, this is precisely the suspicion that sometimes troubles and perplexes the untheoretical participant who is moved to ask the questions from which we began this inquiry. Finally, let it be noticed, and put down to the credit of the framework being commended, that within this it was entirely predictable that the question would be there to be asked.

9.  The non-cognitivist's answer to the question can now be considered under two separate heads, value judgments (strict valuations) in general (this §) and deliberative judgments in general (§11).

For the non-cognitive critique of the assertibility predicate as it applies to value judgments I propose to employ a formulation given by Bernard Williams in 'The Truth in Relativism', *Proceedings of the Aristotelian Society* (1974/5).

Relativism will be true, Williams says, just in case there are or can be systems of beliefs $S_1$ and $S_2$ such that:

(1) $S_1$ and $S_2$ are distinct and to some extent self-contained;

(2) Adherents of $S_1$ can understand adherents of $S_2$;

(3) $S_1$ and $S_2$ exclude one another—by (a) being comparable and (b) returning divergent yes/no answers to at least one question identifying some action or object type which is the locus of disagreement under some agreed description;

(4) $S_1$ and $S_2$ do not (for us here now, say) stand in real confrontation because, whichever of $S_1$ and $S_2$ is ours, the question of whether the other one is right lacks the relation to our concerns 'which alone gives any point or substance to appraisal: the only real questions of appraisal [being] about real options' (p. 255). 'For we recognize that there can be many systems S which have insufficient relation to our concerns for our [own] judgments to have any grip on them.'

If this is right then the non-cognitivist critique of valuations comes to this. Their mere assertibility as such lacks one of the truistic properties of plain truth: for an assertible valuation may fail even under favourable conditions to command agreement (*cf.* truism (2) §8). Again, there is nothing in the assertibility property itself to guarantee that all one by one assertible evaluations are *jointly* assertible (*cf.* truism (5)). Nor is it clear that where there is disagreement there is always something or other at issue (*cf.* truism (4)). For truth on the other hand we expect and demand all of this.

The participant will find this disturbing, even discouraging. But is Williams right about the compatibility of his four conditions?[31] He mentions among other things undifferentiated judgments of 'right' and 'wrong', 'ought' and 'ought not'. Here, where the point of agreement or disagreement or opting one way or another lies close to action, and radical interpretation is correspondingly less problematical, I think he is on strong ground. We can make good sense of conditions (2) and (3) being satisfied together. We can easily imagine condition (4) being satisfied. But for valuations in the strict and delimited sense, such as 'brave', 'dishonest', 'ignoble', 'just', 'malicious', 'priggish', there is a real difficulty. The comparability condition (3) requires that radical interpretation be possible. But radical interpretation requires the projection by one person upon another of a collection of beliefs, desires, and concerns that differ from the interpreter's own only in a fashion that the interpreter can describe and, to some extent, explain: and the remoter the link between the word to be interpreted and action, and (which is different) the more special the flavour of the word, the more detailed and delicate the projection that has to be possible to anchor interpretation. Evaluations raise both of these problems at once. (And one of the several factors that make the link between strict valuations and action so remote is something that Williams himself has prominently insisted upon in other connections—the plurality, mutual irreducibility, and incommensurability of goods.) The more feasible interpret-

---

[31] Both for Williams's purposes and for ours—which is the status of the assertibility concept as it applies to value judgments, and then as it applies (§11) to deliberative or practical judgments—we have to be able to convert a relativism such as this, concerning as it does overall systems $S_1$ and $S_2$, into a relativism concerning this or that particular judgment or class of judgments identifiable and reidentifiable across $S_1$ and $S_2$. Williams requires this in order that disagreement shall be focused. I require it in order to see whether it is possible to distinguish judgments in $S_1$ or $S_2$ whose assertibility conditions coincide with plain truth from other judgments where this is dubious.

ation is here, the smaller must be the distance between the concerns of interpreter and subject.[32] But then the harder condition (4) is to satisfy.

In the theoretical framework of radical interpretation we shall suddenly see the point of Wittgenstein's dictum (*Philosophical Investigations*, §242) 'If language is to be a means of communication there must be agreement not only in definitions but, queer as this may sound, agreement in judgments also.'[33]

10. The difficulty the non-cognitivist is having in pressing his claim at this point is scarcely a straightforward vindication of cognitivism. If the case for the coincidence of truth and assertibility in evaluative judgments is made in the terms of §9, then truth itself is in danger of coming in the process to seem a fairly parochial thing. It is strange to be driven to the conclusion that the more idiosyncratic the customs of a people, the more inscrutable their form of life, and the more special and difficult their language to interpret, the smaller the problem of the truth status of their evaluations.

It would be natural for someone perplexed by the question of the meaning of life to insist at this point that we shall not have found what it takes for individual lives to have the meaning we attribute to them unless we link meaning with rationality. He will say that the threat of relativism does not depend on Williams's condition (3) in Section VIII being satisfied. The threat is rather that, contrary to the tenor of §5, the reasons that impress us as good reasons have no foundation in reason at all. Or as Hume states the point in a famous passage of the First Appendix to the *Inquiry concerning the Principles of Morals*:

> It appears evident that the ultimate ends of human actions can never, in any case, be accounted for by *reason*, but recommend themselves entirely to the sentiments and affections of mankind, without any dependence on the intellectual faculties. Ask a man

---

[32] There are valuations which are so specific, and so special in their point, that interpretation requires interpreter and subject to have in some area of concern the very same interests and the same precise focus. But specificity is only one part of the problem.

[33] *Cf.* §241 and the rest of §242. *Cf.* also p. 223 (*passim*): 'If a lion could talk, we couldn't understand him.'

*why he uses exercise*; he will answer, *because he desires to keep his health.* If you then enquire, *why he desires health,* he will readily reply, *because sickness is painful.* If you push your enquiries farther, and desire a reason *why he hates pain,* it is impossible he can ever give any. This is an ultimate end, and is never referred to any other object.

Perhaps to your second question, *why he desires health,* he may also reply, that *it is necessary for the exercise of his calling.* If you ask, *why he is anxious on that head,* he will answer, *because he desires to get money.* If you demand *Why? It is the instrument of pleasure,* says he. And beyond this it is an absurdity to ask for a reason. It is impossible there can be a progress *in infinitum*; and that one thing can always be a reason why another is desired. Something must be desirable on its own account, and because of its immediate accord or agreement with human sentiment and affection.

Not only is it pointless to hope to discover a *rational* foundation in human sentiment and affection. It is not even as if human sentiment and affection will *effectively* determine the difference between the worth while and the not worth while. Each culture, and each generation in each culture, confronts the world in a different way and reacts to it in a different way.

This scepticism pointedly ignores all the claims I made earlier, in §5. Rallying to their support, I ask: What does this scepticism show about our own judgments of significance or importance? After all there is no such thing as a rational creature of no particular neuro-physiological formation or a rational man of no particular historical formation. And even if, inconceivably, there were such, why should we care about what this creature would find compelling? It is not in this make-believe context that we are called upon to mount a critique of our own conceptions of the objective, the true, and the worth while.

So much seems to hang on this, but the reply comes so close to simply repeating the words of the relativist whom it is meant to challenge, that there is no alternative but to illustrate what happens when we do try to think of rationality in the absolute impersonal or cosmic fashion that it seems our interlocutor requires.

It is interesting that, so far as rationality in theoretical beliefs is concerned, it is by no means impossible for us to conceive of thinking in the impersonal way. Suppose we take a Peircean view of Science as discovering that which is destined, the world being what it is, to be ultimately agreed by all who investigate.[34] Let 'all' mean 'all actual or possible intelligent beings competent, whatever their conceptual scheme, to look for the fundamental explanatory principles of the world'. Then think of all these theories gradually converging through isomorphism towards identity. Cosmic rationality in belief will then consist in conforming one's beliefs so far as possible to the truths that are destined to survive in this process of convergence.[35]

Perhaps this is all make-believe. (Actually I think it isn't.) But the important thing is that, if we identify properties across all theories that converge upon what are destined to be agreed upon (by us or any other determined natural researchers) as the fundamental principles of nature, then the only non-logical, non-mathematical predicates we shall not discard from the language of rational belief are those which, in one guise or another, will always pull their weight in all explanatorily adequate theories of the world. As a result, and corresponding to predicates fit and not fit so to survive, we shall have a wonderful contrast between the primary qualities of nature and all other qualities. We can then make for ourselves a fact-value distinction that has a real and definite point. We can say that no value predicate stands for any real primary quality, and that the real properties of the world, the properties which

---

[34] *Cf.* C.S. Peirce: 'How to Make Our Ideas Clear', *Popular Science Monthly* vol. 12, 1878, pp. 286–302.

> Different minds may set out with the most antagonistic views, but the progress of investigations carries them by a force outside themselves to one and the same conclusion. This activity of thought by which we are carried, not where we wish but to a foreordained goal, is like the operation of destiny. No modification of the point of view taken, no selection of other facts for study, no natural bent of mind even, can enable a man to escape the predestinate opinion. This great law is embodied in the conception of truth and reality. The opinion which is fated to be ultimately agreed to by all who investigate is what we mean by the truth, and the object represented in this opinion is the real. That is the way I would explain reality.

[35] Inasmuch as there is a reality which dictates the way a scientific theory has to be in order that what happens in the world be explained by the theory, the difficulties of radical interpretation, attempted against the background of the truth about the world and the unwaveringly constant desire of speakers of the language to understand the material world, are at their slightest. Or so the upholder of a modest realism might maintain.

inhere in the world *however it is viewed*, are the primary qualities.[36]

This is a very stark view. It expresses what was an important element of truth in the 'external' perspective. Seeing the world in this way, one sees no meaning in anything.[37] But it is evidently absurd to try to reduce the sharpness of the viewpoint by saying that meaning can be introduced into the world thus seen by the addition of human commitment. Commitment to what? This Peircean conceptual scheme *articulates* nothing that it is humanly possible to care about. It does not even have the expressive resources to pick out the extensions of predicates like 'red', 'chair', 'person', 'famine'. . . . For none of these has a strong claim to be factual by the scientific criterion. The distinction of fact and value we reach here, at the very limit of our understanding of scientific understanding, cannot be congruent with what the non-cognitivists intended as their distinction. It is as dubious as ever that there is anything for them to have intended. Starting out with the idea that value properties are mental projections, they have discovered that, if value properties are mental projections, then, except for the primary qualities, all properties are mental projections.

We come now to practical rationality for all conceivable rational agents. (Cosmically valid practical rationality.) The idea here would be, I suppose, that to be serious about objective reasons, or why anything matters, one must try to

---

[36] One should talk here also of the fundamental physical constants. *Cf.* B.A.W. Russell, *Human Knowledge* (London, 1948), p. 41:

> These constants appear in the fundamental equations of physics . . . it should be observed that we are much more certain of the importance of these constants than we are of this or that interpretation of them. Planck's constant, in its brief history since 1900, has been represented in various ways, but its numerical value has not been affected . . . Electrons may disappear completely from modern physics but *e* [charge] and *m* [mass] are pretty certain to survive. In a sense it may be said that the discovery and measurement of these constants is what is most solid in modern physics.

[37] *Cf.* Tolstoy, *Anna Karenina*, Penguin, p. 820: '[Levin was] stricken with horror, not so much at death, as at life, without the least conception of its origin, its purpose, its reason, its nature. The organism, its decay, the indestructibility of matter, the law of the conservation of energy, evolution, were the terms that had superseded those of his early faith.' This is a description of what might pass as one stage in the transition we have envisaged as completed.

ascend closer to the viewpoint of an impersonal intelligence;[38] and that the properties of such an intelligence should be determinable *a priori*. A great deal of time and effort has been channelled into this effort. It might have been expected that the outcome would be the transformation of the bareness of our conception of an impersonal intelligence into the conception of an impersonal intelligence of great bareness. What was not so plainly to be expected was that the most elementary part of the subject should immediately collide—as it has—with a simple and (within the discipline thus *a priori* conceived) unanswerable paradox—the so-called 'Prisoner's Dilemma'.[39] What underlies the paradox (or the idea that there *is* here some paradox) is the supposition that it is simply obvious that an *a priori* theory of rational action ought to be possible—that some cosmic peg must exist on which we can fasten a set of concerns clearly and unproblematically identified *independently* of all ideals of agency and rationality themselves. First you have a set of projects; then you think of a way that they might be best brought about. That was the picture. But, in a new guise, it was nothing other than the absurd idea that all deliberation is really of means.[40]

11.    I conclude that there is no such thing as a pure *a priori* theory of rationality conceived in isolation from what it is for us as we are to have a reason: and that even if there were such a

---

[38] Compare Thomas Nagel 'The Absurd', note 8, *op. cit.*, pp. 720 and 722, 'the philosophical judgment [of absurdity] contrasts the pretensions of life with a larger context in which *no* standards can be discovered, rather than with a context from which alternative overriding standards may be applied'.

[39] I take this as a 'paradox' in the following sense: a general principle of decision-theoretic prudence, generalizable to any agent whatever caught in the relevant circumstances, will lead in a wide variety of applications to what must be agreed by everybody to be a situation which is worse than it might have been for each participant if he had not acted on the generalizable principle.

To say this is not to 'solve' the paradox. It cannot be solved. But it could only be accounted a real paradox if there were some antecedent grounds to suppose that it *should* have been possible to construct an *a priori* theory of rationality or prudence such that 'rational (A)' is incompatible with 'rational (not-A)', and such that that rationality is definable both independently of morality and ideals of agency and in such a way as to have independent leverage in these ancient disputes. (*Cf.* Plato, *Republic*, 445a.)

For an illuminating account of some of the asymmetries it is rational to expect between an *a priori* theory of belief and an *a priori* theory of practical reasonableness, see Ronald de Sousa, 'The Good and the True', *Mind* vol. 83, 1974.

[40] That practically all interesting deliberation relates to ends and their practical specification in the light of actually or potentially available constituents, and that the place of means-ends reasoning is subordinate in practical reason, is argued by A.T.

thing, it would always have been irrelevant to finding a meaning in life, or seeing anything as worth while. What we need is to define non-cognitivist relativism in a way that is innocent of all dependence on a contrast between our rationality and some purer rationality, yet restates the point we found in Taylor.

It now says: Perhaps all strict valuations of the more specific and interesting kind have the interesting property that the interpretation of the value predicate itself presupposes a shared viewpoint, and a set of concerns common between interpreter and subject. Let it be admitted that the exclusive fact-value distinction then fails. If a cognitivist insists, nothing need prevent him from exploiting the collapse of that distinction in order to redescribe in terms of a shift or wandering of the 'value-focus' all the profound changes in valuation that have occurred in history, when the Greek world became the Christian world, or the Christian world the Renaissance world. The relativist will not forbid the cognitivist to say with Nicolai Hartmann, as John Findlay reports him, that these changes were all by-products of an intense consciousness of new values, whose swimming into focus pushed out the old: that such newly apprehended values were not really new, only hitherto ignored.[41]

All this the non-cognitivist may let pass as harmless, however eccentrically expressed; and may in less colourful language himself assert. He may even allow *totidem verbis* that, just as the world cannot be prised by us away from our manner of conceiving it, so our manner of conceiving it cannot be

---

Kolnai, 'Deliberation is of Ends', *Proceedings of the Aristotelian Society* (1962), and in Essay VI, a divergent interpretation of Aristotle's thought on this point, but an account similar to Kolnai's of the problem itself.

[41] See J.N. Findlay, *Axiological Ethics* (London: Macmillan, 1970). *Cf.* William James, *Talks to Teachers on Psychology: and to Students on some of Life's Ideals* (Longman, Green & Co., 1899), p. 299.

> In this solid and tridimensional sense, so to call it, those philosophers are right who contend that the world is a standing thing with no progress, no real history. The changing conditions of history touch only the surface of the show. The altered equilibriums and redistributions only diversify our opportunities and open chances to us for new ideals. But, with each new ideal that comes into life, the chance for a life based on some old ideal will vanish; and he would needs be a presumptuous calculator who should with confidence say that the total sum of significance is positively and absolutely greater at any one epoch than at any other of the world.

prised apart from our concerns themselves.[42] Again, it is open to him to assert the compatibility of anthropocentricity with the only thing that there is for us to mean by objectivity, and to concede that the differences between higher and lower forms of life are not fictitious. They are even objective, he will say, if you use the word 'objective' like that. But here he will stick. Where he will not back down from Taylor's original position is in respect of Taylor's denial that these differences are *decisive*. Such differences may be important to us. But they depend for their significance upon a framework that is a free construct, not upon something fashioned in a manner that is answerable to how anything really is.

Here at last we approach the distinctive nucleus of non-cognitivism (married, without the consent of either, to Williams's relativism). What the new position will say is that, in so far as anything matters, and in so far as human life has the meaning we think it has, that possibility is rooted in something that is arbitrary, contingent, unreasoned, objectively non-defensible—and not one whit the less arbitrary, contingent and indefensible by virtue of the fact that the unconstrained inventive processes underlying it have been gradual, unconscious, and communal. Our form of life—or that in our form of life which gives individual lives a meaning—is not something that we as a species ever (as we say) found or discovered. It is not something that we can criticize or regulate or adjust with an eye to what is true or correct or reasonable. Even within the going enterprise of existing concerns and deliberations, it would be a sad illusion to suppose that the judgment that this or that is worthwhile, or that life is worth living (or worth leaving), would be simply and plainly true. That sort of *terra firma* is simply not to be had.

The doctrine thus reconstructed from the assets of bankrupted or naïve non-cognitivism I shall call the doctrine of cognitive underdetermination. Unlike the positions it descends from, this position does not contradict itself. It is consistent with its own rationale. It can be explained without entering at all into the difficulties and ineffabilities of cultural relativism. It can

---

[42] *Cf.* A.J. Ayer, *The Central Questions of Philosophy* (London: Macmillan, 1974), p. 235: 'we have seen that the world cannot be prised away from our manner of conceiving it'.

even be stated in a manner innocent of the commoner confusions between the idea that morality and culture are constructs and a more questionable idea, that the references (content/truth-value) of the judgements that these things make possible are constructs. (A sort of sense reference confusion.)

Suppose someone says: 'For me it is neither here nor there that I cannot prise my way of seeing the world apart from my concerns. This does nothing to answer my complaint that there is not *enough* meaning in the world. My life doesn't add up. Nothing matters sufficiently to me. My concerns themselves are too unimportant, too scattered, and too disparate.' Equally devastatingly to the naïve cognitivism that the doctrine of cognitive underdetermination bids us abandon, another one may say he finds that the objects of his concern beckon to him too insistently, too cruelly beguilingly, from too many different directions. 'I have learned that I cannot strive after all of these objects, or minister even to most of the concerns that stand behind them. To follow more than a minute subset is to be doomed to be frustrated in all. The mere validity—if it were valid—of the total set from which I am to choose one subset would provide no guarantee at all that any subset I can actually have will *add up* to anything that means anything to me.'

It is the undetermination theorist's role to comment here that things can never add up for the complainant who finds too frustratingly much, or for the complainant who finds too inanely little, unless each of us supplies something extra, some conception of his own, to make sense of things for *himself*.

The problem of living a life, he may say, is to realize or respect a long and incomplete or open-ended list of concerns which are always at the limit conflicting. The claims of all true beliefs (about how the world is) are reconcilable. Everything true must be consistent with everything else that is true (*cf.* truism (5) of §8). But not all the claims of all rational concerns or even of all moral concerns (that the world *be* thus or so) need be actually reconcilable. When we judge that this is what we must do now,[43] or that that is what we'd better do, or that our life must now take one direction rather than another direction,

---

[43] I have put '*must*', because *must* and *must not*, unlike *ought* and *ought not*, are genuine contraries.

we are not fitting truths (or even probabilities) into a pattern where a discrepancy proves that we have mistaken a falsehood for a truth.[44] Often we have to make a practical choice that another rational agent might understand through and through, not fault or even disagree with, but (as Winch has stressed)[45] make differently himself; whereas, if there is disagreement over what is factually true and two rational men have come to different conclusions, then we think it has to be theoretically possible to uncover some discrepancy in their respective views of the evidence. In matters of fact, we suppose that, if two opposing answers to a yes/no question are equally good, then they might as well have been equally bad. But in matters of practice, we are grateful for the existence of alternative answers. The choice between them is then up to us. Here is our freedom. But here too is the bareness of the world we inhabit. If there were practical truth it would have to violate the third and fifth truisms of truth ((3) and (5) of §8 above). In living a life there is no truth, and there is nothing *like* plain truth, for us to aim at. Anybody who supposes that the assertibility of 'I must do this' or the assertibility of 'This is the way for me to live, not that' consists in their plain truth is simply deluded.

Aristotle wrote (*NE* 1094a23): 'Will not knowledge of the good have a great influence on life? Shall we not, like archers who have a mark to aim at, be more likely to hit upon the right thing?' But in reality there is no such thing as *The Good*, no such thing as knowledge of it, and nothing fixed independently of ourselves to aim at. Or that is what is implied by the thesis of cognitive underdetermination.

12. If there is any common ground to be discovered in

---

[44] See B.A.O. Williams, 'Consistency and Realism', *Proceedings of the Aristotelian Society Supplementary Volume*, 1966 and *cf.* J.N. Findlay, *op. cit.*, pp. 74–5:

> What is good [Hartmann tells us] necessarily lies in a large number of incompatible directions, and it is intrinsically impossible that all of these should be followed out into realisation. One cannot, for example, achieve pure simplicity and variegated richness in the same thing or occasion, and yet both incontestably make claims upon us . . . in practice we sacrifice one good to another, or we make compromises and accommodations . . . such practical accommodations necessarily override the claims of certain values and everywhere consummate something that in some respect [ideally] ought not to be . . . a man [ideally should] be as wise as a serpent and gentle as a dove, but that does not mean that . . . it is *possible* for him to be both of them.

[45] Peter Winch, 'The Universalizability of Moral Judgements', *Monist* vol. 49, 1965.

modern literature and one broad stream of modern philosophy it is here. What philosophers, even philosophers of objectivist formation, have constantly stressed is the absence of the unique solutions and unique determinations of the practical that naïve cognitivism would have predicted.[46] They have thus supplied the theoretical basis for what modern writers (not excluding modern writers who have believed in God) have felt rather as a void in our experience of the apprehension of value, and have expressed not so much in terms of the plurality and mutual irreducibility of goods as in terms of the need for an organizing focus or meaning or purpose that we ourselves *bring* to life. The mind is not only a receptor: it is a projector.[47]

At the end of *Anna Karenina* Levin says to himself: 'I shall still lose my temper with Ivan the coachman, I shall still embark on useless discussions and . . . express my opinions inopportunely; there will still be the same wall between the sanctuary of my inmost soul and other people, even my wife . . . but my life now, my whole life, independently of anything that can happen to me, every minute of it is no longer meaningless as it was before, but has a positive meaning of goodness with which I have the power to invest it.'

However remote such declarations may appear from the language of the non-cognitivist philosopher, this need for autonomous making or investing of which Levin speaks is one part of what, in my presentation of him, the non-cognitive philosopher means by cognitive underdetermination. The familiar idea is that we do not discover a meaning for life or strictly find one: we have to make do with an artifact or

---

[46] The plurality and mutual irreducibility of things good has been stressed by F. Brentano (*Origins of Our Knowledge of Right and Wrong*, see especially para. 32); by N. Hartmann (see J. Findlay, *op. cit.*); by Isaiah Berlin, see, for instance, *Four Essays on Liberty* (Oxford University Press, 1969), Introduction p. xlix; by A.T. Kolnai and B.A.O. Williams (*op. cit.*). See also Leszek Kolakowski, 'In Praise of Inconsistency' in *Marxism and Beyond* (London, 1969); Stuart Hampshire, *Morality and Pessimism* (Cambridge University Press, 1972); and Essay VII below.

[47] For the seed of this idea in Plotinus' theory of cognition and for its transplantation and subsequent growth, see M.H. Abrams, *The Mirror and the Lamp* (Oxford University Press, 1953), Plotinus, *Ennead*, IV. 6.2–3: 'The mind affirms something not contained within impression: this is the characteristic of a power—within its allotted sphere to act.' 'The mind gives radiance to the objects of sense out of its own store.'

construct or projection—something as it were invented.[48] And, whereas discovery is answerable to truth, invention and construction are not. From this he concludes that a limited and low-grade objectivity is the very best one could hope for in predications of meaning or significance.

The non-cognitivist takes two steps here and the assessment of the second step concerning objectivity depends markedly on the notion of truth that is employed at the first. What is this notion, we need to know, and to what extent does the cognitivist's position depend upon a naïve and precritical understanding of it? Give or take a little—subtract perhaps the more indeterminate among subjunctive conditionals—the precritical notion of truth covers empirical judgments fairly well. But it consorts less well with conceptions of truth or assertibility defended in mathematics by mathematical intuitionists or mathematical constructivists. It is well worth remarking that, for someone who wanted to combine objectivity with a doctrine of qualified cognitivism or of underdetermination, there might be no better model than Wittgenstein's normative conception of the objectivity of mathematics; and no better exemplar than Wittgenstein's extended description of how a continuing cumulative process of making or constructing can amount to the creation of a shared form of life that is constitutive of rationality itself, furnishing proofs that are not compulsions but procedures to guide our conceptions, explaining, without explaining away, our sense that sometimes we have no alternative but to infer this from that.[49]

---

[48] For a remarkable expression of the non-cognitivist's principal point and some others, see Aldous Huxley, *Do As You Will* (London, 1929), p. 101:

> The purpose of life, outside the mere continuance of living (already a most noble and beautiful end), is the purpose we put into it. Its meaning is whatever we may choose to call the meaning. Life is not a crossword puzzle, with an answer settled in advance and a prize for the ingenious person who noses it out. The riddle of the universe has as many answers as the universe has living inhabitants. Each answer is a working hypothesis, in terms of which the answerer experiments with reality. The best answers are those which permit the answerer to live most fully, the worst are those which condemn him to partial or complete death . . . Every man has an inalienable right to the major premiss of his philosophy of life.

If anything need be added to this, presumably it is only that, concerning what 'living most fully' is for each man, the final authority must be the man himself. There is something right with this; but there is something wrong with it too.

[49] *Cf.* L. Wittgenstein, *Remarks on the Foundation of Mathematics* (Oxford: Blackwell, 1956), III–30.

Perhaps this is a million miles from ethics. Or perhaps Wittgenstein's philosophy of mathematics is completely unsuccessful. But if the subject-matter of moral philosophy had any of the features that Wittgenstein attributed to the sort of subject-matter he thought he was treating, then the issue whether the assertibility of practical judgments was truth, and did or did not sufficiently approximate to the truth of statements universally agreed to be factual, might become relatively unimportant.[50] We could measure the distance, assess its importance, and think how to live with it. (Is there an independent case for tampering in certain ways with the received truisms of truth? Or should we leave them to define an ideal that practical judgment must fall far short of? How important really is the shortfall?)

Of course, if practical judgments were candidates to be accounted simply true, then what made them true, unlike valuations,[51] could not be the world itself, whatever that is.[52] But, saying what they say, the world is not really what they purport to characterize. (Compare what Wittgenstein, whether rightly or wrongly, wanted to say about statements of

---

[50] There is a cheap victory to be won even here of course. For it has proved much easier to achieve convergence or reflective equilibrium within our culture about the value of, say, civil liberty than about how exactly printing extra bank-notes will act upon conditions of economic recession. But this is not the point I am making.

[51] Note that the distinction proposed at §4 between evaluation and practical judgment is observed both here and throughout this essay.

[52] Everything would be the wrong way round. *Cf.* B.A.O. Williams, 'Consistency and Realism' (*op. cit.*, n. 44), p. 19:

> the line on one side of which consistency plays its peculiarly significant role is the line between the theoretical and the practical, the line between discourse which (to use a now familiar formula) has to fit the world, and discourse which the world must fit. With discourse that is practical in these terms, we can see why . . . consistency . . . should admit of exception and should be connected with coherence notions of a less logical character.

This whole passage suggests something important, not only about statements of what ideally should be, but also about deliberative judgments,—namely that the exigencies of having to decide what to believe are markedly dissimilar from the exigencies of having to decide how to act. What the argument does *not* show is that the only truth there could be in a practical judgment is a peculiar truth which transposes the onus of match on to the world. (Still less that, if one rejects that idea, then the onus of match would be from the sentence or its annexed action to an *ideal* world.) Williams has illuminatingly glossed (1) precisely why truth in a practical judgement would not be like that; (2) the reasons why 'Ought (A)' and 'Ought (not-A)' are actually consistent; and (3) why 'must (A)' (which *is* inconsistent with 'must (not-A)') is only strictly assertible or true if A is the unique thing you must here do.

arithmetic.) In the assertibility (or truth) of mathematical statements we see what perhaps we can never see in the assertibility of empirical (such as geographical or historical) statements: the compossibility of objectivity, discovery, *and* invention. (See further p. 350 below.)

If we combine Wittgenstein's conception of mathematics with the constructivist or intuitionist views that are its cousins, then we find an illuminating similarity. One cannot get more out of the enterprise of making than one has in one way or another put there. ('What if someone were to reply to a question: "So far there is no such thing as an answer to this question"?' *Remarks on the Foundations of Mathematics, IV. 9.*) And at any given moment one will have put less than everything into it. So however many determinations have been made, we never have a reason to think we have reached a point where no more decisions or determinations will be needed. No general or unrestricted affirmation is possible of the law of excluded middle. But then anyone who wishes to defend the truth status for practical judgments is released from claiming that every practical question already has an answer. For reasons both independent of the practical and helpful to its pretensions, we may doubt how mandatory it ever was to enter into the system of ideas and preconceptions that issues in such declarations as truism (6*) of §8 above.

I shall break off from these large questions with two points of comparison and contrast.

(i) It seems that in the sphere of the practical we may know for certain that there exist absolutely undecidable questions—*e.g.*, cases where the situation is so calamitous or the choices so insupportable that nothing could count as *the* morally reasonable answer. In mathematics, on the other hand, it appears to be an undecidable question even how much sense attaches to the idea of an absolutely undecidable question. This is a potentially important discrepancy between the two subject matters. If we insist upon the actuality of some absolute undecidability in the practical sphere, then we shall burst the bounds of ordinary, plain truth. To *negate* the law of excluded middle is to import a contradiction into the intuitionist logic which our comparison makes the natural choice for practical judgments. The *denial* of '((A would be right) or not (A would be right))' contradicts the intuitionist theorem '(not (not (p or not p))).

(ii) If a man makes an arithmetical mistake he may collide with a brick wall or miss a train. He may bankrupt himself. For each calculation there is some risk, and for each risk a clear mark of the worst's having befallen us. There is nothing so definite with practical judgments. But surely it is begging the question to require it. Equally, it is begging the question to shrug this off without another word.

13. Let us review what has been found, before trying to advance further.

However rarely or often practical judgments attain truth, and whatever is the extent and importance of cognitive underdetermination, we have found no overwhelming reason to deny all objectivity to practical judgments. That practical questions might have more than one answer, and that there is not always an ordering of better or worse answers, is no reason to conclude that good and bad answers cannot be argumentatively distinguished.

It is either false or senseless to deny that what valuational predicates stand for are properties in a world. It is neither here nor there that these value properties are not primary qualities, provided that they be objectively discriminable and can impinge upon practical appreciation and judgment. No extant argument shows that they cannot.

Individual human lives can have more or less point in a manner partially dependent upon the disposition in the world of these value properties. The naïve non-cognitivist has sometimes given the impression that the way we give point to our lives is as if by blindfolding ourselves and attaching to something—anything—some free-floating commitment, a commitment that is itself sustained by the mere fact of our animal life. But that was a mistake. There is no question here of blindfolding. And that is not what is said or implied by the reconstructed doctrine of cognitive underdetermination.

In as much as invention and discovery are distinguishable, and in so far as either of these ideas properly belongs here, life's having a point may depend as much upon something contributed by the person whose life it is as it depends upon something discovered. Or it may depend upon what the owner of the life brings to the world in order to see the world in such a way as to discover meaning. This cannot happen unless world and person are to some great extent reciprocally suited. And unluckily, all claims of human adaptability notwithstanding, those things are often not well suited to one another.

14.   To get beyond here, something now needs to be said about the connection of meaning and happiness. In most moral philosophy, the requirement to treat meaning is commuted into the requirement to specify the end; and the end is usually identified with happiness. One thing that has seemed to make this identification plausible is the apparent correctness of the claim that happiness is the state of one's life having a point or meaning. But on any natural account of the relation of point and end, this claim is actually inconsistent with the equation 'Happiness = The End'. (Unless happiness can consist in simply having happiness as one's end.) It is also worth observing that, in the very special cases where it is straightforward to say what the point of someone's life is, we may say what he stands for, or may describe his life's work. (I choose these cases not because I think they are specially central but because they are specially clear.) The remarkable thing is that these specifications are not even categorially of a piece with happiness. That does not prove that happiness is *never* the point. The works of practical moralists are replete, however, with warnings of the difficulty or futility of making happiness the aim. If they are right then, by the same token, it would be futile to make it the point.

The misidentification—if misidentification it is—of happiness and end has had a long history. The first fully systematic equation of the end, the good for man, and happiness is Aristotle's. The lamentable and occasionally comical effects of this are much palliated by the close observation and good sense that Aristotle carried to the *specification* of happiness. And it may be said in Aristotle's defence that the charge of misidentification of happiness and the good for man is captious, because his detailed specification of *eudaimonia* can perfectly well stand in—if this be what is required—as a description of the point of human existence: also that Aristotle meant by *eudaimonia* not exactly happiness but a certain kind of success. But that is too quick. Unless we want to walk the primrose path to the trite and solemn conclusion that a meaningful life is just a sum (*cf. Nicomachean Ethics*, 1097b17) of activities worth while in themselves, or self-complete (in the sense of *Metaphysics*, 1048b17), the question is worth taking some trouble over. Not only is this proposition trite and solemn. Read in the way Aristotle intended it is absurd.

Out of good nature a man helps his neighbour dig a drainage ditch. The soil is hard but not impossibly intractable, and together the two of them succeed in digging the ditch. The man who offers to help sees what he is doing in helping dig the ditch as worth while. In so far as meaning is an issue for him, he may see the episode as all of a piece with a life that has meaning. He would not see it so, and he would not have taken on the task, if it were impossible. In the case as we imagine it, the progress of the project is integral to his pleasure in it. But so equally is the fact that he likes his neighbour and enjoys working with him (provided it be on projects that it is within their joint powers to complete).

Shall we say here that the man's helping dig the ditch is instrumental and has the meaning or importance it has for the helper only derivatively? Derivatively from what, on the non-cognitivist view? Or shall we say that the ditch-digging is worth while in itself? But it isn't. It is end-directed. If we cannot say either of these things, can we cut the Gordian knot by saying both? In truth, the embracing of the end depends on the man's feeling for the task of helping someone he likes. But his feeling for the project of helping equally depends on the existence and attainability of the end of digging the ditch.

This is not to deny that Aristotle's doctrine can be restored to plausibility if we allow the meaning of the particular life that accommodates the activity to *confer* intrinsic worth upon the activity. But this is to reverse Aristotle's procedure (which is the only procedure available to a pure cognitivist). And I doubt we have to choose (*cf.* §6). At its modest and most plausible best the doctrine of cognitive underdetermination can say that we need to be able to think in both directions, down from point to the human activities that answer to it, and up from activities whose intrinsic worth can be demonstrated by Aristotle's consensual method to forms of life in which we are capable by nature of finding point.[53]

15. It might be interesting and fruitful to pick over the wreckage of defunct and discredited ethical theories and see what their negligence of the problem of life's having a meaning contributed to their ruin. I have little to report under this head. But it does seem plain that the failure of naturalistic theories, theories reductively identifying the Good or the End with some natural reality, has been bound up with the question of meaning. Surely the failure of all the reductive naturalisms of the nineteenth century—Pleasure and Pain Utilitarianism, Marxism, Evolutionary Ethics—was precisely the failure to discover in brute nature itself (either in the totality of future pleasures or in the supposedly inevitable advance of various social or biological cum evolutionary processes), anything that the generality of untheoretical men could find reason to invest with overwhelming *importance*. These theories offered nothing that could engage in the right way with human concerns or give point or focus to anyone's life. (This is the cognitivist version of a point that ought to be attributed to David Hume.)

Naturalistic theories have been replaced in our own time by

[53] Surely neither the consensual method nor the argued discussion of such forms would be possible in the absence of the shared neurophysiology that makes possible such community of concepts and such agreement as exists in evaluative and deliberative judgments. Nor would there be such faint prospects as there are of attaining reflective equilibrium or finding a shared mode of criticism. But nature plays only a causal and enabling role here, not the unconvincing speaking part assigned to it by Ethical Naturalism and by Aristotelian Eudaemonism. Aristotle qualified by the addition 'in a complete life' (1098a16) the equation *eudaimonia = activity of soul in accordance with virtue*. And, tempering somewhat the *sum of goods* conception, he could agree with my strictures on the idea that the philosopher describes a meaning for life by building upwards from the special condition of its meaninglessness. But, as J.L. Austin used to complain, 'If *life* comes in at all, it should not come into Aristotle's argument as an afterthought'. And no help is to be had here from Aristotle's idea that, just as an eye has a function f such that the eye's goodness in respect of f=the good *for* the eye, so a man has his function. Eye:body::man:what? *Cf.* 1194b12. What is it for a man to find some function f that he can *embrace as his*, as giving his life meaning? Nature does not declare.

Prescriptivism, Emotivism, Existentialism, and Neutral (satis-faction-based) Utilitarianism. It is misleading to speak of them together. The second and third have had important affinities with moral Pyrrhonism. The first and fourth are very careful and, in the promotion of formal or second-order goods such as equality, tolerance, or consistency, rather earnest. But it is also misleading not to see these positions together.

Suppose that, when pleasure and absence of pain give place in an ethical theory to unspecified merely determinable satisfaction (and when the last drop of mentality is squeezed from the revealed preference theory which is the economic parallel of philosophical Utilitarianism), someone looks to modern Utilitarianism for meaning or happiness. The theory points him towards the greatest satisfaction of human beings' desires. He might embrace that end, if he could understand what that satisfaction consisted in. He might if he could see from his own case what satisfaction consisted in. But that is very likely where he started—unless, more wisely, he started closer to the real issue and was asking himself where he should look to find a point for his life. But, so far as either question is concerned, the theory has crossed out the infantile proposal 'pleasure and lack of pain',[54] and distorted and degraded (in description if not in fact) the complexity of the structure within which someone might improve upon that childish answer for himself. For all questions of ends, all problems about what constitutes the attainment of given human ends, and all perplexities of meaning, have been studiously but fallaciously transposed by this theory into questions of instrumental means. But means to what? The theory is appreciably further than the nineteenth-century theory was from a conceptual appreciation of the structure of values and focused unfrustrated concerns presupposed to a man's finding a point in his life; and of the need to locate correctly happiness, pleasure, and a man's conception of his own unfolding life within that structure.

If we look to existentialism, we find something curiously similar. Going back to the formation of some of these ideas, I found André Maurois's description in *Call No Man Happy*

<hr>

[54] For the thought that this might be literally infantile, I am indebted indirectly to Bradley and directly to Richard Wollheim, 'The Good Self and the Bad Self', *Proceedings of the British Academy*, 1975.

(trans. Lindley: Cape; London, 1943, p. 43) of his teacher Alain (Emile-Auguste Chartier):

> what I cannot convey by words is the enthusiasm inspired in us by this search, boldly pursued with such a guide; the excitement of those classes which are entered with the persistent hope of discovering, that very morning, the secret of life, and from which one departed with the joy of having understood that perhaps there was no such secret but that nevertheless it was possible to be a human being and to be so with dignity and nobility. When I read in *Kim* the story of the Lama who sought so piously for the River of the Arrow, I thought of *our* search.

What goes wrong here—and remember that Alain was teacher not only of Maurois but also of Sartre—goes wrong even in the question 'What is *the* meaning of life?' We bewitch ourselves to think that we are looking for some one thing like the Garden of the Hesperides, the Holy Grail . . . Then finding nothing like that in the world, no one thing from which all values can be derived and no one focus by which all other concerns can be organized, we console ourselves by looking inwards, but again for some one substitute thing, one thing in us now instead of the world. Of course if the search is conducted in this way it is more or less inevitable that the one consolation will be *dignity* or *nobility* or *commitment*: or more spectatorially *irony, resignation, scorn* . . . But, warm though its proper place is for each of these—important though each of them is in its own non-substitutive capacity—it would be better to go back to the 'the' in the original question; and to interest ourselves afresh in what everybody knows about—the set of concerns he actually has, their objects, and the focus he has formed or seeks to bring to bear upon these: also the prospects of purifying, redeploying or extending this set.[55]

Having brought the matter back to this place, how can a theorist go on? I think he must continue from the point where I

---

[55] *Cf.* Williams, 'Persons, Character and Morality' (pp. 208ff.), in Amelie Rorty (ed.), *The Identities of Persons* (University of California Press, 1976):

> The categorical desires which propel one forward do not have to be even very evident to consciousness, let alone grand or large; one good testimony to one's existence having a point is that the question of its point does not arise, and the propelling concerns may be of a relatively everyday kind such as certainly provide the ground of many sorts of happiness (*cf.* p. 209).

myself ought to have begun if the products of philosophy itself had not obstructed the line of sight: labouring within an intuitionism or moral phenomenology as tolerant of low-grade non-behavioural evidence as is literature (but more obsessively elaborative of the commonplace, and more theoretical, in the interpretive sense, than literature), he has to appreciate and describe the working day complexity of what is experientially involved in seeing a point in living. It is no use to take a going moral theory—Utilitarianism or whatever it is—and paste on to it such *postscripta* as the Millian insight 'It really is of importance not only what men do, but what manner of men they are that do it': or the insight that to see a point in living a man has to be such that he can like himself: or to try to superimpose upon the theory the structure that we have complained that Utilitarianism degrades. If life's having a point is at all central to moral theory then room must be made for these things right from the very beginning. The phenomenological account I advocate would accommodate all these things in conjunction with (1) ordinary anthropocentric objectivity, (2) the elements of value-focus and discovery, and (3) the element of invention that it is the non-cognitivist's distinction to have imported into the argument. (Nb. now pp. 350, 205 inf.)

Let us not underestimate what would have been done if this work were realized. But ought the theorist to be able to do more? Reluctant thought I am to draw any limits to the potentiality or enterprise of discursive reason, I see no reason why he should. Having tamed non-cognitivism and made of it a doctrine of cognitive underdetermination, which allows the world to impinge upon but not to determine the point possessed by individual lives, and which sees value properties not as created but as *lit up* by the focus that the one who lives the life brings to the world; and, having described what finding meaning is, and described it in a manner which respects the possibility of someone's discovering the inner *necessity* to do this or that, it will not be for the theorist as such to insist on intruding himself further. As Bradley says in *Appearance and Reality* (450):

> If to show theoretical interest in morality and religion is taken as setting oneself up as a teacher or preacher, I would rather leave these subjects to whoever feels such a character suits him.

# IV

# Truth, and Truth as Predicated of Moral Judgments*

> A proposition *shows* how things stand *if* it is
> true. And it says that they do so stand.
> WITTGENSTEIN

> We despise obvious things, but from obvious
> things unobvious ones follow.
> LEIBNIZ

1. Do moral judgments admit of plain truth? And how is the answer to this question to be decided in a way that does not leave the feeling that, if we had gone about answering it in some other way, then the answer might have been exactly the opposite one? In his article 'Truth' (*Proceedings of the Aristotelian Society* 1959) Michael Dummett wrote:

> Classifications do not exist in the void, but are connected always with some interest which we have, so that to assign something to one class or another will have consequences connected with this interest. . . . At one time it was usual to say that we do not call ethical statements 'true' or 'false', and from this many consequences for ethics were meant to flow. But the question is not whether these words are in practice applied to ethical statements, but whether, if they were so applied, the point of doing so would be the same as the point of applying them to statements of other kinds, and, if not, in what ways it would be different.

* This essay, not previously published in English, is based on an address delivered to the Anglo-Polish Colloquium held in Balliol College, Oxford in January 1983. A Polish translation of it is forthcoming in *Etyka*. Some parts of the essay derive from the author's paper 'What would be a substantial theory of truth' in Z. van Straaten (ed.), *Philosophical Subjects* (Oxford University Press, 1980) in which bibliographically fuller acknowledgement is made to some of the scholars (*e.g.*, Donald Davidson and John McDowell) who have established the results exploited in the construction attempted in Sections 3–6 below. See also my 'Truth and Interpretation' in *Language, Philosophy & Logic, Proceedings of the 4th International Wittgenstein Symposium* (August 1979), eds. Leinfellner, Haller, Hübner, Weingartner (Vienna: Hölder-Pichler-Tempsky, 1980).

The passage is often quoted. But perhaps the point it makes is almost as frequently disregarded now as it was in 1959. So many discussions of our question turn even now upon some preconception about truth that works silently within the arguments that are offered or is imported as the unspoken presupposition of the use of some term that sounds familiar but actually behaves in the manner of a technical term.[1] If we are to have regard for Dummett's observation, we must take special care from the outset to invest the question about truth in morals or aesthetics with its full content and interest before we even attempt to answer it.

In the first place we must avoid any method that rests on stipulation (*e.g.*, stipulation about what a truth of fact is). And then, in spite of the cost in trouble, we must be prepared to postpone the moral or the aesthetic or whatever else entirely until we can reach them by a detour through the concept of truth itself, a detour within which we refrain scrupulously from question-begging use of the idea of a fact. What a fact is is something we may hope in the end to cast light upon, if *en route* we deliberately abstain from relying on the idea in our account of truth. This detour must also be made without any positive reliance upon the idea of correspondence.[2] Finally, having in this way not foreclosed upon the question of the status of moral (or aesthetic or whatever other) judgments, we need to be prepared to take these judgments piecemeal or kind by kind, in case we may surprise ourselves by discovering that, among the judgments we persist in wishing to affirm, those that belong to some kinds have a better chance of attaining to the status of plain truth than those that belong to other kinds.

Before going any further, a note on terminology. By moral cognitivism I shall mean here the doctrine that, where a moral

---

[1] And a technical term whose definition would, if it were given, be *creative*, in the sense current in formal logic. (Cp. *e.g.* Patrick Suppes *Introduction to Logic* (Princeton: Van Nostrand, 1957) p. 154.)

[2] Perhaps the only fool-proof way of understanding what philosopers have meant by 'correspond' is to draw on the idea of truth itself. This is to say that the philosophical use of the word is *almost entirely* technical. But proceeding, as I now propose, by indirection, we may yet cause any residue that is non-technical and indispensable to us in the idea of correspondence to show itself. Let me say in advance that this residue has nothing to do with truth as copy, facsimile, representation, mirror or counterpart.

judgment is found to be worthy of being affirmed, (a) the judgment is a candidate to be known and a candidate for plain truth, and (b) the judgment stands or falls for acceptance according as it attains to that status. Unrestricted or strong moral cognitivism will replace the *where* in this formulation by an emphatic *wherever*; and will want no qualification or restriction of either (a) or (b). There is some point in calling this latter position moral realism, though I try myself not to make a habit of this, because the label imports unwanted associations. (See note 25 below.) On the other hand, moral cognitivism in its weakest recognizable form, which I sometimes call under-determinationism, will have no particular concern to replace the *where* by *wherever*. And it will explicitly refrain from asserting (b)—without denying that truth is the proper *aspiration* of all moral judgments.

2.   First then truth. Consider the biconditional equivalence, proposed (in effect) by Frege and Wittgenstein:

> Sentence *s* has as its literal use to say declaratively that *p* (henceforth for short, *s* means that *p*) just if whether *s* is true or not depends upon whether *p*.

The interest that is normally attributed to such formulations derives from the promise that they hold out of eludicating meaning in terms of truth.[3] Here of course our real interest runs in precisely the opposite direction. But if we want to understand more about truth and we think we understand more than nothing about what declarative meaning is (and surely we do), then one thing we can attempt is to shift our weight from the right to the left side of the Fregean biconditional, and look for any elucidations that it will then provide, not on this occasion of declarative meaning by reference to truth, but of

---

[3] For Fregean and Wittgensteinian formulations, cp. Frege, *Grundgesetze der Arithmetik* 1.32; Wittgenstein *Tractatus Logico-Philosophicus* 4.022, 4.024, 4.061; *Philosophische Bemerkungen* IV, 43. For subsequent deployments and redeployments of the insights, see Dummett 'Truth' *op. cit.*; Donald Davidson 'Truth and Meaning', *Synthese* vol. 17, 1967; John McDowell, 'On the Sense and Reference of a Proper Name', *Mind* vol. 85, 1977, and 'Truth-Conditions, Bivalence and Verification-ism' in Evans and McDowell (eds.), *Truth and Meaning: Essays in Semantics* (Oxford University Press, 1976).

truth by reference to declarative meaning, the latter being taken as already to some modest extent understood. We shall not arrive in this way at an 'analysis' of truth.[4] But, even if such an analysis were possible, we should not need it for our advertised purpose. All we need in order to answer our question about ethics is to determine what properties are possessed by every sentence that expresses a truth, or the *marks* (as one might say in Frege's terminology) of the concept *true*.[5] Naturally, the Fregean biconditional is only at its best for these heuristic purposes (*i.e.*, least question-begging) when we consider sentences that are perfectly unproblematic candidates for truth and falsehood. But I predict that the intuitive appeal of the marks we shall actually arrive at by starting from the point I am proposing, and then asking what truths uncontroversially agreed as such have to be like in order to count as truths, will greatly mitigate the risk we should otherwise run of prejudging the whole question of the plausibility or implausibility of moral cognitivism. For once we arrive at these marks, we shall recognize their affinity with the property of truth intuitively and directly; and, whatever the difficulties of deciding the question, there will then be a chance to see in a new way what it *turns on* whether moral judgments have these marks or lack them.

3.   Our Fregean biconditional will only help us to elucidate what truth is like, however, and what its marks are, if we are prepared in the interim to see the formulation given as the starting point for a *simultaneous* elucidation of declarative meaning and truth, and if we improve it in the light of certain entirely general objections.

The first of these objections is this. Whether 'it is cold here' is true or not may depend in some irrelevant and unhelpful

---

[4] One alternative to analysis is *elucidation*, as Frege and Wittgenstein conceived this. (For the continuity between their respective views of it, see Mark Helme 'An Elucidation of *Tractatus* 3.263' in *Southern Journal of Philosophy* vol. 17, 1979, pp. 323–334.) For present purposes, it will suffice to say that an elucidation illuminates a concept by employing it in a set of true judgments that involve it revealingly and interestingly with distinct, coeval, collateral concepts.

[5] For Frege's use of 'mark', see for instance the explanations he gives in his essay 'On Concept and Object'. A mark of the concept F is a property that anything has if it falls under F. So the marks of a concept F are concepts of the same level as F.

sense on whether the heating engineer called last week. But this sentence doesn't *mean* that the heating engineer failed to call.

To ensure that the equivalence holds, it seems we need to have recourse to the idea of *semantical* dependence. It would be consistent with a very modest construal of 'elucidation' to accept this and make it a stipulation that the dependence be semantical dependence. But before we can accept that defeatist conclusion, there is something else we can try.

Drawing upon Tarski's conception of a theory of truth for a particular object-language L, the instrument *par excellence* for generating truth-in-L-conditions of the sentences of L, let us rewrite the right side of the Fregean equivalence so as to obtain:

> *s* means in L that *p* just if it is a consequence of a correct account of truth in L that *s* is true in L if and only if *p*.

Read as it is intended, this is completely faithful to the Fregean conception of meaning. But now of course there is another circle we must take due note of. For even if we can only trace out a larger circle in its place, the larger circle may furnish a more illuminating basis for the elucidation of the marks of truth. What is an account or theory of true-in-L? Well, whatever else it is or does, it must fasten down the extension of the predicate 'true-in-L' both non-accidentally correctly and in a way that does not depend on any particular object-language sentence's being true. But in that case, *either* a Tarskian theory of truth-in-L must postulate for each object language sentence *s* a two-way conditional in the form of

True-in-L 'snow is white' if and only if snow is white,

or (better) the theory of truth-in-L must furnish the axioms that are needed to derive one such Tarskian conditional for each object language sentence *s*; and, in each case, the meta-language sentence used on the right of 'if and only if' must mean the same as the sentence mentioned on the left.[6] Or (as

---

[6] See Alfred Tarski, [35[b]] in [56[m]], 'The Concept of Truth in Formalized Languages' in *Logic, Semantics and Metamathematics* (Oxford, 1956) section 3. I call these biconditionals Tarskian to distinguish them from the general Frege-Wittgenstein biconditional and its variants that are our chosen instruments for eventually elucidating the concepts of meaning (*simpliciter*) and truth (*simpliciter*). (Note continues p. 144)

Tarski says in his statement of 'Convention T') it must *translate* it. (Unless the theory proceeds like this, either it may turn out to be an accident if the extension of truth-in-L is got right, or the theory will not be properly neutral with respect to what object language sentences are true.) And now the circle mentioned earlier makes itself manifest. What has appeared is that we cannot say what we mean by 'a correct account (or theory) of truth-in-L' without surreptitious and so far unelucidated use of 'means' or 'translates' or a synonym of these. Given Tarski's special aims (none of which depends on the elucidation of declarative meaning), this point does him no harm, and is in any case clearly acknowledged in his criterion for what counts as a materially adequate theory of truth for an object language.[7] But the point does count against the use that *we* have wanted to make of Tarski's idea, and it frustrates our first attempt at improving the Fregean conception of meaning as truth-conditions. In proposing that improvement we do need to be able to say what counts as a theory of truth-in-L, for arbitary L. That is the price of solving the very first difficulty by making explicit mention of an account (or theory) of truth-in-L.

In advance of any attempt to solve the difficulty in another way, let it be clear that this difficulty, the difficulty that the idea of meaning already lurks in the idea of a theory of truth,

---

It greatly assists in understanding the uses to which Tarski's theory began to be put from the nineteen sixties onwards to distinguish more carefully than Tarski paused to do between two distinct contributions Tarski made. There is Tarski's *general* approach to definitions of 'true-in-L' for arbitrary object-language L (his theory of theories of true-in-L, as one might say), together with the rationale he gives for such definitions, his criterion of material adequacy *etc.* All this one might call Tarski's general framework, or even his philosophy of truth. And then there is Tarski's practical demonstration of how to meet the criterion of adequacy in drawing up a definition of truth-in-L for a *particular* language L (*e.g.* as in the test case chosen by Tarski, the language of the elementary algebra of classes). In this latter task Tarski forbids the use of semantical concepts. But the notion of meaning is not forbidden in Tarski's philosophy of truth. Witness the occurrence of the word 'translation' in Tarski's Criterion of Material Adequacy for definitions of 'true-in-L' for object language L ('Convention T'). [See below, p. 333 ff.]

[7] Tarski can acknowledge the point because it does not show that the definition of truth-in-L, for particular L, needs to avail itself of semantical concepts. It only shows that the theory of truth-definitions and the criterion for the evaluation of such definitions must do so. See note 6 above.

scarcely impugns the *correctness* of our Fregean biconditional. Even if a certain employment of it is involved in a circularity, that biconditional records an important fact about meaning and truth. Nor is it excluded that, without spoiling any of this, we should mend matters by other means—if we can recast the equivalence a second time, more drastically, and find some replacement for the idea of meaning that lurks on the right hand side.

Let us see then if we can make an idea of making sense of people that is less specifically semantical, even if irreducibly social, do duty for our present purposes, and let us replace the two earlier attempts by the following revised, neo-Fregean equivalence:[8]

> *s* means in L that *p*
> if and only if
> for any theory θ of truth-in-L that combines with a descriptive anthropology to make sense of the shared life and conduct of L-speakers and that makes better sense than any rival combination consisting of a variant theory of truth and variant descriptive anthropology, it is derivable from θ that *s* is true in L if and only if *p*.[9]

By a 'descriptive anthropology' has to be meant here a mode of describing and understanding (in the broadest sense) which draws upon the full store of everyday predicates of human subjects, of features of the environments that impinge on subjects, and of the events that are counted as the actions or conduct of such subjects, and seeks, in response to circumstances

---

[8] This redeployment draws particularly on the ideas to be found in Donald Davidson 'Radical Interpretation', *Dialectica* vol. 27, 1973; Richard Grandy 'Reference, Meaning and Belief', *Journal of Philosophy* vol. 70, 1973; and especially John McDowell, cited at note 3 above.

[9] Strictly speaking, we should require that the biconditional to the effect that *s* is true if and only if *p*—the Tarskian biconditional that the Fregean biconditional exploits the possibility of—should be derivable from θ by a certain canonical, shortest proof-procedure that discharges semantical vocabulary in a systematic way and then halts—lest we end up manufacturing a logical equivalent of *s* (e.g., a truth-functional equivalent) that does not *mean* what *s* means.

Truth being a property of utterances or particular judgments and meaning being a property of sentence types and their constituents, the connexion between them needs to be further systematized. See M. Davies, *Meaning, Quantification, Necessity* (London: Routledge and Kegan Paul, 1981) p. 36.

including the speech or conduct of subjects, to distribute predicates of these and other kinds across features of reality, mental states and actions in such a way that: (1) the propositional attitudes it ascribes to subjects, specifying the content of these attitudes, are intelligible singly and jointly in the light of the true descriptions that the anthropology gives of the reality to which it takes subjects (or their informants, or their informants' informants . . .) to have been exposed; and (2) the actions (and actions of speaking) that it ascribes to subjects are intelligible in the light of the propositional attitudes it ascribes to them.[10]

What is envisaged is a gradual, trial and error process in which the descriptive anthropology starts out without having recourse to any theory of truth for L, but comes to rely more and more upon the construction of a theory of truth in L as we look for more detail and finer and finer grained intelligibility in the interpretations that we are prepared to accept of the speech, thought and conduct of speakers of the language. Obviously then the definition of truth in L and the descriptive anthropology it is paired with will be brought into being simultaneously, adjusted simultaneously, and tested simultaneously against rival pairs. Equally obviously, the Fregean biconditional, as given in the form in which we now have it, must inherit all the well-known difficulties of the ideas of understanding, explaining, making intelligible, imaginative projection or identification, *Verstehen* and the rest. These difficulties are there anyway, and within this new framework some new progress may even be made upon them.

4.    So much for truth and meaning and their connexions. But how can we bring the connexion thus fixed between them into some productive conceptual relation with our preliminary question 'What are the marks of the concept *true*'?

Here is a suggestion. If we have some sort of grasp of all the other concepts that occur essentially in the new and reformulated statement of the connexion between meaning-in-L and truth-in-L, then, if we look at these ideas as they work in concert, they can tell us a great deal about what we want to

---

[10] See again here McDowell *op. cit.*: also for some further suggestions, David Wiggins, *Sameness and Substance* (Oxford: Blackwell 1980) p. 222.

know. For the Fregean biconditional gives us a fix upon the property that any theory must seek to characterize if it is to combine with an anthropological characterization of the life and conduct of L-speakers to determine what the sentences of L mean, and if the combination is to make better total sense of that life and conduct in determining this than any rival combination makes. The thing we have to ask is, 'What must sentences that are true in L be like (what properties must they have) if a sentence's being such as to mean in L that $p$ is to consist in the best (or equal best) sense-making theory's delivering a Tarskian equivalence in the form '$s$ is true in L if and only if $p$'?

So far it appears that we are only dealing with truth-in-L, and are confined to asking, 'What must the property of truth as restricted to L-sentences be like and what other properties must L-restricted truth confer on those things that have it?' The most we may seem to have got is that property $\varphi$ counts as a mark of truth-in-L if possession of $\varphi$ by true-in-L-utterances is a *sine qua non* for the truth-in-L predicate's playing the said role in the interpretation of declarative L-sentences. But now we may note that here the L in 'true-in-L' is variable. We are speaking of how it is with *arbitrary* restrictions of 'true': and we cannot speak of these without committing ourselves to a view of that which they restrict, which is nothing other than truth itself.

5.   If this is right so far, then I think we ought to expect that among the marks of the concept of truth will be the following:[11]

(1)   If $x$ is true, then $x$ passes muster in that dimension of assessment in which $x$ demands to be assessed by virtue of being the sort of thing it is, thus in the primary dimension of assessment for $x$;

(2)   If $x$ is true, then $x$ will under favourable circumstances command convergence, and the best explanation of the existence of this convergence will either require the actual truth of $x$ or be inconsistent with the denial of $x$;

---

[11] Having set out my arguments for these claims elsewhere, I now seek to correct and consolidate these arguments. See 'What would be a substantial theory of truth?' *op. cit.* and 'Truth and Interpretation' *op. cit.* Here I have also tried to answer some of the points made by Anthony Price in his 'Varieties of Objectivity and Values', *Proceedings of the Aristotelian Society* vol. 82 (1982/3).

(3)  For any $x$, if $x$ is true then $x$ has content; and if $x$ has content then $x$'s truth cannot simply consist in $x$'s being itself a belief, or in $x$'s being something believed or willed or. . . .

(4)  Every true belief (every truth) is true in virtue of something;

(5)  If $x_1$ is true and $x_2$ is true, then their conjuction is true.

6.  *Mark (1)*. When someone believes truly that $p$ we may predicate truth of his state of belief, then of the object of his belief, i.e. the proposition or judgment; and then we may predicate truth of the sentence that expresses or reports the belief. Taking each of these usages as derivative in turn from its predecessor, I argue for the first mark of truth as follows.

Suppose truth were not the primary dimension of assessment for *beliefs*, so that falsehood were not a cardinal defect in them. Then there would be no reason to suppose it was a constitutive norm for beliefs as such to aim at truth. But then it would not be the case that the belief that $p$ had as such to carry with it any state of sensitivity to the question whether indeed $p$. And if the belief that $p$ did not have as such to carry that sensitivity with it, then we could not interpret beliefs by asking: How do things have to be for *this* state of mind to succeed in its aim or be correct? What does this state of mind have, *qua* the belief it is, to be differentially sensitive to?

It may be suggested that beliefs could be interpreted by their linguistic expression. But we have already seen that the interpretation of what sentences mean must itself go via the propositional attitudes, conspicuous among which is belief.

But is truth the primary dimension of assessment for *sentences*? Suppose truth were not a primary dimension of assessment for declarative utterance. Suppose then that there were nothing in the practice of speakers to sustain the idea that it was a norm for speakers to aim at truth in what they said. Then, even under some standard sort of circumstance, the utterance of a sentence would give no ground, however defeasible, for the expectation that the speaker believed what he was saying. But then there would be nothing to connect utterances with the one thing that can give an interpretation of them independent empirical support, namely what it would be reasonable for anyone to believe if he were placed as this subject is placed and liable to be impinged upon as he is liable to be impinged upon.

This argument depends, as will some others, on at least three assumptions: (a) that there can be no such thing as meaning unless there is the possibility of the interpretation of subjects by interpreters (and interpreters by subjects); (b) that interpreting subjects have to see one another as party to some however tenuous norm of rationality all departures from which stand in *prima facie* need of explanation; (c) that the idea of such a norm of rationality imports the idea of information, where the discrimination of good from bad information has its rational culmination in belief. The conveying of what is believed being conspicuous among the functions of language, it is surely no accident if it falls to the idea of belief to play this role in organizing interpreters' efforts to determine what is being said.

*Mark (2)* This wears a fugitive appearance. If something that we suppose we need to persist in affirming fails so evasive and slippery-seeming a condition, that must be something remarkable.[12]

First let us abandon interpretation for a moment and think about this matter from the inside. Suppose I am convinced that something is so. Then it is disturbing to me if nobody else can be brought to agree with me. Why? Well, if something is so *either* it must be capable of impinging on others in the way it impinged on me or I shall have in principle to account for its inaccessibility to all others. And if I could have accounted for that, then I should never have been disturbed in the first place by disagreement. If however there were no prospect at all that arguments founded in what made me think it true should have non-random efficacy in securing agreement about whether *p*, I should be without protection from the idea that (unless I was simply wrong) there was just nothing at issue. (And in that case it would be hard to see how a community of speakers could regard either the sentence *s* or its negation as a fit

---

[12] Some truths may be unknowable. In that case there are no sufficiently favourable conditions of investigation. The claim that Mark (2) is a mark of truth leaves it open whether such favourable conditions always exist.

expression for any belief, and hard to see how any interpreter could regard them as regarding it as one.)

Secondly, and pressing on with the problem of interpretation, consider the view from the outside. Suppose we have a subject predicate sentence 'item *t* is F'. To interpret this sentence one who does not yet know what it means has to find a propositional attitude such as belief that the sentence or its negation is good for the expression of, and then determine what condition that propositional attitude is keyed to, or has to be sensitive to the obtaining or non-obtaining of. For a belief to *be* the belief that item *t* is F the belief has to be both *en rapport* with item *t* and answerable to whether or not the item *t* really has the property F. (If a mental state were in no way sensitive to whether or not item *t* really was F, the state couldn't be the *belief* that item *t* was F.)

Now, as we have already in effect seen, a subject or interpreter has to try to see other subjects as constantly adjusting their beliefs to something—as responding constantly to the ins and outs of some reality or other (and, wherever this applies, as responding to any changes in these ins and outs).[13] But if we see other subjects in this sort of way, then the failure by these subjects to apprehend a truth that is there to be apprehended is the kind of thing that calls for explanation—by reference to subjects' cognitive deficiences, for instance, or by reference to adverse conditions of inquiry. So the better we then envisage the conditions of inquiry becoming, the more mysterious it is if no convergence is achieved upon the belief that item *t* is F—if item *t really is* F. And here it is important to note that the convergence that is in question—the convergence the lack of which would need explaining—is not a *mere intersubjectivity* or a chorus of agreement in which each new voice that is added sings the note it joins in upon just for the sake of unison, reinforcing thereby the voices that are already singing that note. If the convergence in the belief that item *t* is F is to be relevant to truth—if this is to be a case of the

---

[13] Of course the construction being attempted here specifies no limits in advance on what can count as a reality, or as the ins and outs of such. It cannot do so if any unprejudiced understanding is to emerge from it of what can count as objective fact or as part of reality.

interesting, significant convergence that truth commands—then what puts that belief there and holds it there has to be nothing more and nothing less than the fact that the item *t* really *is* F. Or dispensing, as we must show is possible, with the language of 'facts', we have the truth-relevant sort of convergence where *the statement of the best explanation of the agreement in the belief needs a premise to the effect that item t is indeed F, and the explanation would be simply invalidated by its absence.* Or, relaxing this very slightly, and prescinding from the example, we have the kind of convergence in belief that truth commands where *the best explanation of the agreement in belief that p is inconsistent with any denial on the explainer's own part that p.*[14]

*Mark (3).* Suppose that *x* is a state of believing. Then, by the argument given in the course of making the case for Mark (1), there must be something distinct from *x*, namely how things have to be for *x* to succeed in its aim or be correct, if there is to be any interpretation of *x* as the belief that it is.

Suppose that *x* is a sentence. Then finding a content for *x* involves seeing *x* or its negation as fit for expressing a belief that interpreters can envisage finding the right sort of licence to project upon subjects. But, if so, then the conceptual requirements on the fixation of belief will interact illuminatingly with the requirements that we impose upon a sentence's expressing something that is a matter for belief: and consideration of this interaction will suggest that the truth of a sentence cannot ordinarily consist (even in the case of the judgment that one is in pain, which might have been taken for a sort of counter-example to our third thesis) in the bare fact that the judgment it expresses is judged—or that its content is willed. If it did,

---

[14] There is a form of the Argument from Illusion that seems to depend on the idea that if a thing were really F it would not appear not-F to anyone. The idea is itself absurd. But perhaps what has lent the Argument its charm is some confused sense that what really moves it along is a principle much weaker (actually too weak to make the Argument from Illusion work) but much more plausible. This is the principle, which seems to be nothing less than constitutive of what we ought to mean by a reality or something to which someone's beliefs can be answerable, that if a thing is really F, then it will *tend* to appear F to any qualified judge, and its appearing not F to such a judge stands in *prima facie* need of explanation. On the strangeness of the argument from illusion, see Myles Burnyeat 'Conflicting Appearances', *Proceedings of the British Academy*, 1979/80.

then an interpreter could find no content for the sentence.[15]

*Mark (4).* The statement of Mark (4) simply condenses the statement of Marks (1), (2), and (3).

*Mark (5).* The argument for Mark (5) goes by a similar route to that for Mark (3). Suppose $x_1$ were interpreted in a way that made it fit for the expression of the belief that $p$, and $x_2$ were interpreted in a way that made it fit for the expression of the belief that $q$. And suppose that Mark (5) were not a mark of truth. Then interpretation could not proceed on the assumption that the beliefs by reference to which $x_1$ and $x_2$ were to be interpreted were themselves answerable to the principle that he who believes that $p$ and also believes that $q$ commits himself either to believe that ($p$ and $q$) or to go back on the belief in one or the other conjunct. It is not a universal (still less analytic) principle that if A believes that $p$ and A believes that $q$, then A believes that $p$ and $q$. But it is a norm of rational belief that one is committed to conform one's belief to this requirement; and the interpretation of beliefs as beliefs has to see beliefs as answerable to it. A propositional attitude that could not be taken as in any way sensitive to this requirement could not be taken for belief. Perhaps we should look afresh at the alternately platitudinous and mysterious principle that anything that is true (however we come by it) is consistent with anything else that is true (however we come by it). [See now p. 339, n. 31.]

7.   So much for the detour. Now let us move back in the direction of our original question. Can any moral judgments have all the marks of truth?[16] I suggested in §1 that the question was one that we must divide, because moral judgments make up a very heterogeneous class. But, even in advance of the division, it may appear that much more still needs to be said

---

[15] Light is thrown upon the approach that this would force upon us in the special case of so-called 'performative' utterances by Julie Jack in her 'Stating, Asserting and Otherwise Subscribing', *Philosophia*, December 1981.

[16] Postscript (1997). Since writing this essay, I have restated the case for the marks of truth construction that is advocated here. See my reply to Wilfrid Hodges in S. Lovibond and S. G. Williams (eds.), *Essays for David Wiggins: Identity Truth and Value* (Blackwell, Oxford 1996).

about the idea of convergence quite generally. How could moral beliefs (or aesthetic beliefs—but these have special features that would in the end require special treatment) *possibly* tend to converge in the special, interesting way we have insisted upon as a condition of the plain truth of true declarative utterances? How can there be values and obligations 'out there' that will account for such agreement as we achieve in our moral and aesthetic beliefs?

Well, there is at least one general way in which we might try to conceive of the prospects for moral judgments' commanding the sort of convergence that truth requires. This is by analogy with the way in which arithmetical judgments command it. There is an impressive consensus that $7 + 5 = 12$; and, when we rise above the individual level and look for the explanation of the whole consensus, only one explanation will measure up to the task. There is nothing else *to* think that seven and five add up to. (A full-dress explanation will prove this.) Since any other answer besides 'twelve' will induce a contradiction in arithmetic, no wonder we agree. We believe that $7 + 5$ is 12 because $7 + 5$ *is* 12. We have no choice.

By complicating our conception of the ties between *because* and 'cause', and between truth and 'the world', such examples lessen the grip of certain wrong ideas about what it would take for moral judgments to attain to truth; and (at least so far as I am concerned) that is the main force and importance of the analogy between arithmetic and ethics.[17] But someone may be tempted

---

[17] This force and importance becomes evident when we realize that the explanation 'People generally believe that $7 + 5 = 12$ because there is nothing else to think' does not invoke causality in any way that commits the theorist to postulating, absurdly, the existence of some causal relation between minds and the series of natural numbers. In so far as causality comes into such explanations at all, it holds only between mental states such as believings, thinkings, endorsings, willings. (See my 'Freedom, Knowledge, Belief and Causality' in *Knowledge and Necessity* ed. G. Vesey (London: Macmillan, 1970) especially at page 142-3.) There is nothing 'queer' about such explanations if we understand them for what they are. (The only problem, if there is one here, relates to something else, namely the referentiality of the *de re* thinkings about numbers which figure in such explanations as this.) For a long-standing misconstrual of this kind of explanation see Gilbert Harman's *The Nature of Morality* (Oxford University Press, 1977) pp. 9-10; Paul Benacerraf, 'Mathematical Knowledge', *Journal of Philosophy* vol. 70, 1973. I have used the word 'queer' here in allusion to John Mackie's 'argument from queerness'—and in opposition to it. See J. L. Mackie, *Ethics: Inventing Right and Wrong* (Harmondsworth; Penguin Books, 1977).

to go further and declare that, despite anything that Kant himself intended, Kant's formal theory of practical reason in the *Groundwork of the Metaphysics of Morals* supplies precisely the materials that are required to support a closer parallelism between arithmetic and ethics. The judgment 'He must X' will be true just if, in X-ing, the agent would be acting in accordance with a subjective maxim that he could at the same time will to become through his will a universal law for all rational beings, and the attempt to will the negation of the maxim results either in a 'contradiction in conception' or a 'contradiction in willing' [424]. Since this 'could' is not supposed to be psychological or contaminated in any way with the egoism or special pursuits or preferences of anybody in particular—only with the standard necessary conditions of there being the intention to act on a maxim—the claim may then be advanced that the content of judgments of this type will be testable by an *a priori* procedure. The said content will render the judgments that pass the test suitable to command just the kind of convergence that arithmetical propositions command among rational men. Wherever a moral judgment or verdict upon an agent's conduct commands actual consensus, we ought to be prepared to discover that the best explanation of the consensus is that there is nothing else that *could* have been willed as a law for the rational will.

This may seem like a tempting prospect. But unluckily it is as yet no more than a bare possibility, for reasons that Kant himself sometimes confronted. ('Maxims of actions might be arbitrary, and are only subject to the restricting condition of fitness for a universal lawgiving, which is a formal principle of actions.') We have no guarantee that, for every practical predicament, there is one and only one relevant maxim that could be willed as a universal law for rational beings in that predicament. Until more is said, we have no assurance that divergent or even conflicting maxims will not compete to answer the question 'What must I do?' Until this hole in the argument is stopped, there cannot be any assurance that truth as predicated of practical judgments will enjoy the fifth mark of truth. And, recalling the second mark, we must note that the best explanation of any consensus there is with respect to practical judgments may prove to be one that invokes cultural considerations and bypasses the whole need there might otherwise have been for the theorist to commit *himself* to the judgment.[18] For instance, one important constituent of such explanations may prove to be some account of why one universalizable maxim rather than another held the agent's attention, and was tested by him. The theorist may have no need at all to say *in propria voce* 'the best explanation for the consensus that *p* is that there is nothing else to think about this matter'. In that case, the explainer's explanation of the prevalence of the belief that *p* will leave *him* with a substantial undiminished freedom to deny that *p*. He does not have to ratify the belief itself.

8.  So much for what needs to be done and the general character of the difficulties that any kind of moral cognitivism must confront. But now I want to concentrate on two particular specimen cases. In order to get some better sense of the strengths and weaknesses of unrestricted cognitivism, I shall concentrate first on the class of judgments that seem to constitute the smallest problem, namely particularized, specific value judgments '*x* is beautiful/graceful/funny/charitable/ cruel/kind.' (Because they are in certain ways illuminating, I give temporary hospitality here to certain aesthetic valuations, whatever may finally distinguish them from moral valuations.) After that, I shall come to the class that probably constitutes the largest problem for any generalized moral cognitivism, namely particular practical judgments in the special forms 'I must ___', 'I must not ___', 'I had better ___', 'It is all right for him to ___' 'He must ___', 'He must not ___', 'He had better ___'. (In these forms '___' is to be replaced by an uninflected verb phrase, with or without 'to', relating to a particular time and place and a particular agent's situation.) It would repay the trouble to study many other classes (most conspicuously perhaps the class of statements of particular need and the class of general statements about the virtues). But I have to hope that a discernible shape will emerge from the scrutiny of these cases.

9.  In Chapter One of *The Nature of Morality*, Gilbert Harman

---

[18] Compare here Gilbert Harman, *The Nature of Morality, op. cit.*, chapter one.

presents a striking contrast between the 'testability' of moral judgments and the testability in respect of truth of scientific hypotheses:

> If you round a corner and see a group of young hoodlums pour gasoline on a cat and ignite it, you do not need to conclude that what they are doing is wrong: you do not need to figure anything out: you can see that it is wrong. But is your reaction due to the actual wrongness of what you see or is it simply a reflection of your moral 'sense', a 'sense' that you have acquired perhaps as a result of your moral upbringing?

Harman's claim is that, so long as the latter is a possibility, there must be an important contrast to be made with the scientific case. A scientist sees a vapour trail in a Wilson cloud chamber, and he says 'there goes a proton'. The scientist counts as observing a proton because the best explanation of his visual state is that there is a vapour trail, and the best theoretical explanation of the vapour trail itself is a proton.[19] In contrast, suppose now that we say that, in the case of setting fire to the cat, you and I simply see its wrongness. Or, since 'wrong' is not a pure evaluative predicate and we want to focus first on these, suppose we say that you and I simply see the callous, gratuitous, unimagining cruelty of the action. And suppose we try to claim that we count as observing this cruelty because the best explanation of our taking the episode in the way that we did is the *actual* callous, gratuitous, unimagining cruelty of the hoodlums' action. Then Harman will say this explanatory claim is wide open to the objection that the best explanation of our seeing the episode in that way can *dispense altogether* with

---

[19] Not only that. Harman could have added that the cognitive state of *belief* about protons that purports to result from observation is a straightforward candidate for objective correctness or plain truth precisely because it is the kind of state that may be explained, and invites us to explain it, as resting on an observation that cannot itself be correctly explained without reference to protons. The point of adding this would be to bring out the continuity between Harman's discussion of observationality and the moves that were made in connexion with our second mark of truth.

In what follows we shall have to explore an analogy, with respect to explanation, between commitment to entities like protons and commitments to entities like properties or the references of predicates. For the view I take of the last, see my 'The Sense and Reference of Predicate Expressions', *Philosophical Quarterly*, July 1984. See also note 20 of Essay V.

the claim that the act was wrong, or callously and gratuitously cruel. For Harman says that our reaction to our perception is to be explained by our 'psychological set'. The act had some non-evaluative property φ, say, and φ is a property that observers like you and me have been schooled to abhor. So the putative moral qualities of the treatment of the cat are simply irrelevant to why we saw the action as we did. Our seeing it in that way bears only upon the state and character of your and my moral sensibility. ('There does not seem to be any way in which the actual rightness or wrongness of a given situation can have any effect on your perceptual apparatus'; or in Harman's words again, 'Moral principles might help to explain why it was *wrong* of the children to set the cat on fire, but moral principles seem to be of no help in explaining your thinking that that is wrong.')

This is a challenging line of objection, and congruous with the approach we have been pursuing towards truth. The pressing, outstanding question we must begin with is how well the objection works when the observational judgment is given in the form 'that was callously cruel'. Harman's reference to how we were schooled raises the question *why* we were so schooled, and whether the mores and institutions that make up the context of the schooling are not themselves a response to something that is simply *there*. (There to be found by anyone, or by anyone who is sufficiently attuned to what bears upon the matter.) Compare the answer to the question why we are schooled that $7 + 5 = 12$.

In the second place, how exactly does the alternative explanation go? To measure up to what seems to need to be explained here, a general theory of some sort will be required, and this will have to place our particular reaction in the face of what the hoodlums did in some relation to our responses to a whole heterogeneous collection of events whose only common property is that they are cruel in some degree. (Or so one is tempted to put it. What else after all do the following have in common?—A man snubs a child; the courtiers steal Rigoletto's daughter; the hoodlums set fire to the cat. . . .) Whatever else such a theory might do or be, it seems that it would have to treat of its subjects' psychological states not in isolation, but in a way that arises out of the production of a convincing account of the *whole range of objects* that provoke or arouse the various states. And it seems certain, considering the very fine discriminations effected by real human subjects, that this theory could not avoid involving itself quite deeply in the classification of the features of the world at large (or conditions of the environment) that *excite* this or that sentiment or belief or reaction on the part of subjects. It would need to describe the standard of correctness that has currency at a given time for the application of any ethical or aesthetic predicate. And it seems it would have to be such as to entail a potentially counterfactual claim that this or that kind of object or situation would, in the absence of error by subjects, bring down upon itself this or that kind of reaction from subjects. If so, the psychologist who applied the theory would even have to be in a position to alert his subjects to oversights or mistakes (at very least to the extent that one normal subject can alert another normal subject).

Such a theory is in one way terribly easy to imagine, if we will dignify with the name of 'theory' the descriptive anthropology that we can sketch of ourselves for ourselves. For this is something we already have. But if this is the theory that the psychologist uses to account for our response to the hoodlums' action, then he is badly placed to deny that what provokes our responses is simply the callous cruelty of the act.

He can distance himself from cruelty, having once grasped what cruelty is. He can say instead 'what they call the callous cruelty of the act', if he likes. But this phrase itself, as he uses it, will need to have the same Fregean *reference* as 'callously cruel' as they are apt to use that. So he can scarcely deny that the property itself exists—unless he wishes to undo the psychological theory he is himself making use of. He need not take the same final view of cruelty as we take, once he has grasped what we mean by 'callously cruel'. But he has left himself with no freedom at all to deny that we have based our thought that the hoodlums' action was callously cruel upon something that is there to be perceived in it. If so, there is still room for plain truth.

There is one other possibility, and this will put Harman's theorist in a better position to explain *and explain away* our reaction. Perhaps the behavioural scientist is not to try to match 'cruel' by a complex scientific property with the same extension. He is to offer explanations that bypass that requirement altogether. He may look for a theory which describes the relevant phenomena in terms that are proprietary to psychology as he conceives it and account for all that needs to be accounted for without postulating any one connexion between events that are taken as cruel and the response 'that was callously cruel!'. Perhaps there are distinct, complex, scientifically palpable properties here each of which would suffice to bring down that particular 'projection'. It may even be suggested that the scientific theory has no need to categorize reality in a way that corresponds at all to the moral agent's own way.

I want to emphasize that, so far as I am concerned, there will be nothing wrong in principle with explanations that explain away in this fashion. If someone finds the smell of (say) winter jasmine *rank*, we can readily explain this otherwise than by postulating actual rankness in that jasmine. We can say he finds the jasmine rank because of his personal or psychological history. (Perhaps there was a strong smell of jasmine in a certain garden where he underwent a traumatic sequence of experiences.) For such an explanation to work, all that is needed is for the theorist to call the shrub in question 'winter jasmine' and its smell 'the smell of winter jasmine', and then to speak of the particular subject's psychological 'set' with respect to winter jasmine and its smell. The theorist need commit himself to no more, and even less may suffice. ('Rank' then occurs only in the theorist's description of his subject's reaction.)

What I question is whether one can imagine a psychological theorist's dispensing entirely with value-properties not just in the case of non-standard reactions but in *every* case (even in the cases where there are standard shared responses to supposedly standard moral qualities), and whether one can imagine him dispensing altogether with predicates that possess non-accidentally the same extension as his subjects' evaluative predicates do. That is what will be required by the thorough-going denial of substantial truth to pure value judgements. What stands in the way of taking the possibility of such a *tour de force* fully seriously is the sheer unimaginability of someone's supplanting by clinical modes of explanation most if not all of our everyday modes of rendering actions and beliefs intelligible; and the prejudicial conceptions of explanation—queer conceptions, I yield to the temptation to say—that are almost always called upon when philosophers seek to interest us in the possibility that *all* valuation rests upon some sort of error or illusion or when they declare, less strikingly but equally prejudicially, that a philosopher falls into illusion if he supposes that moral subjects' idea of correctness in moral judgment might coincide with plain truth. [Cp. p. 355.]

10. The argument just presented needs to be guarded from three misconceptions it may otherwise encounter. First there is nothing here about how one can tell 'from the inside' whether a particular evaluative standard that one is party to is securely grounded in anything or not. We have been concerned exclusively with the statement in terms of explanation of *what it is* for such a practice to be grounded, and what it is for the associated predications to be candidates for plain truth.

Secondly, this defence of cognitivism for the case of pure relatively specific evaluations like 'cruel' is not committed to deny the *essential contestability* of such predications. If the idea of explanation itself is thereby contaminated with the very same affliction of essential contestability, perhaps this is a fair reflection of how matters really stand in the explanation of human cognitions and responses. (Note that the degree of contestability for predicates as specific as 'cruel' is relatively low.)

Thirdly, this defence is not committed to the claim that, wherever there is a genuine value predicate backed by a coherent going practice that makes the sense that its participants think it makes, there must be the prospect of a convergence among *all rational intelligences whatever*, or convergence among *all rational creatures of human fabric and constitution*, about the extension of the property it stands for. The expectation of convergence can be legitimately confined to people of a certain culture who have what it takes to understand a certain sort of judgment—provided of course that one is prepared in principle to undertake to spell out what their special sensitivity is, and to submit to any test there may be the claim that *there is* something that they are thus sensitive to. Austere Peircean convergence (the predestinate opinion of all rational, methodical inquirers or whatever)[20] is not required, only that judgments be open to criticism, and that criticism should always import the question of the prospects of interesting or principled convergence.—Compare here the situation in literary criticism. Longinus writes

> To speak generally, you should consider that to be truly beautiful which pleases all people at all times. For when men who differ in their habits, their lives, their tastes, their ages, their date, all agree together in wholly one and the same view about the same writings, then the unanimous verdict as it were of such discordant judges makes our faith in the admired passages strong and indisputable. (*On the Sublime* Ch. VIII)

It is irrelevant to this phrasing of the 'test of time' criterion that the moment is approaching when nobody will have what one needs to have any opinion at all about the many fine passages from classical authors that Longinus quotes in his treatise *On the Sublime*.

11. Such a defence of moral cognitivism for the case of specific particular pure valuations may embolden a champion of the further determination of the cognitivist outlook that I call strong cognitivism and is often called moral realism to enter a more general and I think more questionable claim, embracing in its scope of application not only pure valuations but everything else that falls within the provinces of the prudential, aesthetic and moral.

He will begin by pointing out that, if the answerability of the judgments of a given class to an objective standard of correctness does not need to create the expectation of Peircean convergence, because we need not expect every rational person to be party to the norms and shared sensibility that gives these judgments their distinctive content, then this creates a presumption that the same will go for practical judgments. He will also be encouraged to say that there (as everywhere else) much care is required in the interpretation of

---

[20] For Peirce's conception of convergence see for instance 'The Fixation of Belief', *Popular Science Monthly* 1877, Section 5; 'How to Make Our Ideas Clear', *Popular Science Monthly*, 1878. [See also Postscript p. 340 ff.]

what passes for disagreement. Even the most striking difference of *mores* and institutions between two societies and the consequential discrepancies in practical judgment need not show very much about any *disagreement* between them, he may say.[21] What does it signify if, for different people in different times and places, practical situations and predicaments are differently conceptualized, or if they prompt different maxims from those that other men will at other times apply to their moral experience? It will take more than that to demonstrate that there is something that these people are in any strict disagreement about. Does one group hold that *p* and another group hold that (strictly) *not-p*? Is there a common problem to which they are offering competing answers or an agreed end that they have found discrepant means to? Evaluative and practical questions are questions that arise in the here and now, and they take on their full sense from the historical and social circumstances that give rise to them. But if so, then what really matters, as regards the truth and objectivity of a practical judgment and its prospect of commanding the interesting and significant kind of convergence, is only that the judgment should represent an answer to a question asked with respect to a given place and time, that the question should have a sense held fixed by reference to the historical context and circumstances of that place and time, and that the answer should be

---

[21] This claim comes in different strengths, and in very different colourations, which it is well worth distinguishing. On the one hand there is the old idea of a *unitary* morality expressed in locally different practices (cp. *e.g.* Aristotle *Nicomachean Ethics 1134b29–30*; Leibniz *New Essays* 1.2.1–13), together with the complementary or corrective idea that there is some constant nucleus (cp. Vico *New Science* §144, §333; Hume *Treatise* III.8, *Enquiry Concerning the Principles of Morals* sect. IX part one). This is the idea of which a writer such as Aurel Kolnai may be viewed as the modern inheritor. (See for instance section 3 of Kolnai's 'Moral Consensus' in *Ethics, Value and Reality*, eds. Klug and Dunlop, (London: Athlone, 1977).) The great interest of Kolnai's conception of moral consensus is its capacity to accommodate and explain divergent practical judgments and divergent moral emphases by reference to the consensus there is with respect to certain other kinds of moral judgment.) On the other hand, there is a distinctive declension from this tradition. This rests on claims of the *incommensurability* (or limited commensurability) of different 'forms of life'. This is the thought exploited in the proposal under discussion in the text. For more on this see for instance the writings of Peter Winch; for muted versions of the thought see Essay III §8, §10; John McDowell 'Aesthetic Value, Objectivity and the Fabric of the World' in E. Schaper (ed.) *Pleasure, Preference and Value* (Cambridge University Press, 1983) esp. pp. 2–3.

better than all competing answers to that question, *so understood.*[22]

12. The pressing question here is whether this extension of the pro-cognitive argument of §9 can prevail against all the difficulties that flow from moral disagreement. Pure specific evaluations, which were the subject of that first argument, are closely associated with special sensibilities for which there can be something approaching an agreed test. But many moral judgments appear to lack this feature, and especially perhaps practical judgments lack it. 'Must', 'may', 'right', 'wrong', 'morally possible' have less local colour than specifically valuational predicates, and in their characteristic use they figure in judgments that lie very close to action. There is no manifest difficulty in finding them some cross-culturally common meaning. (If someone claims that 'must' is always 'must$_s$', or 'must for a given society S', how does he avoid relativizing truth itself? Certainly this *for* is obscure.[23]) However different one community is from another, there are at least some practical questions that they will each face. Surely they will not always find one another's practical problems unintelligible.

What then ought it to mean for an outright cognitivist or moral realist to claim that, given a practical question whose interpretation is properly fixed by reference to a given time and

[22] Bernard Williams would have maintained at the time of writing his 'The Truth in Relativism' (see *Moral Luck* (Cambridge University Press, 1981)) that, once a moral or practical question is properly understood and understood in its application to a context that is too remote, the intelligent response on the part of one not in practical confrontation with the belief system of the members of the group who have to answer the question is to recognize that their own vocabulary of appraisal can gain no grip on the matter, and to abstain from judgment. It is important to see that the reason that Williams himself gives for this abstention—contrast that of a strong cognitivist with would-be relativist sympathies—constitutes the most negative outcome of all to the issue on which the realist rested his hopes. For it is tantamount not to the avowal of insufficient understanding of what is at issue, but to the claim that there is really no fact of the matter to be understood. 'To raise seriously questions in the vocabulary of appraisal about this culture considered as a concrete historical reality will not be possible for a reflective person. In the case of systems [of moral beliefs] that stand in merely notional confrontation is to lack the relation to our concerns which alone gives any point or substance to appraisal.'

[23] Note that, if the cognitivist relativizes in this way he does not necessarily intend the same thing as Gibert Harman has intended by it (see 'Moral Relativism Defended', *Philosophical Review* vol. 74, 1975)—even if the two positions have some common difficulties.

place and situation, there is only one thing to think is the answer to it? That the only convergence that counts as relevant for truth is local? This at least seems tantamount to a 'local reality' that simply *shuts out* alien minds. (A first person plural version of the position that Plato attributes to Protagoras and represents Socrates as refuting in the *Theaetetus*.[24]) Standing by our present formulation of the second mark of truth, we have rather to persist in taking the claim as amounting to the declaration that, within the class of particular practical judgments, there are significantly many judgments passing for correct such that, when their sense is held fixed for a given time, place and situation, they will command a convergence among those independently assessed as competent to understand them, and the best explanation of this convergence commits the explainer himself to the judgment.

If this will do as an account of what is at issue, then given the strength and interest of the realist contention, the dispute loses any semblance it ever had of being merely verbal. And where the cognitivist offers no restriction or qualification of his position (see §1 above), there seem to be two difficulties.

Suppose that A was an agent placed in certain circumstances who reached the decision that it would be right for him to φ. It may be easy to imagine a consensus forming among those who learn about the circumstances and understand them that there was nothing else *for A* to think than that it was right for him to φ. Such a consensus will represent a ratification of A's reasons for thinking what he thought. But perhaps it is one thing to say that there was nothing else *for A* to think, another to say that there is *nothing else to think*. It seems important that one can ratify A's reasons as good for him there, yet still hold back from affirming *in propria voce* that it was right for him to φ, and important that for certain critical purposes (see below §16) one had *better* refrain from that judgment. (Alternatively, one can set such a high standard for 'there was nothing else for him to think' that the consensus we have been imagining disappears.)

The second apparent difficulty is this. Given some definite practical situation or predicament, it is often essentially contestable how it is to be described or conceptualized and what matters or does not matter about it: but to find that the convergence available is convergence of the sort that truth requires we always need to look into the explanation of the convergence. But the more informative and convincing we make this explanation, the more we shall need to say about agents' processes of conceptualization, and the more we shall have to say about the perspective from which they view it and their prior evaluations. But then the more room it seems there will be for the explainer to distance himself from the beliefs that he is explaining his subjects' convergence in. If so, then the harder it becomes for the explainer to sum up his own explanation in the declaration that his subjects have converged in the belief that *p* because there is nothing else to think in this matter except that *p*. There will be cases where the most that we can expect agreement about is that there was nothing else *for the agent* to think. [Cp. p. 348 below.]

13.  Perhaps both difficulties can be appreciably mitigated, if we can confer a special moral authority on one perspective. The only one that seems privileged is the perspective of the agent or participant. If those outside a situation fail to concur in a moral belief that those within it tend to converge upon, and converge upon seemingly non-accidentally relative to the content of their judgment, have the ones outside fully grasped the situation? If those close by all *find* that *p*, it may be said, then surely those further away ought to ask whether that finding is not in itself some sort of *evidence* that *p*.

There is a point here that every proper account of these matters must respect. But it is not enough simply to assert that, where there is a disagreement, those nearer are always (or *ex hypothesi*) better placed than those further away. Much more needs to be said about what confers priority upon the participant perspective, and what sort of priority this is.[25] To

[25] Note also how important it is for the strong cognitivist/moral realist to distance himself from Williams' totally different kind of reason for according a certain priority to the participant perspective ('no fact of the matter' *etc*). What the strong cognitivist/moral realist must develop is the thought that the participants can see better because, by being nearer, they can do something analogous to 'getting a better look'.

NB. One who controverts realism in the sense in which we are using the term here is

make progress we have first to develop the account that the strong cognitivist seems to need of the priority of the agent perspective; and then we have to engage him and test his defences, in a non-legalistic spirit, on the ground where he ought to be most secure, namely within that participant perspective.

14. In the task of further explaining and illustrating the primacy of the agent's perspective, I shall draw upon Peter Winch's essay 'The Universalizability of Moral Judgment'.[26] In this essay, Winch examines the events narrated in Herman Melville's *Billy Budd*, a story set on a British frigate *HMS Indomitable* at a tense moment during the Napoleonic Wars. The drama turns upon a conflict between two sets of demands, the demands of natural justice, forbidding the execution of Billy Budd, an innocent man of angelic character who has been provoked beyond endurance by the perjurious accusation of conspiracy made against him by Claggart the Master at Arms, and the demands of a necessary and justifiable martial law, the Mutiny Act, inheriting all its rigour from war itself, demanding the punishment of a man who has struck and killed a superior officer—and demanding it instantly, in the Captain's considered view, given the recent unrest in the fleet.

Winch points out that to discuss such conflicts as that which faces Captain Vere in this narrative, we have from the outset to invoke a 'should' that belongs to neither natural justice nor martial law. ('Tell me whether or not, occupying the position we do, private conscience *should* not yield to that imperial one formulated in the code under which alone we officially

---

not an *anti-realist* (which inevitably suggests Michael Dummett's usage, *e.g.*, in his *Frege* (London; Duckworth, 1973)) but a *non-realist*. In this connexion, see Philippa Foot, 'Moral Realism and Moral Dilemmas' *Journal of Philosophy* vol. 80, 1983, pp. 397–8. See also §1 above.

[26] First published in *The Monist*, 1965, and subsequently reprinted in *Ethics and Action*, Blackwell, Oxford 1972.

In this matter I must stress that Winch is not to be blamed for any mishap I suffer in trying to apply his ideas to the question of the truth-status of particular practical judgments. That was not his direct concern. (Winch has recently written about cognate questions—see his 'Im Anfang war die Tat' in Block ed., *Perspectives on the Philosophy of Wittgenstein* (Oxford: Blackwell, 1981)—but in a manner oblique to the approach being attempted here.)

proceed'—Captain Vere says at the drum-head court.) Winch than asks himself what he himself would have said and done if faced with the same circumstances as the Captain. The answer he returns is that, even discounting the possibilities of failure of nerve and softness in the face of a terrible duty, he believes that he *could not* have acted as Vere actually did. He could not have proceeded as Vere did against Billy Budd for striking Claggart, who had persecuted him for so long and then falsely accused him. And by this 'Could not', he does not mean 'Would not have had the nerve to' but rather that he would have found it morally impossible to condemn a man 'innocent before God' under such circumstances. ('Innocent before God' are the words that Vere himself uses in his prosecuting speech at the drum-head court.) The considerations connected with this innocence are simply too powerful to be overridden by any appeal to military duty. So Winch's verdict about the 'should' ('must') that belongs to neither martial law nor natural law is that, if he had been in Vere's position, then he would not and could not have accepted the judgment 'I must here and now exact the penalty laid down by the Imperial Code'.

Does this mean that Winch thinks that, in his capacity as loyal officer, mindful of the great danger of a repetition of the events of the mutiny at the Nore, Captain Vere put all moral considerations aside? No. Winch claims that it is absolutely clear from the story that Vere's decision, whatever we think of it, did not prescind or abstract from moral consideration at all. Moral considerations were present throughout, even if we cannot concur in Vere's weighing of them. Does Winch hold then that Vere simply thought wrongly about what was in front of him and acted wrongly?

> I do not think this. The story seems to me to show that Vere did what was for him the right thing to do. But what makes me say this is not anything that I see in his situation different from what I have imagined myself to be faced with.

Here lies the difference between the 'ought' judgments among which the original conflict arises (which may, for all that is said here, be answerable to Sidgwick's requirement that, if A ought to $\varphi$ in such and such circumstances, then in any relevantly similar circumstances B too, where B $\neq$ A, ought to $\varphi$) and the quite different sort of 'should' (or 'must' or 'it is right') judgments that answer the question 'Which "ought" judgment should I (or must I, or is it right for me to) follow?'. Where the latter question is concerned, Winch says:

> If A says 'X is the right thing for me to do', and if B in a situation not relevantly different says 'X is the wrong thing for me to do', it can be that both are correct . . . It may be that neither what each says, nor anything entailed by what each says, contradicts anything said or implied by the other . . . This certainly does not mean that, if A believes that X is the right thing for him to do, then X is made the right thing for A to do by the mere fact that he thinks it is . . . [Vere] is not merely concerned to decide to *do* something, but also to *find out* what is the right thing for him to do. . . . The deciding what to do is, in a situation like this, itself a sort of finding out what is the right thing to do . . . [A] writer like Sidgwick would have to say that the decision is one thing, the finding out quite another. It is because I think that deciding is an integral part of what we call 'finding out what I ought to do' that I have emphasized the position of the agent in all this.

After rebutting any facile assimilation of his own doctrine to a subjectivism of the kind Plato attributes to Protagoras ('I know that *p* just if *p* is true for me', or whatever), the positive account that Winch is then led to give of the distinctive content of the 'I must' is that

> it seems . . . that what one finds out is something about oneself, rather than anything one can speak of as holding universally. . . . What a man finds out about himself is something that can be expressed only in terms of the moral ideas by consideration of which he arrives at his decision.

Now here we are concerned with 'moral modalities'—with what is morally possible for this or that agent—Winch says, but

> somebody else . . . considering these very arguments, might conclude that the moral possibilities were different for him without necessarily making any further judgment about what the corresponding possibilities were for Vere or for anybody else and without being committed to any further judgment . . .

If we want to *express* in a given situation how it strikes the agent, we cannot dispense with his inclination to come to a particular moral decision . . . The one man was disposed to give precedence to one and acquit, the other to give precedence to the other, and convict. [But] if such dispositions as this have to be taken into account in applying the notion of 'exactly the same circumstances', surely the last vestige of logical force is removed from the universalizability thesis.[27]

15. Now if this is right—and much that is said here seems right[28]—then what we are given here first is the denial that we should always expect principled consensus with respect to the question whether it is right for a man to V in circumstances of the kind *c* (we are invited to relax our interest in this impersonal form); and then we are given reason to expect that, if any principled consensus at all could be obtained with respect to the question whether it was right for Captain Vere to V under the circumstances *c*, well that is a consensus that may depend on our agreeing to accord some special primacy to Vere's own findings and the decision that only he can make. And this is a primacy that the agent's own finding and decision *deserve* to enjoy, according to Winch.

---

[27] Cp. A. MacIntyre 'What Morality is Not' in *Against the Self Images of the Age* (London: Duckworth, 1972):

> *Sometimes* . . . the question 'What ought I to do?' can only be translated trivially into 'What ought someone like me to do in this kind of situation?' This is important because this translation is often not trivial at all. When I am puzzled, it is often useful to pick out the morally relevant features of the situation and of my position in it, and having isolated them from the particular situation, I am in a better position to solve my problem. But, where a situation is too complex, phrases like 'someone like me' or 'this kind of situation' [may] become vacuous. For I [may be] the only person 'sufficiently' like me 'to be morally relevant', and [if so] no situation would be *sufficiently* like 'this kind of situation' without being precisely this situation.

(To make it plain how MacIntyre's discussion bears upon the present issue and with what effect, I have ventured to italicize two words and then to reduce, in the square bracketed material, a certain excess strength in the claims advanced in the passage.)

[28] For my own principal reservation see below § 16. But, waiving that for the moment, I would remark that it is not clear that even on his reading of the story, Winch ought to have said that the story shows that Vere did what was the *right* thing for Vere to do. All Winch really needs to say for his purpose of defeating universalizability is that the story (a) does not show that Vere did the *wrong* thing for Vere to do, although (b) it shows enough for him (Winch) to be clear that what Vere did would have been the wrong thing for him (Winch) to do.

This argument, which I for one am prepared to salute as deeply interesting, offers to someone who is a strong cognitivist with respect to the whole class of practical judgments the prospect that, if he can complete the case in favour of Winch's agent-oriented view of practical judgement, and if he can vindicate it as some sort of a conceptual truth that an agent does what is right for him just if he can meet certain requirements that Winch imposes, then the strong cognitivist position can escape all the difficulties that it seemed it had with convergence and the second mark of truth. (The requirements Winch imposes are (i) that the agent should not mistake, but recognize the moral quality of the issue; (ii) that his decision should not arise from a moral outlook that seems profoundly mistaken; and (iii) that the agent should not be insincere.)

Let us be clear that there is no threat to truth in the mere shift from the unrelativized practical judgment to the person-relativized practical judgment. If this is subjectivism, then it is only subjectivism in the good sense of introducing a subject or agent. There is no question here of any irreducible 'true-for-Vere' and 'not-true-for-Winch', for instance. The difficulty for one who has no qualms at all about applying 'true' to practical judgments is rather this. If we try to translate Winch's observations into an elucidation of the apparent *content* of 'It is right for A to V', in terms say of what it was morally possible for A to do, then it seems that what we the non-agents have to ask may be different from what the agent Captain Vere has to ask. By Winch's account, one part of what it may turn on for us is Vere's decision. But that cannot be anything it turns on *for Vere*! Surely this asymmetry is puzzling. But isn't it also one part of the price of securing the convergence requirement within Winch's framework?

What in Winch's view does the decision turn on for Vere? Well, nothing that is in principle unknowable by us. Yet it matters in a special way, on Winch's account, what Vere makes of the considerations in front of him—how things strike *him*. For while many ways of being struck by the situation are no doubt excluded as morally misguided or maniacal or simply purblind, what we always may lack reason to assert (if we follow Winch's doctrine of the primacy of the agent's perspective and if we refrain from expanding Winch's three requirements in a way that subverts his impressive critique of the doctrine of universalizability) is that there is just one way it must strike him if he is sincere.

Again, if we say that what makes all the difference between this non-misguided way and that non-misguided way—what takes in this slack—is that *this* is the way that things actually struck the agent, then it becomes a question whether we are preparing to exempt some of the particular practical verdicts that we endorse as true from the strict rigour of the requirement that was entailed by our formulation of the third mark of truth. For this entailed that the correctness of a judgment should be independent of its author's actually arriving at it.[29]

The outcome of this development so far of the agent-perspective is not yet then any straightforward vindication of unrestricted cognitivism, even if we exercise the option to stay within the area that an adherent of the 'moral realism' we have reconstructed ought to consider the most favourable. For even within that area, it seems that the realist must guard against the danger of securing one of the marks of truth at the expense of the others. Of course, when we prescind from difficulties of cultural relativity, the difficulty in the idea of practical truth only appears clearly for the special case of dilemmas.[30] But what appears there is only a straightforward case of the very general difficulty that exercised us previously, namely the doubtful prospect of finding *enough* convergence of belief, principled convergence that is, among those who have or can get what it takes fully to understand an agent's predicament.

16.   This is at best an interim finding, however, because it is a

---

[29] Cp. Thomas Nagel p. 100 of 'The Limits of Objectivity' in *Tanner Lectures on Human Values* Vol. I ed. McMurrin (Cambridge University Press, 1980):

> In deliberation we are trying to arrive at conclusions that are correct in virtue of something *independent* of our arriving at them. If we arrive at a conclusion, we believe that it would have been correct even if we *hadn't* arrived at it. And we can also acknowledge that we might be *wrong*, since the process of reasoning doesn't guarantee the correctness of the result.

[30] The realist would be wrong to try to secure his position by representing real dilemmas as 'ties', or by withdrawing his interest from so large and important (not to say ill-defined) a class of practical judgments as these. Practical judgments that emerge from dilemmas constitute substantial moral responses to substantial moral perplexity.

real possibility that a more meticulous presentation of Winch's position—designed to attend to points that did not figure among Winch's own preoccupations (which were different from ours)—would not jeopardize the third mark of truth. Such a presentation might attend to another point, which may have troubled the reader already. Whether we are optimistic or pessimistic about the truth-status of practical judgment, there was always something unsatisfactory in letting the agent's own finding count for quite so much.[31] Even when the agent meets Winch's three requirements—see §15 para 2 *ad fin*—, we surely ought not to treat the agent's finding as *above criticism*. Indeed, we cannot do so if we are interested in Melville's book. It is true that in his article Winch has caught well one part of Melville's thinking, which is Melville's desire to discourage us from condescending to the point of view that is alien to our own but more closely caught up in the actual predicament ('Says a writer whom few know, "forty years after the battle it is easy for a non-combatant to reason about how it ought to have been fought. It is another thing personally and under fire to direct the fighting while involved in the obscuring smoke of it. Much more so with respect to other emergencies involving consideration both practical and moral, and when it is imperative promptly to act" '). But there is another equally important trend in Melville's thinking to which Winch pays insufficient attention; and this is the thought that war makes men like Captain Vere selectively but dangerously *mad* ('These men are madmen and of the most dangerous sort, for their lunacy is not continuous but occasional, evoked by some special object; it is protectively secretive, . . . self-contained'). It was not quite right for Winch simply to declare 'The story seems to me to show that Vere did what was for him the right thing to do'. Even if it is out of place to lay the whole blame for any of this madness and its doings at the feet of individual men, criticism still has to reach down to their particular practical judgments, and the route by which they were arrived at. (If only

---

[31] And unsatisfactory even if we are pessimistic in the (limited) way in which I am pessimistic about this kind of practical judgment and we think that the particular practical judgments we have to live with can fall short of plain truth. For even at its darkest this pessimism does not entail that anything goes, or that all objective grounds for preferring one judgment over another must lapse.

because criticism that exempted these judgments from its attention could have no purchase at all in the real world.) Criticism often involves finding the right distance from the point of view of a direct participant; and there is no limit that can in advance be set upon that right distance, except that it must not reach into incomprehension. In the case of war, for instance, criticism must be ready to raise the question whether a civilization can repel its real enemies by conducting itself at battle in ways that discredit the very values it embodies and seeks to protect. It must interest itself in the question whether there is any other way for the question of responsibility to arise than at the level of the accountability of individuals. Naturally, we must acknowledge that there will be participants for whom such thoughts are out of reach, and that among those, some cannot be blamed for this fact. But it was not out of reach of Vere. And even if it had been, there is *one* important form of criticism we still need to engage in that prevents us, even on the strength of such thoughts being out of Vere's reach, from simply acquiescing in Vere's decision not to wait till *HMS Indomitable* rejoined the rest of the fleet, to elide the normal procedures, and to dispense with a hearing of Billy's case at a properly constituted court martial. Of course, Vere's own finding is important, and integral to a morally informed narrative. But so is the disquietude that is evoked by his precipitancy.[32]

17.   So now, having refined the statement of the primacy of the agent-perspective, and having due regard both for what an agent authentically finds and for the need to hold that finding open to criticism from any distance that may prove to be necessary, but not shutting out the deliverances of any non-participant potentially non-convergent consciousness (even if the weight that is attached to its non-divergence has to be proportioned to the independent likelihood that it is sufficiently

---

[32] And is even evoked within Melville's narrative itself, not only in the reservation felt by some members of the drum-head court but also in the subsequent private reflections of the ship's surgeon—reservations and reflections that Melville surely intended the reader to notice and to enlarge upon for himself from a greater critical distance.

informed to understand what is at issue), let us return to our master question, and ask whether it is something intrinsic to the subject matter of moral decision that raises the doubt whether all sufficiently informed intelligences ought to be expected to converge in a sufficiency of cases[33] on a practical judgment of rightness, permissibility, *etc.*, and to converge in such a way that the best explanation of their adherence to the judgment commits even the giver of the explanation to accept it.

Shouldering the onus of proof here,[34] but in anticipation of an equal willingness on the part of those committed to the full realist position, I venture the following answer to this question. We have no assurance, not even ordinary assurance that, always, wherever there is a practical judgment that survives criticism at the level of the reflective, self-critical agent who has attained the distance that seems to him (then and later) to be the right distance, all sufficiently informed intelligences that understand his predicament (and understand it as if from that same distance) will converge on that judgment (or a correction of it) and will converge in a way that leaves everyone who properly explains that convergence with no alternative but to concur in the judgment. The reason why there is a special difficulty in conceiving of such assurance is this. Human interests and concerns are as indefinitely various and heterogeneous as are human predicaments. Even moral interests and concerns are indefinitely various and heterogeneous. Therefore, in a world which was not made for us, and is in any case replete with economic and social conflict as well as conflicts of personality and preference, there is simply no general reason to expect that a common moral consciousness will issue in some rational disposition to single out just one from among all the moral/practical alternatives apparently available in any situation. Where a matter depends on a competition of opposing analogies, one analogy may triumph. There may be no other analogy to back. But why need it *always* be so? (And where it is not, why suppose that the choice between the colourable

---

[33] *E.g.* all or most of the cases where there are practical judgments that we as agents do after criticism *etc.* persist in wishing to affirm, do not regret afterwards, and which other people concur in both at the time and later.

[34] Rather, the onus of making a positive suggestion.

analogies becomes simply indifferent?) Nor is there reason to expect the emergence of any general disposition among men to agree with respect to the question how to go about finding an accommodation in a given case between conflicting demands that are agreed to be real demands. The claims of all true beliefs about how the world is are reconcilable. As we are reminded by the fifth mark of truth (§6 *ad fin.*), everything true must be consistent with everything else that is true. The pieces fit together because they are made for one another. Even when we come to the conclusion that p on the basis of some 'balance of probabilities', we still have to suppose that the truth itself would explain away all the evidence against that conclusion— would show it was not really *counter*-evidence at all: every fact about what stands in front of us must be *reconcilable* with the fact that p and with every other fact that stands in front of us. In contrast, surely the relation of considerations for and against a course of action is unlike the relation between evidence and judgment.[35] We must not expect the discovery of a good course of action to *explain away* the claim of all considerations that support other courses of action. (Indeed when one claim overrides another claim in the determination of a decision to act, we ought *not* to explain away the overridden claim.)[36] If there is no one answer to a practical question whose authoritative revelation can dissipate the force of all other answers, then it is hard to deny that there will be room for different kinds of answers, each answering to a different personal choice of the kind of life to lead, or each

---

[35] Another point against this assimilation—a point in no way proprietary to the underdeterminationist view that I advocate—is that one of these grounding relations is between a *course of action* and its 'pros and cons' and the other is between a *judgment* and its 'pros and cons' (in what is emerging as a different sense of 'pro and con'). On these matters, see also Williams, *op. cit.*, at note 52, p. 129 above.

[36] Or so I think we must acknowledge if we do not believe in a Providence which will secure just compensation for all the claims small and large that an agent is bound to find against if he pursues steadfastly the stringent and narrow supposedly unique path marked out by the temporally unfolding sequence of overriding obligations. Where a philosopher believes in such a Providence because he believes in God, I feel no desire to make fun of this idea. But the curious thing is that almost all philosophers who now write *as if* they subscribed to it are of an utterly secular cast of mind. Anyone who wants to hold onto the idea of Providence and who actually disbelieves in an extramundane God that made us and the world to suit one another (or at least morally to consist with one another) must find some other justification for it.

determining a distinct valuational emphasis. Or so we may hold once we entertain the following reflection. Not only was the world not made for us or to fit our concerns; we have not made our moral concerns (that the world be thus or so) simply in order to fit the world, or even to perfect the accommodation between our very best intentions and that which we shall definitely, despite contingency, be able to achieve. Even if we had the power and the foresight to do this, we might still despise to do so. What else ought we ever to have expected then but a diversity of equally defensible practical conceptions of the good life for man and of the good life for a society?—As well of course as a chaotic profusion of indefensible conceptions of these. This is something we could have worked out for ourselves from within ordinary twentieth century life, even if there had been no anthropologists or historians to tell us what men do or did at remote places or times.

18.    Perhaps the best or most eirenic way to put the difference between me and the strong cognitivist is as follows. He thinks the answer to the question about convergence is favourable to truth oftener than I can feel sure it will. He need not think the condition will be satisfied *wherever* an agent arrives at a practical judgment that survives the critical scrutiny of the agent and those in practical confrontation with him. I for my part do not need to claim that the new condition is *never* satisfied.[37] For, however strong the convergence requirement

---

[37] And, relativist as I may now appear, I do not need to fall into the *vulgar* relativist error that Aurel Kolnai pointed out in the following passage of 'Moral Consensus' (*op. cit.*).

> Since men are not uniformly nothing but moral but always something else as well and many different things also, [relativists conclude that] moralities themselves must be different and at loggerheads with each other. This may appear to relativists all the more plausible as, in fact, tension and conflict between different moral *demands* often arises by reason of circumstances, and is apt to create the illusion of multiple moralities.
> Relativism is guilty of confusing morality with 'ethos', *i.e.* the variable and particular vividness of moral *emphasis* as displayed in locally and chronologically differentiated ideals, idols and ideologies, traditional code-phrasings and fashionable slogans, whose moral tenor is intimately amalgamated with the indefinite multeity of non-moral concerns, particular interests and aspirations, self-loves and selective sympathies, and the never wholly extra-moral but always mixed valuations attached to historically established institutions and emergent projects generally embodied in predominant or unfolding human 'types'.

is, it may be that there are certain practical judgements, especially judgments of the morally prohibitive kind, that pass it easily.[38]

What I have now to add to the reservations I have expressed against unrestricted cognitivism is that our commitment to practical judgments (moral, non-moral, and mixed) and our willingness to follow the course that they mark out for us (corrigibly and revisably) simply cannot lapse at the point where the convergence requirement ceases to be satisfied. To give someone the kind of criticism or advice he can take a live interest in, it may be neither necessary nor sufficient either to excite possible doubts, or to put to rest possible doubts,[39] whether a given judgement (considered, as always, in its proper context) is such that just anyone who really understood it and the circumstances that gave rise to it would accept it and accept it for reasons that committed the explainer himself not to reject the judgement. Nor, again, would one ever give up the search for that which one would oneself be satisfied was the right thing for one to do (here and now) *simply* on the strength of becoming convinced that no answer to the question 'what is it right for him to do?' would ever command principled convergence. The point is scarcely new even among objectivists. Indeed it was insisted upon by Socrates, when he declared to Crito that this conviction that it is unjust to requite evil with evil was the whole basis of his argument against escaping from prison, but then warned Crito:

---

> Relativists err in concluding . . . that ethics cannot be anything but a differential description of kinds of ethos, with or without the addition of the thinker's own personal tastes and arbitrary one-sided preferences.

What I insist, in opposition to one part of this, is only that it is difficult, *pace* Kolnai, to find the whole of the moral in the area where the convergence condition and other conditions upon truth are definitely satisfied. The point where they cease to be satisfied comes before the point where morality passes over into *ethos*. Nor of course is *ethos* itself *more ethos*. It is integral to human life and to moral motivation itself (as Kolnai indeed insists).

[38] Contrast the tenor of Essay III, §10.

[39] Surely, it may be said, it is at least sufficient (however rare this might be) to be able to show that the condition was satisfied. But one has still to find for himself in favour of the judgment. Indeed until he has done so, the condition itself is not yet, strictly speaking, satisfied.

> Look well whether you agree with [this conviction]: for few
> persons do agree to it or ever will: and between those who do
> and those who don't there can be no common deliberation: they
> must of necessity despise each other (Plato, *Crito* 49d).

Behind this uncompromising formulation there lurks a more
general philosophical finding without any special ties to
mutual despising, to intolerance, to irrationalism or to the
moral foundationalism that Socrates sometimes talks as if he
embraces. This is the true thing in the doctrine of cognitive
under-determination—and our elucidation of the concept of
truth (§§3–6) confirms the intuitive appraisal of the point's
relevance to truth. What it does *not* confirm is the supposition
that, wherever it seems that all convictions will fall short of
their aspiration to plain truth (truth being the property which
the second mark is a mark of, and this mark being something
Socrates is prepared to go ahead without), there argument and
criticism must simply fall away.

19.   The realist could scarcely accept quite all of this. Yet it is
still my hope that the formulations (§18 *ad init.*) that precede
the claim I have made last in my opposition to the realist can
serve to diminish mutual incomprehension between the strong
unrestricted position and the weak underdeterminationist
position. Surely there is some sort of resting point here. Yet I
realize that to some of the friends of unrestricted cognitivism
and to moral realists some of what has been said in the last few
sections about what remains to be decided may still appear like
sheer error or blatant irrationalism.

One sort of realist, a utilitarian, for instance, or a neo-
Kantian or some other sort of foundationalist, might say that
the only reason why underdetermination has been allowed to
win through to this point is that I have ignored the possibility
that *moral philosophy itself, e.g.* in the shape of his (the
Kantian's, the Utilitarian's or some other) theory, might take
up the slack that prevents the convergence conditions from
being satisfied; and that, when a more perfect moral philosophy
emerges, human beings will then begin to converge in their
moral beliefs, and will converge in their judgments precisely
because there will then be nothing else to think.[40] To this I
should respond that there is this bare possibility; but as

yet no position has shown signs of mustering even one distinctive, substantial premise that will possess the second mark of truth.

20.  A cognitivist who preferred not to let his objection to my position depend on any particular first order philosophical morality might espouse a very different line of objection: 'You have not in the end denied truth-status to all practical judgments. You have only doubted that ordinary human life can restrict its commitments to those that pass the test of truth. In so far as these commitments outrun what plain truth can sustain, no doubt you will have to say that the empty space is filled on the social level by habit, *ethos*, custom and, on the individual level, by individual character.[41] But this thing that you have to say fills the empty space is itself one part of the very reality to which practical judgments constitute the reponse'. And then he may continue, less plausibly (I think) but filling out the objection as one moral realist has done:

> The target of Winch's article was the *usefulness* of universalisability in moral reasoning; he never claims that two cases which are known to be *exactly* alike can be resolved differently. His point was simply that, when all the evidence is considered, few if any cases will be alike and this is because the character of the agent is a significant element in our understanding of the concrete reality of moral cases. I can understand a man's decision 'through and through' in a case like one I am faced with and yet decide differently. But since I am not just like the

---

[40] Note that professed anti-cognitivists are keenly interested in meeting this condition, *e.g.* R. M. Hare in his recent book *Moral Thinking*. If or when they do meet it, the disputation can be staged about the truth, truth-conditions and declarative meaning of moral judgments.

[41] Cp. E. Pincoffs' 'Quandary Ethics', *Mind* 1971:

> We must ask, not how we find ground in the void, but why we think that we are in one. Who are 'we' who are supposed to be in a void? Are we not concerned to find answers to our repeated demands for grounds? We are not morally featureless, but we have concerns. The intuitions are ours, the discoveries ours, the introspection ours . . . we cannot describe the problem by describing an anonymous collision situation. Aristotle did not give open lectures. St Paul did not write open letters. When they used the word 'we' they spoke from within a community of expectations and ideals: a community within which character was cultivated. In part, the problem of the featureless 'we' arises out of a sense that somehow a universal ethic must be created.

other man the cases are different; and thus the realities are different.[42]

I doubt the interpretation of Winch. Certainly my own has placed no such emphasis on a 'moral realist' component in Winch's thinking, stressing rather Winch's rejection of Sidgwickian universalizability and Winch's special sort of subjectivism. But the pressing difficulty is that, if it is by these means that we meet the requirement of convergence in the belief that *p* among those who properly understand the question to which *p* is the answer, and if we count among the facts or realities of the case such things as the very dispositions that sustain the belief that he ought to X, then the question that the agent is deciding will diverge from that which would-be convergers are answering. The objector speaks as if Vere could treat his own character, and his duty and function as a naval captain holding the King's Commission and his view of that duty and function, as among the realities of the case. Certainly these things were settled facts up to the time of deliberation, and *that* is significant—highly significant. But for purposes of the future *from then on* even these things needed reappraisal or confirmation and renewal. Even if Vere would really have put his commission at risk in not proceeding so summarily against Billy Budd (because there was some just appreciable risk of indiscipline or disorder ensuing, for which he would have been held responsible), well—in the name of natural justice, never mind Vere's mental dispositions or the orderly unfolding of his life-plan (doomed in any case, to judge from the story)—perhaps that risk ought to have been taken. And the thought that it ought to have been taken was open to Vere. For the purposes of his deliberation, one of the pressing questions was whether he *should* treat his own life and character and his attitude to his naval duty and function as boundary conditions for the problem, or should treat them as things that were at least in principle and in the last resort still open. Certainly they were not mere *data*. Only a man demented by the conduct of warfare could think of them like that! Nobody who wants to retain the right not to acquiesce in Vere's decision—indeed

[42] S. Guttenplan 'Moral Realism and Moral Dilemmas', *Proceedings of the Aristotelian Society* (1979/80), p. 74.

nobody who takes Vere seriously as a moral agent or whose concurrence in either answer is worth anything—can simply take these things as simply 'given among its realities'.

21. It may be objected that, if I say this and if I accept the subjectivist account of what fills the space in practical judgment that plain truth cannot always fill, then, however much I qualify Winch's account in order to make more room for the criticism of decisions that are as indefensible as I think Vere's was, I still end up in a position of rank irrationalism. For, in effect, I have been willing to allow that, at least in theory, there can be a pair of cases $C_1$, $C_2$, like this. In $C_1$ and $C_2$ the circumstances (in the strict and delimited sense of 'circumstances') are exactly alike, and all the further facts about the agent that he may *legitimately* treat as fixed for purposes of his deliberation are alike; but the agent decides in $C_1$ that it is right for him to V: and in $C_2$ he decides[43] that it is right for him to W (where V-ing and W-ing exclude one another); and our own verdict, after scrutiny of everything in the circumstances and scrutiny of all other deliberatively admissible facts, is that we endorse for $C_1$ 'It is right for the agent to V', and we endorse for $C_2$ 'It is right for the agent to W', the whole difference in our endorsements for $C_1$ and $C_2$ being owed to a difference in each agent's own finding.

As a limiting case, I am indeed committed to this. In the presence of any case where neither finding is open to the sort of decisive criticism we have found we can mount of Vere's, and where the agent's actual finding is one we can make sense of (if only retrospectively) in the light of what the agent becomes, I am prepared to treat this finding as morally decisive of what was right for him. But I have explained what draws me in this direction, namely my sense of the scarcity of unique solutions to problems of individual or social choice.[44] And I have made the corresponding qualification to the doctrine of moral cognitivism.

The position may seem *arbitrary*. Surely there must be

---

[43] He who decides is either this same agent, or another agent who is not distinguishable in any of the relevant respects such as the capacities, obligations, commitments, etc., that deliberation can treat as fixed.

something about case $C_1$ that made that turn out the other way and differently from $C_2$. Perhaps. Let me not quarrel here with this well-worn dogma. But that which explains the difference in the outcome need not have any place in a rational reconstruction of the facts that were *deliberatively admissible*. In which case it need not impinge upon our grounds for endorsing one verdict in $C_1$ and the other verdict in $C_2$. Our grounds relate to the subjectivities of the agents in $C_1$ and $C_2$.[45]

The position may seem *self-contradictory*. But it is not. There is no question of one agent's coming to both conclusions, and our endorsing each conclusion! And if we imagine two different agents $x_1$ and $x_2$ in $C_1$ and $C_2$, then our verdicts are not given in the form 'It would be right to V [or to W]' but 'It would be right for $x_1$ to V' and 'It would be right for $x_2$ to W'. If it seems to my critic to be self-contradictory for us to issue these verdicts where the circumstances are exactly alike and everything else that can be treated as fixed for purposes of deliberation is also alike, then this critic is taking some substantive thesis of universalizability as a *logical* thesis. Since I do not take it so, I suppose I have to suggest that he should argue more convincingly for the logical claim.[46] Until such time as this happens, I am apt to take him as clinging grimly, and against all sense of what is possible in philosophy, to an idea which has nothing to do with logic (a miss is as good as a mile where infringement of the law of non-contradiction is concerned)—the idea that the discovery of a 'universal ethic' is the only proper role for practical philosophy.

---

[44] I hope I have also explained well enough already why even in such limiting cases I think it wrong to rush in with the verdict 'a tie'. I note here that Winch spoke of self-*discovery*, in preference to self-*determination*. But he deliberately blurs the effect of this by refusing to distinguish the process of discovery from that of decision—and in a manner presumably most unwelcome to unrestricted cognitivists. In dialogue with these or moral realists it is better I believe to say that the place where self-discovery comes in is that it supervenes on the deliberated decision and need not be part of the build-up to that decision. One's nature influences how a situation strikes one, no doubt. It can help to explain the decision. But it is not *part of what strikes one* in that situation.

[45] Cp. E. Pincoffs, *op. cit.*

[46] I note in passing my agreement in this with Thomas Nagel who is an objectivist, a cognitivist and a moral realist. He formulates a comparable condition as what he calls *a condition of generality*. ('This is the condition that if something provides a reason for a particular individual to do something, then there is a general form of that reason

22.    One more problem. (See clause (b) of the statement given in §1, final paragraph.) If this is what subjectivism involves when it addresses the problem of truth, drawing one part of its support from considerations that derive from value pluralism, then what does the subjectivist critic who 'endorses' the one verdict in case $C_1$ and the other verdict in case $C_2$ 'endorse' them *as*? As *true-for-the-agent*? As *true for the agent then, in those circumstances*?[47] We have long since dismissed these suggestions. *True* does not cohere well in these combinations. But truth can still be its own plain self in the combination 'endorsing the proposition that *p* as the best approximation to truth we shall find in this kind of matter'. (And other formulations are surely possible.) What changes here, if this is the dimension in which judgments are assessed, is not the idea of truth but the ideas of endorsing, accepting, believing, assenting that remain open to anyone who has appreciated the possibility of cognitive under-determination and charted the extent of essential contestability in human affairs. The attitudes that remain possible for such a person are no doubt cooler than those which were possible before this was seen. But they need not be negative or irresolute. They can consist in ordinary consciousness with the commitment to some recognizable form of ordinary morality. And they do not thrust against the limits of significant language.[48] It is not moral scepticism but this sort of subjectivism, oriented towards truth but tilted to allow for essential contestability, that will be the real

---

which applies to anyone else in comparable circumstances'), but then he remarks, in a manner that seems to me most sensible, that this condition is 'not tautological', 'is a rather strong condition which may be false, or true only of some kinds of reasons' (p. 101, *op. cit.*).

I should stress that the failure of this condition would not necessarily impugn the possibility of publicly intelligible criticism of an agent's response to a predicament, even where there is no unique best. If criticism is threatened, under this condition, with a certain restlessness, well, this is one part of what we have in mind when we speak of essential contestability. But a matter can be essentially contestable without there being any contestability about the inadequacy of certain responses to it.

[47] Or as *assertible*, though not true? Cp. Essay III. In the light of our characterization of truth, and the difference now further elaborated between evaluation and practical judgment, the suggestion now seems pointless, and (worse) calculated to blur similarities and differences that are interesting and important.

[48] I take the phrase from Wittgenstein's 'Lecture on Ethics', *Philosophical Review*, 1965.

foundation of any philosophical liberalism that can make out its title in the secular age to be the philosophical inheritor of the glorious achievements of toleration in the age of religion. It is the corresponding attitude that will be the foundation of any political pluralism that can distance us even a short way from the noise of ideological conflict, and might in the field of international politics (if we were very lucky) mitigate terror with salutary boredom.

# V

# A Sensible Subjectivism?*

I cannot see how to refute the arguments for
the subjectivity of ethical values, but I find
myself incapable of believing that all that is
wrong with wanton cruelty is that I don't like
it.

BERTRAND RUSSELL

1. Usually—if only for the purpose of having the position
summarily dismissed as soon as possible—the doctrine of
subjectivism is reported as claiming that '$x$ is good' or '$x$ is
right' or '$x$ is beautiful', as uttered by speaker S, says that S
approves of $x$, or that $x$ induces in S a certain sentiment of
approbation.

The first and perhaps most obvious objection, that 'good',
'right', and 'beautiful' do not themselves mean the same, might
be countered by distinguishing different species of approbative
sentiment. But there is a more familiar and more considerable
second objection: at least when it is given in this form,
subjectivism makes a difficulty for itself about disagreement.
If, where John says $x$ is good, Philip denies that $x$ is good, Philip
is not on this account necessarily disagreeing with John.
Certainly, if they are disagreeing, the purported subjectivist
analysis of '$x$ is good' does not really bring out what they are
disagreeing about.

To attend to this fault, the doctrine might be modified, by a

* Not previously published. I am indebted to Anthony Price for detailed comments
on the penultimate version. In notes 17, 21, and 27, acknowledgement is made to
unpublished writing of Hidé Ishiguro, Michael Smith and Edward Hussey. The essay
was originally conceived as a justification and expansion of the claims made in 'Truth,
Invention, and the Meaning of Life' at §V (= §6 of Essay III in this volume). In the time
that has elapsed since that essay was written I have benefited especially (if insufficiently)
from reading Warren S. Quinn's essay 'Moral and other Realisms: some initial Difficulties' in Goldman and Kim (eds.), *Values and Morals* (Dordrecht: Reidel, 1978). The
*strictly* valuational predicates singled out in §4 of Essay III will be the most conspicuous
verifiers, if there are any, of the subjectivist doctrine to be developed here.

shift from *me* to *us*, so as to claim that '*x* is good', as uttered by John, says that *x* is approved of by those whom John calls 'us'. If Philip is one of these persons, there can then be disagreement between John and Philip. But now the risk is that the disagreement in question will appear as merely sociological, whereas the disagreement that always needed to be accounted for and made room for was not disagreement about what we value, but disagreement *in valuation*. Rival attempts to speak for us as a community (if that is how the subjectivist ought to see disagreement) cannot be plausibly reduced to rival accounts of what, if anything, the community does already say.

2. Emotivists may be expected to butt in at this point to suggest that disagreement in valuation can be seen as disagreement in attitude *expressed* (Stevenson). But this suggestion, and the whole idea of an emotive meaning reckoned separately from cognitive content, does insufficient justice to our feeling that divergence of attitude must itself be founded in something, and reflect a prior or coeval disagreement in something not itself reducible without residue to emotive attitude (*i.e.* in something the sentence is *about*, which is not so far accounted for). Even if it were plainer what emotive meaning was and clearer how it could work in concert with ordinary meaning (and more evident that in the end one will have to settle for it), there would still be something deeply unsatisfying about the suggestion.[1]

3. At this point I think we ought to feel the need to look again at the subjectivists who wrote before G.E. Moore's celebrated and influential critique of subjectivism—and especially at Hume, an author whom Moore cautiously refrains from mentioning by name in this connexion.[2]

---

[1] The dissatisfaction was of course anticipated by C.L. Stevenson, but not, one may feel, answered by him. *Cf.* 'The Emotive Meaning of Ethical Terms', *Mind* 1937, especially page 30.

[2] See *Philosophical Studies* (Routledge, 1922) pp. 329–339; *Ethics* (Home University Library, Thornton Butterworth, London, 1912) Chapters III, IV. For the apparently paralysing effect of this critique, see Russell's 'Notes on PHILOSOPHY January 1960' *Philosophy* vol. 35, 1960, pp. 146–7, and his difficulty, surely consequential upon Moore's discussion, in seeing his way past the dilemma I have quoted at the head of this essay and shall discuss in §18 below.

In so far as Hume ever came anywhere near to suggesting a semantical account of 'x is good/right/beautiful' (which is not, one may think, very near—even at the points where he speaks of 'defining' this or that), it may seem that the best proposal implicit in his theory of valuation is that this sentence says that x is the kind of thing to arouse a certain sentiment of approbation. This is not my approbation, or your approbation, or Hume's or society's approbation. If we want a form of words that can be the focus of real valuational disagreement as it was open to Hume to conceive this, then we do best *not to specify* whose approbation. x is simply such as to arouse that sentiment. (Note that it can still count against 'x is good' that x in fact arouses a sentiment of approbation in nobody. Just as the claim that x is desirable falls into difficulty if nobody at all desires x. This is a point that one may register without making the error John Stuart Mill is often accused of making about 'desired' and 'desirable'. Compare Essay IV, §6, mark (2).)

Not only is such subjectivism free from Moore's well-worn criticism about disagreement. It comes close to escaping Moore's earlier 'open question' argument. If x is such as to merit a certain feeling of approbation [when taken as one among the fs], the question is not *wide* open whether or not x is [a] good [f]. (For if x is such as to arouse that sentiment, this surely need not be without influence upon the will.)

Hume might have been easier to satisfy on this point than Moore would have been. But since the escape is still a rather narrow one, perhaps we should consider another suggestion that Hume could have made. If he had considered a question he does not consider and if he had disclaimed any intention to provide analyses of the ordinary terms of approbation, then Hume could have said that x is good/right/beautiful if and only if x is such as to make a certain sentiment of approbation *appropriate*.[3]

4.    It may appear that this second account of Hume's theory makes it viciously circular in a way that it previously was not.

---

[3] Compare John McDowell's discussion of the phrase 'such as to merit' in 'Values and Secondary Qualities' in *Morality and Objectivity*, ed. Ted Honderich, (London: Routledge and Kegan Paul, 1985), pp. 117–120. Compare also A.J. Ayer, *Freedom and Morality* (Oxford 1984), p. 30.

But I reply that, on a proper understanding of the point of subjectivism and its having no need to supplant valuational by non-valuational language, the circularity is benign (see below and §9); and that in any case no *new* circularity has been introduced. There was already a kind of circle before this adjustment was made. What after all is a sentiment of approbation? (Or if the point of the word 'certain', sometimes inserted by Hume, is that there are different, phenomenologically distinguishable kinds of approbation, numerous enough to differentiate the good, right, and beautiful, then what *are* sentiments of approbation?) Surely a sentiment of approbation cannot be identified except by its association with the thought or feeling that x is good (or right or beautiful) and with the various considerations in which that thought can be grounded, given some particular item and context, *in situ*.

Whether such circularities constitute a difficulty for subjectivism depends entirely on what the subjectivist takes himself to be attempting. If we treat it as already known and given that '*x* is good' (or 'right' or 'beautiful') is *fully analysable*, and if '*x* is such as to arouse the sentiment of approbation' (or '*x* is such as to make that sentiment appropriate') is the subjectivist's best effort in the analytical direction, and if this equivalent fails to deliver any proper analysis, then subjectivism is some sort of failure.[4] Certainly. But, even if classical subjectivists have given this impression to those who want to conceive of all philosophy as analysis, analysis as such never needed to be their real concern. What traditional subjectivists have really wanted to convey is not so much definition as commentary. Chiefly they have wanted to persuade us that, when we consider whether or not *x* is good or right or beautiful, there is no appeal to anything that is more fundamental than actually possible human sentiments

---

[4] Observe that by this failure, if it were a failure, nothing would have been established against the *truth* of the biconditional '*x* is good just if *x* is such as to arouse a certain sentiment of approbation'. Consider the statement 'If *x* is the same as *y* then, if *y* is the same as *z*, then *x* is the same as *z*.' As a contribution to an analysis of the meaning of 'same' (or 'identical') this is circular because it employs the word or a mere synonym. But, in pointing this out as a defect in the sentence when it is put forward within an analysis, we do nothing to show the falsity of the sentence. Indeed it might well serve in a partial elucidation of sameness. For elucidation, as contrasted with analysis, see §§2–4 of Essay IV.

—a declaration that seems both contentious and plausible (but more plausible when we take into account the intentionality of the sentiments, cp. §14–15). Circularity as such is no objection to it, provided that the offending formulation is also *true*. But what use (I shall be asked) is such a circular formulation? My answer is that, by tracing out such a circle, the subjectivist hopes to elucidate the concept of value by displaying it in its actual involvement with the sentiments. One would not, according to him, have sufficiently elucidated what value is *without* that detour.

5.    In all these matters, an analogy with colour is suggestive. '*x* is red if and only if *x* is such as to give, under certain conditions specifiable as normal, a certain visual impression' naturally raises the question 'which visual impression?' And that question attracts the answer 'an impression as of seeing something red', which reintroduces *red*. But this finding of circularity scarcely amounts to proof that we can after all appeal to something beyond visual impressions to determine colour authoritatively. It only shows that 'red' stands for something not in this sort of way *analysable*. Surely it is simply obvious that colour is something subjective; and just as obvious that the unanalysability of colour words represents no difficulty in that claim.[5] The mere unanalysability or indefinability of colour terms does not release us from the task of finding means to elucidate these terms in a way that will bring out their subjectivity. Until one has done this much, one has not even reminded anyone of what he or she already knows about what colours are.

---

[5] The analogy can be taken one point further. When asked what red is like, we can say how dark a pure unsaturated shade of red is compared with how light a pure shade of yellow is. This doesn't say what red is. But, while presupposing our colour categories, it does say something more about what red is like. Similarly, given a particular *x* and the question of its title to have some particular determination of good ascribed to it, we can say some more about what it is about things like *x* that makes them such as to arouse a particular species of sentiment of approbation when taken as among the *f*s. Explanations as such do not give out altogether; but those we find will tend to *presuppose* some relevant standard for thinking about the merits and demerits of *x* and things like *x* as among *f*s.

For the non-significance of unanalysability, see further Essay III §8, paragraph 3.

How then, without traducing it or treating it unfairly as a definition or an analysis, are we to develop and amplify the subjectivist claim that $x$ is good if and only if $x$ is such as to arouse/such as to make appropriate the sentiment of approbation? There are two main ways.

6.   The first way is to follow Hume's lead and say that, just as in the colour case 'the appearance of objects in daylight to the eye of a man in health is denominated their real and true colour, even while colour is . . . merely a phantasm of the senses',[6] so value is merely a phantasm of the feelings or a 'gilding or staining' of 'natural objects with the colours borrowed from internal sentiment',[7] (or in terms alien to Hume but in one way illuminating, value is the intentional object of *une certaine folie à presque tous*); and that to the extent that there is a standard of correctness in morals, this is determined by the verdicts of whoever judges 'most coolly',[8] 'with the least prejudice', and on the basis of the fullest information—all of which, 'if we consider the matter aright', is 'a question of fact, not of sentiment'.[9] When men argue and dispute in valuation, and when they succeed in instructing one another, what they are really seeking to do is to approximate to the verdicts of that judge.

What is remarkable here, among many other merits in Hume's explicit defence of this position as it applies in the case of aesthetic taste, is his anxiety to describe and make room for something that an ordinary or vulgar sceptic would simply deny or explain away. This is the remarkable degree of consensus that is sometimes achieved in the view that is reached about works of art and literature that survive the test of time:

> The same Homer, who pleased at Athens and Rome two thousand years ago, is still admired at Paris and at London. All the changes of climate, government, religion, and language have not been able to obscure his glory. Authority or prejudice

[6] 'Of the Standard of Taste', paragraph 12.
[7] *Inquiry concerning Principles of Morals*, Appendix I.
[8] See (*e.g.*) Hume's essay 'Of the Delicacy of Taste and of Passion'.
[9] Cp. 'Standard' *op. cit.* paragraphs 24–5.

may give a temporary vogue to a bad poet or orator; but his reputation will never be durable or general. When his compositions are examined by posterity or foreigners, the enchantment is dissipated and his faults appear in their true colours. On the contrary, a real genius, the longer his works endure, and the more wide they are spread, the more sincere is the admiration which they meet with.[10]

Hume contends that for a subjectivist simply to declare that 'all sentiment is right because sentiment has reference to nothing beyond itself'—which might seem a little close to the position he had himself taken up in the *Treatise*—is for him to invite charges of advancing an 'extravagant paradox, or rather a palpable absurdity'.

It is one of the strengths of Hume's subjectivism that he distances himself from this paradox and works so hard to show how a standard of correctness is possible in taste and morals and to explain our many and frequent lapses from it. No plausible or life-like subjectivism can do less. It is however a difficulty in his execution of the task—and a further difficulty in extending Hume's account of the aesthetic case to the general case and the moral case in particular—that he has to place so much weight at certain points on an analogy between aesthetic taste and ordinary sensory (gustatory, *etc.*) taste:

> Some particular forms or qualities, from the original structure of the internal fabric, are calculated to please, and others to displease, and if they fail of their effect in any particular instance, it is from some apparent defect or imperfection in the organ. A man in a fever would not insist on his palate as able to decide concerning flavours; nor would one affected with the jaundice pretend to give a verdict with regard to colours. In each creature there is a sound and a defective state; and the former alone can be supposed to afford us a true standard of taste and sentiment. If, in the sound state of the organ, there be an entire or a considerable uniformity of sentiment among men, we may thence derive an idea of the perfect beauty.

[10] Paragraph 11. Compare the passage quoted in Essay IV from Longinus *On the Sublime* Ch. VIII, 'when men of different pursuits, lives, ambitions, ages, languages, hold identical views on one and the same subject, then that verdict which results so to speak from a concert of discordant elements makes our faith in the object of admiration strong and unassailable'.

For the pleasures of the table such claims might just pass. But our chances of making the requisite analogy with an organ of perception, or of something a bit like an organ of perception (a sound judge, or organism or whatever) first weaken and then disappear altogether as we pass with Hume from the gustatory to the aesthetic-perceptual and thence to the aesthetic in general and the moral. And it is not enough, so long as we take the problem on Hume's official terms, to respond to this problem as Hume does (in effect) when he answers the question where the true judges and critics are to be found 'whose joint verdict is the true standard of taste and beauty', by saying that:

> Where doubts occur men can do no more than in other disputable questions which are submitted to their understanding: they must produce the best arguments that their invention suggests to them; they must acknowledge a true and decisive standard to exist somewhere, to wit real existence and matter of fact; and they must have indulgence to such as differ from them in their appeals to this standard. It is sufficient for our present purposes if we have proved that the taste of all individuals is not upon an equal footing, and that some men in general however difficult to be pitched upon will be acknowledged by universal sentiment to have a preference above others.[11]

For one happy to speak the language of objects and their properties (as well as of their judges) such a stance may be sustainable. (See below §8.) But for Hume's own purposes the answer is not good enough—not so much because of the epistemological difficulty (which here, as always, one must learn to live with), but because, in the absence of any possible story about something comparable to sound organs of perception, it leaves us with insufficient grasp, and an insufficient account of our actual grasp (which I take to have regard for the properties attributed to objects within the critic's or judge's sentiment of approbation) of what *constitutes* a good critic or judge.

7.   If Hume holds true to his doctrine that values are merely phantasms of the feelings, or gildings or stainings with colours

---

[11] Paragraph 25.

borrowed from internal sentiment, then strictly speaking, he must never look to objects and properties themselves in characterizing the difference between good and bad judgments in taste and morals. (If he could do this then we should not need the independent standard, or the 'sound organ' story.) So Hume looks instead to the *condition of the judge* (his 'strong sense, united to delicate sentiment, improved by practice, perfected by comparison, cleared of all prejudice'), and this he then takes himself to need to see as (in his terms) a real existence or matter of fact. So that it suddenly appears that, if we pass over the properties of the object itself, then a life-like philosophical subjectivism requires a *non*-subjective foundation as well as the support of a substantial conception of a nearly homogeneous human nature.

This paradox deserves to be conjoined with another kind of puzzle. Our subjective reactions to objects or events will often impose groupings upon them that have no purely naturalistic rationale. (That, in a way, is the point of subjectivism—cp. §8 below.) But, at least for subjectivists who are serious in the fashion of Hume, there are good and bad ways of effecting such groupings. We are not simply to fire off *at random* in our responses to things. A feeble jest or infantile practical joke does not deserve to be grouped with the class of things that a true judge would find genuinely funny. How then in the case of a responsible judge are we to envisage Hume's process of gilding and staining? When the mind of such a judge spreads itself upon objects, does it first determine that *x* really belongs in the non-natural[12] class of genuine specimens of the funny—first determine the similarity-link of *x* with items a true judge would find funny—and then, when all is over bar the shouting, 'gild and stain' *x*, or 'project' or 'discharge itself' upon *x*?[13] That seems a ludicrous suggestion. Is it not rather

---

[12] For 'non-natural' cp. the explanation given by G. E. Moore in *Principia Ethica*, pp. 40–41 ('By nature then I do mean . . . that which is the subject matter of the natural sciences, and also of psychology'); also my *Sameness & Substance* (Oxford: Blackwell, 1981), p. 183 with note 40.

[13] Cp. *Inquiry* (Appendix I) '. . . *after* every circumstance, every relation is known, the understanding has no further room to operate, nor any object on which it could employ itself. The approbation or blame which *then* ensues cannot be the work of the judgment, but of the heart . . .' (italics mine).

that there is something in the object that is *made for* the sentiment it would occasion in a qualified judge, and it brings down the sentiment upon the object as so qualified? Surely this feature of $x$, whatever it is, impinges on perception and sentiment simultaneously; and the time has come to enrich our ideas about what can fall under *each* of perception and sentiment in their engagement with the object.[14]

8.   Does the subjectivism that we found reason in §4 above to search after admit of some alternative formulation? Let us seize for this purpose upon a Humean suggestion that has no clear place in his official theory:

> It must be allowed that there are certain qualities in objects which are fitted by nature to produce particular . . . feelings.[15]

In Hume's official theory, this is not meant to count against the Humean denial that virtue, viciousness, merit, *etc.* are in the object itself. But let us now abandon Hume's aspiration to secure the standard of correctness in valuation from outside the domain of values, or by sole reference to the qualified judge. And let us restore to its proper place the ordinary idea in its ordinary construal that the criterion for a good judge is that he is apt to get things right. (If questions of value were not questions of real existence or matters of fact, then how could the criterion for being a good judge have that status?)

---

[14] Something similar is conceded—indeed insisted upon—in Richard Wollheim's psycho-analytically motivated enrichment of subjectivism in *The Sheep and the Ceremony* (Cambridge University Press, 1981), and in Essay VI ('Art & Evaluation') in the second, expanded edition of *Art and its Objects* (Cambridge University Press, 1980). If anything at all puzzles me in this treatment, it is only how it can see itself (if it does) as able to resist the attractions of the alternative version of subjectivism that is sketched in §8 and further refined in §12 below. See also in this connexion Thomas Reid, Essay VIII, *Essays on the Intellectual Powers of Man* (Edinburgh, 1785).

[15] Hume, *op. cit.*, paragraph 16. Compare and contrast Thomas Reid's insistence upon the point, in opposition to the view he complained had become 'a fashion among modern philosophers', ('even those who hold it, find themselves obliged to use language that contradicts it'):

> This excellence [in an air in music] is not in me; it is in the music. But the pleasure it gives is not in the music; it is in me. Perhaps I cannot say what it is in the tune that pleases my ear, as I cannot say what it is in a sapid body that pleases my palate; but there is a quality in the sapid body which pleases my palate, and I call it a delicious taste; and there is a quality in the tune that pleases my taste, and I call it a fine or excellent air. (*op. cit.*, chapter 1, §1.)

Suppose that objects that regularly please or help or amuse us . . . or harm or annoy or vex us . . . in various ways come to be grouped together by us under various categories or classifications to which we give various avowedly anthropocentric names; and suppose they come to be grouped together as they are precisely *because* they are such as to please, help, amuse us, . . . or harm, annoy, vex us . . . in their various ways. There will be then no saying, very often, what properties these names stand for independently of the reactions they provoke. (The point of calling this position subjectivism is that the properties in question are explained by reference to the reactions of human subjects.) But equally—at least when the system of properties and reactions diversifies, complicates and enriches itself—there will often be no saying exactly *what* reaction a thing with the associated property will provoke without direct or indirect allusion to the property itself. Amusement for instance is a reaction we have to characterize by reference to its proper object, via something perceived as funny (or incongruous or comical or whatever). There is no object-independent and property-independent, 'purely phenomenological' or 'purely introspective' account of amusement. And equally there is no saying what exactly the funny is without reference to laughter or amusement or kindred reactions. Why should we expect there to be such an independent account?[16]

Of course, when we dispute whether $x$ is really funny, there is a whole wealth of considerations and explanations we can adduce, and by no means all of them have to be given in terms simply synonymous or interdefinable with 'funny'. We can do a little better than say that the funny is that which makes people laugh. (Since laughter can come about in quite other ways, no doubt that is just as well.) What is improbable in the extreme is that, either singly or even in concert, further explanations will ever add up to a *reduction* of the funny or serve to characterize it in purely natural terms (terms that pull their weight in our theoretical-cum-explanatory account of the mechanisms of the

---

[16] Indeed how could there be? By hypothesis, the linked properties and responses we are speaking of are arrived at by a historical process. How then could these things be *defined*? (Cp. Nietzsche, *Genealogy of Morals* II. xiii, cited at pp. 67–8.)

It is along the lines of the speculations in the text that I should explicate the metaphor of properties and sentiments being 'made for one another'.

natural world). If so, the predicate 'funny' is an irreducibly subjective predicate. These diverse supporting considerations will however serve another purpose. By means of them, one person can improve another's grasp of the concept of the funny; and one person can improve another's focus or discrimination of what *is* funny. Furthermore, the process can be a collaborative one, without either of the participants to a dialogue counting as the absolutely better judge. The test of improvement in this process of mutual instruction and improvement can be at least partially internal to the perceptions of its participants. For, as Protagoras might (almost) have said, after the process has begun, those who participate in it may report not only that they discriminate more keenly, make more decisions and are better satisfied with the classifications and subclassifications they now effect, but also that they get more and more cognitive-cum-affective satisfaction in their own responses.[17] Finer perceptions can both intensify and refine responses. Intenser responses can further heighten and refine perceptions. And more and more refined responses can lead to the further and finer and more variegated or more intense responses *and* perceptions.

9.    When this point is reached, a system of anthropocentric properties and human responses has surely taken on a life of its own. Civilization has begun. One may surmise that at any stage in the process some <property, response> pairs will and some will not prove susceptible of refinement, amplification and extension. One may imagine that some candidate pairs do and some do not relate in a reinforceable, satisfying way to the subjectivity of human life at a given time. Some pairs are such that refinement of response leads to refinement of perception and *vice versa*. Others are not. Some are and some are not capable of serving in the process of interpersonal education, instruction and mutual enlightenment. Those pairs that do have this sort of advantage, we may expect to catch on and survive, and then to evolve further, generate further <property, response> pairs and make room for the discovery of yet further

---

[17] Cp. Plato *Theaetetus* 166–7. A similar point is urged by Hidé Ishiguro in an unpublished manuscript, and made out in intriguing detail for the application of the Japanese predicate 'monono awaré'.

properties that lie at a progressively greater distance from specific kinds of affect. Those pairs that do not have this sort of viability will no doubt fall by the wayside.

If we see matters in this sort of way, we are surely not committed to suppose that the properties that figure within these <property, response> pairs will bear to natural properties any relation of supervenience that could be characterized in terms that were both general and illuminating of the particular properties in question. Rather they will be primitive, *sui generis*, incurably anthropocentric, and as unmysterious as any properties will ever be to us.[18]

Now, however, in order to embrace the great majority of the valuational predicates in common use, there is need to make room in the story for at least one further complication. Suppose that a point has been reached where a <property, response> pair is well established, the response is corrigible by reference to the question whether whatever is required for the presence of the property is present, and various supplementary considerations have become available that make possible the criticism, explanation, and vindication of attitudes and responses to a given thing. Suppose therefore that we are past the stage at which the critics of classical subjectivism like to see the position as stuck, where the non-accidental occurrence of some simple response is seen as simply sufficient for the presence of the property. (That is the stage where it can be said that any actual nausea caused by *x* suffices to prove that *x* is nauseating, and the claim may be preserved against doubt or difficulty by simple restriction—'*x* is nauseating *for John* even if not *for Philip*', or as in Heraclitus' example 'Sea water is good *for fishes* and most poisonous *for men*'.) Suppose then that the language

---

[18] This is not to deny of course that, in a given context with a given object, evaluative properties will rub shoulders with, and have relations of compossibility and non-compossibility with, other properties. That is the normal condition of properties from different ranges converging upon a single object. But this familiar circumstance will shed no particular light upon value-properties either in particular or in general.

In deference to established philosophical usage, I use the word 'property' here and throughout to denominate what predicates stand for, instead of using the Fregean word 'concept' (which I should have greatly preferred). On this point, and the reality of properties (concepts), see the defence-cum-amendment of Frege's doctrine given in my article 'The Sense and Reference of Predicate Expressions', *Philosophical Quarterly*, July 1984.

of evaluation is past the point at which some semi-valuational predicates (such as the predicates like 'nauseating' that we can qualify by explicit relativization) have stuck. Then something else also becomes possible. Instead of fixing on an object or class of objects and arguing about what response or responses they are such as to evoke, we can fix on a response—one that we value or disvalue for itself or value or disvalue for what it is a response to—and then argue about what the marks are of the property that the response itself is made for. And without serious detriment to the univocity of the predicate, it can now become essentially contestable what a thing has to be like for there to be any reason to accord that particular appellation to it and correspondingly contestable what the extension is of the predicate.[19] (This was part of the point of the end of §3.)

Once we have the possibility of an attitude's being held relatively fixed, the attitude's being paired with some reciprocally appropriate property that is made for it, and its being essentially contestable what the marks are of the property, we shall have a sketch for an explanation of something that cognitivists have said too little about. We can explain the phenomenon that Stevenson (who was not the first to notice it—cp. Plato *Euthyphro* 8d, Aristotle *Nicomachean Ethics* 1107a, though Stevenson was first to see it so speech-functionally) called the 'magnetism' of value terms. This is the same phenomenon as Hume notices in the second and third paragraphs of 'Of the Standard of Taste'

> There are certain terms in every language which import blame, and others praise, and all men who use the same tongue must agree in their application of them. Every voice is united in applauding elegance, propriety, simplicity, spirit in writing, and in blaming fustian, affectation, coldness, and false brilliancy. But when critics come to particulars, this seeming unanimity vanishes; and it is found that they had affixed a very different meaning to their expressions. In all matters of opinion and science it is different ... The word *virtue*, with its equivalent in every tongue, implies praise: as that of *vice* does blame; and no man without the most obvious and grossest impropriety could affix reproach to a term which in general

---

[19] See *Longer Note* 19.

acceptation is understood in a good sense or bestow applause
where the idiom requires disapprobation . . .

No philosophy of value can ignore this phenomenon. Stevenson
tries to account for it by his doctrine of emotive meanings.
Richard Hare would approach the phenomenon by characterizing the meaning of value words in terms of their commendatory function. If what I have just been saying is
anywhere near right, however, perhaps we need not go to these
lengths or involve ourselves in the difficulties they involve. If a
property and an attitude are made for one another, it will be
strange for one to use the term for the property if he is in no way
party to the attitude and there is simply no chance of his finding
that the item in question has the property. But if he is no
stranger to the attitude and the attitude is favourable, it will be
the most natural thing in the world if he regards it as a matter of
keen argument what it takes for a thing to count as having the
property that the attitude is paired with.

10. If we imagine that what the moralist or aesthetician
always confronts is the end-product of a long and complicated
evolutionary process of the sort I have described, we shall
certainly find ethical naturalism an unattractive position (at
least if we mean by naturalism what Moore started out meaning,
cp. note 12), and we may well find subjectivism an overwhelmingly attractive one. If so, then I think we ought to prefer the
second of our two formulations, that is the one described in
§8-9 above. There is still place for the sentient subject in our
subjectivism—this is a subjectivism of subjects and properties
*mutually* adjusted. But if we despair of letting the whole matter
of correctness depend on the analogy between a sound, healthy
sense-organ and a sound judge or organism, then we shall need
to give up the idea of achieving any simple or single statement
of the standard of correctness along the lines envisaged by Hume
(or the lines sometimes envisaged by Aristotle, cp. *NE* 107a2).
In which case we must keep faith in another way with Hume's desire to maintain the sovereignty of subjects simultaneously with
the distinction between sound and mistaken judgment. We
shall do this by insisting that *genuinely* [funny/appalling/
shocking/consoling/reassuring/disgusting/pleasant/delightful/
. . .] things are things that not only [amuse/appal/shock/

console/reassure/disgust/please/delight/ . . .] but have these effects precisely because they *are* [funny/appalling/shocking/consoling/reassuring/disgusting/pleasant/delightful/. . .][20]— at the same time insisting that this 'because' introduces an explanation that both explains and justifies. (In *something like* the way in which 'there is a marked tendency for us all to think that $7+5=12$, and this tendency exists because there is really nothing else to think about what $7+5$ is' explains a tendency *by* justifying it. On request, the justificatory aspect can be made yet more evident by filling out the explanation with a calculation, or a proof. Cp. Essay IV, §5, §10. A similar complement for the valuational case could consist in an argued vindication of the claim that $x$ is indeed funny, shocking . . .)

If this is how we work out the second approach, then the subjectivist who is committed to prefer the more Humean formulation of the subjectivist position will ask by what right I characterize the funny/appalling/shocking/consoling/reassuring/disgusting/pleasant/delightful . . . in these terms, and how I can propose to extend this method of elucidation to the good, the right and the beautiful. If he accepts Hume's own criterion of plausibility, however, then there is now a prospect of replying to him as follows: Hume has given the only imaginable external standard of correctness, but it appears more and more implausible the further we move from the gustatory and olfactory cases. If the only other standard we can imagine is an internal one, that is a subject-involving *and* property-involving, piecemeal standard, then we must conclude

---

[20] For various further defenses of this sort of formulation, see Essay III, §5; Essay IV, §5, mark (2) and §10 following; Ishiguro, *op. cit.*; John McDowell 'Aesthetic Value, Objectivity, and the Fabric of the World' in E. Schaper (Ed.), *Pleasure, Preference, and Value* (Cambridge University Press, 1983), especially his section IV. The 'because' is meant literally, with the full sense that is conferred on it by the English language in this context. 'Because' introduces explanations. So questions of causality come into consideration, but only by virtue of the way in which statements of causation can figure within explanations. (Cp. Donald Davidson 'Causal Relations' in *Journal of Philosophy*, 1967; also, on a connected point, McDowell, *loc. cit.*, note 3 above.) Certainly what the predicate 'funny' stands for (cp. note 18) enters into the truth-conditions of 'John laughed because what Philip said was funny'; for certainly the backing for that particular explanatory 'because' comprises something causal. Philip's remark's being funny was causally responsible for John's amusement, let us suppose. Is it necessary to go on to claim that the value-property *funny* itself causes the response of amusement?

that what makes possible those discriminations that Hume insists upon our being properly impressed by is just what we think it is, *viz.* the properties of objects as they impinge on us. Such a standard must be essentially contestable and internal to the thoughts and practices it relates to—indeed all of a piece with the practice of criticism, and vulnerable to anything that that can establish. But then (as Hume says, and we have the better right to say this) when critical doubts occur, 'men can do no more than in other disputable questions which are submitted to the understanding; they must produce the best arguments that their invention suggests to them'. The practices and the standards stand or fall (or, having fallen, are shored up again) together. Perhaps it is a shame that nothing vindicates the standard once and for all. But, conceiving the standard in these humble terms, at least we can prefer the obvious to the devious in stating it, and in doing so speak boldly of objects and their subjective properties. Either we hold our ground in making the discriminations that Hume insists that we contrive to make or (cp. §17 below) we don't. If we do, the standard itself —for that sort of evaluation—is surviving another day, and we can continue to employ it in distinguishing between what is really φ and what is not really φ. It is not inevitable that the standard will withstand criticism. But it does not need to be inevitable that it will. So the response to the objection I envisaged at the beginning of this paragraph is that if there is a problem about this 'really', or if its natural link with the ideas of truth and objectivity ought to be severed, then the onus is on him who prefers the first, more Humean formulation of subjectivism to say what the problem is, to make out the case against these natural appearances, and also to show how, even if talk of objects were only a *façon de parler*, Hume's criteria of adequacy could be satisfied. For the following possibility has now become visible: that we should characterize the *subjective* (and then perhaps the valuational) positively, in terms of a subjective judgment's being one that is however indirectly answerable for its correctness to the responses of conscious subjects; that we should characterize the *objective* positively, in terms of an objective judgment's being one that is a candidate for plain truth: and that, having characterized each of these categories of judgment positively and independently, we need to be ready for the possibility that a judgment may fall into both, may both rest upon sentiment *and* relate to a matter of fact.

I should not for my positive preference call such a position *realism*, as if to contrast it with *mentalism* or whatever. Nor should I claim that this preliminary elaboration and defence can go anywhere near to showing the final tenability of the position itself. What is much more urgent than any final assessment of the position is some fuller appreciation of its motivation and commitments. In this essay I attempt little more than this.

11. (a) Whether we prefer the first or the second of the two ways of expounding subjectivism, it will be appropriate and natural to declare with Protagoras the sophist, the first systematic subjectivist,

Man is the measure of all things,

restricting the Protagorean doctrine to valuational things, and taking 'man' to mean not 'this man' or 'that man' or 'any man'[21] but 'men in so far as we can reach them or they can reach us and are not alien to us'.

(b) Given our development of the position at sections 8 and 9 it will be equally natural to say that, where the ascription of value is concerned, *finding* $x$ to be $\varphi$ is prior to (or at least coeval with) *thinking* $x$ to be $\varphi$.

(c) It will also be natural to say that what is $\varphi$ (simply, not '$\varphi$ for us' or '$\varphi$ here') is *relative*, in a special sense to be explained. An object's or person's or event's being $\varphi$—or $\varphi$ in our sense, if you will (but that of course is what the predicate will mean in this sentence, the sentence being our sentence)—consists in its being such as to evoke in the right way or such as to make appropriate some response, call it A,—still no relativity so far, but now it comes—where A is *our* response, or the response

---

[21] Note that the reading we give to Protagoras' famous formula (Plato, *Theaetetus*, 151e6–152c7) is not the undoubtedly authentic individualistic interpretation but the possibly equally authentic intersubjective social interpretation which I for one believe he was aware of and *also* intended. I am fortified in this belief by an unpublished essay 'Protagoras and the Theory of the Natural Consensus' by Edward Hussey. Hussey translates Protagoras' doctrine as follows: 'A man is a measure of all things: of those which are that and how they are, and of those that are not that and how they are not'.

that *we* owe to it if it really is φ. The relativity to us that is here in question consists in the fact that it is we who owe *x* the response A and owe it that even though one who is not party to the set of associations of paired <property, response> associations to which the <φ, A> association belongs may fail to respond in that way. What this relativity imports is the possibility that there may be simply no point in urging that a stranger to our associations owes the object this response.[22] Even if a stranger can, by an imaginative effort, get himself some idea of what the property φ is and what the associated reaction A is, this may not suffice to effect the connexion between his discerning φ in a thing and his participating fully in A. It may not result in his identifying or associating himself with that sort of response. Even when the response A becomes possible for him, then, this may not trigger any readiness on his part to participate in all the collateral aesthetic or practical responses normally associated with A. (It is for investigation whether that means that he has an imperfect grasp of what φ is.)

A relativity of this kind was always to have been expected if it is by the process speculatively reconstructed in §§8-9 above that we get our value terms. For this process was a historical and particular one, and it comprised some contribution by the mind unlike that which is postulated in Kantian epistemology. What imports the relativity is a contribution that need not be everywhere the same or similar in its content.[23] There is the possibility (at least) of distinct and different moral and aesthetic worlds whose inhabitants need to struggle long and hard to appreciate the differences. They must understand not only the nature and extent of these differences, but also

---

[22] Compare the formulation Williams gives of a connected point in his 'The Truth in Relativism', *Moral Luck*, pp. 141-2.

[23] For an account of the way in which Kant's epistemology suggested to Herder and others the possibility of this different sort of contribution, see P.L. Gardiner in *The Monist*, 1981. For another aspect of this matter, see also Kenneth Burke, *Grammar of Motives* (University of California Press, 1969), p. 59.

> [We] seek for vocabularies that will be faithful *reflections* of reality. To this end, we must develop vocabularies that are *selections* of reality. And any selection of reality must, in certain circumstances, function as a *deflection* of reality. Insofar as the vocabulary meets the needs of reflection, we can say that it has the necessary scope. In its selectivity, it is a reduction. Its scope and reduction become a deflection when the given terminology, or calculus, is not suited to the subject matter.

something of the way in which these differences are shaped substantively by the conditions of human life, before it is even an option for them to come properly to disagree with one another in their valuations.[24] (And when they disagree they are not thereby committed to dwell on the Humean question whether the differences are 'blameless' or 'not blameless'. The various circumstances that make up the differences may condition the sense and proper understanding of judgments.)

12.    At this point I should expect the intuitionist objectivist and the champion of Hume's version of subjectivism (and several other parties perhaps, *e.g.*, the emotivist) to combine forces in a joint protest: 'In something like the way we each expected, you have now talked yourself into a really impossible position: you are trying to ground a distinction that you like to describe as the distinction between what is really $\varphi$ and not really $\varphi$ upon what are by your own account mere responses— upon a convergence in the inclinations various people feel or do not feel to say that $x$ is $\varphi$ or that $x$ is not $\varphi$. Surely this distinction between the really $\varphi$ and not really $\varphi$, like everything else that is distinctive of your subjectivism, is either plain bluff or a mere *façon de parler*. (No wonder you disclaimed the title 'realist'.) In a phrase Williams uses in criticism of intuitionism, you are confusing resonance with reference. Surely the relativity you have now deduced from your subjectivism and described in terms that are both object-involving and blatantly metaphorical ('owing an object a response' and the rest) precisely demonstrates the necessity to treat all such talk as a *façon de parler*. It is no less a *façon de parler* for sounding like the natural continuation of the ordinary language of evaluation.'

It would be a defeat if this were so. We were trying to formulate a variant upon classical subjectivism both positively and literally. Pending a more challenging statement of the objection, however, I believe that I can defend the subjectivist position as we now have it by pointing out that these responses we have been speaking of are not 'mere' responses. They are responses that are correct when and only when they are

---

[24] See *Longer Note* 24.

occasioned by what has the corresponding property φ and are occasioned by it because it *is* φ. If the objector persists: 'How can human agreement in these responses decide what *really* is φ or not φ?' I reply that the sort of agreement that is in question here is only agreement in *susceptibility* to respond thus and so to φ things. It is agreement at most (as one might say, evoking a very familiar passage of Wittgenstein)[25] in what property/ response associations we are able to catch onto and work up into a shared way of talking, acting, and reacting. Since this agreement is not in itself agreement in *opinions* about what is φ or not φ (even though the existence of the shared language presupposes the possibility of such agreement), there is no question of the agreement in the belief that *x* is φ being the *criterion* for *x*'s really being φ. *x* is only really φ if it is such as to evoke and make appropriate the response A among those who are sensitive to φ-ness. That is a far cry from agreement about the φ-ness of *x* simply constituting the actual φ-ness of *x*.[26]

Agreement figures in the story of the formation of the *senses* of value predicates, not in any story about their references.

13. The response is likely to excite another sort of objection: 'You have spoken of morality's depending, at least in part, upon agreement in susceptibility to respond thus and so to certain things. But what if these susceptibilities changed? Could that make what is now right wrong, what is now good bad. . . ? Again, you suggested at the very outset that Hume could be read as proposing that *x* is good if and only if *x* is such as to arouse or make appropriate a certain sentiment of approbation. But whether *x* is such depends not only on the condition of *x* but on the nature and range of susceptibilities of the subjects of the sentiments. What sentiment is appropriate to a thing of a given character will depend at least in part upon what the range is of the sentiments themselves. But how can goodness, goodness itself, depend on anything of this sort?'

The objection is instructive and demonstrates the importance of detaching any development of Humean or Protagorean subjectivism from the Moorean conception of philosophy. I believe it also casts further light upon relativity.

---

[25] L. Wittgenstein, *Philosophical Investigations* §241, discussed at p. 350, below.
[26] See *Longer Note 26*.

The objection would be dead right if the subjectivist were saying that '*x* is good' may be paraphrased as '*x* is such as to arouse or make appropriate [a certain] sentiment of approbation', and if he were saying that this paraphrase could then be intersubstituted with 'good' *salvo sensu* (or more or less *salvo sensu*). But the subjectivist need not be saying that. His distinctive claim is rather that *x* is good if and only if *x* is the sort of thing that calls forth or makes appropriate a certain sentiment of approbation *given the range of propensities that we actually have to respond in this or that way;*[27] or generalizing a little, and still disclaiming the attempt to provide an equivalent, his claim is that, for each value predicate φ (or for a very large range of such), there is an attitude or response of subjects *belonging to a range of propensities that we actually have* such that an object has the property φ stands for if and only if the object is fitted by its characteristics to bring down that extant attitude or response upon it and bring it down *precisely because* it has those characteristics.

To take the matter any further would involve an articulation of the response or attitude and of the associated marks that are annexed to particular value predicates. This articulation would have to be given in a way that threw into relief the organizing point of applying the predicate to anything or withholding it. The existence of a substantial body of attempts at what used to be called the theory of laughter (see the instructive review of these in D.H. Munro's *Argument of Laughter*[28]), all devoted to the understanding of just two or three such predicates, is evidence of the potential difficulty and of the interest of this sort of work. But such a theory need not promise to carry us even one inch nearer to an intersubstitutable equivalent for the predicates that stand for the properties that it studies. It may or may not succeed in this.

14. But does the subjectivist want to remain perfectly satisfied with the actual condition of our actual response to

---

[27] Cp. M.K. Davies and I.L. Humberstone, 'Two Notions of Necessity', *Philosophical Studies* vol. 38, 1980, especially pp. 22–5; also Michael Smith 'An Argument for Moral Realism', unpublished; and for the general point, see Saul Kripke, *Naming and Necessity* (Oxford: Blackwell, 1980), p. 140, n. 71.

[28] *The Argument of Laughter* (London and Melbourne, 1951).

the objects of moral and aesthetic attention? What of criticism and progress?

It was for this reason that I tried to secure the irrelevance of a change in human nature and susceptibilities, by stressing not the relativity of value to the *totality of our actual responses* but its relativity to our *actual propensities*, these being propensities that are answerable to criticism, *etc.*, to respond in this or that way to this or that feature of things. But to fill out this answer, I must hark back to the claims in §9 about the essential contestability of valuational language, and also to the claim that the standard of correctness for each predicate is all of a piece with the day to day practice of using it and criticizing or vindicating the uses that are made of it. In prosecuting that practice (in adjusting the mind's spread upon objects, you can say if you insist—but remember then that the account offered here will construe this process in terms of the discovery of properties or the lighting up of properties that are there, and not in terms of projecting properties onto the black, white, and grey of the presubjective world) in prosecuting that practice, we shall reach wherever we reach, for such reasons as seem good and appropriate. Subjectivism itself prescribes no limit to the distance that reflection (*e.g.* reflection on themes such as those treated in Essays I and II) can carry us from the starting point in the sentiments. (No more than cognitivism does, cp. Sabina Lovibond in *Realism and Imagination in Ethics.*) It does not imprison us in the system of evaluations we begin with; nor does it insulate from criticism the attitudes and responses that sustain glib, lazy or otherwise suspect predications.

15.  But someone will now ask: what if, by a sequence of minute shifts in our responses, an evil demon were to work us round to a point where we took what is actually evil to be good? Perhaps the demon might do this without our even noticing it. Yes, I reply, he might. But this is not an objection to sensible subjectivism. It would not follow from our not noticing the magnitude of the shift and everything that went with it that the very same thing that once told the presence of good was now fastened constitutively upon evil. For the subjectivism we have envisaged does not treat the response as a criterion, or even as an indicator. In the full theory of the last stage of the processes

we have been describing, it counts as nothing less than an act of judging a content; it is a judgment indispensably sustained by the perceptions and feelings and thoughts that are open to criticism that is based on norms that are open to criticism. It is not that *by which we tell*. It is part of the telling itself.

What the objection does do, however, is to point clearly at the thing that has given subjectivism a bad name. This is all the associations that are commonly imputed to subjectivism with the thought that evaluative judgments may be assimilated to 'mere responses' and with the idea that the responses the subjectivist interests himself in are autonomously inner states—or states such that, if you are in one of them, you can tell and tell infallibly, without looking outward, whether you are in it or not. (These really would be states that 'have no reference to anything beyond themselves'.) These associations are made explicit by the objection. But they were already under acute pressure in Hume's more mature statement of ethical subjectivism, and none of them is maintained in the position as we have defended it.

16.   What needs to be emphasized again at this point is that subjectivism ought not to be represented as offering any guarantee that for most (or for any) of the predicates and properties we put our trust in, the very best judgments that we can make involving them *will* gather a consensus such that the best explanation of the consensus is that those who take $x$ to be $\varphi$ do so precisely because $x$ is $\varphi$. (Cp. Essay IV, §6.) Of course our shared linguistic practice commits us strongly to that belief. But our practice can operate without any special or philosophical guarantee that truth and correctness *will* stay around in this way. Our practice can even continue to operate in full awareness of the flimsiness and contingency of the natural facts that it reposes upon, in the awareness that so often impinges upon valuation as we know it of our proneness to error and self-deception, even in awareness of the theoretical possibility that our minds and nervous systems may have been poisoned or perverted. What we can do about that danger is only to take ordinary precautions, and to have ordinary regard (regard not insulated from thoughts about the subject matter itself) for the credentials with which and conditions from out of

which people's judgments are made. Better, we can take ordinary precautions, and then, in deference to the inherent difficulty of the subject matter, a few more. And it is well worth remembering that, by preferring over Hume's subjectivism a subjectivism that was object and property-involving, we did not disqualify ourselves from insisting upon its also being *conscious subject*-involving. If there is something fishy in either the agreements or the disagreements that we encounter, then we must investigate their etiology case by case, and as best we can, having proper regard for everything, not excluding the characters and sensibilities of those participating in the agreements and disagreements.

17.   If nothing can exclude in advance the possibility that the very best judgments we can arrive at involving this or that predicate will fail to gather any consensus, let alone underwrite a consensus such that the best explanation of the consensus is that those who take $x$ to be $\varphi$ do so because $x$ is $\varphi$, then what is to be said about such failure? Well. Where we seem to encounter such a thing, it may be that what we call $\varphi$-ness is different things to different people. That is one possibility. If so, there is less strict *disagreement* than may appear. But it may be that there is no escape by that route. It may not be possible to establish any sufficient difference in the 'value-focus' of those who appear to be in disagreement.

In that case there are two other possibilities. We may simply give up on the predicate; or we may remain undeterred (cp. Essay IV, §22). Sometimes, of course, where the latter seems to be the right attitude Hume's formulation of subjectivism may seem superior to the cognitivist formulation of subjectivism that I have advocated (especially if the Humean version can be freed of the difficulties I have claimed there are in it). It is strange, however, that the pull towards Hume's formulation should be at its strongest precisely where the sense of the predicate gives the appearance of being in danger of the kind of collapse from which Hume himself believed that he needed our shared human nature and our shared proclivity towards certain sentiments to protect it. So long as it is Hume's struggle to make the sovereignty of moral subjects consist with the distinction he wanted between sound and unsound judgments

that remains at the centre of Hume's theoretical concern, I
think there is no clear advantage for him in the shift back to the
first formulation.

In truth, whatever difficulties there are in the possibility of
irresoluble substantive disagreement, no position in moral
philosophy can render itself simply immune from them. We
should not tumble over ourselves to assert that there is irresoluble substantive disagreement. We should simply respect
the possibility of such disagreement, I think, and in respecting
it register the case for a measure of cognitive underdetermination. (Cp. Essay IV, §20.) Some have wished to find a philosophical position that ruled out this possibility in advance, by
espousing some anti-subjectivist theory—a Kantian or intuitionist or utilitarian or dogmatically realist theory. But how
can such a possibility be simply ruled out? And why on the
other hand should the subjectivist be deemed to have *ruled it in*?
In this matter the subjectivist really has to do the same as everyone else: he can only urge that, in spite of the possibility of irresoluble substantive disagreement, but in a manner partially
conditioned by that possibility, we should persevere as best we
can in the familiar processes of reasoning, conversion, and
criticism—without guarantees of success, which are almost as
needless as they are unobtainable.

18.   In 1960, Bertrand Russell wrote 'I cannot see how to
refute the arguments for the subjectivity of ethical values, but I
find myself incapable of believing that all that is wrong with
wanton cruelty is that I don't like it'.[29] How close have our pro-
subjectivist efforts carried us to the answer to this difficulty?
First, reverting to Hume, we can drop the first person. What is
wrong with cruelty is not, even for Bertrand Russell, just that
Bertrand Russell doesn't like it, but that it is not such as to call
forth liking given our *actual* collectively scrutinized responses.
Those responses are directed at cruelty, and at what cruelty
itself consists in on the level of motive, intention, outcome . . .
To be sure, we should not care about these things, these things
would not impinge as they do upon us, if our responses were
not there to be called upon. In the presence of a good reason to

---

[29] *Op. cit.* at note 4 above.

call them in question, we should not be able to trust them or take too much for granted about the well-foundedness of the properties they are keyed to. But, in the total absence of such a reason, it will not be at all question-begging for Russell simply to remind himself as thoroughly and vividly as he can of just what it is that he dislikes, abhors, detests . . . about cruelty and its ancient and hideous marks.

# Longer Notes

### Longer Note 19: Essential contestability

By showing (if it will show) how essential contestability can come to attach to a predicate and how questions of appropriateness get in (cp. §4 and note 3 above), the argument of §9 will complete the subjectivist's vindication of his right to give the 'such as to make approbation appropriate' elucidation proposed in §3 above. But of course it is at this point that I shall be asked how can I claim it is possible for the process described in the text to occur without serious detriment to the univocity of the predicate. If people disagree about the extension and disagree about the marks of the property that serve to collect its extension (*i.e.*, the property the predicate stands for), surely they can only focus their disagreement (can only disagree, instead of simply talking past one another) if they agree in what the attitude of response itself is. But the trouble is that there is no saying—or so I have insisted—what that attitude *is* except by reference to the property that is its proper object.

The right response to this objection is not to seek to explode it, but simply to suggest that it depends for its whole force on a certain quantum of exaggeration. To get an attitude that can be held sufficiently fixed to focus disagreement about the marks of the property it is made for, we do indeed need to effect some delimitation or further determination of the attitude. Only in this way can a subjectivist distinguish different senses for 'good', 'right', 'beautiful'. Approving of some $x$ had better not be a barely determinable state, approving *tout court*. It had better be approving of $x$ as a good $g$, as a good $f$, or as a good $fg$, . . . . Certainly if even this cannot be supplied, the parties may be talking past one another when they dispute about the marks of the property. But then the case we have to be interested in is the case where this much *can* be made clear, and there is *still* room for disagreement about what it takes to be good, a good $f$, a good $fg$ . . . or whatever. So my answer to the question about univocity is simply that you do not need complete agreement about the marks of the property, or total coincidence in your conceptions of it, in order to mean the same by the predicate that stands for the property, or to be concerned with the same attitude directed towards it. (Do you need complete agreement about magnetic compasses—do we all have to have identical conceptions of a magnetic compass—in order to mean the same by 'magnetic compass'? Surely not.) This is a complicated terrain I am trying to make a short cut through. But I cannot help thinking that what my critic is finding hard to accept is really the mutual inextricability I continually insist upon of the anthropocentric properties of an object and the attitudes towards it that are made for these properties. But why should not the ball be rolled as tightly as this: so tightly that nothing will count as unrolling it. (Contrast with unrolling a curled up hedgehog trying to untwist the volutes of a snail's shell.) Remember that we are not inventing these predicates. We have found them already in occupation.

### Longer Note 24: Relativity

Let us distinguish the relativity that subjectivism appears to import from others that are in the offing here and frequently compresent with it.

In the first place, any particular item $x$'s goodness (say) will almost always consist in its being, for some $f, g$ . . . a good $f$, or a good $g$ or. . . . And this 'attributivity' may either come down to $x$'s being good *relative to a comparison-class*, as among whose members it is assessed (the more straightforward sort of attributivity), or, as in the case of 'good man', 'good thing to do', it may consist in $x$'s being good *relative to a certain specifiable point of view*, the moral point of view or whatever (as well perhaps as relative to a comparison class).

In the second place, such goodness-as-among-the-fs and goodness-relative-to-such-and-a-point-of-view may themselves be relative to the circumstances, the actors, the patients, the cultural context. (Indeed, if we didn't have regard for these things we sometimes might not be assessing that very item.)

These two kinds of relativity can of course interact with one another, but neither singly nor in concert could they ever be rationally conflated with the relativity introduced in §11. I announced this as relativity to us. But the kind of relativity I intended there does not (I emphasize) introduce *us* as the value of an extra parameter. Nor does it search out some potentially explicit extra argument-place, as in '*x* is [a] good relative to us [*f*]' or '*x* is [a] for-our-purposes good [*f*]' or whatever. . . . Once the point is passed that we described at paragraph 3 of §9, and once the option disappears of vindicating judgements of φ-ness by simply restricting them as φ-ness for such and such person, nothing like this can be what is at issue. (There is less wrong with '*x* is [a] good [*f*] on our view', precisely because this version makes *oratio obliqua* manifest. What it means is 'According to us, *x* is [a] good [*f*]' or 'In our scheme of things, *x* is [a] good [*f*]'. In this form 'us' or 'our scheme of things' precisely does not fill an extra *argument*-place belonging to 'good [*f*]' and made available by the mode of combination '*x* is [a] good [*f*]'.)

If it is not obvious why the hidden argument place would be a wrong approach, then consider the following dilemma. Suppose two cultures or subcultures $S_1$ and $S_2$ differ with respect to the question whether *x* is a good f, and suppose that their names are to be written into the new slot, subscript 'S', supposedly discovered for the insertion of one or the other—as in '*x* is a good$_S$ *f*'. Now ask: do $S_1$ and $S_2$ really disagree? Either they do or they don't. Suppose they don't and their difference is not a disagreement about the answer to a common question with a common sense. Then there is no point in using the subscripted predicate because there is then the *prior* problem that one of $S_1$ and $S_2$ (or both) is such that its opinion cannot strictly be given *at all* by a content-sentence that either ascribes or denies the property of being [a] good [*f*] to *x*. (For being [a] good [*f*] is the property that '[a] good [*f*]' stands for when used in *our* sense, and this either $S_1$ or $S_2$ does not have available to it.) On the other hand, if $S_1$ and $S_2$ are giving incompatible answers to a common question and they do disagree, then there is some common judgment they disagree about, and *ex hypothesi* there is a common text and the predicate therein comprises neither of these fillings. To make different insertions into the subscript slot would effectively lose us our whole grasp on their disagreement.

It was for this sort of reason that our preferred way of stating the relativity imported by the subjectivity of value was to say that, where we owe *x* the response A in virtue of *x*'s being φ, there will not necessarily be a point in insisting that others not party to the system of associations that comprises the <φ, A > linkage owe *x* that response.

### Longer Note 26: Responses

Anthony Price has pointed out to me that there are *two* sorts of worry that someone may feel in this area, of which only the first is directly addressed in the text. There is the worry the objector actually expresses about 'mere' responses and the attempt to make these validate the reality of that to which they purport to be keyed. And there is another worry. No doubt, *if* the responses in question are ever appropriate, then sensitivity to φ-ness is sometimes certifiable independently of a sensitivity to *x*'s φ-ness. But is the response *ever* appropriate? 'It would seem like lifting oneself up by one's own bootstraps to appeal to φ-ness to justify the shared sensibility and appeal to the shared sensibility to confirm the reality of φ-ness'.

My reply to this would be first that the sensibility and the supposition that there is something it is keyed to are indeed in *joint* danger from the kind of upset that is discussed in §16–17 below. But they may or may not suffer that mishap. They would also be in joint danger from the notion of rationality envisaged in §10 of Essay III if there were any future in that. But that was an illusory notion.

Given that something could count against the sensibility and the property considered jointly, and given that they are not arbitrary constructs but things that have survived the evolutionary process described in §9, and continue to survive criticism (albeit criticism internal to a whole whirl of going practices, cp. Essay Three §5), there need be no question of having to justify the claim that what seems to be a sensibility really is a sensibility (*i.e.* a sensibility *to something*)—not at least *ab initio* or from a standing start. What is required is the readiness to take criticism seriously, and to recognize a case where we do have the situation described in §§16–17.

# VI

# Deliberation and Practical Reason*

> The matter of the practical is indefinite,
> unlimited.
>
> ARISTOTLE

## 1. Three theses of Aristotelian Interpretation[1]

Consider the following three contentions:

(1) In Book 3 of the *Nicomachean Ethics* Aristotle treats a restricted and technical notion of deliberation, which makes it unnecessary for him to consider anything but technical or so-called productive examples of practical reason. It is not surprising in the context of Book 3 that deliberation is never of ends but always of means.

(2) When he came to write Books 6 and 7 of the *Nicomachean Ethics* and *De Anima* 3.7, Aristotle analysed a much less restricted notion of deliberation and of choice. This made it necessary for him to give up the view that deliberation and choice were necessarily of *ta pros to telos*, where it is supposed that this phrase means or implies that deliberation is only of means. Thereafter he recognized two irreducibly distinct

---

*Proceedings of the Aristotelian Society* vol. 76, 1975/76, with revisions. Because the first three sections of this essay circulated in typescript for more than a decade, I had the inestimable benefit (from which they must have felt I had the time and ought to have had the ability to profit better) of comments from J.L. Ackrill, M.J. Woods, M.F. Burnyeat, R. Sorabji (without the support of whose article 'Aristotle on the Role of Intellect in Virtue,' *Proceedings of the Aristotelian Society* vol. 74, 1973/74, pp. 107–129, I might have felt I had to postpone publication yet further), J.C. Dybikowski, T.H. Irwin, Martha Craven Nussbaum, and G.E.L. Owen. To the last-named I also owed the invitation to continue the first three sections into §§4–6, and into a treatment of *akrasia* (see Essay VII), as James Loeb Visiting Fellow in Classical Philosophy at Harvard in Spring 1972.

[1] It is possible that no scholar holds to all three. See also note 3.

modes of practical reasoning, *means-end* deliberations and *rule-case* deliberations.[2]

(3) The supposed modification of view between the writing of Book 3 and that of Books 6–7, and the newly introduced (supposed) 'rule-case' syllogism, bring with them a radical change in Aristotle's view of the subject—even something resembling a satisfactory solution to the problems of choice and deliberation. Thus 6–7 do better in this way than vaguely suggest what complexities a lifelike account of practical deliberation would have to come to terms with.

Taken singly these doctrines are familiar enough in Aristotelian exegesis[3]. But my submission is that, both as a whole and in detail, the view constituted by (1) (2) (3) is damagingly mistaken. It obstructs improvement in our understanding of the real philosophical problem of practical reason. The examination of (1) (2) (3) will lead (in §§4–6 of this essay) into some general consideration of that problem and Aristotle's contribution to it.

I shall begin by trying to show that for all its simplicities and over-schematizations, Aristotle's Book 3 account is in fact straightforwardly continuous with the Book 6 account of deliberation, choice, and practical reasoning. Both accounts

---

[2] I think that those who employ these or similar terms usually intend the distinction of two kinds of reasoning, and the two distinct kinds of non-theoretical syllogism allegedly recognized by Aristotle, to correspond in some way to Aristotle's distinction of production (poiēsis) and practice (praxis).

[3] The conjunction of (1) (2) (3) is not intended to catch the flavour of a more subjectivist interpretation that has had some currency. This enlarges the role of moral virtue at the expense of intellect and, so far as possible, assimilates *NE* 6 to *NE* 3—where *NE* 3 is read in an exclusively means-end fashion. (1) (2) (3) is closer to the reason-oriented naturalist interpretation I shall commend and, like my interpretation, it owes much to Professor D.J. Allan. See his 'Aristotle's Account of the Origin of Moral Principles', *Proceedings of the XIth International Congress of Philosophy, Brussels, August 20–26, 1953* (Amsterdam, 1953), 12:120–127 [hereinafter referred to as Allan (1)] and 'The Practical Syllogism,' in *Autour d'Aristote: Recueil offert à Mgr Mansion* (Louvain, 1955), pp. 325–340 [hereinafter referred to as Allan (2)]. These publications represent so considerable an advance in clearing away the mass of captious misinterpretation to which Aristotle's praxeology had been previously subjected that I have preferred to consider the composite view given above rather than dwell on Allan's special version of it. But I shall allude frequently to his treatment of single passages.

attempt to analyse and describe wide and completely general notions of choice and deliberation. Each is dominated, I think, by Aristotle's obsession with a certain simple solution of the kind described in Book 3, 1112b—the geometer who searches for means to construct a given figure with ruler and compass. Aristotle is acutely and increasingly aware of the limitations of this analogy, but (in spite of its redeployment at 1143b1-5) he never describes exactly what to put in its place. Twentieth-century philosophy is not yet in a position to condescend to him with regard to these questions. For all its omissions and blemishes, Aristotle's account is informed by a consciousness of the lived actuality of practical reasoning and its background. This is an actuality that present-day studies of rationality, morality, and public rationality ignore at their cost, and ignore.

## 2. Rejection of the First Thesis. Book 3 of the *Nicomachean Ethics*

The supposition that Book 3 set out to analyse a restricted notion of deliberation[4] or a restricted notion of choice gives rise to some internal difficulties within the book.

One apparent difficulty is this. *Bouleusis* (deliberation) is inextricably linked in Book 3 to *prohairesis* (choice). 'Is the

---

What principally distinguishes Allan's view from the composite view (1) (2) (3) is that Allan is inclined to say that the changes he postulates between the view of Book 3 and the view of Books 6-7 leave Aristotle's analysis of *deliberation* itself more or less unaffected. Against this I say that either the alleged rule-case reasoning, which is admitted by Allan to be *prohairetic*, can be properly termed deliberative or it cannot. If it can, then, if choice needed radical alteration, then so *on Allan's interpretation of it* did the Book 3 account of deliberation. It could not remain unaffected. For precisely the same considerations then operate on both. If we say that choice cannot be termed deliberative, however, we contradict 1140a27-28. *Cf.* also 1139a23, 1141b8-15.

[4] *Cf.* Allan (1), p. 124: '. . . the good propounded may be (a) distant or (b) general. Thus there is fresh work for practical reason to perform. In the former case, we have first to calculate the means which will, in due course, achieve the end. In the latter, we have to *subsume the particular case under a general rule*. Both these processes are analysed by Aristotle in a masterly fashion, *in different parts of his work, the former in the third book* of the Ethics, the latter in Books VI and VII and in his psychological writings' (my italics). And *cf.* (2) 'His *first* position in the *Ethics* is that all virtuous action involves choice, that all choice follows up a deliberation and *that all deliberation is concerned with the selection of means*' (my italics).

object of prohairesis then simply what has been decided on by previous deliberation?' Aristotle asks at 1112a15, later to define it at 1113a10 as *deliberative desire of what is in our power.* About choice Aristotle remarks at 1111b5 'Choice is thought to be most closely bound up with (*oikeiotaton*) virtue and to discriminate characters better than actions do'. Now this is at least a peculiar remark if deliberation is construed as narrowly as some have been encouraged by the geometrical example at 1112b20 to construe it, and if we construe Aristotle's assertion that choice and deliberation are of what is toward the end (*tōn pros to telos*) to mean that choice and deliberation are concerned only with means. The most straightforward way to see it as a cardinal or conceptually prominent fact about choice that it accurately or generally distinguishes good from bad character, and has a certain constitutive relation to vice and virtue, is to suppose choice to be a fairly inclusive notion that relates to different specifications of man's *end.* The choices of the bad or self-indulgent man, the *mochthēros* or *akolastos,* would seem to be supposed by Aristotle to reveal this man for what he is because they make straightforwardly apparent his *misconceptions of the end.* The thought ought not to be that the choices such men make reveal any incapacity for technical or strictly means-end reasoning to get what they want or the ends they set themselves. For these they may well achieve—and, in Aristotle's view, miss happiness thereby. Their mistakes are not means-ends or technical mistakes. (*Cf.* 1142b18–20, and 6.12 on *deinotes.*)

It may be objected that the thought is neither of these things but that by seeing a man's choice one can come to guess what his ends are; and to arrive at a view of what his ends are is to arrive at a view of his character. But this interpretation, which scarcely does justice to *oikeiotaton,* must seem a little unlikely as soon as we imagine such an indirect argument to a man's ends. Typically, *actions* would have to mediate the argument. But actions are already mentioned by Aristotle in an unfavourable contrast. 'Choice . . . discriminates characters better than actions do'.

The interpretation of this passage is not perfectly essential to my argument, however. Let us go on, simply remarking that the onus of proof must be on the interpretation that hypothesizes that *prohairesis* or *bouleusis* means something different in Book 3 and Books 6 and 7. The first effort should be to give it the same sense in all these books. I hope to show that this is possible as well as desirable and that if anything at all gets widened in Book 6, it is the *analysis* of choice and deliberation, not the sense of the words. Each must be one *analysand* throughout. As so often, there has been confusion in the discussion of this issue because a *wider analysis of notion N* has sometimes been confused with an *analysis of a wider notion N*. 'Wider conception' is well calculated to mask the difference between these fatally similar-looking things. But let us distinguish them.

There are certainly reasons of a sort why some scholars have seen the Book 3 notions of deliberation and choice as technical notions that were superseded by wider notions and then by wider philosophical analyses of either or both notions. These reasons derive from Aristotle's frequent assertions that, unlike *boulesis* (wish), choice and deliberation are not *of the end* but of *what is toward the end* (*pros to telos*). See 1111b26, 1112b11–12, 1112b33–35, 1113a14–15, 1113b3–4. If *what is toward the end* in Book 3 is taken (as it is for instance by Ross in his translation) to be a *means to an end*, then that must certainly suggest that as regards prohairesis and bouleusis we have a wider *analysand* as well as a wider analysis in Books 6–7. But I argue that they need not be taken so.

It is a commonplace of Aristotelian exegesis that Aristotle never really paused to analyse the distinction between two quite distinct relations: (A) the relation $x$ bears to *telos y* when $x$ will bring about $y$, and (B) the relation $x$ bears to $y$ when the existence of $x$ will itself help to constitute $y$. For self-sufficient reasons we are committed in any case to making this distinction very often on behalf of Aristotle when he writes the words *heneka* or *charin* (for the sake of). See, for example, Book 1, 1097b1–5. The expression *toward the end* is vague and perfectly suited to express both conceptions.

The first notion, that of a means or instrument or procedure that is causally efficacious in the production of a specific and settled end, has as its clear cases such things as a cloak as a way of covering the body when one is cold, or some drug as a means to alleviate pain. The second notion that can take shelter under the wide umbrella of *what is toward the end* is that of something whose existence counts in itself as the partial or total realization of the end. This is a constituent of the end: *cf. Met.* 1032b27 (N.B. *meros* there), *Politics* 1325b16 and 1338b2–4. Its simple presence need not be logically necessary or logically sufficient for the end. To a very limited extent the achievement of one end may do duty for that of another. Perhaps there might even be some sort of *eudaimonia* (happiness) without good health, or without much pleasure, or without recognized honour, or without the stable possession of a satisfying occupation. But the presence of a constituent of the end is always logically relevant to happiness. It is a member of a nucleus (or one conjunct, to mention a very simple possibility, in a disjunction of conjunctions) whose coming to be counts as the attainment of that end. Happiness is not identifiable in independence of such constituents (*e.g.* as a feeling that these elements cause or as some surplus that can be measured in a person's economic behaviour).

If it commits us to no new interpretative principle to import this distinction into our reading of Book 3 and to suppose that both these relations are loosely included within the extension of the phrase *what is toward the end*, then on this understanding of the phrase Aristotle is trying in *NE* 3 (however abstractly and schematically) to treat deliberation about means and deliberation about constituents in the same way. Optimistically he is hoping that he can use the intelligibilities of the clear means-end situation and its extensions (how to effect the construction of this particular figure) to illuminate the obscurities of the *constituents-to-end* case. In the latter a man deliberates about what kind of life he wants to lead, or deliberates in a determinate context about which of several possible courses of action would conform most closely to some ideal he holds before himself, or deliberates about what would constitute eudaimonia here and now, or (less solemnly) deliberates about what would count as the achievement of the not yet completely specific goal which he has already set himself in the given situation. For purposes of any of these deliberations the means-end paradigm that inspires almost all the Book 3 examples is an inadequate paradigm, as we shall see. But it is not easy to get away from. It can continue to obsess the theorist of action, even while he tries to distance himself from it and searches for something else.

There are two apparent obstacles in Book 3 to interpreting the passages on choice and deliberation in this way and to making the crudities of the book continuous with the sophistications of Books 6–7.

(*a*) Three times Aristotle says 'We do not deliberate about *ends* but about *things that are towards ends*', and the plural may have seemed, to anyone who contemplated giving my sort of interpretation, to rule out the possibility that any part of the extension of *things that are towards ends*, that is, things that are deliberated, should comprise deliberable constituents of *happiness* (singular)—that is ends in themselves. If we do not deliberate about ends (plural), then it seems we do not deliberate about the constituents of happiness, which are ends, or about things that are good in themselves and help to make up happiness (*telē*). So it will be said, 'that which is toward the end' cannot ever comprehend any constituents of happiness— these being according to Aristotle undeliberable. But on my interpretation it may include such constituents. Therefore, it may be said, Ross's translation of *pros* in terms of *means* is to be preferred.

(*β*) To deliberate about that which is toward happiness in the case where the end directly in question in some practical thinking is happiness might, if *that which is toward happiness* included constituents, involve deliberating happiness. But this Aristotle explicitly excludes.

*Reply to* (*a*). The first passage of the three in question, 1112b11 following reads:

> We deliberate (*bouleuometha*) not about ends but about what is towards ends. For a doctor does not deliberate whether he shall heal, nor an orator whether he shall persuade, nor a statesman whether he shall produce law and order, nor does anyone else *deliberate about his end*. They assume the end and consider how and by what means it is to be attained, and if it seems to be produced by several means they consider by which it is best and most easily produced, while if it is achieved by one only they consider how it will be achieved by this, and by what

means that will be achieved till they come to the first cause, which in the order of discovery is last. For the person who deliberates seems to investigate and analyse in the way described as though he were analysing a geometrical construction (not all seeking is deliberation *e.g.* mathematical seekings, but all deliberation is seeking), and what is last in the order of analysis seems to be the first in the order of being brought about.

I submit that the four words I have italicized show that the *bouleuometha* (we deliberate) and the use of the plural *telon* (ends) are to be taken distributively. Each of these three characters, the orator, doctor, or statesman, has *one* telos (for present purposes). He is already a doctor, orator, or statesman and already at work. That is already fixed (which is not to say that it is absolutely fixed), and to that extent the form of the eudaimonia he can achieve is already conditioned by something no longer needing (at least at this moment) to be deliberated. If I am right about this passage, then there seems to be no obstacle to construing the other two occurrences of the plural, 1112b34–35 and 1113a13–14 (both nearby), as echoes of the thought at 1112b15, and taking *toward the end* (singular) as the canonical form of the phrase (*cf.* 1113b3–4, 1145a4–5 for instance). Provided that difficulty (*β*) can be met, this end may (where required) be a man's total end, namely, happiness.

This reply prompts another and supplementary retort to the difficulty. Suppose I were wrong so far and that *that which is toward the end* (singular) had no special claim to be the canonical form of the phrase. Consider then the case where Aristotle is considering deliberations whose direct ends are not identical with happiness. (Presumably the indirect end will always be happiness: *cf.* 1094a).) Such ends need not be intrinsically undeliberable ends but simple ends held constant *for the situation: cf.* 1112b15, 'assuming the end' (*themenoi to telos*).

*Reply to (β)*. It is absurd to suppose that a man could not deliberate about whether to be a doctor or not; and very nearly as absurd to suppose that Aristotle, even momentarily while writing Book 3, supposed that nobody could deliberate this question. It is so absurd that it is worth asking whether the phrase *deliberating about the end* or *deliberating about happiness* is ambiguous. It is plainly impossible to deliberate about the end if this is to deliberate by asking 'Shall I pursue the end?' If this end is eudaimonia, then *qua* animate humans we have to have some generalized desire for it (a generalized desire whose particular manifestations are desires for things falling under particular specifications of that telos). Simply to call eudaimonia the *end* leaves nothing to be deliberated about whether it should be realized or not. That is a sort of truism (*cf.* 1097b25 foll. *homologoumenon ti*), as is the point that if the desirability of eudaimonia were really up for debate, then nothing suitable by way of practical or ethical concern or by way of desire would be left over (outside the ambit of eudaimonia itself) to settle the matter. But this platitude scarcely demonstrates the impossibility of deliberating the question 'what, practically speaking, *is* that end?' or 'what shall *count* for me as an adequate description of the end of life?' And so far as I can see, nothing Aristotle says in Book 3 precludes that kind of deliberation. The only examples we are given of things that we might conclude are intrinsically undeliberable are health and happiness (1111b27). The first is arguably (at least in the philosophy of the Greeks) an undetachable part of the end for human beings. The second is identical with the end as a whole (and no more practically definite an objective than 'the end'). So we are not given examples of logically detachable constituents of the end or of debatable specifications of the end to illustrate Aristotle's thesis in *NE* 3. But on the traditional interpretation of the undeliberability thesis, these were what was needed. So what I think he is saying that one cannot deliberate is *whether* to pursue happiness or health. It is not in any case excluded that (as described in *NE* 6) a man may seek by deliberation to make more specific and more practically determinate that generalized telos of eudaimonia which is instinct in his human constitution.

If this is right so far, then I think another step is taken beyond what was achieved in Allan's discussion to dissociate Aristotle's whole theory of deliberation from that pseudo-rationalistic irrationalism, insidiously propagated nowadays by technocratic persons, which holds that reason has nothing to do with the ends of human life, its only sphere being

the efficient realization of specific goals in whose determination or modification argument plays no substantive part.[5]

## 3.  Rejection of the Second Thesis. The Transition to Book 6

On the reading of Book 3 so far defended, the transition from
*NE* 3 to *NE* 6 is fairly smooth.

> Regarding *practical wisdom* we shall get at the truth by
> considering who are the persons we credit with it. Now it is
> thought to be the mark of a man of practical wisdom to be able
> to deliberate well about what is good and expedient for himself,
> not in some particular respect, e.g. about what sorts of thing
> conduce to health or to strength, but about what sorts of
> things conduce to the good life in general (*poia pros to eu zen
> holos*). [1140a24–28, Ross's translation—note the *pros*.]

And again:

> Practical wisdom on the other hand is concerned with things
> human and things about which it is possible to deliberate; for
> we say this is above all the work of a man of practical wisdom,
> to deliberate well. . . . The man who is without qualification
> good at deliberating is the man who is capable of aiming in
> accordance with calculation at the best for man of things
> attainable by action. Nor is practical wisdom concerned only
> with what is general—it must also recognize the particular-

---

[5] *Cf.* at random, Jeremy Bray, *Decision in Government* (London, 1970), p. 72 '. . .
the individual consumer's own decision processes which are the more complex for not
being wholly rational in any economic sense'. Is there really, or should there be, a
special sense of 'rational' in economics? Bray goes on to suggest that anyone who
thinks there is room for reason in this sphere, or sets much store by the concept of *need*,
must wish to deny freedom: 'However the concept of minimum need may be used in
social security arrangements, it is a poor guide to consumer behaviour whether at the
minimum income or other levels, and whether in an advanced or primitive society. The
particular purchases made by a family reflect not only their immediate tastes such as a
liking for warmth, bright colours, and tinned fruit, but also their spiritual life and
fantasy world—the stone fireplace as a safe stronghold in a morally insecure world, the
Jaguar car to release frustration or bolster a waning virility, the tingling toothpaste as a
ritual purification. Far from being a matter for ridicule, consumer choice is something
to nurture, cultivate and protect.' In the name of liberty, yes, but not because these
ends are really outside the reach of reason or rational appraisal. Lest Bray's seem to be
a purely Fabian doctrine, I quote a Chicago School economist, Milton Friedman:
'Differences about economic policy among disinterested citizens derive predominantly
from different predictions . . . rather than from fundamental differences in basic
values, differences *about which men can only fight*' (my italics) (*Essays in Positive
Economics* (Chicago, 1953), p. 5). For a protest see Alan Altshuler, *The City Planning
Process* (Ithaca, N.Y., 1965), *ad init*.

ized/specific. That is why some who do not know, and especially those who have experience, are more practical than
others who know. [114b8–18, Ross]

Aristotle is saying here, among other things, that practical
wisdom in its deliberative manifestations is concerned both
with the attainment of particular formed objectives and also
with questions of general policy—what specific objectives *to*
form. He contrasts the two components, and in doing so he
commits his investigation to the study of both (*cf.* 1142b30).
On my view of *NE* 3, we ought not to be surprised by this. But
there is a philosophical difficulty about this kind of deliberation
which becomes plainer and plainer as *NE* 6 proceeds.

Aristotle had hoped in *NE* 3 to illuminate examples of
nontechnical deliberation by comparing them with a paradigm
drawn from technical deliberation. The trouble with both
paradigm and comparison is this. It is absolutely plain what
counts as my having adequate covering or as my having
succeeded in drawing a plane figure of the prescribed kind
using only ruler and compass. The practical question here is
only what means or measures will work or work best or most
easily to those ends. But the standard problem in a non-
technical deliberation is quite different. In the nontechnical
case I shall characteristically have an extremely vague description of something I want—a good life, a satisfying profession,
an interesting holiday, an amusing evening—and the problem
is not to see what will be causally efficacious in bringing this
about but to see what really *qualifies* as an adequate and
practically realizable specification of what would satisfy this
want. Deliberation is still *zetēsis*, a search, but it is not
primarily a search for means. It is a search for the *best
specification*. Till the specification is available there is no room
for means. When this specification is reached, means-end
deliberation can start, but difficulties that turn up in this
means-end deliberation may send me back a finite number of
times to the problem of a better or more practicable
specification of the end, and the whole interest and difficulty of
the matter is in the search for adequate specifications, not in
the technical means-end sequel or sequels. It is here that the
analogy with the geometer's search, or the search of the
inadequately clothed man, goes lame.

It is common ground between my interpretation and the interpretation of those who would accept the three tenets given at the outset, contentions (1) (2) (3), that Aristotle sensed *some* such difficulty in his dealings with practical reason. But according to the other interpretation [see (2) and (3)], Aristotle was led at this point to make a distinction between the situation where the agent has to see his situation as falling under a rule and the situation where the agent has simply to find means to encompass a definite objective.

Professor Allan gives the most argued form of this interpretation. Speaking of the practical syllogism he says 'in some contexts actions are subsumed by intuition under general rules, and performed or avoided accordingly. . . . In other contexts it is said to be a distinctive feature of practical syllogisms that they start from the announcement of an end [he then instances *NE* 1144a31, 1151a15–19, and *EE* 1227b28–32]. . . . A particular action is then performed because it is a means or the first link in a chain of means leading to the end' (2). In support of this he claims to find Aristotle making such a distinction in the syllogisms mentioned at *De motu animalium* 701a9ff. In Forster's Loeb translation that passage reads as follows:

> The conclusion drawn from the two premises becomes the action. For example, when you conceive that every man ought to walk and you yourself are a man, you immediately walk; or if you conceive that on a particular occasion no man ought to walk, and you yourself are a man, you immediately remain at rest. In both instances action follows unless there is some hindrance or compulsion. Again, I ought to create a good, and a house is a good, I immediately create a house. Again, I need a covering, and a cloak is a covering. I need a cloak. What I need I ought to make: I need a cloak, I ought to make a cloak. And the conclusion 'I ought to make a cloak' is an action. The action results from the beginning of the train of thought. If there is to be a cloak, such and such a thing is necessary, if this thing then something else; and one immediately acts accordingly. That the action is the conclusion is quite clear; but the premises which lead to the doing of something are of two kinds, through the good and through the possible.

Now I think Allan understands this passage in a strange way. For he writes 'Aristotle *begins* with an example of the former [*sc.* rule-case] type [the walk syllogism]. . ., but includes among other examples one of the latter type [the cloak syllogism] . . . and he adds that the premises may be of two forms, since they specify either that something is good, or how it is possible (*hai de protaseis hai poietikai dia duo eidon ginontai, dia te tou agathou kai dia tou dunatou* [the premises that lead to the doing of something are of two kinds, concerning the good and the possible])'[6]. This is a strange reading. The walk syllogism, like the next syllogism, will need in any case to be treated as a dummy syllogism, a mere variable. For even if Allan's distinction between two kinds of syllogism could stand, the syllogism would be an idiotic example of either. No conclusion could safely rest on its 'rule-like' appearance. It would also be difficult to settle which sort the house-syllogism belonged to if any such distinction were intended.

In truth, the sentence about two kinds of premises seems to be no more than an allusion to the general form often manifestly displayed and always present (I believe) in Aristotelian action-syllogisms. The first or major premise mentions something that can be the subject of desire, *orexis*, transmissible to some practical conclusion (*i.e.*, a desire convertible via some available minor premise into action). The second premise details a circumstance pertaining to the feasibility, in the particular situation to which the syllogism is applied, of what must be done if the claim of the major premise is to be heeded. In the light of these *De motu* examples nothing could be more natural than to describe the first premise of a practical syllogism as *pertaining to the good* (the fact that it pertains to some good—either a general good or something which the agent has just resolved is good in this situation—is what beckons to desire) and to describe the second or minor premise as *pertaining to the possible* (where 'possible' connotes the feasibility, *given* the circumstances registered by the minor premise, of the object of concern mentioned in the first premise). I can find no textual support for Allan's attempt to make the distinction into a distinction between different kinds of major premises. Indeed, no syllogism could be truly practical or be appropriately backed by orexis if its major premise were simply of the possible.

So much for the alleged presence of the distinction between rule-case and means-end syllogisms in the *De motu* passage. But even if I were wrong (and even if a distinctive rule-case type of syllogism were found at *NE* 7), contention (3) would still founder on other rocks. Allan's distinction of syllogisms is not the right distinction to solve Aristotle's problem, or *the* problem, of practical deliberation. The deliberative situations that challenge philosophical reflection to replace the means-ends description do not involve a kind of problem that anybody would think he could solve by subsuming a case under rules, whereas the comparatively trivial technical problems that are treated by Allan as means-end cases might often be resolved by recourse to rules. Nor can this difficulty be avoided by suggesting that if a policy question becomes too general or all-embracing, then there is no longer any rational deliberation about it. For Aristotle there is. He is convinced that the discovery and specification of the end is an intellectual problem, among other things, and belongs to practical wisdom. See 1142b31–33, for instance:

> If excellence in deliberation, *euboulia*, is one of the traits of men of practical wisdom, we may regard this excellence as correct perception of that which conduces to the end, whereof practical wisdom is a true judgment.

It is one of the considerable achievements of Allan's interpretation to have resolved the dispute about this sentence and to leave the relative clause meaning what the ancient tradition took it to mean and what it so obviously does mean. The good is the sort of thing which we wish for *because we think it good*, not something we think good because it is what we wish for. Thought and reason—not without desire, I must add—are the starting point.[7]

If all this were not enough to refute contentions (2) and (3),

---

[7] See *Politics* 1332b6–8 and *Metaphysics* 1072a2–9: 'We desire it because it seems good to us, it doesn't seem good to us because we desire it'. It is the beginning of wisdom on this matter, both as an issue of interpretation and as a philosophical issue, to see that we do not really have to choose between Aristotle's proposition and its apparent opposite (as at *e.g.*, Spinoza, *Ethics*, pt. III, proposition 9, note). We can desire it because it seems good *and* it seem good because we desire it. Cp. Essay V, *passim*.

then Aristotle's own remarks elsewhere about the character of general rules and principles would be enough to discredit the rule-case approach. There *are* no general principles or rules anyway—except in so far as these are condensations of the judgment of aisthēsis (on which see the paraphrase of 1143a26 to be offered at §4):

> Matters concerned with conduct and questions of what is good for us have no fixity, any more than matters of health. The general account [of practical knowledge] being of this nature, the account of particular cases is yet more lacking in exactness; for they do not fall under any art or precept, but the agents themselves in each case consider what is appropriate to the occasion, as happens also in the art of medicine and navigation (1104a3–10 *cf.* 1107a28).

From the nature of the case the subject matter of the practical is indefinite and unforeseeable, and any supposed principle would have an indefinite number of exceptions. To understand what such exceptions would be and what makes them exceptions would be to understand something not reducible to rules or principles. The only metric we can impose on the subject matter of practice is the metric of the Lesbian rule:

> In fact this is the reason why not everything is determined by law and special and specific decrees are often needed. For when the thing is indefinite, the measure of it must be indefinite too, like the leaden rules used in making the Lesbian moulding. The rule adapts itself to the shape of the stone and is not rigid, and so too a special decree is adapted to the facts [1137b27–32, *cf. Politics* 1282b1–6].

I conclude that what Aristotle had in mind in Book 6 was nothing remotely resembling what has been ascribed to him by neo-Kantian interpreters. Certainly contention (3) must seem absurdly overstated if the only new material which we can muster on Aristotle's behalf for the hard cases of deliberative specification is the 'rule-case' syllogism.

## 4. The Books 6–7 Treatment of Deliberative Specification—a General Framework for its Interpretation and Evaluation

*NE* 6 can be seen in a more interesting light than this. On the interpretation to be presented I admit that the new materials largely consist of sophistications, amendments, and extensions of the means-end paradigm. Nor is the alleged problem of the 'validity' of the practical syllogism solved. But Aristotle has a number of ideas to offer that seem to me to be of more fundamental importance than anything to be found now in utility theory, decision theory, or other rationality studies, however sketchily and obscurely he expressed them. That Aristotle's ideas are inchoate, however, is only one part of what is troublesome in establishing this claim. There is also the difficulty of finding a perspective or vantage point, over a philosophical terrain still badly understood, from which to view Aristotle's theory, and the difficulty (in practice rarely overcome) of sustaining philosophical momentum over a prolonged examination of a large number of obscure but relevant passages of the *Ethics* and *De Anima*.

To these difficulties my practical response is to adjourn all discussion of *akrasia* and, proceeding as if Aristotle had avoided what I regard as the errors of *NE* 7, to give the bare outline (a)–(g) of a neo-Aristotelian theory of practical reason. After that I shall amplify one point in this theory by giving an expanded paraphrase of two of the most obscure and most important passages about practical reason in *NE* 6. The reader's best defence against so prejudicial a method of exposition will be to compare the paraphrase with the Ross translation.

(a) There are theories of practical reason according to which the ordinary situation of an agent who deliberates resembles nothing so much as that of a snooker player who has to choose from a large number of possible shots the shot that rates highest when two products are added. The first product is the utility of the shot's success (a utility that depends in snooker upon the colour of the ball to be potted and the expected utility for purposes of the next shot of the resulting position) multiplied by the probability $P$ of this player's potting the ball. The second product is the utility (negative) of his failure multiplied by $(1 - P)$. It is neither here nor there that it is not easy to determine the values of some of these elements for purposes of comparing prospects. There is no problem about the end itself nor about the means. The end is to maximize points. Of course, there do exist deliberative situations, apart from snooker, which are a bit like this. But with ordinary deliberation it is quite different. There is nothing a person is under antecedent sentence to maximize; and probabilities, though difficult and relevant, need not be the one great crux of the matter. One usually asks himself 'What shall I do?' not with a view to maximizing anything but only in response to a particular context. This will make particular and contingent demands on his moral or practical perception, but the relevant features of the situation may not all jump to the eye. To see what they are, to prompt the imagination to play upon the question and let it activate in reflection and thought-experiment whatever concerns and passions it should activate, may require a high order of situational appreciation, or, as Aristotle would say, perception (*aisthesis*). In this, as we shall see, and in the unfortunate fact that few situations come already inscribed with the names of all the concerns that they touch or impinge upon, resides the crucial importance of the minor premise of the practical syllogism.

(b) When the relevant concerns are provisionally identified, they may still be too unspecific for means-end reasoning to begin. See the account of 'deliberative specification' in §3. Most of what is interesting and difficult in practical reason happens here, and under (a).

(c) No theory, if it is to recapitulate or reconstruct practical reasoning even as well as mathematical logic recapitulates or reconstructs the actual experience of conducting or exploring deductive argument, can treat the concerns an agent brings to any situation as forming a closed, complete, consistent system. For it is of the essence of these concerns to make competing, inconsistent claims. (This is a mark not of our irrationality but of *rationality* in the face of the plurality of ends and the plurality of human goods.)[8] The weight of the claims represented

---

[8] Jonathan Glover speaks of 'the aesthetic preference most of us have for economy of principles, the preference for ethical systems in the style of the Bauhaus rather than Baroque' (*The Aristotelian Society, Supplementary Volume 49*, 1975, p. 183). Against this I say that only a confusion between the practical and the theoretical could even purport to provide reasoned grounds for such a preference. (For the beginnings of the distinction, see Bernard Williams, 'Consistency and Realism', *The Aristotelian Society, Supplementary Volume 40*, 1966, pp. 1-22.) Why is an axiom system any better

by these concerns is not necessarily fixed in advance. Nor need
the concerns be hierarchically ordered. Indeed, a person's
reflection on a new situation that confronts him may disrupt
such order and fixity as had previously existed and bring a
change in his evolving conception of the point (*to hou heneka*),
or the several or many points, of living or acting.

(d) Someone may think it clear to him in a certain situation
what is the relevant concern, yet find himself discontent with
every practical syllogism promoting that concern (with major
premise representing the concern). He may resile from the
concern when he sees what it leads to, or what it costs, and start
all over again. It is not necessarily true that he who wills the end
must will the means. The same would have to apply to public
rationality, if we had that. In a bureaucracy, where action is not
constantly referred back to what originally motivated it, the
acute theoretical and practical problem is to make room for
some such stepping back, and for the constant remaking and
reevaluation of concerns: also for the distinction that individual
citizens make effortlessly for themselves between (i) ends that
deliberation can realize by making projects and (ii) the constraints or concerns that delimit the space within which deliberation can operate freely. In this difficulty of referring back, and
in the chronic inability of public agencies to render the relation
*is found better overall than* transitive between situations envisaged and/or actually brought about by planning, lies one of
the conceptual foundations for a reasoned hatred of bureaucracy, and for the demand for 'public participation' in planning.

---

foundation for practice than, *e.g.*, a long and incomplete or open-ended list of (always
at the limit conflicting) *desiderata*? The claims of all true *beliefs* (about how the world
is) are reconcilable. Everything true must be consistent with everything else that is true.
But not all the claims of all rational concerns or even all moral concerns (that the world
*be* thus or so) need be reconcilable. There is no reason to expect that they would be; and
Aristotle gives at 1137b the reason why we cannot expect to lay down a decision
procedure for adjudication in advance between claims, or for prior mediation. By the
dragooning of the plurality of goods into the order of an axiom system I think practice
will be almost as rapidly and readily degraded (and almost as unexpectedly perhaps) as
modern building, by exploitation of the well-intentioned efforts of the Bauhaus, has
been degraded into the single-minded pursuit of profit. (The last phase of Walter
Gropius's architectural career, and the shady and incongruous company into which
his ambitions for modern architecture drew him so irresistibly, will repay study by
those drawn to Glover's analogy.)

If one dislikes the last, or has no stomach for the expenditure of time and effort that it entails, then one should go back to the beginning, defy certain demands often represented as imperatives, and reexamine the ends for which a bureaucracy of such a size was taken to be needed, or at least the means chosen to realize the said ends.

(e) The unfinished or indeterminate character of our ideals and value structure is constitutive both of human freedom and, for finite creatures who face an indefinite or infinite range of contingencies with only finite powers of prediction and imagination (*NE* 1137b), of practical rationality itself.

(f) The person of real practical wisdom is the one who brings to bear upon a situation the greatest number of genuinely pertinent concerns and genuinely relevant considerations commensurate with the importance of the deliberative context. The best practical syllogism is that whose minor premise arises out of such a one's perceptions, concerns, and appreciations. It records what strikes the person as the *in the situation most salient feature of the context in which he has to act*. This activates a corresponding major premise that spells out the general import of the concern that makes this feature the salient feature in the situation. An analogy explored by Donald Davidson[9] between a *judgment of probability*, taken in its relation to judgments of probability relative to evidence, and a *decision*, taken in its relation to judgments of the desirability of an action relative to such and such contextual facts, will suggest this idea; the larger the set of considerations that issue in the singling out of the said feature, the more compelling the syllogism. But there are no formal criteria by which to compare the claims of competing syllogisms. Inasmuch as the syllogism arises in a determinate context, the major premise is evaluated not for its unconditional acceptability, nor for embracing more considerations than its rivals, but for its adequacy to the situation. It will be adequate for the situation if and only if circumstances that could restrict or qualify it and defeat its applicability at a

---

[9] *Cf.* 'How is Weakness of Will Possible?' in *Moral Concepts*, ed. Feinberg (Oxford University Press, 1969).

given juncture do not in the practical context of this syllogism obtain. Its evaluation is of its essence dialectical, and all of a piece with the perceptions and reasonings that gave rise to the syllogism in the first place.

(g) Since the goals and concerns that an agent brings to a situation may be diverse and incommensurable, and may not in themselves dictate any decision, they need not constitute the materials for some psychological theory (or any empirical theory above the conceptual level of a theory of matter) to make a prediction of the action.[10] Nor need anything else constitute these materials. There is simply no reason to expect that it will be possible to construct an (however idealized) empirical theory of the rational agent to parallel the predictive power, explanatory nonvacuity, and satisfactoriness for its purposes of an economic hypothesis—*e.g.* that under a wide variety of specifiable circumstances individual firms will push every line of action open to them to the point where marginal cost and marginal revenue are equal. If prediction were essential, then a phenomenologist or someone with a strong interest in the value consciousness of his subject might do best. But what is needed here is not prediction, but the subject's own decision processes, constantly redeployed on new situations or on new understandings of old ones.

## 5.   Two paraphrases of Aristotle

My first paraphrase is of 1142a23 ff.:

> That practical wisdom is not deductive theoretical knowledge is plain. For practical wisdom is, as I have said, of the ultimate and particular—as is the subject matter of action. In this, practical wisdom is the counterpart or dual of theoretical intuition. *Theoretical* intellect or intuition is of the ultimate, but in this sense—it is of ultimate universal concepts and axioms that are too primitive or fundamental to admit of further analysis or of justification from without. [At the opposite extreme] practical wisdom [as a counterpart of theoretical reason] also treats of matters that defy justification from

---

[10] See Donald Davidson, 'Mental Events' in *Experience and Theory*, ed. Foster and Swanson (London, 1971). Also 'Towards a Reasonable Libertarianism', Essay VIII below.

without. Practical wisdom is of what is ultimate and particular in the distinct sense of needing to be quite simply perceived. By perception here I do not mean sense perception but the kind of perception or insight one needs to see that a triangle, say, is one of the basic or ultimate components [of a figure which one has to construct with ruler and compass]. [For there is no *routine* procedure for analysing a problem figure into the components by which one may construct it with rule and compasses.] The analysis calls for insight, and there is a limit to what one can say about it. But even this sort of insight is more akin to sense perception than practical wisdom is really akin to sense perception.

*Comment:* On this reading the geometer example turns up again. The method which the geometer discovers to construct the prescribed figure has a property unusual in a technical deliberation and ideal for making the transition to another kind of case, that of being in some sense constitutive of the end in view. It counts as the answer to a question he was asked (and would be proved to count so). *Caution.* Paraphrase and interpretation is not here confined to square-bracketed portions.

The other paraphrase I offer is of *NE* 1143a26 follg.:

... when we speak of judgment and understanding and practical wisdom and intuitive reason, we credit the same people with possessing judgment and having reached years of reason and with having practical wisdom and understanding. For all these faculties deal with ultimates or particularized specifics; and being a man of understanding and of good or sympathetic judgment consists in being able to judge about the things with which practical wisdom is concerned; for the equities are common to all good men in relation to other men. Now all action relates to the particular or ultimate; for not only must the man of practical wisdom know particular facts, but understanding and judgment are also concerned with things to be done, and these are ultimates. And intuitive reason is concerned with ultimates in both directions [i.e., with ultimates in two senses and respects, in respect of extreme generality and in respect of extreme specificity]. For intuitive reason [the general faculty] is of both the most primitive and the ultimate terms. Its proper province is where derivation or independent justification is impossible. In the case of that species of intuitive reason which is the theoretical intuition pertaining to demonstrative proof, its object is the most fundamental concepts and axioms. In its practical variety, on the other hand, intuitive reason concerns the most particular and contingent and specific. This is the typical subject matter of the minor premise of a practical syllogism [the one which is 'of the possible']. For here, in the capacity to find the right feature and form a practical syllogism, resides the understanding of the reason for performing an action, or its end. For the major premise and the generalizable concern that comes with it arise from this perception of something particular. So one must have an appreciation or perception of the particular, and my name for this is intuitive reason. [It is the source both of particular syllogisms and of all the concerns however particular or general that give a man reason to act.] . . . we think our powers correspond to our time of life, and that a particular age brings with it intuitive reason and judgment; this implies that nature is the cause. . . . Therefore we ought to attend to the undemonstrated sayings and opinions of experienced and older people or of people of practical wisdom not less than to demonstrations; for, because experience has given them an eye, they see aright.

*Comment.* It is the mark of the man of practical wisdom on this account to be able to select from the infinite number of features of a situation those features that bear upon the notion or ideal of existence which it is his standing aim to make real. This conception of human life results in various evaluations of all kinds of things, in various sorts of cares and concerns, and in various projects. It does not reside in a set of maxims or precepts, useful though Aristotle would allow these to be at a certain stage in the education of the emotions. In no case will there be a rule to which a man can simply appeal to tell him what to do (except in the special case—see 1129b19 follg.— where an absolute prohibition operates). The man may have no other recourse but to invent the answer to the problem. As often as not, the inventing, like the frequent accommodation he has to effect between the claims of competing values, may count as a modification or innovation or further determination in the evolution of his view of what a good life is. *Caution.* As before, paraphrase has not been confined to square-bracketed sentences.

## 6. Conclusion

Against this account, as I have explained it, it may be complained that in the end very little is said, because everything that is hard has been permitted to take refuge in the notion of aisthesis, or *situational appreciation* as I have paraphrased this. And in aisthesis, as Aristotle says, explanations give out. I reply that, if there is no real prospect of an ordinary scientific or simply empirical theory of all of action and deliberation as such, then the thing we should look for may be precisely what Aristotle provides—namely, a conceptual framework which we can apply to particular cases, which articulates the reciprocal relations of an agent's concerns and his perception of how things objectively are in the world; and a schema of description *which relates the complex ideal the agent tries in the process of living his life to make real to the form that the world impresses, both by way of opportunity and by way of limitation, upon that ideal.* Here too, within the same schema, are knitted together, as von Wright says, 'the concepts of wanting an end, understanding a necessity, and setting oneself to act. It is a contribution to the moulding or shaping of these concepts'[11]. I entertain the unfriendly suspicion that those who feel they *must* seek more than all this provides want a scientific theory of rationality not so much from a passion for science, even where there can be no real science, but because they hope and desire, by some conceptual alchemy, to turn such a theory into a regulative or normative discipline, or into a system of rules by which to spare themselves some of the torment of thinking, feeling and understanding that can actually be involved in reasoned deliberation.

---

[11] G.H. von Wright, *The Varieties of Goodness* (London, 1963), p. 171. Both for the quotation and in the previous sentence I am indebted to Martha Nussbaum. In her *Aristotle's 'De Motu Animalium'* (Princeton, 1978) she writes: 'the appeal of this form of explanation for Aristotle may lie in its ability to link an agent's desires and his perceptions of how things are in the world around him, his subjective motivation and the objective limitations of his situation . . . animals are seen as acting in accordance with desire, but within the limits imposed by nature'.

# VII

# Weakness of Will, Commensurability, and the Objects of Deliberation and Desire*

> It is hard to struggle with one's heart's desire.
> It will pay with soul for what it craves.
>
> HERACLITUS

1. Almost anyone not under the influence of theory will say that, when a person is weak-willed, he intentionally chooses that which he knows or believes to be the worse course of action when he could choose the better course; and that, in acting in this way, the weak-willed man acts not for *no* reason at all—that would be strange and atypical—but irrationally.

The description just given appears to be a consistent description of the inconsistent (not necessarily perverse) conduct that is characteristic of weak will. In this paper something will be done to show that it is a sat sfiable and frequently satisfied description. But there are philosophers of mind and moral philosophers who have felt a strong theoretical compulsion to rewrite the description, rather than allow the

* *Proceedings of the Aristotelian Society* vol. 79, 1978/9, with minor revisions. In October 1975 I read to the Aristotelian Society the paper called 'Deliberation and Practical Reason', which is Essay VI here. The present paper was a reworking with new beginning and ending of what had to be omitted from that. The acknowledgements to Essay VI carry over to this essay. There were new debts to J.H. McDowell, M.F. Burnyeat, and C.A.B. Peacocke. I benefited from discussion and correspondence with all of them in reworking this material, and by the exchange of manuscripts on germane topics. McDowell's 'The Role of Eudaimonia in Aristotle's Ethics' appeared in *Proceedings of the African Classical Associations* vol. 15, 1979/80, and was reprinted as Chapter 19 of *Essays on Aristotle's Ethics* Ed. A.O. Rorty (ULCA, 1981)—as were Essay VI and VII here. Burnyear's paper 'Aristotle on Learning to Be Good' is chap. 5 of the same volume. Peacocke's paper 'Intention and Akrasia' is in *Essays on Davidson: Action and Events*, ed. Merrill Provence Hintikka and Bruce Vermazen (Oxford University Press, 1985). I also incurred new obligations to Professor J.L. Ackrill, who tried to reduce the overall quantity of errors I committed here. I would direct the reader to a book I regret I did not know at the time of writing the original version of Essays VI and VII, namely, his *Aristotle's Ethics* (London, 1973). See esp. pp. 30, 32–3, and 272.

phenomenon of weakness of will to appear as an incontrovertible refutation of the theories of mind or morality that they are committed to defend. It is not, I suppose, inconceivable that this pretheoretical description of weakness of will should be strictly and literally true of nothing; but he who values his pet theory above the phenomenon and wants to hold that weakness of will as I have described it simply does not exist will surely need to command some formidable conceptual-cum-explanatory leverage in the philosophy of value and mind—and an Archimedean fulcrum of otherwise inexplicable facts of human conduct. Pending the emergence of such a theoretician—a man of some different stuff from any ordinary philosopher, psychologist, decision theorist, or economist—perhaps we should feel some provisional gratitude for the rich philosophical suggestiveness by which *akrasia* compensates us for the harm it so repeatedly does us.

In the first place, the phenomenon of weakness of will helps us to adjudicate certain ideas that have important dependencies in moral theory:

(1)   that there is something one invariably acts to maximize;

(2)   that one invariably acts in order to maximize something;

(3)   that there is something such that all actions we have reasons to do are actions that will maximize that.

If I am right in the principal contention of this paper, then (1) (2) and (3) can all be traced to the same oversimplified conception of value (and consequentially mind) as can (5) and (6) below. (See §8.) But the doubtfulness of (1) (2) (3) does not exhaust even the moral philosophical interest of weak will. The phenomenon also makes doubtful certain variants of the idea.

(4)   that, whatever the assertibility condition of a normative judgment may lack in objective factuality, this deficit can be made up by some affect in the maker of the judgment, whose seriousness or sincerity may be ascertained by testing whether he acts out the commitment that his judgment purports to express.[1]

---

[1] I try here to catch many variants upon an idea whose canonical and different expression is to be found in the well known writings of Richard Hare.

In the philosophy of mind there are at least two positions that are impugned by weakness of will as pretheoretically conceived (in formulations influenced by Christopher Peacocke[2]):

(5) is the position that results from conjoining two principles, the principle (a) that the desire one acts on intentionally is the strongest deliberated desire, and the principle (b) that it is irrational to act against the strongest deliberated desire.

(6) is the position that results from combining principle (a) above with the principle (c) that the best criterion for someone's making the deliberated judgment that course $x$ is better than course $y$ is his wanting more strongly to choose $x$ than he wants to choose $y$.[3]

Only the conjunctions (a) *and* (b), (a) *and* (c) are directly impugned by weakness of will. But anybody who takes it seriously will suspect each of (a) and (c). (Especially perhaps if he is disposed to accept (b); but, even if he thinks (b) arises from a flawed conception of rationality, he may be led to suspect both of the other principles.) Such a philosopher is likely, I think, to recover the following picture of the progress from thought to action:

(i) Faced with choice between courses of action $x$ and $y$ one may appraise or evaluate each. (In a favourable case it may be possible and desirable to compare them in respect of one simple or complex feature: but let us bracket the question whether that is always possible.)

(ii) By whatever deliberative route, one may come to decide that $x$ is the better course. In a favourable case one may decide that $x$ is better *all things considered*.[4] But an agent may disbelieve altogether in the possibility of arriving at such a judgment—in which case, if he is able to decide at all, then he dispenses with the 'all things considered' and goes straight to the next stage.

[2] *Op. cit.* at note * above.
[3] *Cf.* Donald Davidson, 'Weakness of Will,' in *Moral Concepts*, ed. Feinberg (Oxford University Press, 1969), p. 2.
[4] The statement that $x$ is the better course all things considered is to be read here not with a technical sense but with the ordinary sense which English invests it with.

(iii) One decides *to* follow course *x;* and thereafter one has the intention to do that. There is no need for a chronological differentiation between this and phase (ii) above. But some conceptual differentiation seems imperative. One can decide for *x* rather than *y* without thinking either of them the better. And, where there is a judgment of comparison, it is surely one thing to think that *x* is better than *y* [phase (ii)], and another to *find it so* and, finding it so, to choose it.

(iv) Having decided in favour of *x*, one may stick by the decision when the relevant moment comes—or not stick by it and change one's intention. This is usually weakness. But when one sticks by the decision even where the original deliberation and judgment stand in need of review (*e.g.*, in the light of new perception), that is obstinacy. If one holds the judgment open to relevant new perception and, subject only to that, one abides by the practical decision, then that is continence, or strength of character. It may even be temperance. In the special case where fear obtrudes, it is courage.

Continence and courage are states of character. If states of character are dispositions (as I suppose they are), then it will help to allay some gratuitous perplexities about the failures that have just been rehearsed under (iv) to remember what certain ordinary dispositions are like.[5]

Just occasionally a horse that is surefooted may miss his step. He may even trip at the point where a less surefooted animal was lucky enough to have passed recently without slipping. Again, aviation spirit is very inflammable. But, just once, someone may get away with it when he throws a lighted match into a tankful of the stuff—even as someone far less rash pays with his life for the risk that he took in throwing a match into a tankful of paraffin.[6] When these things happen, we think that there is always an explanation to be found. We do not always find it (and there is no one place where we always need to look). Nor can we write down a list of conditional sentences

---

[5] I am indebted here to J.C. D'Alessio, 'Dispositions, Reduction Sentences, and Causal Conditions,' *Critica*, 1, 3 (1967), and to his thesis on dispositions (Oxford D. Phil., 1968).

[6] People say that Lord Brabazon of Tara was in the habit of doing just this, in order to demonstrate the relative safety of paraffin as a fuel for aeroplane engines.

(still less a list of reduction sentences in the manner of Carnap) such that a horse is surefooted—or a stuff is inflammable—if and only if these conditionals are true. In special cases we can leave all that behind and give a scientific account of the secret nature of the disposition in question. In ordinary cases the most we can do is to specify the disposition as that disposition in virtue of which *normally*, if for instance . . . be the case, then ___ will be the case, leaving theory, anecdotal knowledge, and whatever else to lend content to the 'normally' and the 'for instance'.

Similarly (*somewhat* similarly, rather, see below §5), when a man of some character fails to persevere in his decision, we look for an explanation. But the task of the philosophy of mind is not to chronicle in advance the conditions under which this failure will happen, or to provide one explanation schema to cover all cases. It is to describe such phenomena as weakness of will in such a way that there is room for the case-by-case explanations that we normally accept. Some of the explanations that we sometimes accept describe what happens from the inside. They give the man's *reason* for departing so weakly from his decision. In that case it is of capital importance that our philosophy of value should accommodate such reasons *as* reasons, even as the philosophy of mind measures up to the question of what quality and degree of weakness is evidenced by the lapse, and the even harder question of what it shows about character. ('Moral insight, as communicable vision or as quality of being, *is* something separable from definitive performance, and we do not always, though doubtless we do usually, require performance as, or allow performance to be, the test of the vision or of the person who holds it.'[7])

We can make perplexities for ourselves in moral philosophy and philosophy of mind by promoting arbitrary construction in invented vocubulary to the place that should be occupied by ordinary description of mental phenomena, or by ignoring the special character of dispositional concepts. But above all we perplex ourselves by failing to heed the subject matter of deliberation and decision. To ignore the nature of the scheme of values between which deliberation and decision have to arbitrate is

[7] Iris Murdoch, 'Vision and Choice in Morality', *The Aristotelian Society, Supplementary Volume* 28, 1954, p. 42.

the most potent source of perplexity about weakness of will.

2.  If we are to describe phases (i)–(iv) at all, then we need autonomous and mutually irreducible notions of believing, desiring, deciding *that*, deciding *to*, intending. And, in correspondence with these, we must speak not only of someone's capacity for evaluation and appreciation, his nerve and resolve, but also of his executive virtues or dispositions, like courage and continence.[8] Or so I should argue. Once we are embarked on this descriptive project, and once we seek to draw out the mind's picture of the mind, it is like building one's own house and then economizing on ink and postage stamps in order to offset the mounting expense, to try to describe all this exclusively in terms of belief and desire. But how do wanting and desiring fit into the picture? I described phases (i), (ii), (iii), and (iv) as if wanting scarcely figured at all—a salutary exaggeration or defect, perhaps, but scarcely one that can be allowed to go uncorrected. To fill the lacuna will bring us just one step closer to Aristotle,[9] though the account of weakness of will that would result if the picture were made complete is not Aristotle's own account.

In the first place, desire or something that brings in desire is involved at phases (i) and (ii). It is hard to conceive of there being an evaluation of *x* and *y* in the absence of a structure of preexisting concerns that will *direct* the imagining of what *x* amounts to and of what *y* amounts to and that will *focus* the evaluator's attendant perceptions of the circumstances. I cannot see that such standing concerns, which jointly determine what Aristotle called a conception (*hupolepsis*) of the good, have necessarily to be *identified* with desires. But I concede that such concerns cannot exist unless there are some standing desires that they organize. Again, although I should insist that the imagination and perception that phases (i) and (ii) call for are needed to *prepare* desire to embrace course *x* at phase (iii), I

[8] For the notion of an executive virtue see not so much Aristotle as D.F. Pears 'Aristotle's Analysis of Courage', *Midwest Studies in Philosophy Volume* 3 (1978).
[9] See especially *De Anima* 433b29–30, *De Motu Animalium* 702a18–19, 700b17–25; and the account of *phantasia* offered by Martha Nussbaum in Essay V in her *Aristotle's 'De Motu Animalium'* (Princeton, 1978).

concede that deliberative imagination and the other cognitive capacities involved do have to be energized by something that belongs on the side of affect—if only the readiness and capacity to *form* desires that will make real that which is judged to be good.

It must then be conceded to the side of desire that both imagination and perception at phase (i) and deliberative integration at phase (ii) will require an organizing conception that is in some sense (the sense just given) sustained or held in place by desire. But, so long as we avoid all technical uses of 'want' and 'desire', we shall not be in the least tempted simply to *identify* any constituent of genuine evaluative or integrative thinking with desire. Nor, I would add, do we need to hasten to the conclusion that an organizing conception, which is not itself a desire, is sure to be ineffective at either the integrative or the subsequent stages (iii) (iv) if there is a desire contrary to the desire for course $x$, and this contrary desire (the desire to escape danger now, for instance) presents itself as stronger than the desire for $x$.

As regards this last claim, everything depends on what one ought to mean by strength in a desire.[10] There is one sense in which a strong desire is a desire that is a winner; the desire either knocks out its rivals or defeats them on points. Just as the strongest fighter is the fighter who is such as to win, so the strongest desire is the desire that is such as to get itself acted upon (so to speak). Philosophers have noted this usage and gone so far as to make it analytic that the strongest desire is the desire that wins. What is unfortunate about this is not so much the stipulation of analyticity—ill-advised though it seems (consider—by an unseen foul or by bad luck, the stronger fighter can lose against the weaker)—as the bad effect the stipulation appears to have had upon the comprehension of the other sense of 'strong' as predicated of desires.

In the other and commoner sense of 'strong', a desire is strong if, in respect of vividness or appeal to the imagination, exigency, or importunity, it is *like* a desire that is a strong desire in the first sense. A strong desire is a desire that has the

---

[10] *Cf.* Susan Khin Zaw, 'Irresistible Impulse and Criminal Responsibility' in *Human Values*, ed. G.N.A. Vesey (Hassocks, Sussex, 1978).

subjective character typically enjoyed by desires that do in fact get their way. But a desire can have this felt character without getting its way. And a desire can get its way without having this subjective character.

I strove to keep phases (ii) and (iii) apart. But, even when (iii) itself is achieved and when there is the normally consequential desire to implement the decision in favour of x (so much we should expect), I think one can now see that there is still no reason why the desire to do that which is involved by x should invariably or automatically be stronger than all other desires— unless this simply means that, where the decision *is* actually adhered to, this desire is shown to have been the strongest. So stage (iii) can be reached without there being any guarantee (even if there is some presumption) that some desire is present that will *see to it*, no matter what, that the decision will be implemented. And hence the need for the executive virtues of which I spoke under (iv), virtues that can refresh and recollect deliberations under (i) (ii) (iii) but are conceptually distinct from anything we find there. The more a man needs to overcome subjectively stronger desires to keep to his decision, the more need he will have of continence. The less susceptible he is to attractions that run counter to the desires that support his decision at (iii) and supervene upon that, and the less susceptible he is to pleasures that compete with the distinctive pleasures that are accessible to the man of temperance and fortitude, the less need he will have of continence as such. *At the ideal limit*, perhaps he will have no need of it, according to Aristotle, because all counterattractions are simply 'silenced', as John McDowell has put it.[11]

3.  It may seem that what is most required to conclude this description of the passage from thought to action is an account of the distinctiveness and desirability of the objects of the particular kinds of desire that a man needs continence to insure him against the attractions of, and an account of the content of the *hupolepsis* of the good that can steer him past these attractions. The comparison between cowardly and incontinent

[11] See 'Are Moral Requirements Hypothetical Imperatives?' *The Aristotelian Society Supplementary Volume* 52, 1978, pp. 13–29; Cp. 'Virtue and Reason' *The Monist*, vol. 62, 1979.

actions and the very Aristotelian character of the notions here employed of desire, disposition, and executive virtue may even suggest that the account of weakness that I recommend as satisfactory is the existing Aristotelian account. But nobody who looks at either account in detail will confuse the account I have started here with Aristotle's own description of incontinence, where 'executive virtue' is not conspicuous.

Aristotle writes in Book 7 of the *Nicomachean Ethics:*

> One may be puzzled how a man with a correct view of a situation can be weak of will. For some deny that this is possible if he really knows what is the right thing to do. For if the knowledge is present, it is strange, as Socrates thought, for something else to overcome knowledge and manhandle it like a slave. Socrates was totally opposed to that view. He denied that there was any such thing as weakness of will. For knowing that it *is* the best, nobody, he said, acts contrary to the best. If he does act contrary to the best, it must be through ignorance. This account of Socrates' conflicts plainly with what seems to be the case and what people say [the *phainomena*]. . . . [1145b21–8]

After such an introduction, someone who read the book for the first time might conceivably anticipate the sort of description of akrasia that was begun in the previous sections of this paper. Such a description would exploit the conceptual riches of *hexeis* (dispositions) that Aristotle was the first philosopher to appreciate, and then build upon Aristotle's own account of the education of the emotions and perceptions and the maturation of such virtues as courage and temperance. If however we follow G.E.L. Owen's analysis of 'phenomena' in the works of Aristotle,[12] then we shall not be altogether unprepared for the possibility that, at the end, Aristotle will conclude that, in at least one important respect, Socrates was more right than wrong about weakness. (*Phainomena* are not necessarily facts.) And an examination of the ensuing text of Book 7 will suggest that this possibility is indeed realized. It is a strangely Socratic account compared with the account Aristotle might have given; and we need to understand how this came about. I shall trace the explanation back to his aspirations for happiness or *eudaimonia* in the theory of action.

[12] 'Tithenai ta Phainomena' in *Aristotle*, ed. J.M.E. Moravcsik (London, 1968).

Aristotle's fullest and final treatment of weakness of will or *akrasia* is at 1147a24–1147b19, and it presupposes the doctrine of the practical syllogism. I shall first declare the general interpretation I accept of the practical syllogism, then cut a long interpretative story short by an expanded translation-cum-paraphrase of the particular passage.

Practical syllogisms offer explanations of actions. These explanations are causal, but they reconstruct the reasons an agent himself has for his action. They usually comprise a major and a minor premise. The first or major premise mentions something for which there can be a desire (*orexis*) transmissible to some practical conclusion (*i.e.*, a desire convertible via some available minor premise into action). The second or minor premise details a circumstance pertaining to the feasibility in the particular situation of what must be done if the claim of the major premise is to be heeded. In the light of the examples Aristotle gives in *De Motu Animalium*, nothing seems more natural than to describe the first premise of a practical syllogism as *pertaining to the good* (the fact that it pertains to some good—either a general good or something which the agent has just resolved is good for this situation—is what can beckon to desire); and to describe the second or minor premise as *pertaining to the possible* (where 'possible' connotes the feasibility *given* the circumstances registered by the minor premise of the object of concern of the major premise).

Aristotle calls such patterns of reasoning 'syllogisms' because of an analogy that interests him between *deductively concluding or asserting* and *coming to a practical conclusion or acting*. He says that the conclusion of a practical syllogizing is an action. What matters most however in this theory is the idea that agents can see in the truth of the minor premise a way of ministering to some concern to which the major affords expression, and that their seeing this explains their doing what they do.

The paraphrase that I offer of 1147a24 following is this:

> Again, we may view the cause of akrasia in the manner of a natural scientist also as follows: The one premise [the major] is general, the other premise is concerned with the particular facts, which are the kind of thing to fall within the province of perception. When a single proposition results from

the two premises, then [in the case of scientific or deductive reasoning] the soul must of necessity affirm the conclusion; while in the practical sphere it must of necessity act. For instance, if one had better eat of anything that is sweet, and the object presented in some specific situation is sweet, then the man who can act and is not physically prevented *must* at the very moment [at which he brings the premises together] act accordingly. So when there is some premise or other [which combines with some minor premise to] constrain the man from eating of something [when for instance a major premise indicating that $\varphi$ things are bad for the health combines with a minor premise that a certain $x$ is $\varphi$]; and when there is another syllogism in the offing with the major premise that everything sweet is nice to eat and a minor premise that $x$ is sweet (this being the premise that is active) and appetite backs this syllogism; then the former syllogism forbids the man to taste but appetite's syllogism pushes him on. (For each part of the soul has the power of originating motion.) So it turns out that a man behaves incontinently under the influence (in some sense) of reason and belief. For he has argued himself to his practical conclusion from true beliefs, and these beliefs are not in themselves inconsistent with reason. It is the appetite itself that opposes reason, not the premises of the appetite's syllogism. It also follows that this is the reason why the lower animals are not incontinent, *viz.*, because they have no universal judgments of the kind that figure in syllogisms, but only imagination and memory of particulars.

The explanation of how this sort of ignorance is dissolved and the incontinent man regains his knowledge is the same as in the case of the man drunk or asleep and is not peculiar to his condition; we must go to students of natural science for it. Since the final premise (the minor) is a judgment deriving from perception and is the hinge on which all action must turn, *it is of this premise that the incontinent man is prevented by his condition from properly possessing himself.* Either that, or, if he does possess it, he does so only in the sense in which possessing does not mean comprehension but only talking, as a drunken man recites the verses of Empedocles. And so, because the second premise is not universal (still less an object of scientific knowledge) in the way the major premise may be universal, the point that Socrates most insisted upon turns out to be correct.[13]

---

[13] It will be worth reckoning up the similarities and differences between Aristotle and Socrates here. Aristotle does not think *akrasia* is an unusable term. He merely

> For passion does not worst [reading *perigignetai* with Stewart]
> anything with the status of demonstrable knowledge. It is not
> demonstrable knowledge that is manhandled like a slave [which
> would be absurd]. What passion overwhelms is a man's
> perception or appreciation *of a particular situation.*

This account of weakness is inconsistent with common sense,
and almost as inconsistent as Socrates' own account with the
account that we should naturally give of the cases where we think
we know we are doing what we should not do. Either the
incontinent man reaches the conclusion of the better syllogism,
or he doesn't. If he does, then there can be no conditional
necessity of the kind Aristotle alleges that he act on the
conclusion. For he doesn't act and he has reached it. Still less
can the conclusion of the syllogism be action itself. On the
other hand, if the agent does not get to the conclusion, then
there is no room for the struggle that Aristotle himself observes
to be characteristic of incontinence (*cf.* 1102b16–18, 1136a32).
There is no ambiguity in 'know' which can reduce the severity
of this dilemma. Nor does it help if the story is that the
conclusion is reached, secures momentary abstinence, and is
then eclipsed by appetite's syllogism. On any premises that
make conceptual trouble for weakness, the two syllogisms
cannot struggle, because they cannot coexist—even for one
moment.

4.   For Aristotle there has to be some important way in which
the incontinent man's cognitive conception of a situation may
be expected to differ from a temperate—contrast a *continent*—
man's conception. (There is allowance for that in our account
of the stages (i)–(iv) of Sections 1 and 2 above). But this is only
half of what was needed. It is important to see that McDowell,

---

redescribes the phenomenon it stands for. Socrates would appear to have thought the
term itself was unusable and irremediably confused. Both think the phenomenon
that goes under this name has to do with culpable ignorance: but the nature of the
ignorance is different. For Socrates the ignorance is typically general in character;
whereas for Aristotle the ignorance is of something particular, something here and
now. (N.B. the careful stipulation *prin en to pathei genesthai* at 1145b30.) Both believe
in the interpenetration of knowledge with virtue, and in *some* form of the thesis of the
unity of virtue. But what Aristotle believes is weaker, and permits him far greater
theoretical freedom in the separate but interdependent characterizations of the
individual virtues.

who is led to concur with Aristotle's view of akrasia, can be right about the interpretation of Aristotle on temperance, and right about what temptation or fear is *at that ideal limit* of temperance, and yet a difficulty can still arise that neither of them acknowledges. The difficulty we are concerned with relates not to the difference between temperance and continence (about which I do not aspire to say anything) but to the difference between continence and incontinence as these occur in ordinary adult people who fall short of the ideal, and the distinction that Aristotle is obliged to postulate between the continent man's and the incontinent man's knowledge and perception of a situation. These two men are neither of them temperate. In a sense, then, they are very much the same sort of men, and *susceptible* at least to the same sorts of excess. (Indeed, on different occasions one and the same man may do the continent thing or the incontinent thing.) How then can it be maintained, even in the face of all the phenomenological findings, that the continent and incontinent man see different things, or *must* see things differently? (Unless the claim is *ex post facto*.) If vertigo or fear prevents someone from doing what he knows it would be best for him to do, must we say that this subverts his *understanding* of why and how it is best?

5. When what I might almost venture to call a more Aristotelian account than Aristotle's promises to be possible (§§2–4), why did Aristotle give such a Socratic account of the phenomena of weakness?

It is true that in order to give another account he would have had to effect some modification of the doctrine that the conclusion of a practical syllogism is an action (because on the rival account the continent and incontinent men have normal, ready access to both competing syllogisms). But why should he have insisted on that doctrine just as it stood? There is also the conditional necessity Aristotle alleges that a man who both gets and puts together minor and major premise should act in accordance with them provided that he is not prevented. But here we must ask what caused Aristotle to insist on this necessity in the first place. I suppose it may be suggested that he thinks that only in this way will either an explanation of action or an analogy between theoretical and practical syllogism be achieved. But neither of these points is enough.

The point about analogy is worthy of respect, but scarcely decisive. If we can find no room for the operation of the will when the two premises of a demonstrative syllogism are seen by him who puts them together to entail their conclusion, then that makes sense enough. For there is nothing the will can add here. Everything that bears on what he will believe is already present.[14] If that is how it is with believing something, however, we ought not to expect the analogy between pursuit and/or abstinence and belief and/or nonbelief to be perfect or complete. (Least of all should we expect this in respect of that which distinguishes the practical and theoretical in the first place, namely, what touches the will.) But, coming now to the first point, about explanation, nor need it weaken the rationalizing role of the practical syllogism (its power to display a course of action under what the agent sees as its rational title to be realized) that the claim made on the agent by the syllogism may be blocked. Why, if Aristotle were to qualify his sentence about the necessity that a man act upon the syllogism unless prevented or unable, would it follow that awareness of the syllogism would lack force in the explanation of behaviour? Surely Aristotle could put in another *unless*. Why should a syllogism-form lack explanatory force in the cases where the man acts by reason of the corresponding thought just because there are allowed to be cases where he might *not* act upon that sort of consideration? (Suppose someone asks why the waiter crossed the room. Suppose it were said that he crossed because I beckoned to him. Is this explanation undermined by the fact that, when he's tired or others are beckoning or whatever, he ignores my beckoning to him?)

If the difficulty Aristotle would have in dropping or further qualifying the 'necessarily' is meant to relate to the fact that all explanations seek after completeness, well, let it be allowed that, to complete the explanation of a man's actual behaviour, we must add that nothing did controvert or defeat the

---

[14] See B.A.O. Williams, 'Deciding to Believe,' in *Problems of the Self* (Cambridge University Press, 1972); or D. Wiggins, 'Freedom, Knowledge, Belief and Causality', cited at note * of Essay VIII.

consideration which, in thinking thus, the agent saw the force of and then acted because of. In the case of explanation the addition is completely otiose, however, because we already know that the action did take place and was not obstructed. If we insist on the symmetry of explanation and prediction, I suppose that some such condition will need to be added in a predictive case. And it is a difficulty, when prediction is insisted upon, that, so long as we stay on the purely psychological level, there is no guarantee that we shall ever be able to attach an operational or predictively useful content to this extra condition.[15] But what that illustrates is not the futility of the psychological sort of explanation given by the practical syllogism, but the real nature of the symmetry between explanation and prediction. At a given level of description the prospect of symmetry only corresponds to the prospect of deterministic description at that level. There is nothing in Aristotle's philosophy or Aristotle's science to mitigate the disappointment that some will feel about this. But the undiminished beauty of explanation of what *has* happened is that it need not wait upon the distant or illusory prospect of fully deterministic description.

We shall come closer, I think, to the real difficulty that Aristotle must have supposed that he perceived in akrasia if we forget these irrelevancies and go back to an earlier sentence of the *NE*, namely 1111b13-15: 'The incontinent man acts from his appetite but not from his choice; whereas the continent acts from choice and not from his appetite'. Indeed, in Aristotle's special philosophical sense of 'choice' (*prohairesis*), the incontinent man acts contrary to choice (1148a9). (Which is not yet to say that he acts non-intentionally in the ordinary sense of the English word *intentionally*.) This is a much more promising clue to what troubled Aristotle and to what would have prompted him to reject the idea of developing the neo-Aristotelian account of incontinence that I began in §§1-2.

In the early books of the *Nicomachean Ethics* Aristotle develops special conceptions of happiness (*eudaimonia*), acting (*prattein*), and choice (*prohairesis*) such that all the purposive

---

[15] Compare here Donald Davidson, 'Mental Events,' in *Experience and Theory*, ed. Foster and Swanson (London, 1971).

acts that a man chooses to do, in the special sense of 'choose' 'act' and 'do', he chooses for the sake of what he conceives as eudaimonia (or as activity in accordance with human excellence).[16] For the agent to embrace a specific conception of eudaimonia just is for him to become susceptible to certain distinctive and *distinctively compelling* reasons for acting in certain sorts of ways. Now the difficulty that incontinence poses is not that it constitutes a counterexample to this generalization. (How could it? The generalization rests on a stipulation that simply excludes the weak-willed doings of the *akrates* from counting as chosen, or as actions in the special sense of 'choose' and 'act' and 'action' employed in Aristotle's construction.) The difficulty is rather that the incontinent man as he was described at the outset is *party* to the Aristotelian conception of activity in accordance with human excellence, and he understands the claims it makes. If he is party to that, then he understands these claims by virtue of being susceptible to them as claims of this sort. How then, understanding *so* much, can he prefer weaker and different claims, or allow himself to pursue a different goal whose pursuit is actually incompatible with what he recognizes as the supremely important goal? If he *can* do this with his eyes open—and if he can act sometimes and speak always in a manner so like the continent man's (so similar even in certain respects to the temperate man's) that there is no alternative but to credit him with a true view of eudaimonia, then his very existence may appear to constitute a quite special threat to Aristotle's construction. What it threatens is the role in which Aristotle casts eudaimonia.

Aristotle exacts from a rational disposition that is directed toward that which is the best of all humanly conceivable goods much more than he would exact from the common or garden physical dispositions that I turned to advantage in Section 1.[17] I

---

[16] As regards these terms and Aristotle's construction I have been both influenced and persuaded by John McDowell's 'The Role of *Eudaimonia* in Aristotle's *Ethics*', *op. cit.* at note * above.

[17] *Cf. NE* 1105a30–33, a requirement going well beyond the conceptual requirements suggested by the need to attend to the point that Socrates is represented in *Republic* Book 1 as making against Polemarchus—that on Polemarchus' definition of justice it might just as well be said that the concept of a just man and the concept of a thief overlap or coincide.

think he exacts so much because, when a man has properly understood what Aristotle has described as eudaimonia, it seems that it must impugn the title of eudaimonia to satisfy the criteria of adequacy announced by Aristotle himself in Book 1 if someone who understands eudaimonia takes himself to have a reason to prefer something that he can see is less important. How *could* he prefer a smaller good when there was an overwhelmingly larger good staring him in the face and he understood what made it overwhelmingly larger? How, understanding the larger thing, could someone fail to pursue it?

Once an end is proposed that is both complete (in the sense of being chosen for itself and never for the sake of anything else, *cf.* 1097a33) and genuinely self-sufficient—in the sense of being such that a life qualifies by virtue of the sole achievement of that as worth living and lacking in nothing (1097b14–15)—, a man has only to understand what is being proposed to him. If this *telos* or *skopos* has been correctly described (and sufficiently persuasively described to convince the akrates), then there ought to be no further problem of single-mindedness. For the man who knows what eudaimonia is will know that, if he attains it, then his life will merit the following description:

> His opinions are harmonious, and he desires the same things with all his soul; and therefore he wishes for himself what is good and what seems so, and does it (for it is characterstic of the good man to work out the good), and does so for his own sake (for he does it for the sake of the intellectual element in him, which is thought to be the man himself); and he wishes himself to live and be preserved, and especially the element by virtue of which he thinks. For existence is good to the virtuous man, and each man wishes himself what is good, while no one chooses to possess the whole world if he has first to become someone else. . . . ; he wishes for this only on condition of being whatever he is; and the element that thinks would seem to be the individual man, or to be so more than any other element in him. And such a man wishes to live with himself; for he does so with pleasure, since the memories of his past acts are delightful and his hopes for the future are good, and therefore pleasant. His mind is well stored too with subjects of contemplation. And he grieves and rejoices, more than any other, with himself; for the same thing is always painful, and the same thing always

> pleasant, and not one thing at one time and another at
> another; *he has just about nothing to regret.*[18]

Where this is the prospect and it is attainable by action, and
where even approximations to this practical ideal represent
approximations to the very same intrinsic goods, nothing else
should hold out any prospect at all to practical reason. Just as,
if water chokes, then there will be nothing else to wash it down
with (1146a34), so Aristotle's notions of practical reason and
of eudaimonia are subverted—or so he seems to fear—if
anything qualifies, with human beings as they are, as a
counterattraction to the attractions of eudaimonia. It ought to
be that, once that is described and understood, the force of
practical reason is utterly spent and the philosopher is *functus
officio*.

6.   It would be a serious misunderstanding of these claims to
see the 'oughts' and 'shoulds' that were needed for their
expression as normatively intended. What they represent are
not requirements upon agents but theoretical conditions for
the delineation of the unitary objective that Aristotle set
himself to describe. Having described it for what Aristotle
thinks it is, and commended eudaimonia to practical reason, it
is not for philosophy to engage in exhortation. In so far as
moral philosophy is to be protreptic at all, the didactic effort is
to be directed solely at the conditions for the proper understanding of the claims that eudaimonia enjoys to our undivided
allegiance. Any claims that are made for eudaimonia have to be
true in virtue of what can be revealed to unblinkered
perception and ordinary human understanding of the actual
constitution of human values. If this actual constitution does
not admit of the delineation of an ideal of eudaimonia with
such an overwhelmingly strong rational claim upon us, then
that is a defeat for philosophy as Aristotle conceives it.

There is another misunderstanding that I should deprecate.
The argument rehearsed in §5 may have reminded the reader
not only of the celebrated Socratic-Platonic arguments of

---

[18] *NE* 1166a13–29 in the translation of W.D. Ross, except for the last sentence, on
which see the translation and discussion of Martha Nussbaum, *op cit.*, pp. 217–9.

*Gorgias* and *Meno* but also of the infamous argument of 'the many' in the *Protagoras* 354d–355d.

> It is not easy to explain the real meaning of what you call being overcome by pleasure [*i.e.*, akrasia], and any explanation is bound up with this point. You may still change your minds if you can say that the good is anything other than pleasure, or evil other than pain. Is it sufficient for you to live life through pleasure and without pain? If so, and if you can mention no good or evil *which cannot in the last resort be reduced to these . . .* you have to say that a man often recognizes evil actions as evil yet commits them . . . because he is led on and distracted by pleasure. . . . the absurdity of this will be evident *if we stop using all these names together, pleasant, painful, good, and evil, and since they have turned out to be only two, call them by only two names.* . . . What ridiculous nonsense for a man to do evil knowing it to be evil because he is overcome by good. . . . By being overcome you must mean taking evil in exchange for greater good. . . .

Let φ be the universal or all-purpose predicate of favourable assessment. A man will only be incontinent if he knows or believes the thing he doesn't do is the thing with most φ to it. But if that is the alternative that has most φ to it, and if nothing else besides φ-ness counts positively for anything, there is nothing to commend any other course of action over the one that is most φ. He could have had no reason, *however bad*, for choosing the other instead. The choice of a smaller amount of pleasure now against a larger amount of pleasure later is explicitly described as a form of ignorance in the supposedly single dimension φ; and the argument can allow for now fashionable complications (which Plato anticipates at 356) such as the rate at which the agent chooses to discount future φ. If everything with any relevance to choice is comprehended in the question how φ a given course of action is, and how φ its competitors are, then no rational sense can be made of weakness of will. This is the *Protagoras* argument.

The misunderstanding I have in mind, and against which I now seek to guard, is to suppose that Aristotle's argument against accepting unqualified, unreconstructed weakness of will would have to be of this reductive character, or would have to depend on the idea that all values are in this sense commensurable. Certainly it would be unfortunate if this were so, because in that case the interpretation I am recommending would have Aristotle contradict himself. He states explicitly at *Politics* 1283a3 that the very idea of universal commensurability is absurd.[19] And in the *Eudemian Ethics* he denies that knowledge and money have a common measure (1243b22). Again, there are no signs in the *Nicomachean Ethics* of Aristotle's supposing that there is a common measure to assess exhaustively the values of the noble, the useful, and the pleasurable (even though the noble and the useful will in the formation of orexis appear to us also under the aspect of pleasure, *cf.* 1104b 35–1105a 1). What he has to maintain is only that, if eudaimonia is to qualify by the formal criteria of autonomy and completeness, then it must be that, wherever a man has to act, he can subsume the question at issue under the question of eudaimonia and discern which course of action is better from that point of view:

> Sensory imagination is found in other animals but deliberative imagination only in those which have reason. For whether one shall do this thing or do that thing it is the work of reason to decide. And such reason necessarily implies the power of measurement by a single standard. For what one pursues is the greater good. So a rational animal is one with the power to arbitrate between diverse appearances of what is good and integrate the findings into a unitary practical conception. [*De Anima* 434a5–10][20]

There is no question even here of supposing that there is just one evaluative dimension φ, and one quantitative measure *m*, such that φ-ness is all that matters, and all courses of action can be compared with one another by the measure *m* in respect of

---

[19] The passage is cited by Martha Nussbaum, *op. cit.*, and by M.F. Burnyeat, op cit., who provides at his n. 29 a comprehensive list of passages of Aristotle that bear on his views about evaluative commensurability.

[20] The last sentence is a paraphrase that depends heavily on Martha Nussbaum's theory, *op. cit.*, Essay V, that the noun *phantasia* holds onto its connection with the verb *phainesthai* and stands for what results from being appeared to by something. In this case it is the good. The deliberator has two or more partial notions of the apparent good and has to harmonize or unify them here and now into a practicable plan for the actual realization of the good.

φ-ness. What is assumed is only the weaker proposition, which is of the ∀∃ not the ∃∀ form, that for any $n$-tuple of courses of action actually available at time $t$ to an agent $x$ there is some way or other of establishing which member of the $n$-tuple is the better course of action in respect of eudaimonia, and (consequentially upon that) the greater good.[21] There is no obvious inconsistency between holding this *De Anima* doctrine and maintaining the thesis of value pluralism or incommensurability in the form of the denial of the ∃∀ sentence.

7.   If the apparent menace of the akrates as unredescribed to the soundness of Aristotle's construction has nothing to do with reductive commensurability in the *Protagoras* sense and everything to do with such formal requirements as the self-sufficiency of eudaimonia, and with the special prospect of having just about nothing to regret that eudaimonia holds out to rational intelligence, then it will be timely to review the question whether Aristotle could not have contrived to accommodate together both akrasia as pretheoretically described and eudaimonia as theoretically described (still appealing solely to reason). This will require some reexamination of the *autarkeia* or self-sufficiency condition that Aristotle seems to impose on happiness, and a preparedness to complicate his account of how contentment can exist in a world of value-conflict.

The *De Anima* passage, taken as I have taken it, claims that there will always be a greater good. It does not imply that there will be no grounds at all for regret about that which is deemed to be the lesser good. And it does not itself imply that everything that matters about an alternative necessarily registers in the measurement of it in respect of eudaimonia. Nor does it imply that, if course $x$ is better in respect of eudaimonia than course y, then there is no important disadvantage that $x$ has in comparison with $y$, or no desirable feature that $y$ offers that $x$ does not offer too, by way of an equal or greater degree of that very feature. One might call this last *the principle of compensation*

---

[21] Similar remarks could be made about the theory of preferability adumbrated at *Prior Analytics* 68a25–b7, cited by Burnyeat. Perhaps 'measurement' is a little overprecise then at 434a9. See below §7, paragraph 7, on 'greater good.'

*in kind.* To insist on such a principle would be to attempt to restore a proposition of the ∃∀ form, taking 'eudaimonia-promoting' or some such dimension as an all-inclusive and sole dimension of assessment. But, so soon as we clearly formulate this principle and see that it is false, I think we shall see the way forward to a more realistic account of happiness, within which there will be room for the akrates to choose the smaller good when he could have the larger, and choose it for a reason that is a *real* reason, for all that it is a *bad* reason. This can happen wherever there is no prospect of compensation in kind, and *y* has some peculiar or distinctive charm that the incontinent man is suspectible to, or when *x* has some disadvantage to which the incontinent man is unlucky enough to be specially averse.

Perhaps Aristotle has some occasional slight tendency to believe something rather like the principle of compensation in kind. Perhaps this underlies his occasional claims that even the purely pleasurable appears to us under the aspect of good. ('The pleasure of the moment appears pleasurable quite simply and good quite simply because of lack of regard for the future'. *De Anima* 433b8–10.) But what is important is that it will take only a very slight change of focus to exempt his construction from this intolerable burden. In the definition of self-sufficiency, we need not take 'lacking in nothing' to mean 'lacking in nothing at all that would be found valuable by anybody pursuing whatever course', only 'lacking in nothing that a man who had chosen the great good of eudaimonia would regard as worth bothering with'. And that surely is all that the Book 9 passage really demands on behalf of eudaimonia. Both temperance and continence are still possible on these conditions. There is still room for some men to be temperate while others are merely continent. And it is not exhortation that makes the difference, but rationality generously conceived (*i.e.*, not the instrumental rationality prescribed by an abstract a priori construction), ruling not a despotical rule but the constitutional rule of a statesman or prince over his free subjects, as Aristotle puts it at *Politics* 1254b4–6. Reason simply reveals the real possibility of eudaimonia.

Conceiving eudaimonia and the philosopher's task in these terms, we relinquish certain prospects we might have thought we ought to have had of proving conclusively the *in all respects* overwhelming superiority of the life or lives that can be shown by Aristotle's consensual-cum-descriptive method to be the best; and we are en route to further and comparable doubts, not only about whether Aristotle's problem of eudaimonia admits of a unique solution but also about whether there are external or independent notions of rationality or happiness to be had such that the other-regarding virtues can be non-question-beggingly represented as rationally required for our happiness. Aristotle's philosophy is not so innocent of all ambitions for unique solutions and invincible reasons as to make him proof against all disappointment here. But the *Nicomachean Ethics* offers the reader all manner of consolation. It describes, elucidates, and amplifies the actual concerns of human life, and makes transparent to theory the way in which these concerns necessitate, where they do necessitate, the actions or decisions in which they issue. I believe that those who find that this is enough in practice to retain their interest in the subject will discover that they can drop Aristotle's doctrine of the akrates' ignorance of the minor premise and complete the neo-Aristotelian doctrine of incontinence that I began in §§1–2. But rather than attempt that here, I shall conclude by attending to two intermediate matters. The first relates to commensurability, and the second to the nature of the philosophical problem of weakness of will—a term I hope to have done something to rehabilitate.

8.    The neo-Aristotelian position would deny the strong, reductive commensurability we find in the *Protagoras*. Explicitly it also denies the nonreductive strong commensurability that is involved in the principles of compensation in kind. These are both $\exists\forall$ principles. It would recommend that Aristotle persevere cautiously in some however qualified form of the $\forall\exists$ thesis of the *De Anima* 434a5–10. (Rather than draft the qualification, I have indicated the nature of serious doubts about the unqualified claim.) But what else would distinguish such a position from the utility-maximizing $\exists\forall$ models of man that are proposed by some social scientists? The question had better be faced because it is a common charge among the tender-minded that economists and others have disregarded the

plurality and mutual irreducibility of goods.[22] And Aristotle himself is sometimes cited as a witness for value pluralism.

The maximizing type of theory with which I have to contrast Aristotle's theory may be seen as a normative theory of rational individual choice (individual choice in the first instance, later social choice, but we shall scarcely touch on that), where the rationality in question is relative to the objective of maximizing utility as that is measured on a scale particularly specified for this or that particular person. Alternatively, the theory may be seen as a specification of the actual motivation of some individual person, this being ascertained and tested on the methodological assumption that he tries consistently to maximize with respect to the said measure. For many purposes it makes no differences in which light the theory is seen. Either way what results is intended as a specification, not only of the subject's actual motivation, that is his springs of action, but also of the constraints under which he is seen as a utility-maximizer; and either way the individual's utility measure is specified as a function from goods ($X_i$) and evils ($A_j$) to total utility, and given in the form $U = f(X_1 \ldots X_g, A_1 \ldots A_h)$. The function $f$ is plotted as an indifference map in $g + h$ dimensions, which orders as lesser or greater various, variably mixed, equally wanted packets of the $g$ types of good and $h$ types of evil.

Meaning can be given to incommensurability within this theory by reference to the case where choices actually made by the subject leave indeterminacy about how certain goods or evils trade off for him under this or that condition against certain other goods or evils. But, insofar as the theory aspires to any completeness in what it undertakes, it would have to aim to state the terms on which anything will trade off against anything else with respect to utility contribution. The commensurability that results is nonreductive, and it can be contrasted fairly sharply with the commensurability mooted in *Protagoras*.[23] One overreaching consideration is postulated, however—namely, maximization of the subject's total utility.

---

[22] For references to modern writings on commensurability see Essay III note 46.

[23] *Cf.* Brian Barry, *Political Argument* (London, 1965), pp. 3–8, which also illustrates the method of indifference maps.

There is something $u$ (namely, utility) such that, for any decision the subject has to make between possible courses of action, there is an indifference curve on which each possible choice can be located for purposes of comparison in respect of $u$ with the other possible choices. This last is an ∃∀ proposition. But it may be suggested that a similar proposition might be attributed to Aristotle if his view were presented as a theory of 'eudaimonia maximization'. And why should it not be?

First, however, even if the Aristotelian theory were seen as an empirically based proposal for an agent's rationality with respect to his eudaimonia, or were seen under another aspect as a theory of the subject's eudaimonia-valuations ascertained and tested on the assumption that he is consistently seeking eudaimonia, this sort of theory does not even attempt to subsume under the agent's pursuit of his eudaimonia his weak or perverse doings, or to predict when they will occur. (*At most* it would explain them after the event, drawing upon the subject's various springs of action, and pointing to the falsehood of the principle of compensation in kind.)

Second, the *De Anima* passage is wholly exempt from the principal difficulty or implausibility of the maximization theory:

> We can derive a rational choice for any given objective and constraint, but we must have both an objective and a constraint, and we must keep clear which is which. . . . the consumer is said to maximize utility, and utility is defined as that which the consumer attempts to maximize. The truism is completely general and cannot be false. Since he is motivated to make choices by a desire to achieve his objective, we can further say that the level of utility achieved depends upon the choice he makes. If he is choosing among goods, utility is a function of the volumes of the goods acquired.[24]

Here what is represented as a truism requires a prior premiss to the effect that there is something the subject seeks to maximize. (What is at issue is no more innocuously truistic than the first premise of a well-known argument that begins 'God is by

---

[24] D.M. Winch, *Analytical Welfare Economics* (Harmondsworth, Middlesex, 1971), p. 17, a work I choose not because of any special vulnerability to the objection I shall attempt to make, but for its signal clarity and philosophical and historical sense.

definition that being which is omniscient, omnipotent, and benevolent [a being than which no greater being can be conceived]'.) The statement that there is something the subject seeks strictly to maximize is not itself a definition, and must be allowed to take its chance with other empirical sentences. It would be indirectly falsified if, in spite of determined efforts to formulate the individual utility functions of the kind that theories of this general form assume or hypothesize that individual agents attempt to maximize, applied-utility theorists encountered no significant success, or no better success than theorists using other methods—psychologists or historians or entrepreneurs and their market researchers. Saying the very specific thing it does say, and the utility function having the special form it does have, the statement that individuals maximize their utility is anything but a truism. [25]

What about the corresponding Aristotelian proposition about eudaimonia? It need not represent itself as immune from empirical upset. It can acknowledge that there may not be any specification of eudaimonia that will muster the appeal which Aristotle's construction depends upon. (See §§5–6, whose conceptual requirements will survive the withdrawal of the principle of compensation in kind.) But, unlike utility, eudaimonia is not built up from a set of packages of goods (or *agatha kath' hauta*) which the theory claims the agent will seek to maximize if he is rational. So the theory does not require what the utility theory will require. The judgment that one course of action is better than another is not arrived at in this way at all, but through the agent's preexisting conception (constantly informed and reshaped by circumstance) of the life that it is good for a man to attempt to realize.[26] The judgment that one

[25] No doubt some theorists will propose that the statement is a regulative maxim or a principle of interpretation of behaviour, and above the mêlée of falsifiable sentences. Such a theorist should study the fate of the so-called Principle of Charity, which was defended by Quine and Davidson as a principle of radical interpretation. It *may* be a truism that, whatever an agent does, we can represent his choices *ex post facto* by indifference maps. But one ought not to expect that such a description of choices will automatically be projectible in Goodman's sense. Nor is the truism equivalent to the claim, which must, if it be significant and true, import projectibility, that there is something an agent maximizes and this is his utility.

[26] See Essay VI §§4–6.

course of action represents a greater good than some other course is *consequential* or *supervenient* upon that.

Third, because its account of the telos of eudaimonia, conceived as the explanation of some actions, reaches behind behaviour and behind the desires that explain behaviour to the thoughts and feelings that lie behind desire, the Aristotelian theory, however discursive, descriptive, non-predictive and low-level it may be, provides a much more intelligible theory of conduct than a utility theory that has practically nothing to say about what organizes the indifference curves that make up an individual's total schedule of preferences—and still less to say about how extrapolation would be possible to the untested counterfactual choices of its subject from observations of the actual choices of its subject taken under quite different circumstances and different constraints. The utility theory needs to be a substantial psychological theory at this point: but it does not even have the form of one, let alone the content.

A fourth and final difference is worth noting. Like the utility theory of individual choice, the Aristotelian theory has its social counterpart. In Aristotle's *Politics* that form of government is held to be best in which every man, whoever he is, can act well and live happily. But the theory does not subserve a program for social action to maximize anything. (See point two above.) *A fortiori* it does not extrapolate into (or project onto) the future, a future supposed to be Utopian,[27] desires conceived by men in circumstances held *ex hypothesi* to be unsatisfactory and intolerably constraining. Insofar as it suggests a social program, the program is for the removal of the public impediments to eudaimonia.

9. It is useful to distinguish between (i) giving an account of mind and value that *leaves room* for weakness of will, (ii) *describing* or *anatomizing* weakness of will in detail, and (iii) *explaining* weakness of will. I have concentrated on (i) and on the discrediting of principles that make (i) difficult. There has been a little of (ii). And on the level of reasons a little about (iii).

---

[27] A *Glanzbild der Zukunft* as Burkhardt put it, with an ambiguity I remember Aurel Kolnai pointing out between 'a resplendent image of the future' and 'the mirage of the future'.

(Here, under explaining itself, there is a further distinction between explanation in terms of reasons and explanation in, say, physiological terms—if that were possible—of why, of two men who saw a situation the same way, one acted weakly and the other matched his action to his evaluation.)

My strategy has been first to reduce the size of the explanandum by giving a nonreductive acount of deciding that, deciding to, and so forth. This account demonstrates the exposure of the process of thinking and then acting to all sorts of mishap; according to the account, none of these breakdowns comes close to threatening a conceptual connection. As a result of our accepting the nonreductive account, I believe that we can then come to be satisfied by a smaller and less ambitious theory of weakness than other philosophical pictures of the phenomenon standardly make it require. (There is in a sense less to explain.) By these means, I have also hoped to offer an explanation that works on the level of reasons but leaves knowledge intact. Incommensurability came into this, but I did not introduce it in order to ascribe any instability to understanding (if such instability be required for the weakness that is *moral* weakness, then that is something quite special to moral weakness) or to excite any skepticism about that which is known. Incommensurability was introduced in conjunction with the idea of the falsity of the principle of strict compensation in kind, and in order to suggest the heterogeneity of the psychic sources of desire satisfaction and of evaluation (both the evaluation consequential upon desire and the evaluation which desire is consequential upon). The notions of 'diachronic rationality' and 'the overall best course' inherit from this heterogeneity *a certain liability to fragmentation.*[28]

The philosopher's business here is with the springs of action in so far as we can clarify these for ourselves as reasons for acting, and with the nature of desire. If I am right (and if I am right to take as central the weakness of will that does give itself reasons), then we cannot understand any of these things until we first understand values and the relation of values that conflict with one another; grasp the nature of the difficulty of finding a

[28] Cp. Thomas Nagel, *Mortal Questions* (Cambridge University Press, 1979), pp. 128–141.

stably incontrovertible best specification of eudaimonia (even of this or that particular person's eudaimonia); and recognize competition between values for the serious and substantial obstacle it is to someone's achievement of the settled disposition to find and then act consistently upon the reason that is the best reason—the hard-won disposition not only to think the overall best reason the overall best, but, despite the attractions of other reasons that are real reasons, to *find* it so, and—just so long as it remains the best reason (this virtue is not a form of obstinacy)—to continue to find it so. Until this disposition be present, there is not even the presumption of a puzzle, a puzzle needing to be dissolved by ignorance of the minor premiss, about weakness of will.

# VIII

# Towards a Reasonable Libertarianism*

His own character is a man's destiny.

HERACLITUS

Very well, my obliging opponent, we have now reached an issue. You think all the arbitrary specifications of the universe were introduced in one dose, in the beginning, if there was a beginning, and that the variety and complication of nature has always been just as it is now. But I, for my part, think that the diversification, the specification, has been continually taking place.

C. S. PEIRCE

## 1. Introduction

One of the many reasons, I believe, why philosophy falls short of a satisfying solution to the problem of the freedom of the will is that we still cannot refer to an unflawed statement of

* Abbreviated from my contribution to *Essays on Freedom of Action* edited by Ted Honderich (London: Routledge & Kegan Paul 1973). I thank Routledge & Kegan Paul for permitting me to reprint it here. This was one part of a paper to the Oxford Philosophical Society in the summer of 1965. A version of another excerpt from that paper appeared as Part II of 'Freedom, Knowledge, Belief, and Causality', p. 13, in *Knowledge and Necessity*, ed. G. Vesey (London: Macmillan, 1970), and is cited at notes 4, 5 below.

§4–§8 represent a rearrangement, revision, and extension of the three concluding sections of the original article.

Every student of Richard Taylor's and Roderick Chisholm's path-breaking efforts to refurbish the credentials of libertarianism will perceive my indebtedness to them, as well as my various reservations about the positions they have taken. See especially Richard Taylor's *Action and Purpose* (New York: Prentice Hall, 1966) and Roderick Chisholm's 'He could have done otherwise', *Journal of Philosophy*, July 1967.

I thank Oxford University Press for their permission to make the quotation in note 16 and the British Academy for their permission to make that in note 29.

libertarianism. Perhaps libertarianism is in the last analysis untenable. But if we are to salvage its insights, we need to know what is the least unreasonable statement the position could be given. Compatibilist resolutions to the problem of freedom will always wear an appearance of superficiality, however serious the reflections from which they arise,[1] until what they offer by way of freedom can be compared with something else, whether actual or possible or only seemingly imaginable, that is known to be the best that any indeterminist or libertarian could describe.[2]

A sympathetic and serviceable statement of libertarianism cannot be contrived overnight, nor can it be put into the two or three sentences that some utilitarian and compatibilist writers have been willing to spare for the position. If they were more anxious to efface libertarianism than to understand and improve available formulations of it, this was natural enough, but ordinary human obstinacy has shown that the issue is too complex for such summary treatment. What follows is offered as a small step in the direction of a more reasonable or less fantastical exposition.

## 2. What the libertarian means by 'He could have done otherwise'

The libertarian insists that a man is only responsible or free if sometimes he could do otherwise than he does do. It must at least sometimes be genuinely up to him what he chooses or decides to do. But what does this mean? Let us begin with three clarifications.

---

[1] By *compatibilism* (or dissolutionism) I mean the position which says that freedom (the freedom of being able to do otherwise) and physical determinism can coexist. By *incompatibilism* the position that they cannot coexist. *Libertarianism* is a species of incompatibilism, one which saves freedom by denying physical determinism. In refurbishing libertarianism I do not myself mean to subscribe to *a priori* or introspective or extra-scientific arguments against physical determinism but to subscribe to an interest in what the libertarian *wanted* by way of freedom, whether or not the world will allow of this freedom. Whether libertarianism is true or false, it is the only good source for the position which it entails (without being entailed by it), viz. incompatibilism. It is true that some classical determinists were incompatibilists of a sort, but for the most part libertarian writings are a better guide for the understanding of incompatibilism.

[2] It is only fair to say that more work has been done on this since the time of the complaint. See, for instance, the collection *The Freedom of the Will* (Oxford University Press, 1984) edited by Gary Watson, and especially his Editorial Introduction.

(i) It is characteristic of the libertarian to insist that, for at least some of the things that the man with freedom does, or plans or decides to do, he must have a genuine alternative open to him. That is, for some act A and some act B, where A≠B, he must be able to do A and he must be able to do B. (In my usage 'act' denotes a thing done, *i.e.*, a *type* that particular actions exemplify. The auxiliary 'do' marks schematically the connexion of act and agent.) But should the same apply to what the man with freedom thinks, believes or infers?[3] In another place,[4] I have given an argument, whatever it may be worth, whose purpose was to show that the notions *open choice, decision, alternative, up to me, freedom* have a different point in the realm of belief, the state whose distinctive aspiration it is to match or represent the world as it is, from their point in the realm of action and volition. The proper province of action and volition is not to match anything in the physical world but to affect or act upon the world. Of course the world and its causal properties, whether or not these constitute it a deterministic world, are the unquestioned framework within which action takes place. But for the libertarian it is typical and proper to insist that nothing in that world should completely determine the ends, objectives and ideals with which the free agent, if he is truly free, deliberates about the changes he would seek to make to it. There is no question of requiring of ends and ideals the vindication by things in the world that a belief about the world requires from things in the world: on the other hand, the libertarian ought to be content to allow the world, if it will only do so, to dictate to the free man who has questions that he wants to put, and is suitably placed to answer them, how the world is.[5] Freedom does not consist in the exercise of the

[3] See, for instance, John Lucas in *Aristotelian Society Supplementary Volume* 1967; Ted Honderich in *Punishment* (London, 1969) (recanted, *Aristotelian Society Supplementary Volume*, 1970).

[4] *Cf.* my 'Freedom', pp. 145-8 (*op. cit.*, at note\*).

[5] Historically speaking and common-sensically speaking, the point of the demand for freedom of thought was not to conceive one's beliefs in a manner untrammelled or underdetermined by external reality, but to remove civil and clerical obstacles to the spirit of enquiry that allows only the way things are to determine belief. The contrast I am drawing here between theoretical and practical does *not* depend on a conception of knowledge or discovery that excludes or ignores intellectual fertility or active invention. It simply imposes conditions upon its workings and possible outcomes. See, 'Freedom', p. 146.

(colourable but irrelevant) right to go mad without interference or distraction by fact.[6] Alternatives of the kind that the libertarian defines and demands are alternatives in the realm not of theory but of practice.

(ii) To say that an agent is doing or will do B, and that there is something else, A, that he can do, is to say something ambiguous, even though (ignoring permissive and epistemic contexts) 'can' itself is most likely univocal (see (iii) below). A may be something the agent can generally do, for instance, or something he can for such and such a stretch of time do, given the opportunity. It is true and important that a claim about a persisting ability to do A is confirmed if the agent's wanting or trying to do A at an appropriate moment during the relevant period is a sufficient condition of his producing a non-fluke performance of act A. But, read in this way, the finding that the agent can do otherwise is irrelevant to the point that troubles the libertarian. What organises the whole dispute, and what holds the libertarian's position apart from his present day opponents' position, is rather his treatment of another question: if physical determinism is true, is there ever something different from what the agent will in fact do at some time $t_i$ such that the agent can at $t_i$ do that other thing at $t_i$ instead? If physical determinism is true, the libertarian maintains, then such an alternative is never really or truly available to the agent (see below §4). Sometimes earlier doings, in their context, completely determine successions of later events and doings. According to the libertarian, however, there can only be true alternatives if there are at least some doings and decidings which, whether or not they completely determine their immediate successors, are not themselves entirely determined by earlier events. Of course this is only a necessary condition of alternatives or freedom of action. And he does not deny that, even if this freedom did not exist, we could, if we wished, having discovered that it didn't exist, continue mechanically to draw our conventional distinctions between different kinds of

[6] It is worth adding that the causal determination by the world of a rational man's particular true belief $p$ cannot in itself entail that the world would have lodged this belief with him *even if it had not been true*—the conditional is both subjunctive and contrary to fact—or that nobody could have told that $p$ was not true if it had not been true.

situations—between acting *voluntarily* and acting *reluctantly*, between *control* and *non-control*, between *freedom* and *constraint*. But determinism largely undermines their point, he says. It prunes off too much that was important. True freedom cannot be vindicated by holding onto distinctions whose rationale would be subverted by the discovery of the truth of determinism. (But of course, he will add, that is not what we have discovered. If anything, the reverse. See §7.)

(iii) Though the sentence schemata *he could have done otherwise* and *he could have done A instead of B* may import varying truth conditions, it is the libertarian's hope to explain all these variations by differences of complementation with respect to (a) the time or period for which the ability subsists, (b) the particular replacements of 'A' and 'B', and (c) the time specification for the acting itself. *Can* itself is, in the libertarian's provisional opinion, a unitary semantical element.[7] But those who have distinguished, *e.g.*, a 'general' *can* from 'particular' *can* have performed an important service in forcing us to be clear about what exactly it is that it is claimed a man could or could not have done. The replacements for 'A' and 'B' must determine this fully. (The provision of two slots (a) and

---

[7] That is to say that the diversity of possible complementations is the *prima facie* best explanation of phenomena that writers have attributed to an ambiguity in the word *can* itself. If the schema 'he can X' has to be unpacked ('he (when?) can [(what?) (when?)]'); and if 'he can X if. . . .' (contrast Austin's discussion of this *if*, to which he gives a very peculiar treatment) has to be unpacked both in these ways and with respect to scope ('(he (when?) can [(what?) (when?)] if (. . .))' and 'he (when?) can [(what?) (when?) if . . .]'); and if there is also the phenomenon of ellipse (which seems to play an important role in sentences about what can and cannot be done *without undue cost* or *harm* to persons or property, etc.) to help explain the apparent diversity of truth-conditions; then I hope the way is open for an attempt to obtain a unified lexical account of *can* (ignoring permissive and epistemic uses).—One that at least comes up to the standard for lexical univocity suggested (for instance) in my 'Sentence Sense, Word Sense, and Difference of Word Sense' in *Semantics: An Interdisciplinary Reader in Philosophy, Linguistics, and Psycholinguistics*, ed., Steinberg and Jakobivits (Cambridge University Press, 1971).

There has been a temptation among those of the compatibilist persuasion to suppose that the commonness in pleas of justification and excuse of the 'cannot' that is to be interpreted as meaning 'cannot without undue cost or harm' counts somehow against the libertarian thesis. But this 'cannot' cries out for temporal specifications: and when these are supplied and the cost or harm in question is made explicit, what we have looks like a further determination of the kind of 'can' that the libertarian is anxious to elucidate.

(c), for the times of the ability and the performance respectively, may seem questionable. But consider the fact that I may now, in Baker Street at 9.55 a.m., be able to catch the train from Paddington to Oxford at 10.15 a.m. Eight minutes later, however, at 10.03 a.m., if I have not progressed from Baker Street, then, given the state of the Inner Circle line and Marylebone Road, I shall certainly be unable to catch the train. What we have in this example is not a special case but a specially clear case. Both slots are always there—we cannot create them specially for cases like the train case—but when they both take the same temporal specification, as they must in 'he could have done otherwise' in at least some important occurrences, then the ellipse of one of them is surely natural and intelligible enough.)

So much for the sentence *he could have done otherwise* as it figures in the dispute, and as the libertarian construes its occurrence in the ordinary interchange of accusation, exoneration, exculpation, and the rest.[8] The other urgent need is for a clarification of the determinism that the libertarian takes to be incompatible with his understanding of the sentence.

## 3.  What determinism signifies

J.L. Austin once maintained that determinism was 'the name of nothing clear'.[9] But as a second-level non-scientific theory that the world admits of explanation by a certain kind of

---

[8] And not only there, but even within the expression of the moral sentiments that it is P.F. Strawson's conspicuous contribution to have insisted on bringing into the area of the controversy about free will. (See his 'Freedom and Resentment', *Proceedings of the British Academy* vol. 48, 1962, pp. 1–25.) Consider Jonathan Bennett's claim:

> If a benefactor was manifesting an insane compulsion to give things away, the beneficiary may welcome the gift but should not be grateful for it. In such cases the agent is not praiseworthy. ('Accountability' p. 15, in *Philosophical Subjects: Essays presented to P.F. Strawson*, edited by Zak van Straaten (Oxford University Press, 1980).)

Consider why the claim might be accepted. We might ask: What was his intention towards me? Answer: that I have the object. Why then did he want me to have it? Answer: because he felt warmly towards me—as no doubt he felt towards others at that time. What then would be the matter with my feeling grateful for his making me a present of the thing? Sole possible answer(?): He couldn't help having that intention and those feelings.

[9] 'Ifs and Cans', *Collected Papers* (Oxford, 1961), p. 179.

ground level scientific theory, the thesis can be made as plain as terms like 'cause' and 'explain' can. Whatever his other difficulties, the libertarian need not find it impossible to indicate what it is that he is afraid of, or the libertarian what it is that he rejects.

Let us say that a scientific theory for a subject-matter s is deterministic if and only if the theory possesses a store of predicates and relation-words for the characterisation of s-items (events, situations, etc.) and the theory affirms lawlike general statements such that for every s-item $s_j$ it can find a description $D_j$, an s-item $s_i$ with description $D_i$ such that $s_i$ occurred some $t$ seconds earlier than $s_j$, and there is some law the theory affirms that implies something in the form (*if a $D_i$ event occurs, then a $D_j$ event occurs $t$ seconds later*).

A deterministic theory is adequate if the law-like statements it affirms are true and will combine with the theory's descriptive categories $D_1, D_2, \ldots D_n$ to form explanations that are correct wherever $D_1, D_2, \ldots D_n$ apply.

As a first attempt, one might then say that determinism is the theory that *for every event (situation, state of the world or whatever) there is a true description and an adequate deterministic theory T that explains the event under that description.*

I suppose the reason for thinking that this might hold is science's spectacular success in extending again and again the number and variety of events for which it can find theories with the title to be in my sense adequate and deterministic. Someone may comment that it is hardly surprising that we have discovered the regularities which were there to be discovered; that our success shows nothing about the residue; nor does the possibility of such success really guarantee the operational or empirical intelligibility of the thesis of determinism. Perhaps it is not intelligible, it may be said. The charge ignores falsification however; and those who want to persist in subscribing to determinism (in spite of, *e.g.* quantum phenomena) might reply to the objection with this question: 'How big *is* the residue? Can there really be, what the objection purports to achieve, an *a priori* estimation of it?'

At this point we stumble upon the widespread idea, presumably shared by the objector, that every situation must be infinitely describable. All we can do in a causal investigation is

to pick out and test causal *strands* from a total physical
background that is provisionally regarded as the 'normal'
background;[10] there is no logical question of this procedure
(the only operational procedure, the objector says) either
terminating or issuing in finished law-like generalizations that
are closed and not subject to a never ending process of
qualification.

Let us first work out the determinist's answer to the difficulty
about generalizations and then return to infinite describability.
Adequacy in our first formulation required the strict and
universal truth of the laws employed in deterministic explanation. If one says all Fs are Gs then one means *all* Fs; and if
some restriction of the conditions under which all $D_i$ events at $t$
are followed by $D_j$ events at $t'$ is needed, then the restriction
must, for purposes of this determinism, be made explicit. A
body falling near the surface of the earth for $t$ seconds will
cover a distance of $16t^2$ feet, for example, provided that it is
in a vacuum and provided it is falling freely. The hypothesis of
determinism that we are considering precisely entails that in
due course such qualifications can be everywhere spelled out
and completed.

It is true, of course, that the objection is making an
important point about the discovery of physical laws, and
about the way in which everyday conceptions of causality lead
into scientific ones. In deference to it, and in deference to Hart
and Honoré's analysis, the determinist could meet the point in
another way, by saying that an explanation holds universally if
*either* (1) there are no apparent exceptions to the predictions
made by the use of the law or laws L which cover it; *or* (2) every
such apparent exception can be explained in terms of an
interference (a) describable by the vocabulary of the body of
theory to which L belongs, and (b) for which there is *in its own
turn* an explanation in terms of an adequate theory, this theory
itself being compatible with L. Whatever one thinks of this
strategy, it enables one to suppose that every causal generalization starts life with a *ceteris paribus* clause, understood by

---

[10] I use here an idea of H.L.A. Hart and A.M. Honoré in *Causation in the Law*
(Oxford, 1959), but there is no intention at all to ascribe to these authors any view at all
about the import, sense, status or significance of the thesis of determinism.

means of (2) in such a way that the escape clause does not trivialize L. Then in the revised set of definitions, deterministic in terms of *adequate*, *adequate* in terms of *universal*, and then *universal* in terms of *adequate* again, there would of course be a circle. It may perhaps be seen as matching a similar circle in the beginnings of a science. It is not necessarily a vicious circle, however, because by conjoining a larger and larger set of good and consistent theories it will become possible, *if determinism is true*, to diminish the apparent exceptions to nil. The determinist can then use the 'no exceptions' condition of clause (1) as a criterion of 'universality' and 'adequacy'.

If either of these replies is to carry the determinist the whole way against the objection, which has the virtue of bringing out just how exigent a thesis determinism is, then the next thing he must do is to combat directly the idea that every situation is without redundancy infinitely describable. This will be best achieved however by our first attending on his behalf to an important shortcoming in the first formulation of determinism. That formulation only undertook to find a theory to explain every item under *some* description or other. The flaw was this. What if the chosen descriptions were thin or uninformative (even as uninteresting as *something which happened at t*)? Such a determinism might leave almost every significant feature of reality perfectly free of determination by physical law.

It is no good for the determinist to try to stiffen the doctrine by requiring that for *every* description of every event there be an adequate deterministic theory T which explains the event under that description. How could *every* conceivable description, however arrived at, of anything, find its way into a law of nature or pull its weight in a serious theory?[11]

Both to amend the determinist thesis and to meet objections inspired by the question of indefinite describability, what the determinist needs, I think, is the notion of a *saturated* description. A description D of item $x$ is saturated, let us say, if and only if (a) D is true of $x$, (b) there is no property P of $x$ which can vary without variation in the property D stands for, and (c) D incorporates every projectible property of $x$.

---

[11] Here, and in the ensuing paragraph, I am indebted to ideas of Davidson. See 'Mental Events', in Foster and Swanson (eds.), *Experience and Theory* (MIT Press, 1970).

(On pain of our new formulations collapsing into the amendment of determinism just dismissed, I emphasise that this idea has absolutely nothing to do with the *reduction* of all properties to saturated properties. If a picture is beautiful and serene and sad it cannot be modified in these respects without a modification in the chemical, structural, or physical properties which would enter into its saturated description. It does not follow at all from this tie between the aesthetic and scientific properties that we can find any complex description couched in the terms of physics or chemistry and satisfied by all and only pictures beautiful and serene and sad—or even by pictures which are these things to the very degree that $x$ is.)

We can now state a sufficient but not necessary description of the holding of determinism. *For every event* (*situation . . .*) *there is a saturated description and corresponding adequate and deterministic theory that explains that event under that description.* Saturated descriptions, if they exist, encode everything that is of any causal or scientific significance. Further refinements of this formulation might classify theories by the degree of computability of the functions they employ, by the degrees of solvability of the equations they invoke, or by other refinements into which there is no need to enter. The general character of the doctrine and the colour of its claims to be a factual doctrine[12] should now be apparent, as should the direction in which one would have to look for its verification or falsification

---

[12] On this point see the problem stated by B.A.W. Russell, 'On the Notion of Cause' in *Mysticism and Logic* (London, 1921) and C.G. Hempel in Sidney Hook (ed.), *Determinism and Freedom* (New York, 1958).

An objection parallel to the plea of infinite describability has found some circulation (see J. Passmore, *Philosophical Review*, Vol. 68 (1959), pp. 93–102, B.A.O. Williams's tentative exposition in D.F. Pears (ed.), *Freedom and the Will* (London, 1963)): that determinism is obliged to treat the universe as a sort of closed system or box, and to take seriously the idea of a total-state description of the world. It is certainly true that the classical Laplacean approach would characteristically have proceeded from outside to inside, from a total world state and total prediction to the prediction of constituent particular phenomena. (See La Place, Introduction to *Théorie Analytique des Probabilités*, Oeuvres Complètes VII, Paris, 1847.) But if the world satisfies the thesis of determinism as I have expounded it by means of the notions of saturated description, adequacy, and universality—*if* this logical possibility is exemplified—then it is as unnecessary to describe the whole world in order to explain a particular event as it is unnecessary to reckon with indefinite describability. The only difficulty is one of establishing, however tentatively, that determinism is true. But in testing this we proceed from inside to out, from smaller to larger tracts of the universe.

—*viz.*, the progress of the sciences of matter. The libertarian thinks modern science shows determinism is false. The incompatibilist hopes that it does. The compatibilist or dissolutionist usually assumes that it is true or as good as true.

Determinism is not always formulated as a thesis about the sciences of matter. So it may be helpful, and it will disarm objections to certain claims to be entered in §4 and §7, to pause here to express an attitude towards the psychological, socio-logical, or economic determinisms that attract some thinkers and have a powerful effect on the institutions, practice and methodology of the social sciences.

It is not unusual to find social scientists who believe that some day, somehow, their sciences will grow up and produce results comparable in their way with the splendid things which in its maturity physics has achieved. In its adolescence, we are to suppose, social science practises and rehearses the methods of dispassionate enquiry and conscientious and accurate measurement that are the *sine qua non* of the spirit of science: but when the time comes, society will receive the instruments of stability and the dividend for which it has so presciently invested—namely applications of sociology, economics, psy-chology which will bear the same certain relation to the disciplines they apply as the products of modern technology do to chemistry, physics and the rest.

Unless what this really means is only that we shall in due course see some of the predictions of social scientists actually brought about by the trend-planning that is 'based' upon them, or that certain sorts of social science can already be employed, without the benefit of any notable insight or understanding but to sinister effect, to protect our managers against the dangers of our facing the more open future that it might be more desirable for us to face, there is no very awesome reason to believe it. The only general argument I know for the likelihood of what social scientists hope (and libertarians disbelieve and incompatibilists fear) goes something like this. The physical sciences give good reason to believe that, at least on the macroscopic level, the world is a deterministic system. But every event economically described or sociologically described is also a physical event, so how could sociological events or economic events fail to make up a deterministic system themselves? They are physical events. So there must be universal laws and functional correlations out there awaiting the researcher who can make accurate enough measurements and can master (or hire enough computational brute force to master) the multitude of variables required to hit upon and solve the relevant equations.

This argument, which rests on a greater confidence than many people can muster in physical determinism itself, comprises an instructive and fundamental mistake. Economic events say, or commercial events, could be part of a larger deterministic system without themselves (or as such) comprising a self-contained deterministic system. And it would not follow from the fact that any system they helped to make up was deterministic that the laws in virtue of which it was deterministic would be *laws of economics* or *laws of sociology*.[13]

What determinism of the sort earlier envisaged says (where $e_i$, $e_j$, ... range over events, S represents all properties including sociological, economic, *etc.*, ones and P is the property of being physical, *i.e.* satisfying a description of a science of matter) is this:

$$(e_i)S(e_i) \rightarrow (\exists e_j)(P(e_j) \& (e_i = e_j))$$

*For every economically or sociologically described event, there is a physical event identical with it.*

Now when K ranges over natural or scientifically significant kinds,[14] $K_s$ ranges over economically or socially categorized kinds, and $K_P$ ranges over kinds of physical events, this no doubt entails

$$(e_i)((e_i \in K_s) \rightarrow (\exists e_j)(\exists K_P)[(e_j \in K_P^j) \& (e_i = e_j)])$$

*For every event of a sociological or economic kind there is*

---

[13] Cp. the situation in genetics. My parents' genotypes limit my genotype and hence my phenotype, but their phenotypes do not have anything like the same control over my phenotype. This is not the only kind of comparison possible, nor of course is it well calculated to gladden those who long for a stronger more independent status for social science or who ignore the other aspirations that linguistics or philosophy of language can suggest to social science. But the comparison might explain why it is that William Dray's 'How possibly?' pattern fits the explanations to be encountered in the actual practice of sociology, economics, anthropology, history, *etc.*, better than the covering law pattern fits them.

[14] See, *e.g.*, W.V. Quine, 'Natural Kinds', in *Ontological Relativity and Other Essays* (New York, 1970).

*an event of a natural kind recognized by a science of matter which is identical with it.*

But it does not entail the statement the argument crucially needs

$(K_s)(\exists K_p)(e_i)[(e_i \in K_s) \vdash (\exists e_j)(e_j = e_i \ \& \ e_j \in K_p)]$

*For every sociologically or economically characterized kind of event there is a natural kind of event recognized by a science of matter such that every event of the former kind belongs also to the latter kind.*

## 4. The logical character of the incompatibility of determinism and the ability to do otherwise

So much for serious determinism. It is a shaky hypothesis, and in its strict and literal form wide open to disbelief. (See below §7.) It is not a thesis to be disarmed by *a priori* arguments against its truth or significance. It is manifestly far stronger than the weak, almost undisputable thesis that every event has some cause.[15] Unsurprisingly, therefore, the *denial* of the thesis does not commit one to find any uncaused events, or to see agents, with Chisholm, as 'prime movers unmoved', or to anything else that is strange.

If determinism is true, and if every action of every agent in its particular circumstances is really fixed in respect of its occurrence, in respect of its mode of occurrence, and in respect of the characteristics upon which its character as an action supervenes, and fixed in this way by some antecedent physical condition, then obviously actions cannot be torn free from the nexus of physical effects and fully determining causes.[16] It is

---

[15] Maybe all events have causes but there is nothing in a cause or its circumstances to fix everything about the character of its effect. On this and the problems of event reference and individuation of events see Milton Fisk, 'A Defence of the Principle of Event Causality', *British Journal of Philosophy of Science*, 1967 and Donald Davidson, 'Causal Relations', *Journal of Philosophy* vol. 64, 1967.

[16] If that is the character of the causal nexus we live within, then it makes no particular difference to this point whether or not actions are *identical* with movements of matter. Even if this were the wrong thing to say, actions still could not be constitutively independent of the arrangement of matter or of physical events. On the constriction of freedom which would result from the determinism of physics, whatever one thought of the identity view, see G.J. Warnock, *ab init.*, in *Freedom of the Will*, ed. Pears (London, 1963). It should be added that even if we adopted the mysterious view that mental events do not occur in the physical world, still, if physical determinism were true, then

this that creates the incompatibility that the libertarian alleges between physical determinism and statements of the form 'he could at $t'$ have done otherwise at $t'$'. But this incompatibility needs to be stated carefully.

Richard Taylor writes on page 54 of *Action and Purpose*, 'If however, existing conditions are causally sufficient for my moving my finger, then it follows that it is causally impossible for me not to move [it] . . . Since, however, it is true that . . . I can hold it still, it follows that [this] is not causally impossible.' What is the underlying argument of the first sentence of this passage? For a moment one might suppose that the argument is this. (I) It is a law of nature or a consequence of a law of nature that under conditions C a man moves his finger. If this is a law of nature, it is true for all time. *A fortiori* it is true for this time $t'$ when the man does move his finger. Hence it is causally impossible at $t'$ that C should obtain and the man not move his finger at $t'$. But (II) from $t$ onwards C did obtain. Therefore (III) it was causally impossible at $t'$ that the man should not move his finger at $t'$. Therefore (IV) the man could not at $t'$ keep his finger still at $t'$—it was inevitable at $t'$ that he move it. But (V) he could at $t'$ have kept his finger still at $t'$. Therefore (VI) some premiss must be false. So if we concede (II), the deterministic claim (I) is false.

This can scarely be the argument Taylor had in mind, however. For its pattern at (I) (II) (III) suggests that of the patently invalid argument:

(I) $\Box$ (p is known $\supset$ p is true)
(II) I know q
(III) $\Box$ (q)

Nevertheless, I feel convinced, with Taylor,[17] that there is some

---

bodily movements would fall within its ambit and the autonomy of the mental would be limited to mental events with no proximate physical cause and no practical (acted) outcome. Autonomy would be something utterly inert.

[17] And among many other Hobbes. His suggestive but equally incomplete formulation in the *De Corpore* runs as follows: 'Every act which is not impossible is possible. Every act therefore which is possible shall at some time be produced; for if it shall never be produced then those things shall never concur which are requisite for the production of it; wherefore that act is impossible by the definition; which is contrary to what was supposed.'

valid inference from (I) to (III). The problem is to discover another form for it and to formulate its additional premisses. If this much can be accomplished, then, it will become worthwhile to try to characterise and define the notion of historical inevitability that makes the argument work. First then let us look for a candidate form for the inference.

Suppose that a law of nature assures us that in the conditions obtaining at a particular juncture $t'$

(1)  Inevitable at $t'$ (if C at $t$ then the agent does R at $t'$),

and suppose that we know that if the consequent is true this causally or logically excludes some particular agent's doing A, so that

(2)  Inevitable at $t'$ (if the agent does R at $t'$ then the agent does not do A at $t'$).

Then, if 'Inevitable at $t'$ (if . . . then — )' is transitive, it follows that

(3)  Inevitable at $t'$ (if C at $t$ then the agent does not do A at $t'$).

Suppose for instance that 'R' is replaced by 'extend a finger' and 'A' is replaced by 'keep still'. And suppose the man failed to keep still. The question will be: Could he have kept still, even though, from the earlier moment $t$, C obtained? Proposition (1) is the particular contribution of determinism to the argument. What that thesis implies is that there exists this sort of empirical truth. If the argument depends on (1) and (2) it will not be a fatalistic, but a deterministic argument.

The extra premiss which I believe the argument needs is the uncontroversial modal principle

(4)  $\Box p \supset (\Box(p \supset q) \supset \Box q)$.

Supposing that 'Inevitable at $t'$' is a modality (see below) and abbreviating this as '$\Box_{t'}$', we have as an instance of this;

(4')  $\Box_{t'}(\text{C at } t) \supset (\Box_{t'}(\text{C at } t \supset \text{the agent does not do A at } t') \supset \Box_{t'}(\text{the agent does not do A at } t'))$

Now suppose that the condition C did obtain at $t$. Then by the time $t'$, which is later than $t$, there was nothing to be done about the obtaining of this condition. So we have

(5)   $\Box_{t'}$(C at $t$).

But, given (3), we have

(6)   $\Box_{t'}$(C at $t \supset$ the agent does not do A at $t'$)

So by *modus ponens*

(7)   $\Box_{t'}$(the agent does not do A at $t'$).

But how can this consist with

(8)   He could at $t'$ have kept still at $t'$?

We recognize this incompatibility when we allow the question of what was physically-cum-historically possible to organize our evaluation of excuses and pleas of non-responsibility. Therefore, given (3), and given that the condition C did obtain at $t$, we have

(9)   He could not have kept still at $t'$,

and this is the consequence, not of pure logic and the uncontroversial modal principle by themselves, but of empirical determinism and the nature of time.[18] At any given moment a man has no real alternative but to do what he does at that moment: in which case there is no way for him to exploit the fact that he could, if he were to do A now, do B in the future, and could, if he were to do not-A now, do D in the future. For it is already fixed which of A and not-A he will do. And the same argument will hamper the attempt to find his freedom at some earlier moment.

Nobody will feel happy about this demonstration until more is said about the idea of historical inevitability at a time. But first, we must attend to the premises (1) (2) (3). They rest, amongst other things, on the lawlike generalisation that entails (1) and the analytic truth or lawlike generalisation (as the case may be) that entails (2). But laws of nature themselves will usually be much more general than (1) or (2), and will rarely or never bear much resemblance to (3). Being very specific, (3) will depend heavily upon the particular situation at t'. It does what

---

[18] See *Longer Note* 18.

no proper law by itself would normally do. It links very different kinds of description. That it is possible to conjoin laws of nature, which could not by themselves perform this task, with facts about particular situations and thereby obtain particular statements like (3) is what makes it so difficult to find human freedom in the undoubted fact that there are most likely *no* exceptionless empirical principles at all about the causal antecedents (or consequences) of actions classed by action-kinds. But to make a bridge from propositions like (1) to propositions like (3), we simply do not need any exceptionless principle about the connexion between the condition recorded in 'C' and the sort of movement recorded in 'R at *t*'.

By 'it is historically inevitable at time *t'* that p' is intended something like this: whatever anybody or anything can do at *t'* or after *t'*, it will make no difference to whether *p*, *p* being either a law of logic or a law of nature or at *t'* already history, or being the logical or physical consequence of what is already history. This definition includes the notion of possibility, but this is no objection. The purpose is only to fix from within the circle of modal notions a sense of necessity which satisfies principle (4′) and yields a strict implication which is transitive (for the passage from (1) and (2) to (3)). It is not necessary to break into the circle of modal notions from outside.

Briefly, one might say it is historically necessary at *t* that *p* just if it will hold that *p* whatever can happen at *t* or later (consistently with laws of nature).[19] Or in the sort of language that many people have come to prefer, and that David Lewis uses in his book *Counterfactuals* to characterise modal and counterfactual principles, one might stipulate that $\ulcorner \square_t p \urcorner$ is true if and only if it holds that *p* in every world whose history is indistinguishable from the history of the actual world up to

---

[19] We are not defining a purely technical notion here. If we were it would be all too easy for someone to go back to premiss (6) and question that. We are characterising an existing everyday notion whose dual, historical possibility, figures in such contexts as this one. 'It's too late. *H.M.S. Hermes* can't now intercept the *Bismarck* before *Bismarck* rounds the cape. It's no longer possible for her to get there in time.' And this, I have claimed, is the notion that figures not only in pleas of exoneration and exculpation, but also within the underlying dialectic of the moral sentiments. See note 8 above.

(but not necessarily including) $t$. Here we should have to understand its natural laws as comprising a part of the history of a world.[20]

It remains to verify whether (4) and (4') hold when the modality has its sense fixed in this way. Suppose then that it is historically necessary by time $t'$ that $p$. Then it holds that $p$ in every world indistinguishable from the actual world with respect to times earlier than $t'$. Now suppose also that in every world indistinguishable from the actual world with respect to times earlier that $t'$ it holds that if $p$ holds then $q$ holds. But then in every world indistinguishable from the actual world with respect to times earlier than $t$ it holds that $q$. So under the conditions that it is historically inevitable at $t'$ that $p$ and that if $p$ then $q$, it is historically inevitable at $t'$ that $q$.

This verifies (4) and with it (4') for the temporally indexed interpretation of $\square$.

The reaction of some to this whole exercise will be to say that it fortifies a dislike they had always had for natural necessity—even before it was relativised to a time. I reply that such scepticism must in consistency apply equally aptly to physical possibility, relativised or unrelativised, wherever it outruns actuality. And here we notice a curious thing. This scepticism, by reducing possibility to actuality, seems to undermine 'can do otherwise' *directly*—unless it treats animate possibility, the *can* of human ability, with some special indulgence. But that would be a strange concession to make, especially in the presence of libertarians. Its effect would be to mark off animate agents from the rest of nature in just the sort of way in which at least some libertarians have wished to distinguish them.

[20] It should be noted that none of these definitions makes 'Theaetetus sits at $t'$' historically necessary at $t$ just because Theaetetus sits at $t$. The sentence isn't true *whatever* Theaetetus does at $t$. And, unless determinism happens to be true, there is a possible world historically indistinguishable from ours up to $t$ in which Theaetetus stands and does not sit at $t$. The proof of (9) does not therefore depend on the fatalistic type of puzzle revived at *Analysis*, vol. 25 (no. 4, 1965), or on a special view of truth, but on the absurdity of its being *now* possible for something *in the past* to have been different. I should not deny that the definition might be slightly improved by amending it to read 'indistinguishable from the history of the actual world *appreciably* before $t'$'. This abandons the precision of the Dedekind section in favour of a serviceable and perhaps indispensable vagueness. Two equally intelligible worlds can scarcely resemble one another up to $t$ and differ in that in one Theaetetus sits promptly at $t$, and in the other he promptly stands at $t$. One or other world would involve a discontinuity. See now also *Longer Note* 20.

## 5.   Views open to the libertarian of the self and its abilities

It may be said that the whole preceding demonstration turns on a confusion between what lies in the agent and what lies outside him.[21] It is perfectly absurd, it will be said, to lump together under conditions C items as diverse as the character of the agent, the present state of mind of the agent, the external causes of that state of mind, and the concrete particularities of the conditions under which he acts. It makes as little sense as saying that one of the circumstances under which an agent did some specific thing was the circumstance that he was a man of a mean and murderous disposition. Nothing but confusion can come from such a way of speaking, it will be said; and the only possible philosophical outcome of speaking like this is a far-fetched theory of the metaphysical, totally non-empirical and character-less self whose difficulties match exactly the incoherences of the Lockean doctrine of substance—the thing with the property of having no properties, the substrate that explains the possibility of change by being both unchanged and identical with that which persists through change. Either the libertarian requires (*cf.* §2) that *nothing in the world outside the free agent himself* should determine for that agent how he will change or deliberate to change the world, or the libertarian simply requires that *nothing in the world* determine for the agent how he will change or deliberate to change the world. It will then be said that, if the requirement is stated in the former way, we can and must distinguish what lies within the agent from what lies without. If the requirement is stated in the latter way, however, then even the agent himself is excluded from determining anything—even *for himself*—unless the self is outside the world altogether. This is an unintelligible conception. Finally it may be said that the libertarian's expression 'determining for the agent' is pure rhetoric—the *agent* deliberates and thus determines for himself what change he will import.

I hope this states the objection as dissolutionists or compatibilists want to see it stated. But without the discovery of a specific mistake in the argument above, the absurdities of

---

[21] *Cf.* Aristotle's distinction between what is and is not *en to prattonti* in Book 3 of *Nicomachean Ethics*.

the metaphysical self cannot themselves suffice to disprove the inference from determinism to *nobody can do otherwise than they do do*. How exactly the metaphysical self could be supposed to compensate for physical determinism is not at all clear. But if determinism did really imply that if we were responsible then the doctrine of the metaphysical self would be true, and if the doctrine of the metaphysical self is absurd (as I for one am sure that it is), then either we are not responsible or the doctrine of determinism is not true. But then if determinism is true, the conclusion follows that, in the full sense in which we commonly take ourselves to be responsible—*i.e.*, in the sense of 'responsible' fixed by the question whether a man can do otherwise—we are not responsible. But that after all is exactly what the libertarian said. The conditional 'if determinism is true then we are not responsible' is not *all* that he says. *If* he were also convinced of the antecedent (the truth of determinism), he would climb down to the weaker position (which is incompatibilism) and go on to say a great deal more. But first things first. His first point is that, if our actual notion of responsibility, unreformed, fails of application, then it can only darken counsel to pretend that our notion is another notion—some notion touted by utilitarians and dissolutionists, for instance—or to pretend that we never really had our notion. All sorts of things in our social, judicial, and penal institutions, and all sorts of things in our relations with human beings, depend, he says, upon the supposition that men *can* do otherwise than they do do. Substitution of another notion of responsibility may be called for, but substitution is not the same as the philosophical elucidation of what we have. The practical and metaphysical imports of substitution and analysis are totally different. If a dilemma exists here, it should first be acknowledged and felt as such. Only barbarism and reaction can benefit by concealment, or so he will contend.

There is another way for his compatibilist opponent to move, however. If the conclusion of §4 is simply incredible—incredible regardless of the facts about scientific determinism—then perhaps this shows that *he could have done otherwise* never means what, in stating the doctrine of libertarianism in §§2–3, we took such trouble to make it mean where it occurs in §4. The step from (5) to (7) and the principle (6) are particularly relevant here. In the search for a compatibilist meaning for *can do otherwise*, some philosophers have tried to gain favour for the analysis of *x can at t' (B at t')* as *if(. . . at t) then x does B at t'*; where . . . picks out some conditions distinguished from the rest of the circumstances of action by pertaining specially to what is *in* the agent.

Perhaps the most promising-looking hypothetical analysis may be approached by way of a consideration of the non-animate dispositions. Carnap showed long ago the difficulties of trying to define such dispositions as brittleness or solubility in terms of conditionals like *if x is dropped then x breaks* or *if x is put into water x dissolves*. Instead of these conditionals he proposed 'reduction-sentences' which have the advantage of not verifying brittleness by the falsity of the antecedent. A typical reduction sentence would be *if x is dropped, then if x is brittle x breaks*. But even if a finite number of them could really fix the sense of 'brittle'—which is unclear and dubious—reduction-sentences are open to another difficulty. Brittle things may for various and divers reasons significantly frequently fail to break when dropped: and many things break when dropped even though they are not brittle. No satisfactory correction is obtained by converting the mood of the first or second sort of conditional into the subjunctive. But there is another remedy that suggests itself and has obvious relevance to the problem of animate abilities. Take 'is disposed' or 'tends' as *pro tempore* primitive, and analyse *x is fragile (during period t)* on something like these lines: *x is of a kind to be so disposed (during t) that (if x is hit or dropped then x breaks)*, where the hypothetical is now embedded within the characterisation of a categorically described disposition. The corresponding analysis of *x can at t A at t* might perhaps be *x is so disposed at t (that (if . . . then x does A at t))*, where . . . indicates some condition about something 'in' the agent. It could be the condition that he tries, or that he wants or whatever. (The embedded conditional is subjunctive.)

No doubt this account represents some kind of advance on previous attempts. The specification of the categorical state of ability requires an *if*, but not in the manner of the more usual hypothetical analyses. What is noteworthy, however, is that the improvement in the analysis does nothing at all to block the question of the possibility of . . . , which is the happening mentioned in the antecedent. The analysis seems powerless to trump the circumstantial demonstration of the physical impossibility, taking everything into account, of . . . coming to pass. Till this problem is faced no subtleties about *in the agent* or the agent's *will* or his *will to will* can gain any purchase.

## 6. Hume's fork and the libertarian view of the self

Perhaps it is pointless to debate whether the sentence 'he could at *t'* have done otherwise at *t''* does have the sense I have ascribed to it in the incompatibilist demonstration of §4 above, until it has at least been shown that the argument invoking that sense could ever, even if it were successful, do for the libertarian what he wanted. This problem is often taken to be equivalent to the following question: can the libertarian even specify a possible world in which there are things that people can (in the libertarian's sense) do, but do not do? Hume has been followed by a large number of philosophers in holding that not even a possible world of the right sort can be specified. If it were false that every event and every doing were causally determined, then (it is said) causally underdetermined events and doings would surely, to that extent, be simply random. That a man could have φ-d would then mean no more than that it might at random have turned out that way. It is then asked whether it makes any better sense to hold a man responsible for actions that happen at random than for ones that arise from his character. Surely, the argument ends, if it doesn't, we ought to prefer that our actions be caused. Real freedom *requires* causal determinism.

This objection is question-begging. One cannot prove that determinism is a precondition of free will by an argument with a premiss tantamount to 'everything is either causally determined or random'. This is simply too close to the conclusion, that whatever is undetermined is random. That is what had to be shown. But in the form of a challenge, it may appear that at least something in the objection can stand. If an event is underdetermined, if nothing excluded an event of different specifications from taking the event's place, then what does it mean to *deny* that the event is random? What is it to be justified in ascribing the action identical with the event (or comprised by the event) to an agent whom one holds *responsible* for that action? In the unclaimed ground between the deterministically caused and the random, what is there in fact to be found?

In reponse to this challenge, some philosophers have ventured the idea that, within the field of physically under-determined events, what would make the difference between the random and the non-random is the presence or absence of a prior mental event such as a *volition*. It was in this tradition (which goes back at least as far as the *clinamen* or swerve of Epicurus and Lucretius) that Russell and Eddington tried to deploy the phenomena of quantum-indeterminacy as having a bearing upon the free-will issue.[22]

> If—as seems likely—there is an uninterrupted chain of purely physical causation throughout the process from sense-organ to muscle, it follows that human actions are determined in the degree to which physics is deterministic. Now physics is only deterministic as regards macroscopic occurrences, and even in regard to them it asserts only very high probability, not certainty. It might be that, without infringing the laws of physics, intelligence could make improbable things happen, as Maxwell's demon would have defeated the second law of thermo-dynamics by opening the trap-door to fast-moving particles and closing it to slow-moving ones.
>
> On these grounds it must be admitted that there is a bare possibility—not more—that, although occurrences in the brain do not infringe the laws of physics, nevertheless their outcome is not what it would be if no psychological factors were involved . . . So for those who are anxious to assert the power of mind over matter it is possible to find a loophole. It may be maintained that one characteristic of living matter is a condition of unstable equilibrium, and that this condition is most highly developed in the brains of human beings. A rock weighing many tons might be so delicately poised on the summit of a conical mountain that a child could, by a gentle push, send it thundering down into any of the valleys below; here a tiny difference in the initial impulse makes an enormous difference to the result. Perhaps in the brain the unstable equilibrium is so

[22] B.A.W. Russell, *Human Knowledge: Its Scope and Limits*, Chapter V: 'The Physiology of Sensation and Volition', p. 54.

delicate that the difference between two possible occurrences in one atom suffices to produce macroscopic differences in the movements of muscles. And since, according to quantum physics, there are no physical laws to determine which of several possible transitions a given atom will undergo, we may imagine that, in a brain, the choice between possible transitions is determined by a psychological cause called 'volition'. All this is possible, but no more than possible.

Russell is not enthusiastic, and perhaps the idea is even less free of difficulty than he allows. (Could not the incidence of human acts of 'volition' upon quantum phenomena upset the probability distributions postulated by the quantum theory?) It is perplexing that the theory bases actions on occurrent mental events that it does not relate to personality or character, or even to purpose. If the theory tried to find room for such components as these in the genesis of action, then that would import the mysterious idea of an as it were 'immaterial realisation' of the agent to be the source of the volitions. What is an immaterial realisation? Finally, is it likely that Russell's suggestion can give any clear account of what justifies him in comparing the role of volition to that of the child who gives the stone a *gentle push* in one or other of several possible directions?

If anything is to be salvaged from Russell's and Eddington's thought that the probable falsity of physical determination is relevant to the question of free will, it will be far better for libertarians and incompatibilists to make it clear that their conception need not be so wilfully Cartesian, and that their project is to describe a world that is a clear candidate to be the natural world. This had better be a world in which agents are natural things among others, albeit natural things whose motions and capacities invite appraisal by subtle, exacting (and utterly familiar) standards of practical rationality. Why should there not be actions that are not even in principle uniquely or deterministically derivable from laws and antecedent conditions but can be fitted into practically meaningful sequences? We need not trace free actions back to volitions construed as little pushes aimed from outside the physical world. What we must find instead are patterns that are coherent and intelligible in the low level terms of practical deliberation, even if they are not amenable to the kind of generalisation or necessity that is the stuff of rigorous theory. On this conception the agent is conceived as an essentially and straightforwardly enmattered or embodied thing. His possible peculiarity as a natural thing among things in nature is only that his biography unfolds not only non-deterministically but also intelligibly; non-deterministically in that personality and character are never something complete, and need not be the deterministic origin of action; intelligibly in that each new action or episode constitutes a comprehensible phase in the unfolding of character, a further specification of what the man has by now *become*.

For help with such ideas, we might look first in the direction of J.-P. Sartre, and we should do best to look not at the crazily optimistic positions of the early plays *Les Mouches* or *Huis Clos* or *L'Etre et le Néant*, but to what he tried later, and more soberly, to make of his position.[23] Here is Sartre's 1969 account of it.[24]

> For the idea which I have never ceased to develop is that in the end one is always responsible for what is made of one. Even if one can do nothing else besides assume this responsibility. For I believe that a man can always make something out of what is made of him. This is the limit I would today accord to freedom: the small movement which makes of a totally conditioned social being someone who does not render back completely what his conditioning has given him. What makes of Genet a poet when he had been rigorously conditioned to be a thief.
>
> Perhaps the book where I have best explained what I mean by freedom is in fact, *Saint Genet*. For Genet was made a thief, he said 'I am a thief', and this tiny change was the start of a process whereby he became a poet, and then eventually a being no longer even on the margin of society, someone who no longer knows where he is, who falls silent. It cannot be a happy freedom, in a case like this. Freedom is not a triumph. For Genet, it simply marked out certain routes which were not initially given.

---

[23] Later, he was prepared to be 'scandalised' by his previous assertion (of Resistance times) that 'whatever the circumstances and whatever the site, a man is always free to choose to be a traitor or not. . .'. 'When I read this', he goes on, 'I said to myself: it's incredible, I actually believed that!' See *New Left Review*, no. 58, reproduced in *New York Review of Books*, 26 March 1970, p. 22.

[24] In *New Left Review, op. cit..*

This is not the place to take up everything that is strange or interesting in the passage. It is surely not innocent of confusion where it employs the words *rigorously conditioned*, which belong with a view of the world that Sartre really ought to have seen the life of Genet as refuting. But the capital point that is got across to us is that it may not matter if the world *approximates* to a world that satisfies the principles of neurophysiological determinism, provided that this fails in the last resort to characterise the world completely, and provided that there are actions which, for all that they are causally underdetermined, are answerable to practical reason, or are at least *intelligible* in that dimension. Surely *these* are not random. They are the mark left on the world by conscious agents who have freedom.

## 7.  Hume's challenge re-examined

The developing or accumulating biography of people and their characters goes some way towards convincing at least some philosophers that the libertarian has more than nothing to offer in reply to the Humean challenge.[25] But perhaps the libertarian view is still presenting itself as needlessly peculiar, and as insufficiently liberated from the fixations that are proprietary to compatibilism and 'soft determinism'. What I think really needs even more careful scrutiny is the challenge itself and the understanding of the free-will dispute that insists that it is not enough to expose (as above in §6 *ad init.*) the grossly question-begging nature of the Humean argument from which the challenge seeks to inherit its force.[26] When the

---

[25] See for instance Gary Watson's friendly account in *op. cit.* note 2 above.

[26] That the supposed dilemma is still felt as such may be attested by its occurrence within the argument of one of the most distinguished contributions to the compatibilist viewpoint since Strawson's:

> It is not obviously absurd to think that 'A state of affairs obtained which causally ruled out the non-occurrence of E' entails 'E could not have not occurred'; so it is not obviously absurd to think that determinism implies that nothing which did happen could have not happened, and thus implies that there is no accountability. . . . One (answer) is to suppose that determinism is false. So it probably is, in which case some events 'could have' not happened, in the sense of not being *preceded by causally sufficient conditions* for their occurrence. But this does not help to rescue accountability; for *a chance event*, whose occurrence is a matter of absolutely brute, inexplicable fact, is one for which obviously nobody is accountable. I am assuming that accountability requires intelligibility, and that

dialectical position is clarified, I hope it will be apparent that the libertarian does not really have to have his own special or peculiar way of describing the perfectly ordinary case where an agent is free to do A and free to do B, A is not the same as B, and the agent chooses to do B. The libertarian need not speak of uncaused acts or efforts of the will, for instance, or see agents as unmoved movers, or say anything that ordinary people do not say. *Any* account of acting freely that generally commends itself by its other descriptive, philosophical, and phenomenological merits and commends itself to everyone else (as the Sartrean account might if it were filled out a little in the direction of perfect ordinariness) can commend itself to him too. His real concern is not with providing his own account of that, but with how things have to be in order for the ordinary belief to be vindicated that a person can sometimes, in the sense of the phrase relevant to responsibility, do otherwise than he does do.

The libertarian's account of the dialectical position might, if he wished, be this. Once upon a time, people used the language of deciding, choosing, and acting, the language of practical rationality, and language of moral character, and the language of incrimination and exculpation, quite unself-consciously. At that time, as even now, being fully responsible at *t* for doing A at *t* clearly implied being able at *t* to do something other than A at

---

something which is *not caused* [?preceded by deterministically sufficient conditions] cannot be rendered intelligible or removed from the 'brute fact' category. Causal explanation is not the only kind; but no explanation is possible for an event *for which there is no* [?deterministically sufficient] *causal explanation*. (Jonathan Bennett, 'Accountability' *op. cit.* p. 16.)

As the italics and square brackets that I have added are meant to make plain, this is an interesting specimen. Worrying a little, it seems, about the unargued transition that carries him from 'not deterministically caused' [*i.e.*, not preceded by a strictly and fully sufficient condition that rules out every eventuality except one—note, incidentally, Bennett's commitment to the Millian conception of causation, and, for my Davidsonian preference, see note 15] all the way to 'random', Bennett feels the need for an argument. But then he loses track of what he needs to do, and he writes 'not caused' where he should have written 'not preceded by deterministically sufficient conditions'. Had he remembered to put the latter, he would have seen that what he has committed himself to claiming is that the explanation of human behaviour requires deterministic causation. Where is his argument for that? And how can a follower of Strawson suppose that everyday explanation of human behaviour really rests on something that is so totally unverifiable. (Cp. also Peirce 'The Doctrine of Necessity' *The Monist*, April 1892, which is the source of the sentence quoted at the beginning of §1.)

*t*, or entailed that at some earlier time than *t* there was
something different from what you actually did then that you
could then have done then; and it was sufficient for exculpation
either to show that this condition was not satisfied or to show
that, even if there was something else you could then have done
then, it was then out of the question to do that then, or you
could not then have been expected to know then that there was
this other thing. In that distant age from which we inherit our
present concepts of *decision, action, ability*, and the rest, these
were the thoughts that sustained the grasping of the senses of
the words that stood for these concepts.

But then two things happened. First physiological and
psychological discoveries suggested new possibilities of
exculpation and new doubts whether a more profound
knowledge might produce some conclusive exculpation for
such and such acts done by such and such kinds of agent under
such and such conditions. Secondly, with the arrival of the
scientific conception of the world, the idea made its appearance
that the human conception of the world and the scientific
conception might be superimposed upon one another. At
many points there might be nothing at all that was marked out
by the intersection of the two conceptions (hence not even any
question of inconsistency between the two world views). But
sometimes there might be. It might be that, looking at the way
in which events were articulated by the human conception, one
would find that every event that registered there as a human
action was an event that also registered in the scientific
conception,[27] and registered there as an event that the scientific
conception could envisage itself coming to see as historically
necessary (in the §4 sense). And it might be that every interesting
attribute that the human conception made it possible to ascribe
to the action in question supervened upon, or was fixed by, the
properties that the scientific conception attributed to the
corresponding physical event.

That was how things seemed for a very long time after the
end of the unreflecting first phase. But things need not seem
like that any longer, the libertarian may say. What has now

---

[27] For doubts on this score, see Jennifer Hornsby 'Which Physical Events are Mental
Events?', *Proceedings of the Aristotelian Society* (1980).

happened is that, quite apart from all sorts of doubts about the whole idea of a superposition of the human and scientific conceptions, those who work within the scientific conception have perceived significant limitations upon what could ever be shown therein to be physically-cum-historically necessary. The sorts of premiss employed in the abstract or general demonstration in §4 are simply not available. And in that case the intractable general problem that the incompatibilist and libertarian used to say that there was about physical determinism simply goes away. What is left is only the less general (albeit practically much more real and troublesome) form of exculpatory possibility—the worry about responsibility that arose from quite special physiological and psychological discoveries.[28]

Not only that. It is good that the intractable general problem goes away, the libertarian will claim. It is good because resentment, anger and indignation, gratitude and admiration, guilt, remorse, and the urge to make amends, plus all the other attitudes that make constant reference to what was possible or could in the circumstances have been expected of oneself or of others, are not things painted onto the surface of a going system of moral ideas already fully operational. They are integral to its workings. Of course, it was wrong for the libertarian to declare dogmatically that a reformed notion of responsibility would have to have recourse to the crude causal efficacy of punishment. It is now common ground between compatibilists and incompatibilists that this is not the same thing as the efficacy of moral norms or ideals working through consciousness. But that does not prevent it from being a real question *how* the reformed notion of responsibility, once it is dissociated from the question 'can he do otherwise?' taken in the sense attributed to it by the libertarian, will ever reconstruct a rationale for the remorse or resentment or whatever that human beings direct at actual human doings of this or that or the other kind. When the reformed notion tries to make sense of the looking backwards that seems essential to these attitudes

---

[28] Even though the two ways of raising doubt proceed by radically different routes, they issue in a common interest in 'he could have done otherwise' and 'he could have helped it'. Nothing prevents the *sense* of such phrases from being the same in each context.

as we know them, how can it do otherwise than mimic the unreformed—except on pain of subverting the moral consciousness that arises from the generalization of these attitudes?

## 8. Freedom and Resentment

In his well-known British Academy lecture on this theme, P.F. Strawson claimed that, whatever we knew in favour of the hypothesis of total determinism, it could never be rational for us to opt out from all resentment or anger or gratitude or admiration, or from the conceptual framework of responsibility in which these and like responses or attitudes have their meaning; no one who supposed that it would be rational had thought into what it would really signify for human life to attempt to abandon them.

I hope that it will have struck the reader how much the libertarian whose position I am engaged in reconstructing would find to agree with in this. Even if the libertarian thinks there is more to be said about rationality,[29] what he will chiefly

---

[29] The transition by which Strawson reaches his conclusion is worth quoting.

> Inside the general structure or web of human attitudes and feelings of which I have been speaking, there is endless room for modification, redirection, criticism, and justification. But questions of justification are internal to the structure or relate to modifications internal to it. The existence of the general framework of attitudes itself is something we are given with the fact of human society. As a whole, it neither calls for, nor permits, an external 'rational' justification. Pessimist and optimist alike show themselves, in different ways, unable to accept this. The optimist . . . seeks to find an adequate basis for certain social practices in calculated consequences, and loses sight (perhaps wishes to lose sight) of the human attitudes of which these practices are, in part, the expression. The pessimist does not lose sight of these attitudes, but is unable to accept the fact that it is just these attitudes themselves which fill the gap in the optimist's account. Because of this, *he thinks the gap can be filled only if some general metaphysical proposition is repeatedly verified, verified in all cases where it is appropriate to attribute moral responsibility.* This proposition *he finds it as difficult to state coherently and with intelligible relevance as its determinist contradictory. Even when a formula has been found ('contra-causal freedom' or something of the kind) there still seems to remain a gap between its applicability in particular cases and its supposed moral consequences* (*op. cit.* my italics).

Of course I object to the label 'pessimist' for the occupant of the libertarian/incompatibilist position. But the reason why I quote the passage is to point out that a libertarian with a healthy scepticism about the scientific basis of determinism can *agree* that the attitudes themselves fill the gap. Even better, he can declare that there is no gap. He can also insist that the falsehood of determinism need not be verified—even if there *would be a gap* if determinism were true. Finally—as we have several times insisted—he has no need to speak of such things as contra-causal freedom. Actions are events, and events have causes. What the libertarian dispenses with is only the metaphysical sort of cause that must *qua* cause exclude all outcomes except just one.

insist on pointing out is how singularly effective Strawson's lecture was in articulating, in fresh and novel detail, the full range and variety of things the libertarian always said were put in jeopardy by the classical utilitarian and crude substitutive resolutions of the problem of freedom. Strawson offers no such substitution. That would be wholly alien to his approach. What Strawson maintains is that, from the nature of the case, our ordinary ways of talking about responsibility, agency, human ability, human character and all the rest are best left unreplaced and unreduced. They require no justification at all beyond their manifest viability, and their proven capacity to animate the practices of everyday life. But here again the libertarian would agree, once more saluting the contribution that Strawson has made to the proper understanding of everything that would have been at stake if reform or substitution had been proposed.

Where then is the disagreement? Well, at least here: throughout his article Strawson proceeds as if it were simply obvious—he never argues for this—that, *if* the use of the ordinary language of responsibility, agency, human ability, character, etc. requires no justification, then the *untruth* of sentences in the form 'he could have helped it' ('he could then have done otherwise then') will never represent any threat at all to the sorts of things we express in that sort of language. It is the readiness to assert the consequent of this conditional that principally distinguishes Strawson from an incompatibilist. Indeed, without the conditional claim, Strawson's reconciliation is no reconciliation at all. But taking his position *with* the claim that the untruth of the sentence does not matter— taking it as intended to have the force of a reconciliation, and as a refutation of incompatibilism—Strawson's eirenic conclusion is a *non-sequitur*. The language of action and responsibility is not something one needs reason to opt into. Certainly. We just use it. But it does not follow that nothing could count as a reason to opt *out* of it.

The points I have been urging rest on delicate questions of onus and justification. Let me set them out as explicitly as possible.

(1) From the fact that I engage in a manner of thinking,

feeling, and talking that is conditioned by a certain non-deterministic assumption, it never followed that I had to justify that assumption if I was to continue in that way of thinking, feeling, and talking. I didn't have to, and the libertarian never needed to suggest that I did. After all, there was nothing peculiar or odd about the assumption. (Rather, if the assumption has any peculiarity, the peculiarity is that it is almost certainly true. The thesis that has emerged as special, too special perhaps to be true, is the thesis of determinism.)

(2)    From my not needing to justify the true non-deterministic assumption it does not follow that the *falsehood* of the assumption would have been irrelevant to the practice that was conditioned by the assumption. Maybe, even if the falsehood of the assumption were authoritatively revealed (*i.e.*, if it were authoritatively revealed that strict determinism in the sense of §3 obtained), it would *still* be rational for us to maintain the practices that are conditioned by the assumption. But, in so far as that could ever be shown, and in so far as it would really be rational for us to maintain the practices despite everything, well, perhaps what that really amounts to is this. By hook or by crook, Strawson would have managed to show that there were overwhelmingly good rational reasons—reasons that even outweigh the concern with truth—for us to distract our own attention from the falsehood of the non-deterministic assumption that conditions our practices.

(3)    Under the given headings of the free-will dispute, this last contention can only be classified as a libertarian or incompatibilist doctrine. Reconciliationist or compatibilist it is not.

(4)    The philosophical significance of determinism is that it threatens to subvert or upstage the meaning that an ordinary narration of an agent's acts and reasons shows as inhering in those acts. If determinism is not even true, then there is no such threat.

# Longer Notes

**Longer Note 18: Could have done otherwise**

In the original version of this paper, this proof proceeded not through (4) but through Diodorus Cronus' principle

> If $p$ is possible, and necessarily if $p$ then $q$,
> then $q$ is possible.

Apart from its historical interest, Diodorus' principle only contributed an unnecessary deductive prolixity. The reformulation given here has not been designed to counter the doubts of *e.g.*, Michael Slote 'Selective Necessity and the Free Will Problem' *Journal of Philosophy*, January 1982. (On which, however, *Longer Note* 20 below does have some bearing.) Doubt will also attach to the incompatibility I claim between (7) and (8). It may disarm some of the misgivings that have been expressed if I point out that there is no question here of *analysing* the 'can' of agent ability in terms of historical-cum-physical possibility, or of any grammatical assimilation. All I claim is the incompatibility. Pending the production of another convincing principle to explain away what looks like a reliance on the incompatibility of (7) and (8) in our actual evaluation of excuses, I think that the denial of this incompatibility will continue to astonish those not already immersed in the philosophical controversy.

In his interesting article 'Alternate Possibilities and Moral Responsibility', *Journal of Philosophy* vol. 20, 1969, Harry G. Frankfurt has suggested that

> (i)     He couldn't have done otherwise

is not a necessary condition or a sufficient condition of non-responsibility. What suffices for non-responsibility and will support our practice in the evaluation of excuses is

> (ii)     He did what he did *only* because (i).

What does (ii) mean? If it means that the only good explanation of the occurrence of his action is something like (i), then (ii) is rarely or never true. Its holding is much rarer than non-responsibility. On the other hand, if we omit the 'only' from (ii) and pretend that determinism is true, then we have something which will almost always be true (in so far as 'he couldn't do otherwise' is ever a straightforward causal explanation, which is dubious). So it will follow that there is little or no responsibility.

Suppose that (ii) concerned not causal explanation in general but explanations that go via the agent's own reasons—so that (ii) came down to 'his only reason for φ-ing was that he thought there was no alternative'. Then in this interpretation (ii) is not sufficient for non-responsibility. (Perhaps he *ought* to have realized that there was this other thing that he could do.) In the second place, (ii) then looks off the point in many cases. Many non-responsible acts are non-responsible for reasons quite other than the agent's having thought that he couldn't do otherwise.

**Longer Note 20: Inevitability at a time**

It may appear that in spite of all my protestations about the contingent premisses of the argument that he could not have kept still at t', the step from 'the agent did not A at t'' to

$$\Box_t(\text{the agent did not do A at } t'),$$

could just as well have been simpler and *a priori*; so that the conclusion of the argument is fatalistic in character (a mere logical puzzle).

In the original article I thought it enough first to point to the semantics here specified for □, (namely: True ⌜□, (p)⌝ if and only if it holds that p in every world whose history is indistinguishable from the history of the actual world up to *but not necessarily including t*), and then to indicate the ways in which that stipulation might be rendered more natural. See *Notes* 20 and 18. But more needs to be said about this problem if it is to be rendered at all plausible that normally, and except in the presence of some particular *a posteriori* argument for its contingent truth, the English sentence

(*)   if the agent did not A at $t'$, then it was inevitable at $t'$ that the agent did not A at $t'$

will be false (contingently false).

The contingency of (*) will not spring to the eye if we think of the time $t'$ as a moment or instant. (For the charm of the idea that (*) is necessary, cp. Aristotle *De Interpretatione* 19a23–4. 'The existence of what is when it is, and the non-existence of what isn't when it isn't, is necessary'.) But so soon as we remind ourselves that time indicators like 'when' and '$t'$', so far from needing always to introduce moments or instants, will often have to qualify ordinary imperfective verbs of action, such as *run, write, sleep* . . . , we shall be put in mind of the time indication that they more naturally require, *e.g.* 'on Wednesday', 'on Wednesday morning', or 'between 8:00 a.m. and 9:00 a.m. on Wednesday morning'. And then we shall doubt the necessity of (*). Even though I *am* writing on Wednesday morning, it is not historically-cum-physically inevitable on Wednesday morning that I do. I don't *have* on Wednesday morning to write on Wednesday morning—even though at 11:45 a.m. precisely (the moment I shall complete the last word of this sentence) it will be too late for me to be engaged in anything else at 11:45 a.m. than that which I am engaged in at 11:45 a.m.

The deep point that can be made to surface here is this: that continuous and imperfective aspect verbs naturally require stretch-like time indicators, and it is only in virtue of an abstraction that such verbs can be qualified by the use of the language of moments or instants (which is itself an abstraction). What is more, if we want to understand action and freedom of action, we *cannot* supersede the imperfective aspect. We must take the continuous and imperfective verb for what it is, namely as coeval with and irreducible to the punctual or perfective. To understand the world of change, to understand change itself, we need to descry within the world not only events but also processes, not only instants but also stretches—or, as I would say, times. These are the terms on which, in the matter of being able to do otherwise than one is doing, we shall be able to side with Alice in a celebrated conversational exchange:

'You couldn't have it if you did want it,' the Queen said. 'The rule is, jam to-morrow and jam yesterday—but never jam to-day.'
'It must come sometimes to "jam to-day",' Alice objected.

Lewis Carroll, *Alice through the Looking Glass*

# IX

# The Concern to Survive*

> The conviction which every man has of his
> identity, as far back as his memory reaches,
> needs no aid of philosophy to strengthen it;
> and no philosophy can weaken it, without first
> producing some degree of insanity.
>
> REID

1.  Under the influence of well known thought experiments[1] modern inheritors of John Locke's conception of personhood have recently been led to draw a distinction between questions of the identity of a person and questions about survival. 'Certain important questions [about such matters as survival, memory, and responsibility] do presuppose a question about personal identity. But they can be freed of this presupposition. And when they are, the question about identity has no importance'.[2] 'We can, I think, describe cases in which, though we know how to answer every other question, we have no idea how to answer a question about personal identity. . . . Do they present a problem? It might be thought that they do not, because they could never occur. I suspect that some of them could. . . . But I shall claim that even if they did they would present no problem'.[3]

2.  In another place[4] I have attempted some reassessment of the thought experiments involving the supposed fission and fusion of persons that prompted Derek Parfit to draw these

---

* *Midwest Studies in Philosophy* Volume 4 (1979), with permission.
[1] Sidney Shoemaker, *Self Knowledge and Self Identity* (Ithaca, 1963), p. 22: David Wiggins, *Identity and Spatiotemporal Continuity* (Oxford, 1967), p. 50; Derek Parfit, 'Personal Identity', *Philosophical Review* vol. 80, 1970, p. 5.

[2] 'Personal Identity' p. 4.

[3] 'Personal Identity' p. 3.

[4] David Wiggins, *Sameness and Substance* (Oxford: Blackwell, 1980), Chapters 3 and 6.

strange and disturbing conclusions. I have even suspected sometimes that Parfit's conception of the identity relation rests on a rejection of the idea, which to me at least seems overwhelmingly plausible,[5] that the predicate 'is the same as' is as primitive and irreducible as any other predicate that one can think of. But the present question is neither the status of thought experiments involving the putative division of persons, nor the nature of identity (whether, as Parfit puts it, identity can be 'a further fact' of some matter[6]). It is the separability that Parfit alleges of questions of survival from questions of identity—and not even the whole of that issue.

What it is necessary to discuss is the alleged separability of two *concerns*—the separability, for instance, of a man's 31st December 1978 concern to survive until 31st December 1980 at least and the concern that such a man has on 31st December 1978 that, at every moment between then and 31st December 1980 at least, there should exist something identical with him. I concede that, even as regards survival, this separability or inseparability is only one small part of what needs to be discussed; but nobody can judge the separability question irrelevant who undertakes, as Parfit did,[7] to reach out to our actual concern with death or to distinguish in theory between a legitimate apprehension that lurks in fear of death and something supposedly less rational therein, having to do with identity.

The criticisms I offer will be made from the general position of one who holds that, although experiential memory is one component in an inner nucleus of conceptual constituents of what it is for a person to continue to exist (to persist), there is no non-trivial necessary or sufficient condition of identity through time that we can formulate in terms of experiential memory. Insofar as there is some general disagreement here, it is about the importance of identity in the philosophy of persons and the relation between identity and mental connectedness, not about whether *any* importance attaches to mental con-

---

[5] *Ibid.*, Chapter 2, Section 1, and *Longer Notes* 2.03, 3.19, 4.02.

[6] I doubt that we really know what it is to describe a case for which we know how to answer *every question*, or *every question except one*. Certainly no such case ever presents itself in concrete reality.

[7] 'Personal Identity,' pp. 3 and 27.

nectedness. The disagreement is a disagreement within the wider class of friends of mental connectedness who see something to applaud in Locke's definition of a person as 'a thinking intelligent being that has reason and reflection, and can consider itself as itself, the same thinking thing in different times and places'[8], however much they differ over other things.

3. I have rehearsed these points only in order to set the general scene for the dispute. What I want to argue now is much more briefly stated. Suppose I express the fervent and enduring wish to survive until 1980 at least. Then, so far from its being possible (as a pure mental connectedness account of survival would hold that it was possible) to separate my concern that there should exist something identical with me at every moment between now and 1980 from my concern that my mental life should flow on under the cognitive and affective influence of my present memories, beliefs, and character (even as these themselves evolve between now and 1980), absolutely any adequate description of the second concern will have to presuppose the validity and importance of the first one. This presupposition between the two concerns arises from something central to the phenomenology of these matters— something whose elimination or modification cannot be relied upon to leave undisturbed *the desire itself* to survive into the future. This last desire is not, I claim, a thing that we can treat as a brute datum. It comes with thoughts and conceptions that require philosophical attention and description: and some of these thoughts and conceptions have a content that involves identity inextricably.

4. The first deficiency in the pure mental connectedness account of survival and one's concern for one's survival is that it ignores or redescribes the fact that consideration of who and what he is, or what value he puts upon himself, is sometimes crucial to a person in his deliberations about life and death. If someone dislikes himself very much, that may diminish his desire to survive (or may diminish it subject only to the

[8] John Locke, *An Essay Concerning Human Understanding*, Essay II, xxvii, 11.

countervailing influence of fear of the alternative). Again, an unassuming man in a setting of domestic peace who finds himself faced with a choice between a dangerous act of heroism and living out his days in what he will conceive as dishonour may well come to value simple survival far less highly than he previously did. To describe or understand what happens here we need to see the issue of survival as the issue of the survival of a *continuant* that can be assessed in certain relevant ways. We shall return to this problem at the end of §8. But the pressing question is one of what rational replacement or substitute consideration the mental connectedness theorist can offer for this man's preoccupation with his doubt about what sort of person he would survive *as* in surviving by making the non-heroic choice.

5.   The next thing to consider is consciousness and survival, and the requirement that the mental connectedness theorist will make that the person who survives should know in 1980 that he has got what he wished for in 1978 and should then remember his wishing to survive that long. There is something very plausible in this. But let us approach it *via* the question of desiring things in the future perfectly in general.

Men care about all sorts of future things that they know they will never know about. A grandparent of eighty may care now in 1978 about what his eight-year-old grandchild's life will be like in the 21st century. Normally when we care about something, we must value the opportunity to know how matters turn out. But the concern to know is surely separable in principle from the concern for the thing itself. It is true that a grandparent who was offered by some magic the opportunity to live into the 21st century in order to witness the life and fortunes of his grandchild would have to see that there was *something* to value in this opportunity—that, to the extent that he cared about his grandchild, he would have to regard it as at least in some respect a good thing to be able to know of his grandchild's fortunes. Nevertheless, before he made the choice whether to live that long or not, he would have to weigh in the balance the fact that in the interim he might lapse into the condition of a Struldbrug and that by the year 2000 he might be blind, feeble-minded, and incontinent. In itself, the concern for the grandchild's future is not conditional on *knowing* anything

at all about the actual outcome. *A fortiori* it is not conditional
on any mental or cognitive connectedness between the wishing
and the fulfilment of the wish.

6.   This is the normal case, but no doubt there is something
very special about knowing about the satisfaction of one's own
wish to survive. That which is special about this is indeed one
part of the foundation of the pure mental connectedness theory
of survival. What would it be to live up to 1980 and not know
that in doing so one had got what one wished? Surely, it will
be said, life without the experiential memory required to
remember the wish of 1978 (or any similar and subsequent
wishes to survive) is survival as a mere vegetable, not as a
person. That is what will be said by most neo-Lockean
philosophers, and it is well known where the thought leads. It
leads to that which leads in the end to the pure mental
connectedness theory. But there is an alternative answer to the
question, and this explains no worse than the theory of mental
connectedness the intuitions that underlie the Lockean position.
The alternative answer is that this sort of survival would not be
the survival of enough of what is presupposed to that which
made one value oneself and one's own continued life as dearly
as one did. What made me dear to myself, what made me into
something I thought it was *worth* caring about the survival
of—surely this required and presupposed my still having my
faculties.

7.   At this point one may muster the courage to ask the
question what is so good, either absolutely or for me, about my
own mental life's flowing on from now into the future. Surely
this depends on what kind of person I am or think I am, and
what sort of mental life it is. Well, not quite. There is something
instinctive here and as irreducible as the rational commitment
to make prudent provision for the future. These are things that
we need reasons to opt out of rather than things that we have to
look for deep reasons to opt into. That is how it is with human
rationality. Obviously the instinct for survival has played its
part in the determination of what we mean by 'rational'. But
what is the content of the said instinct? The content is surely
that this animal that is *identical with me* should not cease to be,

but should survive and flourish. If that sounds improbable as an account of the content of an instinct, this is only the result of my attempting to make the involvement with identity perfectly explicit. And what would the pure mental connectedness account be? That these experiences (*which* experiences?—well, never mind now whether we can say which ones without reintroducing personal identity) should give rise in the right way to successors. As an account of the content of an instinct, this is improbable. As an account of the object of a further or post-instinctual rational concern, it does not answer the question what is good about survival, or why it should even matter to anyone. But an account of what survival is *ought* to show this.

8.   Of the two answers implied by §7 above to the question what (when uncertainty is left out of account) is bad about death, it may seem, nevertheless that the more rational answer is the former non-instinctual answer, carrying with it my idea of myself as a continuant with certain moral or aesthetic qualities that command my allegiance. If so, then one is bound to wonder how a man who survives, and gets that which, in wanting to survive, he envisaged himself having, will actually conceive of that survival. One natural answer will be that he envisages that as the persistence of a certain bearer of a certain range of predicates that are irreducibly mental. Such is the answer that is suggested not only by common sense but also by Strawson's thesis of the primitiveness of the concept of a person. (A thesis that can be cited here without any commitment to the particular details of the account given in *Individuals*[9] of the principles of the distinction between M- and P-predicates, without commitment to the disjointness of these ranges, and without commitment to deny that the psychological predicates are indirectly body-involving.) The thesis of the primitiveness of the concept of *person* not only fits our actual conception of what a person is. It has two other relevant virtues. It shows how we might see the body-involving, not purely mental properties of a person as integral to the proper expression of his mental attributes. And

[9] P.F. Strawson, *Individuals* (London: Methuen, 1956).

it structures the dispute we find here in philosophy.

Abandoning Strawson's even-handed treatment of the two ranges of predicate and shifting the emphasis onto one or the other of the two classes of predicate, we arrive at two twin deviations. By relegating body-involving predicates and predicates of the whole organism as an organism to secondary status and demoting some to unimportance we arrive at Parfit's identity-free conception of survival. By promoting the predicates involving the whole organism as an organism to special prominence, we arrive at Bernard Williams's equally notorious and surprising suggestion[10] that one exists so long as one's whole body exists, and that whatever one is or does one's body is or does.[11]

9. If Strawson's sort of answer is the natural answer to the question how the person who wants to survive envisages his survival, we must ask what the theorist of mental connectedness who proposes that we dispense with identity wants to substitute for it. Either he substitutes nothing, because he regards the desire to survive as a brute datum (but it is not); or else he substitutes for the Strawsonian conception of survival a conception of the continuation of a certain line of consciousness. But here we must ask: ought this new idea to command the same allegiance? *Would* it indeed command it—once it was appreciated that the facts themselves were being held to require that we substitute for an ontology of persons an ontology of mental events, and once it was appreciated that within this new ontology there is no real room for the idea of an individual biography? (Indeed so soon as we try to make room within it even for a *line* of consciousness linking mental events, and to reconstruct the evaluation of persons in terms of the evaluation of such lines, we restore identity itself to the content of the concern to survive, contrary to Parfit's intention.) Surely it

[10] Bernard Williams, 'Are Persons Bodies?' in *Problems of the Self* (Cambridge University Press, 1973).

[11] *Identity and Spatiotemporal Continuity*, p. 45, *Sameness and Substance*, Chapter 6, Section 6. I am now content to allow the second (predicability) point to settle the less important (and surely vague) question of how long a person continues to exist. (For the consistency of the vagueness with the definiteness of identity, see my 'Singling out an object determinately' in McDowell and Pettit eds. *Subject, Thought, and Context* (Oxford University Press, 1986).)

was, in the first place, some allegiance to the idea of an individual biography that made Locke's conception of persons interesting to us. It was some chord that this struck in us that made mental connectedness seem important. But if so, any theorist of mental connectedness who has come to the point where he is preparing to sacrifice the notion of an articulated, indefinitely amplifiable, individual biography has cut off the very branch he was sitting on.

10.   It is important not to confuse the considerations that I have just urged with the prediction that, if a man were told that tomorrow there would certainly be nobody who was him, then he would decline all offers to rearrange matters so that tomorrow someone would bear to him Parfit's relation of mental connectedness. The prediction that this would be refused is no doubt false in many cases. But it is irrelevant. For it is not obvious that a man's acceptance of the offer would tell us anything at all about that which motivated the original desire to survive—the desire as that exists among actual human beings.

When the desire not to cease to exist comes to accept its own long-term futility, it can be commuted into all sorts of distinctively different sorts of desire to *leave traces*: to be remembered by friends or pupils, to live on in one's works. 'And now that thou art lying, my dear old Carian guest,/A handful of grey ashes, long, long ago at rest,/Still are thy pleasant voices, thy nightingales awake;/For Death, he taketh all away, but them he cannot take', as Cory translates Callimachus. Again, the desire to leave traces can take the form of desiring that some small improvement one brought about in the world be not instantly eroded, or that someone somewhere learn something from what one learned oneself the hard way. These things can be desired for themselves, but they can also appear as sublimations of the desire not to cease to exist. They are typical accommodations to the certainty of death. What is not clear is how much more there would be to the possession of mentally connected descendants than there is to these more etiolated forms of 'survival'. Indeed I think that I myself prefer the more etiolated forms. What I am certain about is that I do not see how the offer of any of these things, Parfitian *or* etiolated, can be taken for a proper surrogate (equivalent on the level of imagination, conception, and desire) for the continued existence of the one and only person that is me. Unless, of course, I no longer want that continued existence—in which case the etiolated forms of survival are again not equal or tantamount but simply better.

11.   There is real difficulty in the idea that we could purify our actual concerns of every taint of the personal identity concept, and then, with everything else intact, persevere in—or identify ourselves with—the purified desires that emerged.

# Postscript to Essays I–IX

# 1

1.1   In one way or another more than half of the essays
collected here seek to explore and assess the option of
combining an irreductive, 'no foundations' account of the
subject matters of morals and politics (occasionally, *obiter*,
aesthetics) with some sort of cognitivist view of the status of the
judgments that are made there. I have to hope that, when they
are taken together, the relevant essays do something to suggest
how a subject matter can be essentially contestable[1] yet
principled: and how a collection of convictions and concerns
can be the product of system yet resist all efforts of
simplification, because it reposes on a diversity of mutually
irreducible ideas.[2] What I have also wanted to show is that it is
possible for such a subject matter to be rooted at the level of
sense in the actual and contingent condition of human beings,
while being objective on the level of reference and truth-value.

To forestall misunderstanding, I would emphasize again
that the objectivity whose possibility I am holding out for in
these essays has nothing to do with the 'absolute view of reality'
or 'the view from nowhere', but relates only to the exacting

[1] The idea of essential contestability was introduced into philosophy by W.B. Gallie,
in 'Essentially Contested Concepts', *Proceedings of the Aristotelian Society* vol. 56,
1955/6.
[2] If it seems puzzling that I should say that these ideas are mutually primitive or
irreducible even though it is my settled and declared habit to elucidate each in terms of
the others, then perhaps what is needed is the picture of each idea's not being
introduced by a definition, but being thrown up by a practice that presupposes the
presence of a whole skein of other practices the majority of which have come into being
and evolved more or less simultaneously.

standard of correctness that is partially explicated in Essay IV. That standard is in a certain way maximal.[3] But this in itself does not entail that, if our best judgments of value or obligation turn out to fail this standard, they were bound *as such* to fail it. Whether or not this is so is one of the questions that is touched upon in Essays IV and V.

1.2 The 'no foundations' view is one of the common themes of Essay I, 'Claims of Need', and Essay II, 'Universalizability, Impartiality, Truth'. As will be evident, the first of these is concerned with other matters, some of which, I realize, may be of little interest to professional philosophers as such. (All who desire to do so must exercise the option to skip the descriptive passages and footnotes that I have devoted to the discrepancies that interest me between the actual outcomes of political deliberation and the rhetoric of 'need' by which the decisions reached have had, however mendaciously, to be justified.) But there is at least one distinctively philosophical aim that is common to Essays I and II. This is the aim of drawing attention to the copiousness and diversity of what can be discovered by attending to the full range of fully considered and fully deliberated (unreconstructed) moral sentiments (construed here as complex intentional states)—or *could* be discovered if we would only resist the reductive influences that press from everywhere upon them.[4] What I contend is not simply that this range of sentiments is presupposed to complex ideas like that of justice, but also (contrary to the theoretical expectations that some have entertained) that they are presupposed in their fully fledged condition to any 'universalization' test that can strike us as remotely plausible. This range of sentiments is not a mere datum for a universalization test to work upon, but a large part of the substance of morality itself. To seek to put these sentiments to work and simultaneously subordinate them to another level of moral theory will either import

---

[3] For the claim that, whatever else it is, absolute truth is not a higher degree of plain truth, see below note 24.

[4] For the reductive influences that work even from within morality, see Bernard Williams, *Ethics and the Limits of Philosophy*, p. 6 and *passim*. The part of morality that I argue can survive exposure to the philosophical account of what morality itself is no doubt overlaps extensively with the part that Williams prefers to call 'ethics'.

contradiction (the right hand seeks to undo what the left hand has already completed—*i.e.* theoretical morality subverts the findings upon which theoretical morality depended for content) *or* denature the only thing there ever was to sustain ordinary moral motivation. (Consider the way in which, even as it seeks to attend to them, consequentialism actually subverts the simple inhibitions that restrain us from murder, arson, pillage. The inhibition is commuted into the impersonal desire—not at all to be depended upon for the same motive force, least of all in the age of terrorism and blackmail—for as little as possible murder, arson, pillage to occur.)

1.3   I expect it will be said that such an 'intuitionist' outlook is almost as old as moral philosophy; and that, if it were any good at all, the problems of the philosophical subject would not still be with us. What defences can I arm the new intuitionism with against the familiar old objections?

I reply first that there has always been a tendency to blame on moral philosophy what are really the shortcomings (if that is the word) of its subject matter; and that these shortcomings may themselves be inherent in morality itself. Maybe the subject matter furnishes too little (or not the right things) for there to be any general answer to the questions that philosophers and others have felt that philosophy is duty-bound to answer generally. If so, it does not follow that what is furnished is in any other respect meagre. What follows is rather that to make proper use of the plenty that *is* provided we have to abandon the process of greater and greater quasi-mathematical refinement of one or two supposedly promising general principles and cultivate instead a keener sense of how to identify in a given particular case what is at issue there and how to make the best use of everything bearing on it that is furnished in the particular context.[5]

The second point I have to make is that, to the extent that the position I advocate has anything in common with moral intuitionism,[6] it is in the two positions' common interest to

---

[5] The discussion of commensurability and incommensurability in Essay VII §8 exploits this possibility.

[6] And in fact it has more in common with Humean subjectivism than it has with ethical intuitionism.

take advantage of all the improvements brought about by Williams and others in our understanding of what can be expected of any account of the nature of morality, and to encourage some keener sense of the danger that, if we lust for more than that can provide, then we shall probably lose touch with what gives moral philosophy its interest on the level of motivation. Not only that. If a good many of the historic objections to intuitionism were really objections to the actual and inherent condition of morality itself, then morality must learn to live with the philosophical account of its own actual and inherent condition. This accommodation will probably not be effected without loss, because it cannot be effected by morality's turning a blind eye on what it itself is. But this is not to say that global scepticism need be the outcome. Everything depends on what that philosophical account itself says.

Finally, I would urge in defence of intuitionism and its successors that such positions badly need to avail themselves of distinctions like that between practical and evaluative judgments (see Essay III §4, Essay IV §11), which have not always been noted or appreciated in the summary inspections (or even the official visitations) carried out by philosophers who have condemned intuitionist premises as unfit for human habitation. All that these inspectors have been able to perceive is a huge mass of low grade evidence: but in fact (as I try to show in §§11–21 of Essay I, where I am concerned with the ideas of need, right, and just claim) there are elements of order and cohesion to be discovered within this plenitude of apparent confusion. Order and cohesion will only be visible, however, if, having marked the practical/evaluative distinction, we attend to the moral sentiments in their social and historical setting and then prepare to take a livelier interest than we are usually tempted to do in what I call their *stratigraphy*. In this instance, the stratigraphy is illustrated by a conceptual cum phenomenological distinction between something I call *phase one justice*, which is justice as the guardian of rights; *phase two justice*, which is justice as the definer of the limits of aggregative reasoning and vigilant arbitrator between rights and counterrights (*viz.* claims not themselves representing rights that can nevertheless count against rights); and *phase three justice*, which is justice as the custodian, distributor and occasional producer of public goods.

I know that the reader will see much less point than I do in such a stratigraphy, unless he is ready to accept the essential contestability of political and moral judgments, and prepared to have regard for the possibility of their underdetermination. But, once he contemplates granting this concession and once he makes the experiment of trying to see phase three justice as essentially contestably delimited in the sphere of its operation by the non-negotiable claims of phase one justice and phase two justice, I believe he will be rewarded by finding some release from the panic or paralysis of the reasoning faculties that is so easily induced in us by questions that tacitly but illegitimately roll up protective and limitative (phase one and phase two) justice within 'distributive' (phase three) justice. He will be released from trying to take seriously all sorts of utterly iniquitous proposals that are alleged to maximize satisfaction.[7] He will feel that he knows in a principled way why it is that such schemes are not candidates for consideration.

What lies behind the insistence upon essential contestability? Not the desire to rush in and close the question of the exact difference between axiological and scientific objectivity; nor any positive general insistence that *in every case* there will be underdetermination of the practical. (Cp. 3.7 below.) Rather the idea is that with the valuational and practical the determination of truth is a *dialectical* undertaking in which we have to be content for the objectively stronger to defeat the weaker consideration, but without indulging the hope that there is some way by which we can be assured that we have finally arrived at the strongest consideration in the comprehensively best framework. We do best neither to indulge this hope, nor to issue the general denial that such a thing as that consideration and framework ever exist. Even if they do not, that still does not mean that just anything goes.

---

[7] Even if they will pass the compensatory version of the economists' test for being Pareto optimal. On Pareto optimality—which has nothing to do with my reasons for mentioning Pareto in §2.1 below—and on compensation-based reformulations of this criterion, see now John Mackie's fine essay 'Rights, Utility, and External Costs', in *Persons and Values* (Oxford University Press, 1985).

# 2

2.1   As I look back at Essay I, what now disturbs me most is the suspicion that I have gravely underestimated the resistance that anyone must expect who defends a principle of justice like the Limitation Principle given at the beginning of §23.[8] If he puts it forward to be one of the limits of the area within which

[8] The relevant passage runs as follows:

> Perhaps the limitative principle that will regulate both rights/counter-rights arbitration *and* collective reasoning conducted in pursuit of public goods is this. Even if there is nothing unjust in actions of the State or its agencies making one man poorer in a way that makes another man less poor than he was (in kind or money) . . ., it *is pro tanto unjust* if the State or an agency of the State intervenes against contingency, or changes its policy, or confounds citizens' sensible expectations, in a way that sacrifices anyone's strictly vital interests to the mere desires of however many others; and (more speculatively) *it is pro tanto unjust* if, among vital interests actually affected by such interventions, the greater strictly vital need of anyone is sacrificed in the name of the lesser needs of however many others.

It is an urgent matter to improve all such formulations, but I believe that the improvement must be made in the light of the question discussed in Essay I §17. This is a far more sensible focus for the dialogue between conservatism and socialism, I claim, than the question of equality. By socialism I suggest one then ought to mean a position whose central preoccupation is with *counter-claims*, as these are defined in Essay I §12 following. For the way in which the idea of counter-claims will make better sense of some of the more promising questions about equality, see below note 13.

For my use of the expression *pro tanto* in the passage cited, and elsewhere, see Susan Hurley 'Conflict, Akrasia, and Cognitivism', *Proceedings of the Aristotelian Society*, vol. 86 (1985/6), pp. 23ff. For the need for such a term see Bernard Williams' critique of the term '*prima facie*' in 'Consistency and Realism', *The Aristotelian Society Supplementary Volume* 40, 1966.

aggregative reasoning can operate without injustice and announces, as I have, that this principle is to be part of a fence between the justice that concerns rights or counter-rights and a kind of justice that is treated with less respect in that essay and called 'phase three justice' or 'the rest of justice', then he must expect to be closely cross-examined about what vital interests are. When the proponent of the limitation principle goes on to reveal that vital interests are due to be defined in terms of needs that are grave, deeply entrenched, and scarcely substitutable (§9), he is bound to be pressed very hard to face the question exactly how such needs are to be determined, and who is to determine them.

It is often assumed that simply to ask the last question in the right tone of voice suffices to dissipate the whole force of the suggestion that needs are an urgent or central constituent in the idea of justice. Who wants other people to tell him what he needs?

Among the first to have seen this as the difficulty was Pareto. What Pareto wrote was:

> La formule: *à chacun selon ses besoins* se change ainsi en l'autre: *à chacun selon ce que décide l'autorité:* et elle vaut en général ce que vaut l'autorité.[9]

Pareto's objection has not lost its power. Variants of it are still directed with the same expectation of dialectical triumph against champions of the need concept who, unlike Pareto's, have never proposed 'From each according to his ability: to each according to his need' as part of some supreme or all-embracing principle of all justice, are quite innocent of all totalitarian or authoritarian aspirations in politics, and have as their principal transgression nothing worse than this: to find nothing compelling or convincing in any of the descendants or mitigations of the Greatest Happiness Principle that have been intended to minister to our ideas of justice and injustice.

Perhaps the only way to come to terms with the sneer 'And who then is simply to determine vital interests, or needs?' is to pretend that no sneer is intended, to overlook the rhetorical

[9] *Les Systèmes Socialistes* (Paris, 1901) vol. II, p. 167.

intentions with which such questions are so often uttered, and try to provide a literal answer to them, just as they stand, attending *en route* to all the supplementary questions that would be bound to arise in a political or philosophical exchange on the subject. Those not in the grip of Pareto's objection may feel that they wish at this point to skip to §3.1 below.

2.2 How are needs to be determined? Confronted with this question our first task, but not our only one, is surely to say what the question of needing *turns on*, and what is relevant to it, and what is not.

Sections 3–7 of Essay I attempt this task. What the question of needs turns on depends in the first instance on what needing is, and on what people mean when they speak seriously about needs (in the absolute or categorical sense, see §6). So the first part of the first task is the question of meaning. The correctness of §§3–7 and of the use they make of such ideas as harm and necessity chiefly depends on whether the proposals put forward there make better sense of the data than any rival semantical hypothesis.

Once we emerge from that semantical question, if we do, it will appear that the idea of harm is correlative with ideas of human life and flourishing that each age, community and culture has to make the best it can of. These are public property and the fit subject of constructive argument; but, like so many ordinary ideas, they are also metaphysical and essentially contestable. And to some theorists of politics that will seem both dangerous and unnerving. They will search about for reasons to displace these notions by more technical, supposedly more operational, counterparts whose application will occasion less heart-searching and less argument.

If the principles of need comprised some political principle to the effect that a person was to have only what he or she needed, then the essential contestability of need claims would be a troublesome point and the public determination of needs and vital interests would represent an intolerable violation of personal autonomy. But the thing I must emphasize is that no such principle is being offered in Essay I. What is being offered there is a principle that is designed to safeguard the space around the individual, and to protect him and his life chances from certain kinds of injustices that might otherwise be committed against him on some specious pretext of public interest.

In fact even more protection could be afforded to individuals' interests within the needs framework if the protection of the individual from aggregative reasoning were the only sort of protection that was at issue here. But legitimate purposes of the State, most conspicuously the requirements of phase two justice, cannot help but circumscribe what ought to be attempted in this connexion. That which is really required is a way of arbitrating between all sorts of claims—the individual's claim, the community's claim, other individuals' claims.[10]

That this last end has to be achieved *somehow* is common ground. What is controversial is whether the concept of need is somehow pernicious in this connexion. I am claiming that it is not, and that in these conflicts it often clarifies what is at issue on both sides. Surely the idea of need is not disabled from its conceptual role on either side of the argument by the essential contestability that statements of vital interest inherit from the essential contestability of statements of need. For in this area, essential contestability is the condition of all important ideas. Its presence does not entail that just anything goes, or that the process of determination of harm (either to the individual or by the individual) is simply a matter of counting ayes and noes. These ideas of life, harm, flourishing are the focus of wide-ranging, open-ended controversy and of a rich variety of

---

[10] And once phase two justice enters explicitly, we can find a reading that nobody need find too sinister for such familiar observations as Wade's in his *Administrative Law*: 'social needs and ancient liberties are frequently hard to reconcile'; though this is not to say that the phase two interpretation of 'social needs' has been consistently accorded any actual priority by all the great departments of State in which writers on administrative law such as W. Robson were prepared to place such confidence. Not only have phase three considerations come slowly but surely to outstrip all others. These departments have been slow to see the conceptual basis of the profound truth that what real justice usually requires is not that utility should be maximized by whatever means and then 'redistributed' (for the strangeness of this verb see Essay I §17), but that (however hard this is to achieve) it should be made possible for the wealth on which vital interests depend to be produced closer to the point where it is to confer its benefit, and that its presence there, when once it is present, should be actively protected by use of all the judicial and other resources of the State from predations of all kinds, not excluding predations by agencies of the State itself.

opposing analogies which it can still be hoped will converge in an agreement over essentials (either a general agreement, or an agreement among a majority of representatives properly elected) that is both principled and capable of justifying itself. In the present we have to draw credit upon the prospect of drawing closer to that auspicious state of affairs in the future. Certainly the ideas of flourishing and harm are not rendered inapplicable by virtue of being temporally and culturally conditioned. For one might think that notions that are conditioned by one's own time and culture are the ones that it ought to be easiest to criticize in a practical way and, after refinement by criticism, to apply in action.

2.3   But *why*, I may now be asked, are vital interests in $x, y, z$ to be defined in terms of needs that are grave, non-substitutable with respect to $x$, $y$, $z$, entrenched *etc*? To this I answer that these categories, as defined in §§8–9 of Essay I were designed to catch something that I hoped that everyone would recognize as the grounds for a certain sort of concern for an individual whose interests are gravely threatened by our pursuit of some supposedly common good, a concern further enlarged upon in §12 following. But the categories can be displaced by any others that are better designed to fulfil this task and that engage better with the relevant sentiments.

2.4   All right, someone may say. I hear all that. But what states then, with what objects, will deserve the title of grave, non-substitutable, entrenched needs? Once you answer this question, you will be seen in your true colours as an autocrat, or as the willing slave of the autocrat.

I would reply that §12 following give some indication of the states I should single out for this special title: but that it is philosophically important to distinguish here (and I have already assumed that one must distinguish) between the question of how to specify these states, *i.e.* to enumerate them, and the logically prior question of what it *turns on* in a given case whether, under circumstances $c$, $x$ is a vital need or interest of such and such persons. In so far as the theorist has any privileged standing here, it only consists in his claim to have tried to articulate this logically prior thing, and in the liberty (which is not exclusively his) to issue reminders of this, if nobody else will, whenever and wherever argument breaks out over such things as needs, rights and counter-claims. Apart from this, the theorist has no privileged standing. Nor will any other supposed expert, appointed, self-appointed or elected necessarily have a privileged position. The question of the norms of flourishing or harm, and of the subclassification of these, is the exclusive intellectual property of nobody, except in so far as what is proposed is the creation or perpetuation of a system of government that *makes* these questions into someone's mystery or exclusive preserve.

2.5    Who then is to determine, either in a given case or more generally, what are harms, what are needs, what are vital interests?

Pareto envisages that the answer to that sort of question will be 'the authority'; and then he rightly points out that the answer we shall get from that authority about our needs cannot be expected to be worth more than that authority is worth. But since 'from each according to his ability: to each according to his need' is not being put forward by me as the single supreme principle of justice, and all that is being said (contrast the contentions of some of Pareto's opponents) is that the idea of need figures essentially in constituent principles of phase one and phase two justice, it will be apparent that no proposal is in question here to set up some unitary dictatorial authority to determine the needs and/or abilities of each and every person.

Facing the questions we actually face then, let us make the thought-experiment of envisaging in some detail the present pattern of government, judiciary *etc.*, and let us speculate what is the least institutional change that would be required to enforce the Limitation Principle and to make counter-claims stick. I claimed in Essay I that the first necessity here was a further (by no means novel or unexpected) development of our moral and political culture; and that the second necessity might be to make provision (or to take seriously some old provision) by which government or its agencies would be legally required on certain sorts of occasion to demonstrate that this or that public practice or project did not infringe the principles of justice.[11]

Who then would judge that? Well, suppose that on these occasions it was for some member or members of the judiciary to determine the question of infringement or non-infringement. Then on this sort of occasion, the question of determination of vital need would be one for judges. What then would judges themselves rely upon? In the last resort, they would have to rely (as they sometimes have to in matters of equity) on the more durable deliverances of our shared moral and political culture. But what would those deliverances themselves depend upon? Well, indirectly but ultimately, these would surely depend on *us*, on how careful we ourselves were to listen to what we were saying and think what we meant by it, and on how careful we were both singly and collectively to keep track of our own judgments and our reasons for making them.

In this area it turns out that, if public policy were more need-orientated and less preference-orientated, and if the emphasis were shifted from phase three to phase two justice, it would sometimes fall to judges, or legislators or their public servants to determine the substance of certain vital needs. That is in line with Pareto's gloomy general prediction. But note now that the substance of vital needs is not very different from what legislators and their public servants *already* claim to determine. See Essay I, §3. The difference I am interested in is that, under the happier state of affairs I am trying to describe, these legislators and their servants would have not to use the words 'need' or 'vital interest' so lightly or without thinking what they meant by what they said: and that in order to administer phase two justice, they would then have to aim to articulate for this or that particular purpose that which was soundest and most durable in the ideas of needs, vital interest, *etc.* that passed muster then. Hence the importance (already urged) of our understanding as well as we can now what we are talking about

[11] Where counter-claims are concerned, it will probably be necessary to envisage yet a third thing: some sort of procedure designed to draw attention to the condition to which certain people have been reduced by the existing systems of entitlement relations. I shall not weigh down the argument by seeking to specify such a procedure. It will be sufficient to suppose, for the sake of determinacy, that those arbitrating the outcome might be members of the judiciary, or members of the first or second chamber of the legislature.

now when we make arguments in the area of needs, rights and counter-claims—and of our not permitting moral or political philosophers or political scientists or economists to cheat us of our conceptual birthright by reducing questions of social choice and justice to questions that can be dealt with in the impoverished terms of bare desire, revealed preference *etc.*, however mitigated or tempered by the superposition of radical or inspiratory after-thoughts of equality or fraternity. If our own way of thinking becomes over-schematized or over-simplified, or insensitive to the vital interests of the outvoted or outnumbered, then that of our public servants is bound to do so.

2.6　　At certain points in the last answer I pass close to the fear that is sometimes voiced that expert opinion or some wide public consensus about what is a good or wretched life or a vital need might work against the interests of those not party to the consensus and license massive interference in their freedom.

Of course the determination of practical matters by those who represent majorities, or by educated consensus, or (what is different again) by experts subject to educated consensus is always dangerous. It is a dangerous necessity (once given the greater danger of dispensing with government altogether). The only real question is whether, under the condition I have called the happier state of affairs, such things as majorities or experts or consensus would be more dangerous than they have to be, or less answerable to rational control. For, as I have said, this happier state is not a new political arrangement by which some single person or body is newly charged with realizing any supreme principle or with butting into every detail of everyone's life. It is simply a state of affairs differing at specific points from the present by virtue of certain thoughts about justice being taken more seriously, and then followed through.

My claim, as I have said, is that at present experts and ministers or their public servants purport (in effect) to determine what preferences *have* been revealed and then (within limits and constraints no doubt, but with only fitful regard for phase two justice) devise the policies that will optimize relative to these. The great choice we need to find a way to make is not whether a large variety of things will continue to be determined for us, but whether those who determine them shall continue to work to maximize the satisfaction of preferences within the framework of what I call phase three justice: or whether they shall leave rather more of these preferences to find their own satisfaction and concentrate instead, in the frameworks of phase one and phase two justice, on our grave, unsubstitutable, entrenched needs, interpreting our vital interests in the light of what people pursue and say they pursue qua needed, and in the light of what appear as the best ideas to be had about these things. In this matter, *pace* Pareto, the champion of needs has as good a right as anyone else to declare himself as an opponent of despotism and authoritarianism. He can join with others in the contention that it would be a good thing if social deliberations in which appeal is made to our behaviour as evidence of how we conceive of our interests were more often obtruded upon by our own interpretations of our own doings—albeit in defiance of the behaviourism that has shaped the development of our theories of political economy and has made these theories so blind to the question what people might have chosen had there been the option to act out some other choice, in behaviour the economist could then have observed.[12] On any sane view, the human voice is required in any case. But the human voice, where permitted, is no worse adapted to the revelation, expression and constructive criticism of needs than it is to that of preferences (preferences themselves often notoriously failing in any case to effect any unique determination of the correct, or the 'democratic', decision).

2.7 Finally then freedom, and the threat to freedom that is sometimes apprehended from any theory of needs. Here perhaps one can only have recourse to a question. In operation within a non-authoritarian, critical society in which discussion was both free and effective, why should not principles like the Limitation Principle, explicated in terms of vital interests and needs, *restore* freedom or choice or independence to classes whose freedom is now intolerably restricted and narrow, or has

[12] Cp. David Wiggins, *Sameness and Substance*, p. 180.

been substantially diminished? What is more, freedom, choice, and autonomy are themselves vital human needs, and are candidates for precisely the kind of protection that is accorded *qua* needs to other real needs. Is it not within the power of the idea of need to suggest limitations on the purposes of the State, as well as to suggest the desirability, in certain well understood cases that can be carefully defined, of the State's raising taxes for the purpose of giving education, health or self sufficiency (requirements of phase one and phase two justice) to its citizens?[13] The real enemy of human freedom is not the idea of a need—or any other ordinary moral or political idea that we can sustain in a determinate distinctive use—but conceptions of political science that will reduce or simplify the complex vocabulary of politics and political evaluation that is second nature to us and will give undeserved assistance to those already bent on narrowing ignobly the range of political possibilities that can be sufficiently visible even to be considered. (Cp. Essay VIII §3; Essay VI §4; Essay VII §8.)

2.9 Over and over again in these matters, one will find oneself referring to what can by effort be discovered within *us* or *our* valuational consciousness. Who is this *we*? Anyone and everyone is included in it until explicitly (and for good reasons, cp. p. 66) he or she is excluded. To see another as disagreeing is precisely to see him or her as *party* to the effort to construct the point of view that shall be common to one person with another. If things go well, then everyone is party. But even where things go well, we are not simply counting heads. Rather we have concerted our efforts to make it possible for the best considerations to prevail—*as* the best considerations.

[13] With all these things in place, I gladly mitigate some of my strictures on the idea of equality. For what has emerged as a plausible requirement of phase two justice is that in the pursuit of that sort of justice, where it does pursue it, the State must not only delimit the sphere of aggregative calculation but must have regard and equal regard, in its actions as well as its deliberations, for each person's equally vital interest *as* his or her vital interest. Note however that this strong principle still leaves it open what the scope of State intervention is to be, and what further commitment if any the State must have to the further aspects or dimensions of equality. And what I cannot retract is my claim that it is a gratuitously weak (and *de facto* ineffective) criticism of most actual acts or public injustice to say that what is being done is inegalitarian. (Or else it is a gratuitously obscure criticism.) Always so much else is wrong too. Can that not be articulated?

# 3

3.1   Essay II, 'Universalizability, Impartiality, Truth', contends that unreconstructed intuitions and sentiments are as ineradicably presupposed to the operation of a plausible universalization test as they are to our complex and many-layered notion of justice. But this essay also looks forward to Essays III, IV, V. At the time when the first two of these three essays were written, my main aim was to help to restore some sort of cognitivism to the status of a real option in moral and political philosophy, and to suggest various ways in which this option might be redeployed, or modified in response to criticism.

The most extreme of all cognitivist options is, I suppose, a 'moral realism' that takes morality as John Mackie takes it in his formulation of the 'error theory' of morality, and then says there is *no* error here. Since Mackie was not inhibited in his characterization of the content of ordinary morality by any fear of exaggeration, because he felt no temptation to embrace the moral realism that represents its philosophical affirmation, it has been plain for a long time that less strange and less extreme sorts of moral cognitivism must be possible. This terrain has been explored in different ways by John McDowell, Sabina Lovibond, Susan Hurley and others, coming from one side; even as, working from the other side, Bernard Williams, Gilbert Harman, and (in a distinct way) Simon Blackburn have respectively anticipated and/or fortified and/or diversified

Mackie's general offensive against realism. What I have always been concerned to do myself, for reasons that appear in Essays III and IV, is to identify the least extreme distinctively cognitivist option that preserves for some unsanctimonious, unmysterious species of ordinary morality the main features of the picture that that morality has of itself, refrains from any systematic or philosophical redescription of the actual purport of the claims that it advances, but allows all the room to which they are entitled for certain sorts of doubt that cannot help in real life but impinge on practice. The beauty of such a philosophical position, if it could attain to verisimilitude, would reside in its effecting a certain kind of closure. With this we should achieve mutual transparency between philosophy and practice, the transparency of practice to itself, and a clear meet between particular philosophical doubts about morality and particular doubts we are actually prone to about how to see the human world. Cp. Essay III §§11–12, Essay IV §12, §§17–22.

There is a danger, nevertheless, that this may please nobody on either side of the present argument. Some will require moral philosophy to vindicate more of accepted morality, or to play a more interventive or constructional role in moral decision; others will be sceptical whether, once morality and the cognitivist account of morality are exposed to one another in the deliberate fashion I envisage, even as much can be preserved of either as I should claim.[14] But there is at least one misunderstanding I can try to forestall, if I emphasize again how much I should deprecate the choice of the label 'moral realism' for the cognitivist position. Not only does the label suggest a controversy I believe that we should opt out from, because I think 'true' is a better focus than 'real' for what is important here; and not only does the label mislead by

---

[14] The moral some anti-cognitivists will draw is that the whole idea of such confrontation is a mistake. Williams, I take it, would not, and it is his reaction that I am trying to guess in the text. Another reaction to what I am attempting in this book would be to say that the genealogy of values offered in Essay V §9 is insufficiently scientific or naturalistic to be genuinely explanatory. Whereas I should say that anything more reductive would not even characterize, let alone fully explain, the actual phenomenon of valuation. (On 'naturalistic', see Essay V note 12.) Essay II §§5–6 stresses how hard it will be to arrive at any strictly naturalistic account of the real nature or point of the phenomenon. Essay V §8 following stresses how undisturbing we should find this.

suggesting that the denial of the position is Dummett's anti-realism (which it is not; see Essay IV, note 25): the label also renders it difficult to make the kind of contrast between intellectual and practical freedom that is attempted in Essay VIII, §2(i). In the third place, the label 'realism' will tend in practice to insinuate causality at the wrong points into one's account of explanation and principled convergence. See Essay IV §§7–11. Finally, 'realism' seems to promise a safer haven for the heart's most cherished convictions than can really be provided for all of them.

3.2  The principal objections to cognitivism in the philosophy of value have tended to fall under three heads: (a) problems about disagreement; (b) problems about moral motivation; (c) problems about truth and correspondence.

About (a), I say my piece in Essays IV and V. And I return briefly to this below (§§3.6, 3.8).

As regards (b), I have taken it that I can supply one part of what is needed by finding the right subject matter for valuational and practical judgments (see especially Essays III, V), and another part by replacing the sentence-by-sentence 'commitment' that Hare and others provide, which has made *akrasia* into a problem for their theories, with an altogether looser sort of commitment that arises from the way in which the whole range of judgments that a person makes are conditioned by a background of commitments and habits of concern. These are the commitments and habits that make it possible for him to find in the world what will give a meaning for his life and, in grasping the sense of moral language, to focus upon one set of saliencies out of countless possible ones. (For the Aristotelian source of the idea of saliency, see Essay VI §4 following.) Essay III introduces this theme. Essay VI seeks to harvest the possibility of full blown weakness of will.

About (c), much is said in Essays II, III, IV and V—so much that when I now survey it and recall that cognitivism as I assess it depends entirely on taking truth substantially and seriously, I feel that yet more is needed.

3.3  There are still philosophers who will have recourse at certain critical points to the idea that there are different senses and/or uses of 'true', and/or different concepts of truth (or that they can proceed as if there are); and there are other equally reputable and insightful authors who will declare that they are ready to write off the idea of truth, or who will offer for the claim that it is suspect or dispensable arguments that simply take for granted some linkage (a linkage making truth suspect) between ordinary truth (or between truth as a sane realist conceives it) and correspondence as that is conceived by the correspondence theory of truth.[15]

There are altogether too many assumptions here. The only way forward is for us to treat it as a methodological assumption, pending disproof, that there is only one relevant sense of the predicate 'true'; to take this as the sense of the word in ordinary English; and then as calmly as possible, simply forgetting correspondence, to inquire what the property is like that 'true' stands for, admitting technical terms and their associated philosophical preconceptions one by one, and only in exchange for good reasons for the preconceptions and *bona fide* non-creative, non-prejudicial explications (such as have not yet been produced for 'corresponds') of the meanings of the technical terms. In this way let us even try to understand how and why truth is a *value*.

This is the approach that I try constantly to pursue in Essay IV, not quite always (I fear) conforming to the methodological maxim and not without some technicality—though I hope that the explanations of this technicality are non-technical. There is little chance of what happens there being understood as it is intended, however, or of the meet being appreciated that I claim to effect there between semantical and traditional theories of truth unless, *inter alia*, an unusual degree of care is taken to distinguish (i) a theory or definition of 'true-in-L' for some particular object language L, which is the sort of thing Tarski shows how to achieve in certain cases; (ii) the theory of truth-in-L definitions, for variable L; (iii) the theory (or 'definition', if that were so much as thinkable) of truth *tout court*. I do not deny that an account of one of these things may

---

[15] For instance, this is my diagnosis of the underlying assumption of Nancy Cartwright's argument in 'Do the Laws of Physics State the Facts?', *Pacific Philosophical Quarterly* vol. 61, 1980, and 'The Truth Doesn't Explain Very Much', *American Philosophical Quarterly* vol. 17, 1980.

rest upon (or need to exploit) the possibility of one of the others. But these are three totally different things.

Note 7 of Essay IV bears upon one part of this distinction, but I fear it is not enough. And the reader may not see the point of my insistence unless I am prepared to illustrate by examples the damage that is done by failing to make the distinction. Rather than annoy some living person by claiming to produce a present day example of this failure, however, I shall content myself with an older instance, one coming from an author whom Tarski mentions favourably in 'The Concept of Truth in Formalized Languages'. In the new appendix of the translated and expanded version of the book that Tarski cited in his original paper, Tadeusz Kotarbinski writes,

> The semantic conception of truth (Tarski) . . . is a modern continuation, freed from common objections, of the classical interpretation of truth as agreement with reality. By that conception, the truth of a sentence consists in the fact that it is satisfied by all objects, the concept of satisfaction being not defined by reference to truth; but introduced in a different way.[16]

It cannot be denied that there are points at which Tarski himself encouraged such a reading—*e.g.* by his references (often justly criticized as unfortunate) to the 'classical or correspondence' theory of truth and by his expressions of confidence that that very theory is something that his own results can come to the rescue of. But a grave misinterpretation (and underestimation) results from this reading of Tarski. What Kotarbinski is trying to arrive at is too direct a route between what belongs under heading (i) and what belongs under heading (iii).

'Satisfaction by all objects (or sequences)' is a phrase that may be expected to occur within particular Tarskian definitions of 'true-in-L' for this or that particular object language L. But there is not and there cannot be any general notion of satisfaction. Satisfaction by all objects (or sequences) sounds like a definite and technical relation between words and things, a wonderful winnowing of precisely what needed to be

---

[16] *Elementy Teorji Poznania* (Lwow, 1929), translated with additional material as *Gnoseology* (London, 1961). The passage cited is from page 410 of the translation. The Polish original of this addition to the original book dates from 1949.

preserved from 'correspondence'. But, unspecified for language, it is not any relation at all. Satisfaction is defined separately for each object language L. And the attempt to define it generally would make it impossible for any truth definition to meet the criterion of adequacy that Tarski imposes on such definitions (on which see below, §3.4).[17] The proposal '$x$ is true if and only if $x$ is satisfied by all objects' is simply not commensurate with, or a possible rival for, the proposal '$x$ is true if and only if $x$ agrees with reality/$x$ corresponds to a fact/$x$ belongs to the largest coherent system of judgments'. What someone interested in the latter kind of proposal should notice is how much better Kotarbinski himself did philosophically without correspondence *or* satisfaction, when, earlier in the same book, and in the part of the work that was available to Tarski at the time of his writing his classic paper, he characterized truth in the following way:

> Let us pass to the classical doctrine and ask what is understood by 'accordance with reality.' The point is not that a true thought should be a good copy or [fac] simile of the thing of which we are thinking, as a printed copy or photograph is. Brief reflection suffices to recognize the metaphorical nature of such a comparison. A different interpretation of 'accordance with reality' is required. We shall confine ourselves to the following explanation: 'John judges truly if and only if things are so and so; and things are in fact so and so.' (pp. 106–7).

Or, as Kotarbinski could more explicitly have said, spelling out the explanation for the case of a particular sentence and its world-involving truth condition, but with a prolixity that falls away in Tarski's formulation of his Convention T,

> John judges truly in saying 'snow is white' if and only if (1) John is right in saying 'snow is white' if and only if snow is white and (2) snow is indeed white.

Something about truth as such is conveyed here. But nothing at all is defined, and what we grasp is something that can only be generalized schematically, in a manner that involves the use of a device (the schematic letter) whose general explanation must itself, in one way or another, involve the idea of truth. As

---

[17] Such a general definition would not provide what is needed to derive any particular equivalence in the form '$x$ is true in L if and only if $p$'.

Kotarbinski says, what we grasp here—in so far as we grasp anything non-metaphorical—is not the idea of agreement or accordance or correspondence.[18] What we are furnished with—but only on the condition that we do not try to analyse the idea of truth itself[19]—is a way of dispensing with these ideas, as Tarski later dispensed with them, *without* relapsing into the coherence or the redundancy (or, as he says, nihilistic) theory.

### 3.4   Let us start again, recognizing that Tarski's aims were not

[18] Having repeatedly dismissed or postponed the issue of correspondence, let me declare my own conviction that the chief objection to a correspondence account of truth is the objection Strawson put like this (in 'Truth: a Reconsideration of Austin's Views', *Philosophical Quarterly* vol. 15, 1965): we can say if we like that a statement is true if there obtains or exists the particular situation, which, in the making of the statement, is stated to obtain; but this formulation 'abandons altogether the notion of an *identified existing situation* which it is a matter of a statement's identity that it refers to and with respect to which the question arises whether it is or isn't of a certain general type . . . [and] it drops all explicit allusion to conventional (semantical) relations between words and things . . . The semantical conventions (help to) determine what the statement is a statement to the effect that; whereas the statement's being true, if it is, is another matter altogether, *viz.* a matter of that situation's obtaining'. I would add that on these terms ('we can say if we like') nothing is achieved that is not better achieved in Kotarbinski's fashion.

[19] And only on condition that we will put our mind where our mouth is when we displace '*p*'. We must displace '*p*' by a live sentence that comes up to the standard one must impose on a sentence by which we ourselves can *say* anything. See §3.8 below; Essay III §7.

A condition that definitely need not be placed upon replacements for '*p*'—and need not be placed upon it even by a card-carrying realist still in possession of his faculties—is that the replacement be a neutral, eternal, placeless-and-timeless, non-perspectival or standpoint-less sentence. Why should *anyone* require this? There is a long standing tendency in controversy about these matters to burden the scientific realist, who thinks science can aspire to see the world as it is, not only with the correspondence theory of truth, but with this strange unnecessary supposition too. Cp. for instance Richard Rorty *The Consequences of Pragmatism* (Brighton: Harvester Press, 1982) p. 14 (I am indebted for this reference to Adrian Moore); and cp. also a much more benign witness towards realism, Nicholas Jardine, in *The Fortunes of Inquiry* (Oxford University Press, 1986), p. 13 (cp. p. 113), who, in sidestepping the idea of the 'identification of truth in science with representation of the world as it is', feels he must gloss the realist's use of the latter phrase with the words (themselves standing in an ambiguous construction) 'undistorted by the standpoint of any observer'. He thereby implicates the aspiration 'to see the world as it is' with the aspiration to see it from no particular standpoint—as if standpoint were *itself* a distortion. (On this last, see Essay III §7.)

For reasons given in Essays III and IV, there are at least two reasons why I must disown any creed of 'moral realism': but I have to enter a general protest that, where realism is concerned, it seems that almost any stigma will now do to beat this particular dogma with.

exactly the same as the aims either of the correspondence theorists or of the exponents of modern truth-conditional semantics who draw upon them; and let us begin these afterthoughts for Essay IV by seeing what continuity, if any, there may prove to be between Tarski's ideas and more recent uses of them.

Suppose that we take the idea from Frege and Russell of a formal system with formal rules of proof; and suppose that we conjoin this with the philosophically different, specifically semantical idea, originally the property of a distinct school, that a set of sentences $\Sigma$ (whether formalized or not) has another sentence $s$ as its logical consequence if and only if every uniform reinterpretation that verifies the sentences in $\Sigma$ also verifies $s$ (a valid formula being one that is true under every such reinterpretation). These ideas of formal system and of semantic validity can exist in isolation. But once they come together—as they were beginning to at the time nearly sixty years ago when Tarski was preparing his paper on the concept of truth in formalized languages—a flood of new questions present themselves. It becomes natural to ask whether the formally demonstrable formulas of some system of predicate logic will coincide exactly with those that are true in every interpretation and valid in the full intuitive sense. It becomes natural to inquire about the general idea of definability in a formal system; and it becomes natural to ask about the relation between the status of a sentence that is formally provable in the language L of an *a priori* or *a posteriori* theory and the status of an L-sentence that is simply true. Could these two statuses, that of provability in a theory and that of truth, ever coincide exactly? Finally, as a precondition of finding a secure basis for an answer to *any* of these questions, can such notions as *truth* and *truth of* be freed from paradox?

These are problems of what Tarski called the methodology of the deductive sciences. Let us consider the last two of the questions just mentioned. Evidently, one way to answer would be to carry the Fregean distinction of mention and use to the point of distinguishing object-language and meta-language, to show how to construct in a meta-language ML a demonstrably unparadoxical notion of truth for the sentences of a given object language L—that will serve to answer the last of the questions just enumerated—and then, for purposes of comparison, to construct in ML the notion of *provable-in-L*. Where L and ML suffice to express arithmetic, the comparison of the extensions of 'provable-in-L' and 'true-in-L' yields a negative reply to our other question. (The ML definition of formal provability-in-L can under the stated condition be coded back into L. But, if L was demonstrably secure from paradox, then the concept of truth-in-L cannot be coded back into L. It must have a wider extension. There must be true-in-L sentences that are not provable-in-L.)

This would seem to settle that matter—but only in so far as the constructed predicate 'true-in-L' really is a genuine specialization or restriction of what was intended by 'true' in the questions we began with. How is the upholder of intuitionistic formalism (Tarski's philosophical position at that time, see [30e] in [56m], trans. Woodger, p. 62) to be assured of this?

One obvious answer to the question is that 'true-in-L' and the intuitive 'true', if they are proper counterparts, must agree always, and in a principled way, in their applications to the sentences of L. It should be no accident that every ascription of the one predicate to some L-sentence have the same truth-value as the ascription of the other to the same L-sentence. Within the domain of L-sentences the extension of 'true-in-L' must be determined in the same way as that of 'true' would naturally be.

How then is the extension of 'true' generally determined? Again, only one thought readily presents itself. Although there are countless true sentences in the form 'True $x$ iff $p$' that will assign the sentence $x$ to the extension of 'true' on the condition that $p$ ('True "snow is white" if and only if grass is green', for instance), indefinitely many of these assignments to that extension will be, if correct, only accidentally correct. The general condition that will determine the extension non-accidentally correctly for each and every arbitrary $x$ is this:

> True $x$ iff $p$, where the sentence for which '$p$' holds a place *translates* or *means the same as* the sentence $x$.

The technical notion of truth-in-L will be faithful to what is understood by 'true' if and only if the definition of 'true-in-L' delivers as a theorem one biconditional for each sentence of L given in the form

True-in-L $x$ iff $p$,

where '$p$' on the right hand side holds a place for a translation into the metalanguage of the L-sentence $x$ mentioned on the left hand side.[20] (See Tarski p. 188.)

The answer we have just arrived at for our question is of course Tarski's own first formulation of his criterion of material adequacy for truth (-in-L) definitions. It is not an arbitrary stipulation, or even a stipulation that could easily have been different. And this criterion (Convention T, as Tarski calls it), so long as it catches the *general* idea of truth, belongs neither to the object language L nor to the theory of truth-in-L given in a metalanguage, nor in a meta-meta-language for that particular metalanguage. It is a part of the general theory or framework for semantics; and the point it takes off from is a simple general observation about truth as such. It represents one modest but indispensable contribution to the philosophy of truth, with the conspicuous interest of being proprietary neither to the redundancy view (explicitly rejected by Tarski), nor to correspondence (on which Tarski could as well have been totally and utterly silent). Equally interestingly for our purposes, what it looks back to in a new way is a general point about truth that is usually associated with Frege. Frege suggests (*Grundgesetze* I.32) that an account of the meanings of the sentences of a language will have to say under what conditions each sentence is true. Tarski's Convention T suggests that an account of the truth-conditions of the sentences of a language must associate each sentence with a condition that is faithful to its meaning. These two claims stand or fall together, and their generality transcends the special theoretical interests of Frege or Tarski or anyone else. The connexion of meaning and truth is there for anyone to avail himself of. What semantics does is only to draw upon and specialize this general point.

---

[20] Note that if we put the matter like this then we do not need to suppose that the object language and the metalanguage are part and whole. In later writing, *e.g.* 'Truth and Proof' *Scientific American* (June 1969), Tarski does rely on this latter supposition, in order no doubt to reduce his dependence on semantical vocabulary. For the claim that 'translates' is perfectly innocent in Tarski's statement of Convention T, even by Tarski's own standards, see again Essay IV, notes 6, 7.

3.5 Now each statement, Convention T explicitly and the Fregean account of meaning and truth conditions implicitly, invokes a largely unelucidated idea of meaning. Essay IV seeks to elucidate that idea, and it then tries to turn to advantage the resulting, more spelled out interconnexity of truth and meaning in trying to arrive at an informal account of what the marks of truth are—*i.e.* what other, truth-connected properties accrue to anything to which the property of truth accrues. See Essay IV §5.

As I have said, neither these marks nor these taken in conjunction with any others that might be determined will ever amount to an analysis of truth. The search for such marks has to be the search for a better understanding of a property that we already know much more than nothing about. Of course, I hope that in the end this search might help us to tell such things as whether the law of excluded middle is or is not universally valid. But in the meanwhile, with certain issues of formulation still pending,[21] my chief and foremost concern is to be sure whether the search itself has been put on the right basis; to trace the connexions that identification of this basis apparently reveals between the way the problem of truth is perceived in twentieth century semantics and the way it is or was once perceived in the rest of philosophy; and then to exploit these connexions in the positive determination or clarification of meta-ethical questions.

3.6 Now the marks of truth that are developed in Essay IV

---

[21] The third mark in particular has given much trouble and I still doubt that I have it quite right. The fifth gave less trouble, I thought. But Hilary Putnam pointed out to me that in expressing it, I was undertaking to oppose Nelson Goodman's contention in *Ways of World Making* (Hassocks, Sussex, 1978) that there can be 'a diversity of right *and even conflicting* versions of worlds in the making'. But Goodman's examples of such conflicts (I am only objecting to the italicised phrase, not the other insight) have always been modelled on the general pattern that Benacerraf discussed and resolved without any concession to conflicting versions in his 'What Numbers Could Not Be', *Philosophical Review* vol. 24, 1965. In conversation Putnam suggested to me that there were better examples to be found in present day science. I hope that some day he will write about these examples. The crucial question, however, is not whether there are at any moment cases where science makes conflicting (contrast multiple) versions, but whether scientists are wrong to find this as disturbing and unsatisfactory a state of affairs as I gather that they still do, wherever it happens. Can they really be wrong?

can do this last kind of work, I claim, because they can help to determine what exactly is at issue when truth is at issue. But it is crucially important that they do not provide, and are not seen in Essay IV, as providing, any *clear effective test* (palpable sufficient condition) of truth. And unlike Peirce's account of truth, in *e.g.* 'On the Fixation of Belief',[22] they are not part of any *method for finding truth* (truths, that is). I insist upon this because being obliged to see convergence as at least as interesting as Peirce did, and owing him some clear debts, I run the risk of seeing my project assimilated to his, or of seeming to misinterpret Peirce's. I hasten to sort this out a little.

For me the main interest of convergence is this: by the use of this idea, which is one of several that animate the search for the marks of truth, I arrive at a necessary condition for a subject matter's being one that admits of truth. For instance, if I am right to claim, as I do in Essay IV, that if $s$ is true then (i) $s$ will under favourable conditions command convergence and (ii) the best explanation of the existence of this convergence will require (or be inconsistent with the denial of) the actual truth of $s$, then it follows that a subject matter that admits of truth will need to have the wherewithal to create and sustain (in the favourable cases) the beginnings of principled agreement; and it will also need to afford materials for us to describe (though not necessarily to determine effectively) the difference between principled and non-principled agreement. Truth is in jeopardy unless things are like that. For Peirce, on the other hand, our convergence in a belief that will in fact stand up and will thereby end the discomfort of doubt is constitutive (or at least pragmatically constitutive) of our actually attaining truth. This is a use I have never tried to make of convergence. On the account of truth offered in Essay IV, it is still a clear, however remote, possibility that the predestinate opinion of all determined researchers should be false.

There are some other differences that need to be signalled from Peirce. They relate to the question of the aetiology of beliefs, and to certain differences of aim and emphasis in our respective uses of this question of aetiology. To explain this I must supply some Peircean background.

---

[22] *Collected Works* 5.382.

For Peirce, it will be remembered, belief or opinion is the state we seek to attain, and doubt is a state of irritation that we seek to end. The sole object of inquiry is the fixation of belief.[23] His question—not a question properly touched upon in any of my essays—is how we shall conduct our inquiry in order to achieve this fixation. In arriving at the method that he favours—the method of science as he conceives that—Peirce passes in review the method of *dogmatism* (but the social impulse guarantees its ineffectiveness to determine opinion), the method of *authority*, consisting of dogmatism supported by the repression of social impulses that unsettle opinion (but this will not work either, for we should then be bound in the end to see that our having beliefs was 'the mere accident of our having been taught as we have'), and a third method which Peirce calls the *a priori* method. In explanation of this last, Peirce writes

> A different, new method of settling opinions must be adopted that shall not only produce an impulse to believe, but shall also decide what proposition it is which is to be believed. Let the action of natural preferences be unimpeded then, and under their influence let men, conversing together and regarding matters in different lights, gradually develop beliefs in harmony with natural causes.

This *a priori* method, Peirce says,

> resembles that by which conceptions of art have been brought

[23] To understand this as Peirce intended, however, we need to imagine Peirce saying 'Believe what you will, provided only that the belief in that really *will stick*'. What this advice will entail, *given the exigent nature of belief as Peirce will characterize it* when he makes the transition from the third to the fourth of his methods of fixing belief (I shall quote the passage later), is that, if you follow it, then you will hold on to no belief that you do not take yourself to have acquired in a manner non-accidental to its content.—Just as you will desire nothing God would not wish you to desire (or nothing you think he would not wish you to desire) if you do your best to obey Augustine's injunction 'Dilige [deum] et quod vis fac'.

I should add that as I interpret Peirce, the philosophical purposes of his theory of inquiry (the fixation of belief) make it strictly unnecessary for him to give a strict *analytical definition* of truth—still less to misdefine it as the predestinate opinion or whatever. For Peirce, truth can be just the same thing as it is for any other sane person, even the scientific non-correspondist realist (cp. note 19 above). What Peirce does have to do, however, is to find a target for belief, something that, from within his inquiry, the serious inquirer may find it helpful, productive of stable (because well considered) conviction, to see as what he is aiming for. On a sympathetic reading of Peirce, *that* is the point of the *pragmatic equivalence* between truth and the limit of inquiry.

to maturity. . . . As long as no better methods can be applied, it ought to be followed, since it is then the expression of instinct, which must be the ultimate cause of belief. . . . But its failure has been the most manifest. It makes of inquiry something similar to the development of taste; but taste unfortunately is always more or less a matter of fashion. . . . [And] I cannot help seeing that. . . . sentiments in their development will be very greatly determined by accidental causes. . . . Now there are some people, among whom I must suppose that my reader is to be found, who, *when they see that any belief of theirs is determined by any circumstance extraneous to the facts, will from that moment not merely admit in words that that belief is doubtful, but will experience a real doubt of it, so that it ceases in some degree at least to be a belief.* (My italics)

And this last sentence is of course the point of transition to Peirce's celebrated fouth method. This is the method

by which our beliefs may be determined by nothing human, but by some external permanency—by something upon which our thinking has no effect . . . [but] which affects or might affect every man: [by] Reals whose characters are entirely independent of our opinions about them.

That is the background; and it will be obvious how much I owe to Peirce's account of the deficiencies of the third method as he describes it; and obvious that he addresses a question I might have been well advised to address and have not (namely how good opinions are to be arrived at). But there are some differences I must draw attention to.

First, Peirce's way of commending a method that enables our convictions to be determined by circumstances not extraneous to the facts is to point out that nothing else can actually be relied upon *to end the irritation of doubt.* His project of making the pragmatic identification of truth with the predestinate opinion cuts him off from objecting, as I should insist on exercising my right to do, that what is wrong with the third method is that nothing particularly equips it (as it stands in Peirce's characterization) *to produce truths.*

The next point I want to make about Peirce's doctrine—and this is a point I should want to make in general defence of subject matters that Peirce tends to treat unseriously (assimilating morals to taste and taste to fashion) but am glad to make within Peirce's framework—is that the argument I have quoted from 'The Fixation of Belief' plainly underdetermines Peirce's insistence that we should get our beliefs by his fourth method. This last is a method that one cannot help noticing leaves little room for whatever is distinctive of morals or political discourse, or of the discourse of the criticism and appreciation of art. Is there not some space we can occupy between the two conceptions of belief and its fixation that correspond to Peirce's third and fourth methods?

What indicates that there must be this space is that, as literally interpreted, the fourth method seems to relate not to truth as such but to absolute truth—an important, no doubt undismissable idea, but not one for the sake of which we shall be wise to sacrifice every other idea of the distinction between that which deserves to be believed and that which does not, or one for which we are well advised to abandon everything in science itself that fails to measure up to this exacting standard.[24]

The last point is now all too familiar, not least in the historiography and philosophy of science itself. Let me

---

[24] See here Essay III §10. The conception of truth that such a realism invokes is not truth as it inheres or fails to inhere in the great generality of the significant sentences of a whole language. Scarcely any of the predicates in a language—even in the most 'factual' portion of it—will pull their weight in theories of the causal order that come up to such standards. Many predicates exist solely to denominate properties and thing-kinds of purely anthropocentric importance. These can be as factual as you like, but they are only to a negligible degree projectible in Goodman's sense. And how many significant predicates have a use that presupposes no relativity whatever to the perspective and concerns of speakers themselves, or enjoy a sense that is conditioned, corrected and regulated solely by interaction between scientific theory and features of reality that are perfectly indifferent to the point of view from which they are discerned?

An advantage of retaining the fourth method, but annexing it to the limiting function of an elucidation of absolute truth is that one can then accommodate the idea of the world as conceived in independence of provincial or human interests without saying that the only sentences that are genuinely true are sentences of the most abstract and finished theories of the causal order. Both plain truth or truth for the working day and absolute truth make a demand for objectivity. But the second demands it in a way leading to a restriction of vocabulary so stringent as to raise altogether new questions about meaning. Whereas truth that is not absolute requires only the objectivity that is spelled out in the formulation of the five marks of truth. If it is a matter of degree to what extent a species of discourse can satisfy either these or stricter demands, that does not entail that truth itself is a matter of degree. (If it is, then that is owed to some quite different consideration.) Nor does it entail that non-absolute truth is relative. Absoluteness is not a modality of truth. It is a feature of sense, one might say, not reference.

emphasize, however, that to demand that a Peircean method succeeding the third be mitigated in the severity of its requirements is not in itself to demand that we should climb down from the requirement of copying or correspondence. For even Peirce's own fourth method is quite innocent of that idea. Nor is the demand equivalent to the suggestion that we should simply make do with the third method, or take refuge *faute de mieux* in some breezy instrumentalism. What is demanded is only a principle that cures the deficiencies of Peirce's third method without committing us to the more stringent peculiarities of Peirce's characterization of the fourth. And *ad hominem*, I would point out that Peirce himself provides precisely the materials that we need in order to find such a stopping place. What we need is the distinction between states of mind proper to idle supposition, wishful thinking, telling a good story or whatever, for which the third method seems perfectly appropriate, and propositional attitudes like belief that are proper to active inquiry and have, on pain of extinction, to see themselves as answerable to something.

Here let us refer back to the italicized sentence in our quotation from Peirce. Continuing what he says there, let us say that, in so far as we want to settle opinion and end the irritation of doubt, what we have to want is for our belief that *p not* to be determined 'by circumstances that are extraneous to the facts' but to come about precisely *because p*. This, however, is a state we can often attain without our opinion's being determined by 'external permanencies' or 'Reals' that affect every inquirer in the same way regardless of his history or acculturation so that 'any man if he have sufficient experience and he reasons enough about it will be led to the one True conclusion'. There are subject matters where getting a grasp of the sense of the language proprietary to them is not at all independent of specific acculturation. In these subjects we need not look to such a thing as the 'one true conclusion' of *all* inquirers. But nor did Peirce need, by virtue of the logic of his argument, to characterize in such absolute terms as he chooses what it would take to repair the third method. The real mark of a state that is truth-oriented in the way in which belief as Peirce understands it is truth-oriented is simply that the state should be one which, in virtue of being the mental state that it is, seeks to be determined by causes that are *not accidental relative to its content*. Any way of determining belief that permits this to happen non-accidentally relative to content *ipso facto* excels the third method, however short it falls of the fourth. (Or eliminating the reference to such things as facts, let us convey the point by an example from which the reader can then generalize schematically (cp. our discussion of Kotarbinski above): John's belief that the cat is on the mat is vindicated as objectively correct if and only if the best explanation of why John has arrived at that belief depends on (and/or is inconsistent with the denial of) the explanatory premiss 'the cat *is* on the mat'.)

Here, in arguing with Peirce on his own terms, I have allowed myself to be drawn for a moment into his philosophical project. Let me restore a proper distance by emphasizing again that my interest in convergence has nothing to do with the search for a general method of settling opinion: and let me now acknowledge the debt that is owed to Peirce, but do so within my framework.

When we 'converse together' on matters of value and 'regard [these] matters in different lights'; when we seek in this process to enlighten one another and be enlightened in our turn, and when we find collectively (if we do) that in this way we begin to be able to attend to all sorts of distinctions previously unnoticed by us and discover (if we do) that, to some significant degree, we even converge in our judgments and in our way of thinking about values,[25] the question that Peirce could have insisted we should ask is precisely the same as the second mark of truth directs us to ask, namely: is the best explanation of such consensus as we achieve independent—or is it not independent—of the content of that consensus? Can we explain the consensus best in terms that both prescind from, and so leave room to deny, the beliefs that are comprised within the consensus? Or is the best explanation of our consensus in this or that belief *not* like that?

Here, against many current (friendly or hostile) treatments

---

[25] Here of course subjectivist thinkers like Protagoras (see the set speeches in Plato's *Theaetetus* and *Protagoras*, and especially 152 foll., 162 foll. and 320 foll. and 333e–334c respectively) and Hume (see *Of the Standard of Taste*) have both bettered and impressively complicated the account of taste that Peirce seems prepared to assume. See Essay V.

of so-called 'moral realism', what I have insisted is that we cannot combine an indifference to these questions with a realist or a non-realist or an anti-realist or a quasi-realist position. There *is* no way of determining what properties are real and what properties are not real that effectively bypasses this question and all questions tantamount to it. (I return briefly to this matter in §4.2.) On the other hand, against Gilbert Harman's account of the point at issue—an account I admire and see as very much in the spirit of Peirce—what I principally insist is that the questions just formulated cannot be answered so swiftly as he seeks to answer them.[26] Until we take them seriously, we have simply no right to embrace the preconceptions that will lead one to a *prima facie* preference for the so-called *projection* theory of valuation, or Hume's account in terms of 'gilding and staining', over a theory that accounts for the same valuational phenomena in terms of value focus and the anthropocentric-cum-subjective real but non-natural properties that are there for us to discover ('in the world' as one says).[27] The possibility that deserves to be taken seriously is that our subject matter is *subjective*, by virtue of the language proprietary to it having a sense that makes its judgments answerable to what registers upon the critically regulated object-involving responses of human subjects, but also *objective*, by virtue of comprising a substantial number of beliefs that have been determined by circumstances not extraneous to the facts. These are beliefs to the effect that *p* that are best explained either by reference to the very circumstance that *p* or by reference to considerations that leave no room to think anything else but that *p*.

3.7    Two misconceptions about the idea of truth have made the possibility that I seek to describe here so hard to see. One is a fixation (whether this leads one to treat truth contemptuously or respectfully) upon the wrong (*i.e.* the distinctive) part of the correspondence theory of truth, and the other is a confusion about the part played by convention, accident, agreement, contingency *etc.* in the making possible of significant human discourse. To see through both these mistakes (and I return for

---

[26] That is to say that the explanation itself falls short. See above note 14, Essay IV §9 following.
[27] See Essay V §8 following.

a moment to the second below in §3.8) is to take the most decisive step in understanding how there could be such a thing as truth and falsity in matters of value, how moral sentiments, intuitions *etc.* can define the standard of truth in a subject matter that is subjective, even (in some sense of that overworked adjective) relative, on the level of sense, while truth itself is neither subjective nor relative. Having seen through them, we can attain a fairly clear idea of what it is for truth and falsehood to *lose* their foothold within a particular kind of discourse. (However hard it always is to ascertain whether they have.)[28]

Perhaps this seems too easy. But it is not even easy. These questions (of the best explanation of convergence *etc.*) are not questions we shall ever find easy to answer for any particular species of thinking. Nor, I would add, has the answer that I would offer to them turned out to be unqualifiedly favourable to cognitivism—so soon as practical verdicts and final questions of right and wrong come into consideration. Judgments of these kinds seem to enjoy an inter-culturally common meaning. But in different cultures or communities and even more strikingly, in different people in what might be accounted subcommunities of one and the same community, they can collect apparently irresolubly contrary answers.

There is a deep and intriguing temptation to react to this failure of convergence in sophisticated relativist fashion by saying that these answers are not really *contrary*; that the individuals in these communities are not even engaged in the same pursuits, the same game, the same dance, the same whirl of acting and being; that to the extent that the answers they give to these questions are apparently irresolubly contradictory, even the questions they are facing are not really the same.

Where aesthetic and purely valuational predicates are concerned, much can be made of this possibility. But where practical judgments are concerned, I do not think that such a suggestion can explain away enough of the apparent disagreement, or enough of the apparent mutual comprehension between apparently disagreeing parties. (Cp. Essay III §9;

---

[28] As re-deployed, the Peircean contribution can now be seen as this: to have shown how the question of truth and the question of the aetiology and fixation of belief can be connected together so that they have a bite *without* our being required to transcend at time *t* the positive realities that figure as of *t* in our own discourse.

Essay IV §§15–19.) It is true that when we see a clear enough issue between the parties to descry a point of real disagreement (contrast difference) then that will constitute a question for us too; and it is true again that we may then be able to arrive at a point where it seems that there is nothing else *for us* to think. The question that will remain is whether we always dare to venture further and omit the *for us* and say there is nothing else *to think*. I do not myself doubt that sometimes we really can reach this point: nor do I doubt that sometimes, when we do, it will be possible for someone else to say that we think what we think (and that some of the others who think this may think this) not accidentally, but precisely because there is nothing else to think—with a 'because' that simultaneously vindicates and, by vindicating, explains. (See Essay IV §7; Essay V §10.) But what I do have to doubt, *pace* one possible relativist, is that we should start to take more lightly the transition from 'there's nothing else *for us* to think' to 'there is nothing else *to think*'.[29] (See Essay IV §18.) Something in the subject matter of morality as we know it makes this transition a substantial and difficult one. It is this that forces us, in some of our better thoughts about conscience, to institutionalize the respect we feel for the 'there is nothing else *for me* to think' state of mind as sometimes the best *attainable*. (Cp. again Essay IV §18 following.)

Such cases as the last are not uncommon. But nor are they the norm. The mistake of unrestricted cognitivism resides in its determination to see such cases as the reflection of a merely epistemological difficulty. The mistake of anti-cognitivism is to think that, at bottom, *all* cases are like the conscience case. My objection to the anti-cognitivist is that he has insufficient reason to think this. My objection to the unrestricted cognitivist arises from my doubt that we shall *never* find a void where we expected to find the world (the world as we know it), forcing upon us a decision between two different ways of seeing that world, different ways that will lead in the end to different courses of action. (Cp. Essay III §12.)

---

[29] Once we start to take this lightly, we must give up our idea that the conviction we end up with has to be *answerable to how things are* with regard to whatever it is. As Peirce shows, this is really tantamount to the abandonment of conviction.

The conclusion I draw is that, in so far as cognitivism remains an option—and the difficulty can scarcely show that truth is not the constant aspiration of practical judgments—, the position will need the sustenance of certain other philosophical ideas. I hope that the further materials supplied here—see Essay IV §28—have at least one advantage over Mackie's thought that the philosophical comment which needs to be set against morality as commonly conceived is that morality rests on a theoretical error. The advantage I claim for them is that of being able intelligibly, relevantly, and unproblematically to coexist in ordinary consciousness with the commitment to a recognizable residue of ordinary morality.

3.8   What then is ordinary truth on this account?[30] It is not a social construct. What the predicate 'true' stands for is an objective property of a special subset of the sentences that are thrown up by, and then survive in, certain processes of thinking and talking that can stand up, more or less, against criticism—human criticism, that is, not criticism by a race of creatures whose focus upon the world was so different from ours that, even if each race became convinced that the other had a language, there would still be no clear prospect of mutually transparent interpretation. I have said enough already to make it clear that this sort of objectivity is not mere intersubjectivity. Nor is this truth mere human agreement, or human agreement in the long run. No doubt some minimum quantity of agreement in judgments among speakers is a precondition for a set of signs to function as an interpreted language. Without that minimum there would be no entry point for interpretation. But even if one believed (as I need not and do not) that an interpreter had always to interpret his subjects in such a way as simply to maximize agreement between them and himself, it would still not follow that being agreed on and being true were the same thing. And here it is a pleasure to turn at last to Wittgenstein, or rather to mention him by name, even if only to propose a small amendment to the

[30] This section draws on my *Sameness and Substance*, Chapter Five; 'What would be a Substantial Theory of Truth?'; and 'Truth and Interpretation', *op. cit.*

standard English translation of a passage that has become exceedingly familiar:

> So you are saying that human agreement decides what is true and what is false?—It is what human beings *say* that is true and false. Their agreement is in *the language* that they use. This is not agreement in opinions, but in form of life. (*PI* §241.)

If I venture to add anything to this, it is only that, for each predicate of a language, it is a precondition of there being sufficient however minimal agreement for the interpretation of the predicate to be possible (and a precondition of the perpetuation or justified continuance of such agreement in the face of criticism) that interpreters should be able to say that the predicate is assertible of an item *x* if and only if. . . ., where the '. . . .' on the right hand side is a condition on *x* that interpreters can state in *propria voce*, appealing thereby to what interpreters themselves conceptualize as a sufficiently objective feature to peg a predicate upon. Agreement plays its part in fixing senses. We only have a chance of getting to the point where a predicate has a clear public sense if the users of the language are so constituted as to be able to come to agree sufficiently over a sufficiently large area whether the predicate applies or not; and what senses we invest our language with plays its part in fixing what truths we shall be able to give expression to. But that exhausts the role of agreement—just as the size and mesh of a fisherman's net determine what fish he will catch, if he catches any; not what fish are in the sea. The possibility of agreement is the *presupposition* of the sense; and the sense itself is none the worse for that, unless agreement actually breaks down irrevocably.

These matters are pursued further in Lovibond and Williams (eds.) *Identity, Truth and Value: Essays for David Wiggins*, Blackwell, Oxford 1996; see there the reply to Wilfrid Hodges. See also my 'Objective and Subjective in Ethics', *Ratio* VIII, 1995, no. 3.

# 4

4.1 So I end by saying that, where matters turn on the application of strictly valuational predicates in a fully determinate context, the question of truth will both arise and stay around for an answer: but that where practical judgment comes into consideration—and with it the question of *what* categories of evaluation and modes of attention we are to bring to bear upon a given practical question—we must expect truth to be much more problematical. Which is not to say that it is out of the question for truth to be attained.

But in saying this, am I not saying in different words the same as some non-cognitivists? What then is distinctive about moral cognitivism?

To answer this question, and to find the best way of putting any agreement that may already exist among the warring parties, I believe we need to find some new locus for the dispute. The possibility I shall conclude by exploring is that, in the end, both the significance and the success or failure of moral cognitivism will have to turn on the question of what we are to make of the considerations that are urged by authors in a long and readily recognizable tradition, who have seen themselves as offering the 'philosophical explanation' of morality.

4.2   Bertrand Russell writes:

The ethical element which has been prominent in many of the most famous systems of philosophy is, in my opinion, one of the most serious obstacles to the victory of scientific method in the investigation of philosophical questions. . . . Ethical metaphysics is fundamentally an attempt, however disguised, to give legislative force to our own wishes. . . . Ethics is essentially a product of the gregarious instinct. . . . The ends which are pursued by our own group are desirable ends, the ends pursued by hostile groups are nefarious. . . . When the animal has arrived at the dignity of the metaphysician, it invents ethics as the embodiment of its belief in the justice of its own herd. . . . [Both] self-preservation and the preservation of the herd are biological ends to the individual. Ethics is in origin the art of recommending to others the sacrifices required for co-operation with oneself. Hence, by reflexion, it comes through the operation of social justice, to recommend sacrifices by oneself. . . . As compared with science, [ethics] fails to achieve the imaginative liberation from self which is necessary to such understanding of the world as man can hope to achieve. . . .[31]

In a comparable spirit W.V. Quine writes:

Hypotheses less extravagant than that of divine origin account well enough for such uniformity as obtains among moral values, even apart from possible innate components. It is merely that these values are passed down the generations, imposed by word of mouth, by birch rod and sugar plum, by acclaim and ostracism, fine, imprisonment. Values are imposed by society because they matter to society, whereas aesthetic preferences may be left to go their way.[32]

More recently some of the same themes reappear in formulations influenced by socio-biology:

Obviously the emergence of cooperative and altruistic stances is not a mere armchair speculation. It can be filled out by both theoretical and empirical studies. It is noteworthy that the account will insist upon the non-representative, conative function for the stance. The evolutionary success which attends some stances and not others is a matter of the behaviour to which they lead. . . . Animals with standing dispositions to cooperate (say) do better in terms of other needs like freedom from fleas, or in terms of their ability to survive failed hunting

---

[31] *Mysticism and Logic* (London: Allan and Unwin, 1918), pp. 82–3, with omissions as indicated. I am indebted to Mr Paul Johnston for the reference to this essay.

[32] 'On the Nature of Moral Values', *Critical Inquiry*, Spring 1979.

expeditions by cadging meals of others. No right, duty or value, plays any explanatory role in this history. It is not as if the creature with a standing disposition to help those who have helped it does well *because* that is a virtue. There is no naturalistically respectable explanation of any such sort. Its being a virtue is irrelevant to evolutionary biology. . . . The [ethical] state of mind starts theoretical life as something else—a structure, or conative state or pressure on choice and action. Such pressures need to exist if human beings are to meet their competing needs in a social co-operative setting. The stance may be called an attitude. . . . Its function is to mediate the move from features of a situation to a reaction. . . . Someone with a standing stance is set to react in some way when an occasion arises, just as someone with a standing belief is set to react to new information cognitively in one way or another. It matters to us that people have some attitudes and not others, and we educate them and put pressure on them in the hope that they will do so.[33]

Now in one way there is nothing very much here that a cognitivist needs to quarrel with.[34] For the origin of human morality is an interesting question; and that which is instructive and convincing in these accounts relates to the origin of morality; whereas what morality is now may be an altogether different question. (See here Essay II §6.) To explain and describe morality as we now know it may conceivably involve trying to speculate about how it can have started, or involve bringing it into focus with questions of the biological and cultural emergence of mankind. But after speculating about that, the thing we really need to try to describe is what morality *has become*, a question on which evolutionary theory casts no particular light. It is here that the real issue lies between cognitivism and anti-cognitivism. Typically, the anti-cognitivist wants to see in morality nothing very much that qualitatively transcends its reconstructed starting point—whereas a cognitivist has no such reluctance. He is someone deeply impressed by considerations akin to three I shall now enumerate.

First, when authors like G.J. Warnock allude to the way in

[33] Simon Blackburn, 'How not to be an Ethical Anti-Naturalist', *Midwest Studies in Philosophy* Volume 11, 1986.
[34] Except of course for the significance that these writers are apt to claim for their explanations.

which the content of morality is constrained by the need that human beings have to combat the tendency of human affairs to turn out badly rather than well, the cognitivist maintains that we ought to be powerfully struck by the discovery that our moral ideas have already reached a point where there is no longer a question of our being able to say in full what 'well' and 'badly' mean here except in a way that will import reference to the actual content of social morality and social mores themselves. However things may once have been, and whatever may once have been possible, it is no longer possible to see morality as a tool or as an instrument of human welfare whose function might equally well have been served by other tools or instruments. (See again here Essay II §6.)

In the second place, the cognitivist will want to insist upon the special importance of explanations that explain moral subjects' beliefs by vindicating their judgments—explanations that explain these subjects' arrival at an opinion by showing that this was the only opinion that would survive reflection. What the cognitivist typically wants to do is to take fully seriously, and much more seriously than the anti-cognitivist, the aspiration (which he takes to be as strong within morality as outside it) to reach the state of mind where one thinks that $p$ because there is nothing else to think but that $p$. For the cognitivist there is something altogether distinctive about this condition that we aspire to. Hence the key role (for those on both sides of the dispute) of John Mackie's 'argument from queerness', and of the philosophical impulse, which Mackie (really very felicitously from our point of view) would have called moral scepticism, to deny that these vindicating explanations are properly explanatory. For this denial undermines in a general and universal way what at worst deserves to be undermined only locally, and in special cases (see Essay IV §17), namely the passion to get the answer to this or that moral or political question *right*.

Thirdly, the cognitivist will see nothing in modern evolutionary theory, or in any other branch of modern science, that forbids us to allow to thoughts themselves and the standards to which these thoughts are answerable the explanatory role that he himself attributes to them when he endorses as explanatory such claims as: 'Everyone thinks that $7 + 5$ is 12, because, in the end, there is nothing else to think' or 'We converge in the belief that the slaughter of the innocent is wrong because, in the end, there is nothing else to think on this question'. If the cognitivist sticks his neck out anywhere, it is here. What he refuses to allow is that non-natural properties are explanatorily inert.

Let us be careful about this last point. Strictly speaking, properties themselves can cause nothing. Not even the primary qualities can. In that sense all properties are inert. But in another they are not inert. For properties figure indispensably in many explanations that are causal explanations. ('The helicopter crashed because it had a defective gear.') What the cognitivist will insist is that not all properties that enter into good causal explanation need to be natural properties. Non-natural properties as he conceives them (see Essay V Note 12) are the properties that consciousness itself marks out in the world and critically delimits and determines there (cp. Essay V §9); but according to him the explanation of moral phenomena (beliefs and actions) essentially involves such properties; it would be hobbled without the use of the predicates that stand for them. That is his distinctive contention, and it is rooted in his willingness to take our actual explanations seriously, and in his belief that these explanations need not conflict either with real science or with reasoned metaphysics.[35]

4.3 That such mental and value properties as the cognitivist finds in our ordinary thinking should enter into the explanation of that thinking and the explanation of actions that that thinking can rationalize—this can seem like common sense, or if you already have a certain prejudice, like outrageous metaphysics. But whichever it is, this is the claim that shows what it is for consciousness to take on a life of its own in the world. Of course, when such a moment comes in the evolution of mind, that does not signify that all the neural mechanisms of fully conscious beings are suddenly obsolescent or superfluous. What it means is rather that the point has been reached where what happens in the world cannot be properly

[35] I do not mean to suggest by this the claim that real science moves on a different level somehow—compare Essay VIII §7—only that in this case the question science has concerned itself with is different. Cp. again the passage from Nietzsche quoted at pp. 67–8.

understood for what it is by explanations that dwell exclusively upon mechanisms. The story is an old one. Cp. Plato *Phaedo* 98c. What cognitivism does is only to add one new twist. It takes seriously both the possibility that mentalistic explanations will never be supplanted, and the possibility that mentalistic explanations themselves for some actions and thoughts will never be able to dispense with the moral properties that consciousness finds for itself in the world. But for such properties as these to be indispensable and irreducible, and for *vindication* to be one indispensable element in the explanation of thinking and acting, this is surely what it is for consciousness not merely to arrive in the natural world, but for it to make itself at home there. For by critically determining the presence there of valuational properties, we colonize that world; and, by treating the vindication of thought as both indispensable to understanding what happens in the world and irreducible to any other ideas that pull their weight in the description of that world, we demonstrate practically the irreducibility of that consciousness.[36]

[36] Among those who have been kind enough to encourage or advise me in the writing of this Postscript I want particularly to mention Cheryl Misak (with whom I discussed Peirce, especially the points made in note 23), Wilfrid Hodges, Martin Davies and Jennifer Hornsby.

# X

# Incommensurability: Four Proposals*

The gist of the assertion that not all lengths are commensurable . . . may be expressed as follows. If AB, AC be two lengths along the same straight line, it may happen that, if AB be divided into *m* equal parts, and AC into *n* equal parts, then, however *m* and *n* may be chosen, one of the parts of AB will not be equal to one of the parts of AC, but will be greater for some values of *m* and *n*, and less for others; also lengths equal to either may be taken along any given line and with any given end-points.

BERTRAND RUSSELL

Yet the acquisition of wisdom must in a sense end in something which is the opposite of our original state of curiosity. For we begin in astonishment that the matter is so. . . as with the solstices . . . or the incommensurability of the diagonal, where it seems amazing that there should be a thing which cannot be measured by even the smallest unit. But we must end in the contrary and better state, as is the case when men learn the reason. There is nothing which would

* Acknowledgements. This paper, reprinted with the kind permission of Harvard University Press and now revised and cross-referenced to the other essays in this book, seeks to make explicit the view about rationality, reasonableness, commensurability, and incommensurability implicit in the preceding essays. For persuading me to attempt this I am grateful, now that I have done it, to Ruth Chang. The essay was written for her edited collection, *Incommensurability* (Cambridge, Mass.: Harvard University Press, 1997). I thank her for her comments. I also thank Martin Hollis, John Broome, Peter Hammond, Samuel Guttenplan, Michael Hechter, Bernard Williams, and Ronald Dworkin. (The chapter mottoes are from B. A. W. Russell, *The Principles of Mathematics* (London, 1903), pp. 438–9, and Aristotle, *Metaphysics*, 983a12–31.)

> surprise a geometer so much as if the diag-
> onal of a square turned out to be commen-
> surable with the sides.
>
> ARISTOTLE

1.  Technical and recondite though they are—indeed, in the
continuing absence of explicit stipulation, obscure—the ideas
of commensurability and incommensurability have long since
had a life of their own in moral philosophy. Their presence
here reflects fears or expectations that are very familiar.[1] But
it is doubtful even now whether these fears and expectations
can by themselves determine the usage of 'commensurable'
and 'incommensurable'. It is equally doubtful whether, just
as it stands, the language of moral philosophy can sustain an
agreed signification for them. An explicit stipulation would be
the best. On the other hand, so much has now been argued
under their mysterious auspices and believed in their name
that not just any definition will suffice.

In what follows I try to identify some salient ideas that
have had currency among adherents of claims of incommensurability. Then I redeploy these materials in a sequence of
proposals designed to pin down a little better what, given the
concerns of those who have written about things that they
call by this name, we ought to want to mean in ethics and
political philosophy by 'incommensurable'. I hope that whatever survives this process will show the way to simpler, more
refined, proposals that will carry with them the possibility of
more widespread and substantial agreement about what
incommensurability is. Writing as an incommensurabilist, I
have the further aim of persuading the reader that, in some
reasonable and useful sense of the word, there are moral,
political, and aesthetic incommensurables. This aim is important but, strictly speaking, it is subsidiary.

2.  A familiar first proposal (not yet a definition, rather, one
might hope, something potentially following on from a defi-

---

[1] Whether fears or expectations are in question depends on the question of
whether it is feared that consequentialism will prevail or expected that it will, or
what. On these matters, see below, §6.

nition) is this. We are frequently faced with situations where not every claim upon us can be satisfied. If the options A and B make mutually incommensurable claims, then, whether you choose A over B or choose B over A, something will be lost. It is not sensible to expect that always everything that matters about A and matters about B will survive in the outcome of the wise exercise of practical choice between them.

What is the corresponding definition of (in)commensurables? If moralists wish, in describing our confrontation with the objects of appetition and conation, to press into service the celebrated sequel of the theorem whose discovery Pythagoras is said to have celebrated by the sacrifice of an ox, the sequel that Russell states and Aristotle alludes to in the passages I have prefixed to this chapter, then one putative definition is as follows:

> Option A is incommensurable with option B just if A is not commensurable with B.
> Option A is commensurable with option B if and only if there is some valuational measure of more and less and there is some property $\phi$ that is correlative with choice and rationally antecedent to choice or rationally determinant of choice, such that A and B can be *exhaustively compared* by the said measure in respect of being more $\phi$ and less $\phi$;[2] where an exhaustive comparison in respect of $\phi$-ness is a comparison in respect of everything that matters about either A or B.

Wherever A and B made incommensurable claims in this sense—wherever no measure and property simultaneously meeting these exigent conditions was available—it would be reasonable to expect that any choice between them would leave what Bernard Williams calls a residue. Even where one made the choice everyone would agree was (in context) the right choice, something important might be left over for which the winning option could afford no compensation.[3] A

---

[2] 'Such' is an adjective here—as it is everywhere and always in this writer's dialect. (That is to say that, in these pages, 'such that' cannot by itself mean 'so that'—even though 'in such a way that' is equipollent with 'so that'.) In the sentence of text from which this note hangs, 'such' stands in construction with 'measure' and with 'property'. (Ten years ago I should not have thought to write this note. In ten years from now, the explanation itself may be unintelligible.)

[3] Of course, if nothing *important* is left over, then it is not worth insisting that A and B make claims that are incommensurable. I suppose that one more eager than

legitimate claim might go unsatisfied. It would do so wherever it was impossible for the winning option to reflect some
genuine, valid, well-grounded claim of some losing option.

3.   Here it is important not to let a concern with the existence of incommensurables tempt one into the denial that a
practical verdict arrived at by some sensible means or other—
the overall best one for the circumstances C, suppose—will
effect *a ranking* between A and B.[4] That is not the right
denial. Indeed it may be false. The point the would-be incommensurabilist should rather insist upon is this: the ranking
read off a practical verdict made for C will be a ranking in
respect of *overall choice-worthiness under the circumstances* C,
and only that. An overall ranking of this kind, conditioned
by circumstances, will indeed relate to more and less and may
be the soundest, most judicious ranking. But, from the nature
of the case, it need not represent a complete or exhaustive
valuation of the alternatives A and B. It need not be a
valuation of everything that matters at all or in any way
about each of them. Having insisted upon this, moreover,
the   incommensurabilist   is   not   then   prevented   from
registering a new and further point. This is that in real life A
may count as more choice-worthy overall than B—and come
to be seen as such—altogether otherwise than on the basis of
A's representing more of something that B represents less of.
For a comparison in respect of more and less 'overall choice-
worthiness' may issue simply and directly from the scrutiny
of A and the scrutiny of B, or from thoughts quite other than
those of more and less. As a result of an agent's scrutiny of
each of A and B, A may commend itself as simply mandatory, for instance, as an inescapable 'must', and/or option B
may seem to be unthinkable—entirely out of the question.
     That, of course, is a special case. The more general thing
it clearly points towards is that the judgment 'A is more

I am to explain the idea of incommensurability along these lines, or by reference to
the choice between the particularized options available in particular cases, had better take steps to make incommensurability require the importance of this residue.

     [4] I use the word 'ranking' throughout in the ordinary sense that it is fixed by the
language, not in any technical sense. It is the genus of which the recondite or specially defined sorts of ordering employed in the literature of moral philosophy, economics, *etc.*, are species.

choice-worthy than B, overall' may, when it comes after the decision, be the only comparison in respect of more and less that is to be discerned anywhere in the agent's thoughts about the situation. In such a case, it is the choice of A (or the considerations that ground the choice of A) that gives the ranking, not the ranking that gives the choice. The two-place predicate 'X is more choice-worthy than Y' plays no deliberatively useful role. It sums up a deliberation effected by quite other means. This might even be the normal case. The two-place predicate itself is well enough defined. That is close to guaranteed, provided that we are clear that the ranking is simply for C and made under the constraints of C. But the only reason why it is guaranteed is that, wherever necessary, the predicate's extension can be determined by reference to the logically antecedent practical choice that it recapitulates. In other words, it is guaranteed because we can make practical choices in ways not allowed for at all by the 'ranking' conception of deliberation. *A fortiori*, the availability of such a universal predicate in the role here described does nothing whatever to help suggest that there is just one overarching deliberatively substantial property—some single property that grounds practical choice and underlies practical choices.

So, for the would be incommensurabilist, this seems to be the state of play. Even if every practical choice did presuppose a comparison of options in respect of some antecedent and deliberatively substantial property that subsumed all the relevant properties of the alternatives—and we lack any reason at all to believe that, and can readily think of cases where we do not even appear to have recourse to this—*indefinitely many* such properties might (for all that anyone has yet shown) need to be invoked, depending upon the nature of the alternatives, the context *etc*. Indeed, pending some argument to the opposite effect, there would have to be a strong presumption against there being just one deliberatively substantial property of choice-worthiness. (In philosophy, as in mathematics, the normal presumption is not for but against uniqueness.) What is more, once the idea appears that, even on the ranking model, there may be a plurality of such properties in play, the thing we shall immediately expect is that it will become *essentially contestable* which property should prevail in a given case or will trump there all the others there.

4. These reflections put us into a position to formulate a second and in some ways more satisfactory definition of incommensurability, one which will carry us past a defect in the first proposal. Someone might reasonably find fault with that which the first proposal stipulated about exhaustive comparison's requiring the comparing A with B 'in respect of everything that matters about either A or B'. The defect is that, if this means only that an exhaustive comparison between A and B *has regard* for everything that matters, then the denial that A and B were commensurable in the sense defined might come perilously close to the denial that one could choose sensibly between A and B at all. (Do we really want to confine our whole use of the notion of incommensurability to cases like that?) And then of course the positive claim of commensurability would amount to terribly little. It would simply remind us that a good choice must have regard for anything and everything that matters. Who is going to gainsay that? On the other hand, if comparison 'in respect of everything that mattered' about A or B meant that one could *recover* from the verdict 'A is more φ than B' some condensation of all the information about everything that there was in favour of either A or B—if it implied that nothing important in that information would be lost in the passage to a verdict in favour of one or the other—then the claim of commensurability would be improbably strong. In which case, under this alternative interpretation of the phrase 'exhaustive comparison', the *denial* of A and B's commensurability would amount to little or nothing. For it would have been absurd to expect such a mass of evaluative information about A and B to be fully represented in or fully recoverable from the overall verdict in favour of one or other of them.

The second proposal to which one is led by all these considerations runs as follows:

> The set (A, B, C, D, . . .) constitutes an incommensurable set of options if and only if it is *not* the case that there is one property φ and one measure $M$ of φ-ness such that φ and M satisfy all the following conditions:

(a) it is determined by $M$ which is the more $\phi$ member of any pair $(X, Y)$ consisting of options drawn from the set $(A, B, C, D, \ldots)$,

(b) comparisons in respect of $\phi$-ness ground correct deliberative choice between the members of each and every pair drawn from the set $(A, B, C, D, \ldots)$, and are antecedent in reason to choices between them,

(c) comparisons in respect of $\phi$-ness reflect a proper regard for *every* choice-relevant feature of any member of the set $(A, B, C, D, \ldots)$.

5. Does this definition of incommensurability inherit any title to minister to the thought that, where you rightly choose A over B, something important may nevertheless be lost by the choice of B?

Just to this extent. The relevant deliberative property $\phi'$ for the choice between A and B may have had relatively little regard for certain among the properties of B, and these less valued properties might well have counted for much more in connection with a comparison in respect of another property $\phi''$, where $\phi''$ would not have been the right respect of comparison for the choice here between A and B but might have been the right respect of comparison for the choice between A and (say) C.

This second conception of incommensurability plainly can, to this extent at least, cast light on the classic or hackneyed examples, such as the choice here and now between pursuing justice and pursuing commercial efficiency, or the choice posed here and now between a life of contemplation, a life of statesmanship and public endeavour, and a life of relaxation, privacy and pleasure. Perhaps the most important thing about such well-worn examples is that there is no uncontentious choice of standard of comparison. Whatever standard you choose, someone else may, and may in good faith, press for another. The second conception of incommensurability illustrates this vividly enough—just as it illustrates the fact that it may be sensible to refuse to see the different lives that different people choose as competing answers to some stable, unitary and general question, with a stable and unproblematic sense, reference and intended elucidation, namely 'Which of these lives is *the best overall*?' Even if we decide not to quarrel (here or now) with the myth that there is something general called value and comparison in respect of it fixes choice (the more one thinks about it the more certain one becomes that that is a myth, but never mind), we can see that there is a further element of myth-making in the idea that, in respect of sensible choice, there *ought* to be some not essentially contestable notion of 'overall best' (or 'overall best here now') that will serve to gloss the sense of the question that is at issue in the choice.

So the second proposal has some of the virtues that the first proposal was aiming at. It predicts that, for purposes of practical choice and the selection of the right dimension of comparison, it will in some special cases be agonizingly difficult to decide how to hold the right balance between the values that are preserved or promoted by one option and those that are preserved or promoted by the other option. It predicts this on the basis of the plurality of putative dimensions of comparison. Just as the first proposal did, it leads us to expect that the choice may represent a terrible challenge to the chooser. Bernard Williams, Peter Winch, and writers in other traditions, Jean-Paul Sartre for instance, have illustrated in convincing detail the nature and quality of challenges of this kind. There is much more to be said about them in the framework that is to be proposed later in this paper. But for this, see below §§14–15.

One more advantage. Like the first proposal, the second has the effect of drawing attention to an important contrast between ordinary evaluations and practical verdicts. Whereas the verdicts of practical choice must often sacrifice something, the verdicts of pure evaluation, provided it makes a full use of all the resources of valuational thinking and these are not collapsed into valuations on a single scale, need not lose or obliterate anything. Everything can register. We can say 'It would have been kind and it would have been benevolent to do act A, but unjust.' Or we can say 'This work-practice is time-consuming and costly, but it also achieves something distinctive; and it gives more people the experience and insight into reality that come from work; the point of persisting with it, if one did persist, would not be that it was commercially efficient, but that it achieved something distinctive, and/or was more just'.

One last preliminary. The second proposal does not predict that every choice from a set of incommensurables represents a real dilemma or a case where the idea of the right practical choice is problematic. (Real or tragic dilemmas will be touched upon at §§14–15 below.) Its non-prediction of that counts positively in favour of the proposal because, in given particular contexts, with varying senses of loss, we can, and in practice we regularly do, make such choices. (Which is not to say that we always can.) In looking for the right dimension of comparison, we arrive, little by little, at rather specific reasons for our choices. How we do this and arrive at certain distinctive moral emphases in our practical and moral outlooks is an important part of the story of how we become what we become and make for ourselves the various different characters that we come to exemplify. The thesis of incommensurability understood in the light of the second proposal is not a substitute for philosophy's effort to come to terms with all this. But it may usefully complement that effort. It points towards an irreducibly practical element in our practical knowledge.

6.   How does the second of our two proposals relate to the fears and expectations that attach to the philosophical thesis of moral consequentialism? I ask because there are numerous writers who expect the existence of incommensurabilities, if there are any, to represent the chief escape route, if there is one, from the morally repugnant conclusions that flow from the consequentialist idea that practical decisions are to be arrived at by assessing states of affairs in respect of their total net desirability. Incommensurabilists expect such an escape route and commensurabilists have come perhaps to expect that incommensurabilists will expect this.

Nevertheless, it is hard to believe that there is any notion of incommensurability that can by itself provide this way of escaping the consequentialist's dialectic (if once we grant him his opening move). I say this because so often, in cases where consequentialism outrages conviction, the considerations that stand behind the competing practical options seem all too easily comparable. There may be various numbers of deaths, lives, broken promises, etc. on each side of the dilemma. We do not need to force these things or the options that comprise them into a common currency in order to compare and measure what lies within rival options. They may be in a common enough currency already. Comparison may be easy but may all too easily issue in morally repulsive directives.

According to Scheffler, moral consequentialism comes in two parts:

> First, it gives some principle for ranking overall states of affairs from best to worst from an impersonal standpoint, and then it says that the right act in any given situation is the one that will produce the highest-ranked state of affairs that the agent is in a position to produce . . . Anyone who resists consequentialism seems committed to the claim that morality tells us to do less good than we are in a position to do and to prevent less evil than we are in a position to prevent . . .[5]

In so far as our second conception of incommensurability sheds any light at all here, it does indeed cast doubt on the claim that there is just one deliberatively foundational principle of the sort Scheffler describes for ranking overall states of affairs from better to worse. That should never be taken for granted. See §3 above. But how fatal that is to consequentialism is something that would need to be argued with the position's defenders. And in any case, the first and chief question about consequentialism is not so much whether a single overall principle exists for ranking states of affairs as whether there was ever any positive and non-question begging reason to espouse consequentialism in the first place.[6] What positive argument can the consequentialist offer for insisting that the complex and distinctive (already moralized) deliberative procedures of an agent must be merged into some concern with 'the impersonal standpoint'? (Contrast with this 'impersonal standpoint' the 'point of view that one person shall have in common with others', which is not as such a consequentialist point of view at all. See pp. 59, 61, 78, following.) To develop a good notion of incommensurability is a worthwhile aim, but it is no substitute for gaining

---

[5] Samuel Scheffler, paragraph 2, editorial introduction for *Consequentialism and its Critics* (Oxford: Oxford University Press, 1988).

[6] This lack is exposed, albeit only inchoately and in bygone idiom, by W. D. Ross in chapter two of *The Right and the Good* (Oxford, 1930).

an understanding of the distinction between questions of overall goodness/badness of states of affairs impersonally considered (cp. p. 316 above) and questions that immediately engage the agency of a person (questions of what it would be right or wrong, callous or kind, just or unjust, honourable or dishonourable, *for him or her* to do now here).

7.  If the defects of the second proposal do not relate to its contributing so little to the examination of consequentialism, then they chiefly lie elsewhere. I shall place some of these defects on the record.

First, the proposal perpetuates unclarity about what kinds of thing they are that belong to sets of options that are counted as incommensurable.

Secondly, the proposal leaves us without any direct way of saying what we seem to want to say (however obscurely) when we claim that A and B themselves are mutually incommensurable.

Thirdly, the bare claim that there are incommensurable option-sets (A, B, C . . .) is signally unsuggestive about what it is that a reasonable person will collate with what in arriving, by whatever contextually appropriate route, at defensible practical choices. It would be good if we could find an account of incommensurability that more explicitly related the incommensurability of incommensurables A, B, C, . . . both to the dispositions, character-traits, or commitments that sustain a reasonable person's concern with each of A, B, C, . . . and also to the contexts that activate these concerns. We need a proposal that is more deliberate and more explicit in its treatment of the *objects* and of the *occasions* of regret or anguish, for instance. (I mean the regret or anguish that ensue upon the 'payment', as some say, of what they will like to call 'moral costs'.)

8.  To this end, let us try first to revert to the thought that mutual incommensurables are things themselves, A, B, C, not the sets that contain them. Let us try to preserve something too from two other ideas that we began with: namely, (1) the idea that incommensurability results from the way in which complete assessment ('valuations') of option A and option B

may seem to under-determine the decision between A and B; (2) the idea that incommensurability should reflect the way in which a real life practical choice between the options A and B will often be either appreciably less or appreciably more than an all-inclusive valuational comparison between them in respect of more and less.

Reflection and experiment with versions I shall not put onto the page suggest that, in order to achieve these desiderata, we must be prepared to supersede the thought that incommensurable things should be particularized historically determinate rival options. Abandoning these, let us rule instead that incommensurables are the relatively unspecific and rather general objects of concern, the objects of the distinct and potentially rival or conflicting ethical concerns (in the widest sense of 'ethical') which can figure in deliberation at any given moment of choice. Among things A, B . . . that can matter in a situation and may end up making rival claims upon us, A will be incommensurable with B, just if, even though A can be compared with B in a particular context under the constraint of that context and for a particular purpose that obtains there, A and B cannot be ranked in any more general way. In a given case, we may well find some way to collate and arbitrate between the demands that impinge there of (say) impartiality, benevolence, mercy, due process, etc. (if not to satisfy them fully): but there may be no acceptable and general method for doing this. Let us say then that A is incommensurable with B, in the new sense of 'incommensurable' and under the new understanding of what sorts of things A and B are, if there is no *general* way in which the self-sufficient claims of A and of B trade off in the whole range of situations of choice and comparison in which they figure.

One clarification may be needed here. People of different characters will certainly bring to bear certain distinctive moral emphases and seek persistently to promote certain distinctive concerns. There are people who can be reliably depended upon to act and live out these distinctive concerns. But, according to the incommensurabilist, this is not to say that, even for one agent of this kind, any exceptionless (or even helpful) statement, applicable over a full range of situations, can be made of his or her ranking of these concerns, or of his or her relative ranking of various combinations of these concerns. If it could, then that would be a symptom, not of the firmness or distinctiveness of an agent's character, but (very likely) of his or her obstinacy or fanaticism. *A fortiori*, the formation of character cannot be redescribed as the process by which someone settles down to their final choice of something to maximize.

9. Incommensurability in the sense we are now trying to pin down reflects the separateness and mutual irreducibility of the standing concerns that make up our orientation towards the distinct values and commitments (and whatever else) that impinge upon us in different sorts of situations. It reflects the fact that these concerns are not all variations upon a common theme. According to our new account, the idea of incommensurability can indeed (as the first proposal insisted) have application to specific historically determined choices or options, or to sets of them (as the second insisted). But it does so only derivatively from the incommensurability (in the new and improved sense) of more general or persisting concerns to which we have standing, strictly speaking unranked, attachments.[7]

How then, confronting these general concerns as they impinge upon particular historic contexts and situations, *do* we make our choices? Answer: we have to make our choice in the light of our overall practical conception of how to be or how to live a life (both here and in general). We deploy these conceptions even as the variety of the contingencies that we actually confront constantly shapes or reshapes the conceptions themselves. (A two-way flow.) It will be no wonder if choice (as now described) is the exercise of an irreducibly practical knowledge, a knowledge that can never be exhaustively transposed into any finite set of objectives that admit of finite specification.

How then can the incommensurabilist who stresses the practical aspect of choice, and insists upon the unlimitedness,

---

[7] 'Unranked' here, which is simply my response to a technical term used by commensurabilists, is intended to leave room for a distinctive moral *emphasis* among a rational agent's attachments.

distinctness and separateness of the various values, concerns, commitments that we care about, best mark or signal all these things and relate them more precisely to questions about the springs of action? Well, the best I can offer is the following condensation: where A and B are incommensurable in our new and third sense, there is no (however complicated or conditionalized) correct, unitary, projectible,[8] explanatory and/or potentially predictive account to be had of how A and B trade off against one another in some reasonable agent's choices or actions, or within the formation of his springs of action. Where A and B are mutually incommensurable, the attempt to extrapolate from the actual choices that he makes between them under such and such circumstances (and under this or that constraint) and the effort this entails on the theorist's part to surmount the relativity of these choices to those circumstances (and constraints) will not succeed in establishing any determinate and projectible ratio of substitution between them.

10.   Now that incommensurability is restored as something that concerns can have to one another, let us be as explicit as possible. By the usage proposed, an incommensurabilist will not merely disbelieve that there is for each rational agent some in principle predeterminable and constant 'ratio of substitution' that his valuational, ethical, normative outlook fixes, in a projectible and counterfactual-sustaining fashion, between all the standing values or objects of concern that

----

[8] In Nelson Goodman's sense of 'projectible'. See *Fact, Fiction and Forecast* (London: Athlone Press, 1954). An account of how A and B traded off against one another would not be projectible unless it could be applied to non-actual cases and cases in the open future. It would need to underwrite subjunctive conditionals.

In this sentence of the text, am I contradicting anything that any live person would actually assert? I think so. From a variety of possible sources I shall cite the following, with grateful acknowledgement to my colleague James Griffin for the quotation: 'Our basic theory assumes first that, for all the alternative consumption bundles he could conceivably [*sic*] face, the individual has a preference ordering. This reflects his tastes . . . From the opportunities available to him, he does the best he can, best being defined according to his tastes', P. R. G. Layard and A. A. Walters, *Microeconomic Theory* (New York: McGraw Hill, 1978). Such a 'basic theory' may be harmless enough for purposes of describing or explaining some specific class of economic transactions. What I am resisting is the suggestion that the assumption is true, or true enough for our purposes when we ask for a faithful picture of reasoned choice and action as such.

mean anything to him. To disbelieve that is to disbelieve a relatively simple and unbelievable form of commensurabilism. The incommensurabilist will also reject a weaker and potentially more plausible conjunctive claim, namely this: that, given some rational agent possessed of a valuational, ethical, normative (etc.) outlook, there always exists, in principle, some account of how different sorts of objects of concern trade off for him, either at a constant ratio or at a systematically varying ratio of substitution, and this account is *explanatory, projectible*, and *counterfactual-sustaining*. (The incommensurabilist will not, of course, deny that after the event, some such ratio might be hit upon. That claim is nearly vacuous and the incommensurabilist will be foolish to deny the nearly vacuous.[9] It does not give any empirical content to the idea of maximizing anything. It does not represent a falsifiable claim about the agent's springs of action.)

Maybe nobody will see any reason to assert what the incommensurabilist denies here. (If so, then see below §11.) Maybe nobody at all will own up to believing the things the incommensurabilist disbelieves. However that may be, what the incommensurabilist holds (in defiance of any lazy scientism to which his adversaries cling in the privacy of the closet) is that for an ordinary agent to have a sane, reasonable outlook is not (in real life, in the real world) the same thing at all as it is for his outlook to amount to a preference ordering by reference to which the agent's well-considered actions may be seen as maximizing any however complex thing.[10]

---

[9] See B. A. W. Russell, 'The Idea of Cause', p. 148 in the Penguin edition of *Mysticism and Logic* (London: Allen and Unwin, 1917). See also Nelson Goodman's account in *Fact, Fiction and Forecast, op. cit.* of what we should require of any satisfactory account of a predicate's being projectible.

[10] As always, some may respond by emptying 'maximize' of all distinctive content. My claim that it would show nothing to determine a subject's utilities and his ratio of substitution in a manner that was essentially after the event (simply recapitulatory of it) may provoke the response that it is a non-trivial exercise to determine such things as this, even after the event, *if* the postulates of rational choice theory are to be found to be in force. My claim is not so much however that it is *easy* after the event to find (subject to this severe constraint) the utility schedule and the ratio of substitution (or that curve-fitting is *by its nature* an easy exercise) as it is this: that, if curve fitting is *all* that is attempted, if neither phenomenology is advanced nor any properly (n.b.) projectible characterization of the springs of action is achieved, then nothing of any explanatory interest is accomplished—however hard

11. Such then is the idea for the third proposal. The proposal under review could issue in definitions of incommensurability for a given agent and (notwithstanding the essential contestability of the notion of 'rational') of incommensurability for the 'rational agent'. I postpone such refinements, however. It is more urgent to fill out the philosophical background for the denials that the incommensurabilist is issuing. Let us also inquire how reasonable beings do identify what is at issue when they decide in hard cases and arbitrate there between the clamant and mutually inimical rival claims of their various commitments, arriving thus at their choices—choices that may or may not command the acquiescence of other reasonable beings. What is it for them to do this better or worse?

Suppose—with Aristotle and common sense—that the subject matter of the practical is by its nature both indefinite and unforeseeable. Then there does not exist the option, which one might otherwise have supposed there would be, for an agent to measure in advance what exactly any kind of commitment lets him in for, either of itself or in relation to all his distinct commitments (whatever *they* may prove to amount to). It cannot be predicted in the real world how much scope one positive commitment will allow to others. (Contrast perhaps the acceptance of certain prohibitions, on which compare Aristotle *N.E.*1110a29.) Nor can it be predicted what it will take to persist in a given commitment. If such is the condition of human agents, however, then theorists of practical reason ought to leave room for practical reason to propose to agents something other (and better) than that they should make as if to consult their preference function. The preferred picture must be that agents learn to decide about practical things by learning what it is they are to look to and learning

or demanding is the work of curve-fitting. Still less is the ordinary knowledge upstaged that ordinary agents have of themselves and one another. 'He ϕ-ed in order to maximize his utility' tells us no more than we are told by 'there was a reason of some sort why he did what he did'.

The incommensurabilists' negative claim does not (I should add) commit him to the denial of physical determinism. If a determinism stated in strictly physical terms were true—I use the subjunctive conditional advisedly here, see Essay VII—then that would in no way guarantee the truth of any determinism specifiable in terms proprietary to economics or to psychology or to rational choice theory.

how to interpret and reinterpret their given conceptions of the thing they are to look to. What we have to make speculative sense of is agents' making the best sense they can of their own positive concerns and commitments in the space not excluded by accepted prohibitions—and of their striving to do this even in a world for whose countless and not exhaustively classifiable contingencies no decalogue or code of practice or statement of objectives could ever prepare them.

It will be useful to transcribe here, for the incommensurabilist's use, Aristotle's conception of the practical as it subsists in the real world. Aristotle describes this conception in Book Five of the *Nicomachean Ethics*, at chapter ten, which is on the subject of *epieikeia* or equity:

> About some things it is not possible to make a general statement which shall be correct. In those cases then in which it is necessary to speak generally but not possible to do so correctly, the law takes the usual case, though it is not ignorant of the possibility of error. And it is not wrong to do so: for the shortcoming is not in the law nor in the lawgiver but in the nature of the thing, since the subject matter of the practical is like this from the outset. About some things it is impossible to lay down a law, so that a particular decree is needed. For when the thing is indefinite, the rule also is indefinite, as is the leaden rule used in making the Lesbian moulding: the rule adapts itself to the shape of the stone and is not rigid. So too a decree adapts itself to the particular facts.

Somehow, on the shifting ground that Aristotle describes here—his contention in this passage relates to problems of public legislation and adjudication[11] but his perception of the nature of the practical is an entirely general one—individual agents can find a way to make real their conceptions of living and being. For they can deliberate, in the light of the good and the possible, about ends, about the constituents of ends, and about the means to ends. Somehow, despite the intractability and uncertainty of the subject-matter of choice,

---

[11] Where it has lived on in juristic principles that animate English and American systems of case law and in jurisprudential outlooks that grow out of these systems. See Ronald Dworkin, *Law's Empire* (Cambridge, Mass.: Harvard University Press, 1986), pp. 257–8.

agents do arrive at judgements about what is worthwhile or
what can or cannot be done in pursuit of what. And somehow, from out of all this, they arrive at shared, partly inex-
plicit norms of reasonableness. In this way, they can set
standards, not fully verbalized, by which people of good
sense and good character can live. If these norms are only
misdescribed when they are seen as modes of maximization,
then the thing philosophy had best do is to desist altogether
from the attempt to identify something which is to be maximized. It must attend instead, in an ethically engaged fashion, to the various ideas that give the however essentially
contestable content, a content under constant revision and
extension, of reasonable agents' conceptions of the good.
*Pace* the received misinterpretations of Aristotle, the main
business of practical reason is ends and their constituents, not
instrumental means. For an Aristotelian, the idea that a self-
contained part of the concept of rationality can be bitten off
and studied in value-free fashion as the rationality of means,
leaving the rest (that is ends) to the taste or formation of individual agents, is a delusion, and a gratuitous delusion at
that.[12]

12. I expect that a sceptic about everything that passes
under the name of incommensurability or about our freedom
to make and remake constantly our conception of the good
may now join forces with any sceptic who doubts all the
other things to which the new conception of incommensurability is intended to lend succour. The following declaration
may be expected:

> Given any two options or packages and given a rational
> agent with desires and concerns of his own, either the
> agent will *qua* rational ascribe to the items equal over-
> all utility or he will ascribe higher overall utility to one
> of them—where overall utility is the satisfaction of *all*
> the agent's divers concerns, commitments (etc.) and
> relates in the obvious way to all the agent's various

---

[12] The received misinterpretations of *Nicomachean Ethics* rest on the mistransla-
tion of the Greek words *ta pros to telos*. See my 'Deliberation and Practical Reason',
Essay VI above.

reasons to pursue this or that line of conduct. Surely the rational agent is one who unremittingly and consistently (despite difficulties of uncertainty, ignorance, and the rest) pursues this utility.

So far as I can see, this statement treats it as simply obvious that, for every rational chooser, there is something he or she is constantly seeking to maximize, namely the thing the objector calls 'the chooser's utility'. That is to say that the statement ignores almost everything I have said already. Despite that, I shall persevere with the objector, and shall even do everything I can not to repeat myself.

One difficulty for the utility thesis as it appears here I shall mention but shall discount. This is the existence of weakness of will.[13] The objection on which I do want to insist goes as follows: that in so far as the maximizing-cum-commensurabilist account of individual choice is not deprived of all empirical content and all explanatory or predictive interest (a privation that can readily escape notice in the post-positivist or post-logical empiricist phase we have now reached in so much of what passes for the philosophy of social theorizing), no reason has ever been given to believe it. No reason is given in the shape of telling conceptual considerations (for these would depend on the demonstration, still lacking, that the maximizing model furnishes the best way of characterizing a particular person's practical outlook or his springs of action) nor yet in the shape of empirical evidence. Indeed, in actual cases where a predictive or empirical theory is really needed of individual choice (as it exists in the wild, so to speak) and entrepreneurs also have something to lose by getting things wrong—e.g. in connection with their concern to make money by selling things

---

[13] The difficulty is not that weakness makes counter-examples to the thesis. That could be taken care of by saying of the agent that 'there is something he or she is seeking, in so far as s/he is rational, to maximize'. The difficulty is that proper or reflective weakness of will is so hard to understand in these terms. If everything trades off against everything else at some predeterminable (however contextually variable) rate and the trading rate reflects everything that matters about it, what reason could anyone have (and what reason could there be for him or her) to think twice about whether to do the act that scored highest. What reason could there ever be to backslide from the demonstrably optimific act? (Unless, of course, s/he wanted to go back on the calculation.) It will be harder than it ought to be to understand weakness of will *as having reasons* (of a sort) *of its own*.

that might be invented, made, and retailed at a profit—the thing that we observe in the real world (or so I am told by those who inhabit that part of it) is that nobody seriously proposes to make any distinctive use at all of rational choice theory or of its modes of characterization of the springs of action.[14] In practice, the thing that is always deployed in the world of commerce is empirical phenomenology—or market research, to give it a more familiar name. This last is a modest, useful business, but it stands in no more need of the supposition that individual choices and the constraints upon choices derive from the chooser's striving after a maximum than does advertising or any other method of persuasion on whose behalf market research can spy out the ground.[15]

13.   Having come so far, let us recapitulate the third proposal and then paint in one further detail.

Suppose then that (as already claimed) our different valuations and pursuits are grounded in a multiplicity of distinct concerns which are rooted in a multiplicity of different psychic structures which make distinct and mutually irre-

[14] Nobody deploys anything that is *proprietary* to these theories, I mean. Real empirical inquiries can of course, even in the fields I have just mentioned, dress up their results (or even their questions) in the garb of decision theory or rational choice theory, thus enhancing the credentials of the inquirers' professional mystery. This does not mean that any results they actually achieve need to go to the credit of decision theory or rational choice theory. The same goes for the familiar praxeological truisms that see actions as the product of beliefs (*inter alia*) and desires (*inter alia*). These truisms are as old as reflection on the subject of agency itself, and proprietary to nobody, least of all to the theory of action seen as utility maximization. Nor, in any sane sense of 'theory', do they amount to a theory.

[15] There is one kind of case where one might anticipate that theories of individual choice which see agents as would-be maximizers could have real application, namely the case where the activities to be forecast are by their essential, professed and explicit nature maximizing activities, *e.g.* activities in the market place or the bourse. Here one might indeed expect that there could be some impressive predictions to be had and illuminating explanations of outcomes. The same will apply wherever the field to be studied has been non-arbitrarily narrowed down to a specific class of activities that are shown in due course to be candidates to be seen as maximizing of this or that specific end. Nevertheless, successes of this sort would leave it perfectly open how seriously we should take the idea of a theory that will make sense not of a specific class of activities, but of every act of some particular agent, as an act of utility maximizing. They would leave it open how seriously we should take either the idea of an all-embracing theory for all individual agents or the idea of a set of particular and specific theories, one for each agent or even the bare claim to the effect that for each agent *some* such all-embracing theory is possible.

ducible claims upon us: suppose that a particular practical cum ethical outlook is something an agent works out in confrontation with the indefinitely varied contingencies (in the forms of opportunity and constraint) with which the world confronts him as he lives, as he acts, and as he responds to each new contingency in the light of past responses to past contingencies: suppose that there is not for each rational agent some general, predeterminable and/or at least projectible rate (or yet some projectible systematically variable rate) at which different values such as honour, altruism, pleasure, safety, comfort, morality . . . will trade off for him against one another in the manner that is visually represented, for a given case involving n things, in given circumstances, under given constraints (budget, etc.), by an indifference map in n dimensions. Suppose then that there is no *general* (*i.e.* all context negotiating) way of arranging different quantities of honour, pleasure, safety, comfort, benevolence, justice, . . . into bundles that are valued equally by the agent. (As always, the denial depends upon taking projectibility seriously. Note also that the dots, . . . , are not the dots of laziness. Nobody knows, even in principle, how to complete this enumeration.) Suppose finally that we do in fact arbitrate constantly between such concerns in our confrontation with whatever it is to which the world forces us to find our response. Suppose we do this not in the light of a *post factum* construct called our utility but in the light of our ideas, our ideals, and our developing and essentially time-bound conception of that life (among the lives that we think it may be a realizable possibility for us to try to lead) in which we can best find meaning.

14. If we suppose all of this, then it provides precisely that which was (or could have been) presupposed by writers who wanted to dwell upon tragic and/or morally impossible choices. Real dilemmas depend on various values making autonomous mutually irreducible demands upon us. The picture we have offered suggests how, over and over again, in normal life, we may reach accommodations between these demands and live with conviction the accommodations that we find. The picture makes room for the thought that this is

a part of the process by which, as already remarked, we acquire or make our own characters, and so on. The one extra thing that needs at this point to be added is only this: that, despite our capacity so often to make do or get by, there still *cannot be any guarantee* that, no matter what the circumstances may be, we shall always find an accommodation that we can accept or live out. What is more, the picture that was offered earlier left room for that possibility. Where our concerns for A, B (which are incommensurable in the third sense) *cannot* in the given circumstance X be accommodated to our sense of how one should live and what one should do, where *nothing* at all seems to us (the agent), even for the context, bearable or liveable, there A and B are also in a fourth and 'tragic' sense incommensurable in X—or incommensurable for the agent in X.

We need both of these ideas of incommensurability, namely the third which was introduced at §8 and this new sense too. Let us distinguish them as the (common or garden) *incommensurable* and the *circumstantially cum tragically incommensurable*. So for Sartre's young man, in the circumstances of World War II in occupied France, patriotism and filial duty were both incommensurable and also circumstantially cum tragically incommensurable. For the example, see J.-P. Sartre, *Existentialism is a Humanism*.

15.  What then according to this conception is rationality, if there is nothing that rational agents need, simply qua rational, to maximize? Answer: rationality in an agent is the disposition, episodically exercised (and occasionally no doubt not exercised), to prefer (and to persist in the preference for) an act or a belief or an attitude in the light of the standards of evaluation and normative ends and ideals that it is the substantive work of evidential, axiological, moral, and whatever other reflection to determine. (It is a philosophical mistake, analogous to the mistake of which Gödel convicted Hilbert in the matter of mathematical truth, to suppose that it ought to be possible to do better than this and to *circumscribe* practical rationality by enumerating in advance its bases or grounds.) The rich fabric of reason or reasonableness is not to be confected from the thin threads of plain consistency, or

from any elaboration of such materials. (Indeed, consistency only makes practical unreasonableness worse.) What then, with regard to reason and rationality and reasonableness, is the business of philosophy? Surely, to participate in the critique of *reasons*, and to do so in a manner at once participatively engaged yet alert to the need to step off the treadmill, to stand back, or to lower the level of optical resolution and look harder (cp. pp. 100, 113 above) in search of scale, shape and outline. The standards of reasonableness that philosophy can articulate from the critique of lived experience, or by reflection upon the claims that each value makes upon thought, feeling, and appetition, will be a distillation from practical knowledge. Such knowledge is not exhausted by the verbalized generalizations or precepts of either agent or theorist (cp. *Nichomachean Ethics* 1143b). Seeing its standards for what they are, we shall then be prepared, as Aristotle puts it in a passage already referred to, for the decision itself to lie in perception (1126b4, 1109b23). That is to say that we shall be prepared for the decision to depend on the exercise of judgement in confrontation with some actually given particular situation—a situation described very specifically, though not in a way that makes it impossible to inquire for the relevant difference between it and other situations calling forth similar or dissimilar decisions.

16.   The case for adopting the third and fourth accounts of incommensurability, like the evidence for the general picture presented here of action and choice, rests mostly on the evidence of phenomenology and of phenomenological reflection, the last being undertaken in parallel with the philosophical analysis of the language that we already employ in the daily business of practical appreciation and decision. That language embodies the human account of what moves us. It helps us to make sense in our own way of what we all think and do. Of course, this is weak evidence. Rival accounts of individual choice come in a far more impressive scientific cum mathematical livery, with countless new promises of prediction and understanding. Nevertheless, in so far as these rival accounts make substantial empirical claims (which, I repeat, is not a thing to be taken for granted), and in so far as these

claims relate to individual choice and they go beyond the ordinary historical and philosophical platitudes concerning actions, beliefs, and desires—or in so far as these accounts enter normative claims about what it is reasonable for reasonable beings to aim for—well, here let us ask ourselves whether these rival accounts (decision theoretical and/or other) rest upon conceptual considerations or empirical evidence that gives them better support than is enjoyed already by the working, untheoretical, open-endedly phenomenological account. For in this phenomenological account lies the beginning of the understanding of deliberation and choice—a beginning that can be improved, by philosophy, by experience, by self-knowledge . . . , but can scarcely be superseded.

# Postscript to Essay X: Reasoned Choice, Freedom, and Utility

1. So much for incommensurability in moral philosophy, political philosophy, and similar contexts. And so much for the reason why from the incommensurability, so understood, of two or more things that we care about no expectation need arise of an impossibility of choosing, in a given context, between the lines of conduct that favour one thing at the expense of the other. In the ordinary circumstances of a life sustained by ordinary aims and concerns, incommensurability is something entirely commonplace. Outside the situations of tragedy touched upon in §14, we know how to put together a provisional idea of the specific good that is to be realized here, our longer and shorter term aims, our sense of what is mandatory for us and what forbidden to us, our sense of what requirements are sacred and what negotiable. . . . Before we advance to action, we know how and where, in the light of all these things, to reconsider, either not at all or once or twice or as many times as it takes (cp. pp. 225, 232), our provisional identification of the concern to be heeded or the specific good to be realized. In the choices that we make in this way, the springs of action are deployed and redeployed and directed and re-directed, all under the governance of practical thought about the good and the possible (cp. 248), about ends and their constituents (cp. 217–34), about means and ends, about the fit of ends to means and means to ends.

Or so it can be when things go well and the agent is not troubled by weakness of will or loss of nerve or perversity. Our picture of this capacity to choose or decide is part of the larger picture that we have of ourselves—a picture that is in part descriptive and in part normative—in which our individual autonomy is seen as residing, positively, in our pursuit of aims and ideals that are of our own reasonable and citizenly choosing, but residing negatively in the exclusion of the possibility that these particular aims or ideals *had* to be ours. This is to say that it is excluded from our picture that the generality of our individual deliberations or decisions or actions should be (in Essay VIII terminology) historically necessary. When we act at some point in the *now*, we do not normally think there was anything in the world *last year* or even *last week* (say) from which our act had, by virtue of natural laws and given circumstances, to ensue. Indeed it is a condition of human engagement that one should think that this is not so. Compare Kant, *Foundations of the Metaphysics of Morals* [p. 448]. We are happy enough, of course, with the possibility that last week there was something in us from which our present act would ensue. But it is doubtful in the extreme that there exist laws about us, either individually or collectively, that are seriously comparable with the laws of nature (and their applications and specializations) that are required for the holding of historical necessity.

In this general picture, actions and decisions do not lie outside the causal nexus. But the causal nexus underdetermines them—if only because it underdetermines all sorts of things. And the way in which actions and decisions become *explicable* is by being seen as intelligible—and intelligible only by virtue of standing in the right relation to aims and ideals proposed to us by practical reason (cp. Plato, *Phaedo*, 98[d] following). The fullest intelligibility of this latter sort is achieved in the whole story that not only recounts how the agent acted at this or that juncture but says what it was in the world—representing what sort of good or evil and engaging with what idea of the agent's—to which the agent was responding in acting so. In such a story, each succeeding episode in the sequence of the agent's doings will be an intelligible phase in the unfolding of an agent's mentality, a phase at once expressive of what the agent is and constitutive of what he is en route to become. Looking at the agent in this way, letting one part of the sequence impart significance to another, we have no difficulty in seeing the agent as one who exercises choice between alternatives (not necessarily making the choice that others would make). Nor do we have any difficulty in seeing the alternatives as real alternatives. Finally, availing ourselves of the said picture, we can see in the deliberations of agents a part of the culmination of the process by which striving has evolved into thought, and thought not only explores the world but colonizes it (cp. 356). At this point striving emerges finally in consciousness, a consciousness that holds itself answerable in action and reflection to the objects and properties thought discovers, subsumes objects under standards (in some sense) of its own making, yet refrains from hubristically supposing that, just because properties correspond to senses and practices that owe their existence to us, the properties thought finds in the world are its own creation.

2. In a philosophy that was happy to count itself as a recapitulation, extension and critique of ordinary experience, the details of such a phenomenological cum anecdotal cum philosophical account as this could be corrected or made more complete. But, improved and extended, why should it not stand as the best possible account of action and choice—or as the best possible account of action and choice as they are or can be when reason has full sway over us?

Well, I think such an account *can* stand. I should think this even if it were going to have the effect of philosophy's being forced to count as rational lines of conduct in which the decisions or actions of the agent violated some pet axiom of decision theory. (If the agent cannot be seen as a maximizer or as a constrained maximizer, then so what? What is so special about these forms of reason?)

Is there anything in physics or any other science to oppose this account? Nothing in serious science lies at this level. There is however an institutional difficulty. In a world where nobody is sure they are worth their salt any longer unless they can represent themselves as 'theorists' of some sort, where it takes no more than the existence of X to justify the use of the phrase 'the theory of X', and where almost anything will be made welcome if it promises to make the account of X resemble the proper or would-be scientific theory of X, the phenomenological cum anecdotal account of individual choice will appear to be long overdue for replacement. Replacement will seem especially urgent when the subject-matter of the ordinary account, namely *praxis* and *prohairesis* or action and choice by individual agents, is one component in virtually everything that is now submitted to theory in economics, sociology, politics, and the other social sciences.

Despite this difficulty, I persevere in my stand on the intellectual and practical indispensability to us of the ordinary anecdotal picture, as enlarged by the commonplaces of philosophical phenomenology. Why should anyone bother to insist upon this? Chiefly because of the destructive and subversive effect, which this is not the place for me to try to document, upon our life, our work, our new education, our politics and culture (both the form and the substance of these things, not to say their 'management'); of the alternative picture of a human being as *homo economicus, homo consumptor, homo maximum semper appetens, homo tandem charadrios. (Cf.* Plato, *Gorgias* 494[b], with scholion *ad loc.*)

The decision theorist will protest that, if there is any such degradation as I say I am pointing to, then it is not of his making: that in itself his theory is entirely neutral between different specifications of the end.

So far, my reply to him has been to insist that the proposal to replace the commonplaces of thick description by the schematism of maximization or constrained maximization is more than a formal step: that to adopt a schematism of this sort is to deform or abandon a low-level and almost pretensionless form of genuine insight which serves us indispensably well—recklessly, and all for the sake of a promise of theory which, as it relates to the prediction of individual behaviour or to the nature and normative demands of individual rationality, is entirely deceptive. Taken simply as a predictive or empirical theory of individual decision (this reply continues), rather than as the empty promise of one, decision theory has been falsified over and over again, *e.g.* by Tversky and collaborators. Decision theory might yet define a normative conception of individual rationality, and here the theory that is false empirically might seem in another way much more promising. It might, except that the most that the theory then promises is small technical improvements in the recommended modes of pursuit of ends taken as *already* certified—

but how?—as the rational ends to pursue. In other words, decision theory thus reconstrued leaves almost everything still to be said about which ends *are* rational. This abdication of responsibility will appear all the more serious when one reflects that technical enhancements of instrumental rationality may well aggravate the grave effects of a poor choice of ends (or a poor emphasis among good ends). All too often, the exclusive and refined understanding of instrumental rationality promotes an obtuse disrespect for direct and indirect ends and concerns that are not explicit and cannot ever be made operationally, fully, or for all purposes explicit (see Essay X, §11). All too often it undermines the capacity to engage at any level with the *reasons* why the project must fail of making every thing that matters once and for all explicit, and why the practical could not ever be reduced to the theoretical.

3.   Such a reply recapitulates, more or less, the line taken in Essays VII and X about individual decision theory, utility theory, and the rest. I shall not recant it. But I ought never to have given the appearance, if I have anywhere done so, of seeking to deny all the empirical and explanatory insights that have accrued to social scientists' various accounts of phenomena *other* than those of individual choice. Such a denial would be unnecessary, as I shall explain in one moment, and as unnecessary as it would be rash. In this postscript, the further reply that I offer to the decision theorist is quite different, and much simpler. In outline, the reply is as follows. *Homo economicus* and all variants upon it are abstractions, abstractions whose usefulness can be measured by what they offer to studies of the collective effects of theoretically significant aggregations of individual decisions, *e.g.* the over-grazing of the commons, the exhaustion of open-sea fishing stocks (to take some of the oldest and simplest cases), or the behaviour of financial markets. But the evident success of the accepted explanations of these things lends no support at all to the idea that the abstractions which make these explanations possible are *themselves* realities.

4.   Look at the abstractions that pull their weight in the systematic understanding of the collective phenomena studied

most successfully by sociologists, economists, and others. These abstractions work (where they do work) by prescinding from all the individual details and complications that would have to be the stuff of an empirical theory of individual decisions. In the understanding of collective phenomena, individual details and complications are revealed, if only in the light of the success of the explanations such abstractions make possible, as irrelevant to answering the particular kinds of *how* or *why* questions that are actually posed. The variations that make up these details and complications are revealed as insignificant (or as 'cancelling one another out'). My claim is that the *how* and *why* questions that permit such success chiefly relate to collective phenomena lying at a huge distance from the phenomena of decisions and actions considered individually. What has been shown over and over again is only that in many different areas of social life it is theoretically fruitful to pick out large classes of actions which are aimed, whatever else may be true of them, at this or that specified end—the end a peasant has in pasturing his beasts and collecting firewood, say, or the aim of a fisherman in open waters, or the aim of a financial trader. When such classes are singled out to be studied and explanations are drafted of the relevant sorts of behaviour, the expression 'utility' can be harmlessly and uncommittally a *place-holder* for some particular end. It is not a general name, whose introduction has to be effected by manoeuvres or definitions such as I have criticized on pp. 263–4 above. Almost equally uncommittally, we may think of each idealized actor as acting under certain conditions (which the theorist has identified as normal or prevalent) in order to optimize the pursuit under certain standing constraints of that specified end. Finally, there arises the option to investigate in general terms the intended and unintended effects of agents' acts and decisions, the synergetic effects of these acts and decisions, and any mismatch between the intended and the unintended effects.

The success of this form of abstraction and generalization has been undeniable. But the interest of the discoveries that have been made in this way seems to be quite independent of all questions that might be posed about individual psychology, about why and when individuals make the decisions they do, or why and when they embark on the courses of action they do. Only confusion of different kinds of questions, the impulse to build new intellectual empires, or the archaic impulse to find new 'foundations' for old forms of intellectual inquiry in some simple, general, and circumscriptive theory of man as a certain kind of being, could explain anyone's thinking that, just because so many abstractive explanations of large classes of action are successful, each of these abstractions must represent human beings as they really are.

To impute to so many people such confusion may seem rash. Yet it is hard to think of any other explanation of the insistent conviction that idealizations that yield theoretical insight *must* possess greater reality than was afforded by the picture of individual human beings offered in the phenomenological account.

5. To suggest that it is a methodological confusion to try to turn to advantage the successes of the abstractive explanation of aggregative phenomena, or seek to turn them back onto issues of individual minds and mentality, *need* not of course discourage those who have reasons of their own to delight in seeing themselves and their fellows in the utility maximizing picture that is offered to us by political scientists, psephologists, financial economists, or countless other observers of the divers works of the hidden hand. To those who delight in this picture one can only suggest that they should find reasons to do so. Pending such reasons being produced, I claim there is no good reason for anyone who engages in argument on questions of ethics or public policy to transpose into the jargon of utility theory the ordinary terms of ethical or political discourse. To see the distortion that results from this sort of transposition, consider, for instance, what Kenneth Arrow writes in comment upon Richard Titmuss's book about blood donation considered as a gift relation:

> I suggest here a reformulation of [what Titmuss presents as the generalized desire to benefit others, or as a feeling of social obligation] in the language of utility theory. I find three classes which do not correspond precisely to those of Titmuss:

1) The welfare of each individual will depend both on his own satisfaction and on the satisfactions obtained by others. We here have in mind a positive relation, one of altruism rather than of envy.

2) The welfare of each individual depends not only on the utilities of himself and others but also on his contributions to the utilities of others.

3) Each individual is, in some ultimate sense, motivated by purely egoistic satisfaction derived from goods accruing to him, but there is an implicit social contract such that each performs duties for the other in a way calculated to enhance the satisfaction of all. ('Gifts and Exchanges', *Philosophy and Public Affairs*, 1972, vol. 1, no. 4)

Such falsification of Titmuss's findings is as unnecessary as it is lamentable and misleading. Least of all is it scientific.

6.  It is one thing, I have been claiming, to collect up some class of actions or decisions made by all sorts of agents whose differences either do not matter very much or cancel out— classes well made for the generalizations in which social sciences excel precisely because, for these purposes, the barest caricature of a peasant, fishermen, stock-jobber, or institutional investor will do. It is another thing altogether to take one particular agent, that one, and then another, and another, and to seek to subsume the heterogenous sequence of each agent's actions and decisions under theoretical generalizations that short-circuit or supersede or upstage by empirical theory the anecdotal findings of phenomenology. Perhaps it was always obvious that nothing very impressive would be achieved in this attempt. But, if it was not always obvious, then reflection ought to reveal how different these questions about collectivities are (on which see Essay X, §12, with nn. 14, 15) from questions about individuals in all their particularity.

7.  At this point, I am sure further resistance is to be expected against the suggestion that the decision theoretic model of man should be seen not as any sort of preliminary study but as an abstraction, not as a sketch but as a caricature. It will grate yet more on the ears of those who resist to add that nothing more reality-directed than caricature was

ever needed for the purposes of answering the kinds of question that the abstraction has subserved. For it may be protested that the success of the theories that abstraction has made possible and the prospect of further success of this kind, gives hope of an eventual unification of the insights of various social sciences. It will be said that these sucesses *must* lend credence to the models or abstractions that have made all this possible.

The most economical reply to this is to invite those who share in these ambitions to step forth from the arena of controversy and consider the indispensability of the concept of an *ideal gas* to the reasonings by which the kinetic theory of gases was first arrived at and is still explained and understood. The Boyle–Charles Law relating the pressure, temperature, and volume of a gas—$PV=RT$, where R is an empirically identified constant—works by prescinding from all the particularities of particular gases and from most of the empirical properties of molecules. The concept of a gas that results from this prescinding is more or less indispensable to understanding, either historically or conceptually, why the Boyle–Charles Law has the form that it does. Yet it would be a mistake to argue from this success to any theoretical need to project the concept of an ideal gas onto reality itself.

> We assume that our ideal gas is made up of molecules all alike, each of mass M, of negligibly small size and which exert no forces on one another, except in collisions, which are perfectly elastic. We note, at the outset, that these assumptions involve an inconsistency: if the molecules are indefinitely small and do not attract one another, they will never collide. The collisions are [however] a necessary feature of the situation. On the other hand, the inconsistency is logical rather than essential. It results from out stretching our simplifying approximations to the limit. We can relax these sufficiently to meet the logical objection, without inconvenience, as the need arises. Imagine now a volume of gas enclosed in a vessel at a fixed temperature . . . (p. 284 in the Penguin 1959 reprint of *Mass, Length and Time*, Norman Feather, [Edinburgh University Press, 1959])

Is it any wiser to embrace the utility maximizer conception of individual agents than it is to see the success of the

Boyle–Charles Law as confirmation that *in reality* gas molecules exert no force on one another, except in collisions, which are perfectly elastic?

8.   A sketch, whether or not it is finished, is intended to depict, to depict a thing in its givenness or actuality. It points beyond itself to an open-ended plethora of actual attributes. A caricature, on the other hand, capitalizes upon certain designated attributes, as if not even leaving room for others. (Hence no doubt the numbing ugliness of caricature done in stone or bronze or even clay.) To which then should one liken utility theory? Is it a sketch or a caricature of human decisions and actions? By my account, it is not any sketch.

# Index of Persons Cited or Mentioned

# Content Index